MOST VORACIOUS ANIMAL

Meet the vibrant and visually striking caterpillar of the polyphemus moth (*Antheraea polyphemus*) – the perfect record breaker to introduce the new green-themed *GWR 2027* edition. In the first two months after they hatch, these lime-green larvae consume *c.* 86,000 times their own birthweight in food. In human terms, this would be equivalent to a newborn baby devouring 300 tonnes (330 tons) in the same period! We just hope you get your teeth into this year's compendium of superlative treats with the same ravenous gusto as this chomping champion. Bon appétit!

GUINNESS WORLD RECORDS 2027

ICONS
Guinness World Records celebrates a selection of title holders who truly embody what it means to be Officially Amazing. This year's roll call of high achievers includes K-pop stars BLACKPINK, adaptive adventurer Hari Budha Magar, astronaut Christina Koch and baseball talent Shohei Ohtani.

FEB 29 Happy birthday to the children of the Henriksen family (NOR) – Heidi (b. 1960), Olav (b. 1964) and Leif-Martin (b. 1968) – the **most siblings born on Leap Day**!

100% Discover the true scale of some of our biggest and smallest record holders.

Packed with more than 2,000 classic, updated and brand-new records

New record-of-the-day timeline features a year's worth of superlatives. What awesome feat took place on your birthday?

Filled with hundreds of stunning colour photographs

Welcome to *Guinness World Records 2027*! Prepare to face killer plants, spend a day with the world's **tallest man**, get slimed, explore Tutankhamun's tomb, peek inside the *International Space Station*, experience a whirlwind Formula One pit stop and voyage to a much-loved sci-fi galaxy far, far away…

CONTENTS

100%

JAN 1 US president Theodore Roosevelt performed the **most handshakes by a head of state** – 8,513 – at a New Year's Day event in Washington, DC, USA, in 1907.

JAN 2 First posted in 2000, *The Journey* by Adam Kontras (USA) – the **first video blog** ("vlog") – followed his trek to California, USA, in a bid to get into show business.

Junior record stars get their very own chapter! Check out the latest under-16s to have joined the GWR family in the Kids Zone

Science & Technology
Our survey of hi-tech superlatives is out of this world – literally. Alongside a wealth of scientific world beaters – including solar-powered speedsters and cutting-edge nuclear science – you'll discover the vital mechanics of how astronauts relieve themselves in space!

Snapshots
Each of these eye-catching features focuses on one remarkable record holder relocated out of their natural surroundings into a more familiar location. Above, a long-extinct prehistoric giant finds itself strolling through New York City's bustling Times Square. *Make way!*

SCIENCE & TECHNOLOGY

HISTORY

KIDS ZONE

ARTS & ENTERTAINMENT

SNAPSHOTS

SPORTS

As well as a bounty of green flora and fauna and other natural delights in the Green Planet chapter – such as the **largest cut peridot** (above) – keep an eye out for other verdant record holders as you explore *GWR 2027*. The **highest-grossing film based on a play, most leaves on a clover** and **largest knitted diorama** all share an emerald theme. Can you find them in the book?

JAN 3 At 02:26 (UTC) in 2019, the China National Space Administration's *Chang'e 4* spacecraft made the **first landing on the far side of the Moon.**

JAN 4 In 2017, Robert Marchand (FRA, b. 26 Nov 1911) became the **oldest competitive cyclist** in a race held in Saint-Quentin-en-Yvelines, France, aged 105 years 39 days.

Green

Verdant record breakers are getting their moment in the spotlight in *GWR 2027*. Whether it's prodigious plants, quirky animals or beloved figures from folklore and pop culture, let's get things underway with this selection of green heroes…

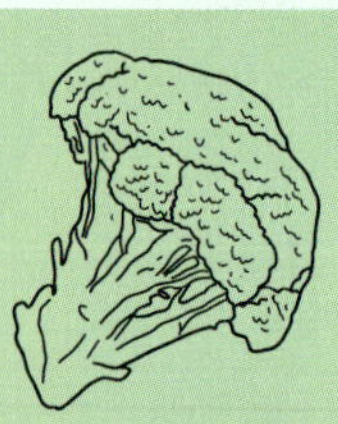

Heaviest broccoli
15.87 kg (35 lb), by John and Mary Evans (both USA) in Alaska, USA, in 1993

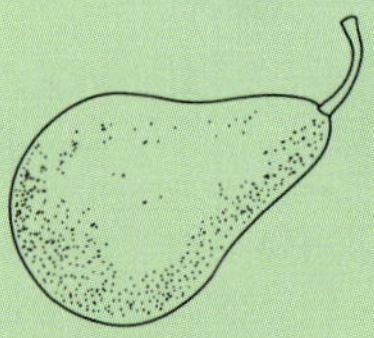

Heaviest pear
2.948 kg (6 lb 8 oz), by JA Aichi Toyota Nashi Bukai (JPN) in Aichi, Japan, on 11 Nov 2011

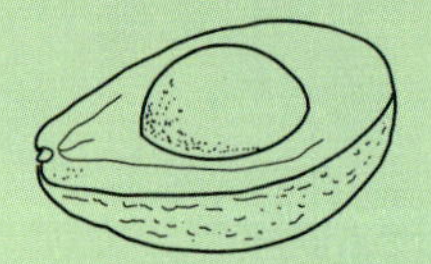

Heaviest avocado
2.55 kg (5 lb 10 oz), by Mark, Juliane & Loihi Pokini (all USA) in Hawaii, USA, on 14 Dec 2018

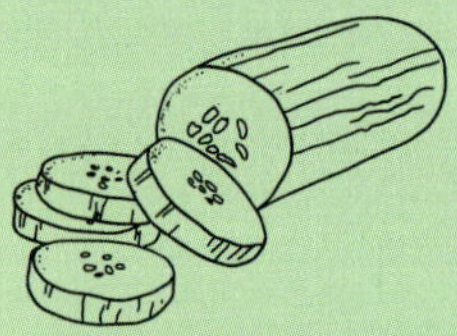

Heaviest cucumber
13.388 kg (29 lb 8 oz), by Vincent Sjodin (UK) in Glamorgan, UK, on 23 Sep 2023

Heaviest celery
42 kg (92 lb 9 oz), by Gary Heeks (UK) in Oxfordshire, UK, on 29 Sep 2018

Most people dressed as the Incredible Hulk
Muckno Mania Festival in Castleblayney, County Monaghan, Ireland, assembled 574 attendees to impersonate Marvel's mean green smashing machine on 13 Jul 2012. This came in the wake of the **most people dressed as cartoon characters**, which the arts event claimed with 905 *Flintstones* cosplayers on 16 Jul 2010.

Fastest marathon dressed as a leprechaun
Fundraising for a homeless children's charity, Sean McIntyre (USA, above) ran the Boston Marathon as an Irish imp in 2 hr 47 min 6 sec on 21 Apr 2025.

The **half marathon** record is 1 hr 19 min 54 sec, set by Melvin Nyairo (USA) in Toronto, Ontario, Canada, on 16 Oct 2022.

Largest human recycling logo
All kitted out in green, 3,373 people united to recreate the emblematic three arrows of recycling in Chennai, India, on 23 Jan 2019. The attempt was coordinated by the Central Institute of Plastics (now Petrochemicals) Engineering & Technology (IND) to raise awareness of its mission to improve plastic waste management and work towards a circular plastics economy in India.

Most powerful electric tugboat
Seeking to haul in a new cleaner era in tugboat technology, the *Bu Tinah* – with its 2,782-kWh battery capacity – exerted 78.2 tonnes-force (86.2 tons-force) of pulling power in Abu Dhabi, UAE, on 23 Oct 2024. The vessel was built by Damen Shipyards (NLD) for the Safeen Group (UAE).

JAN 5 In 2020, the **longest golf club** – at 15.57 m (51 ft 1 in) – swung into action at First Tee in Fort Worth, Texas, USA, wielded by Michael Furrh and Mike Rausch (both USA).

JAN 6 In 2019, the **tallest tropical tree** – a specimen of yellow meranti (*Richetia faguetiana*) in Sabah, Borneo – was measured to stand 98.53 m (323 ft 3 in) by tape drop.

Tallest cactus
The cardón or elephant cactus (*Pachycereus pringlei*) of Mexico regularly grows to the same height as a three-storey house. One particularly giant specimen – spotted by Marc Salak and Jeff Brown while hiking in Baja California in 1995 – topped out at 19.2 m (63 ft).

Longest career as a flatulist
Train driver-turned-professional *f*-artiste "Mr Methane", aka Paul Oldfield (UK), has been breaking wind to tuneful and comedic effect since Dec 1990. The art of flatulism has a surprisingly long history, entertaining the masses – and even royalty – since the 1100s.

Farthest throw of a welly boot
63.98 m (209 ft 10 in), by Teppo Luoma (FIN) in Hämeenlinna, Finland, on 12 Oct 1996

Largest toy-soldier collection
1,020, by Jonathan Perry Waters (USA) in Macon, Georgia, USA, as of 28 Feb 2016

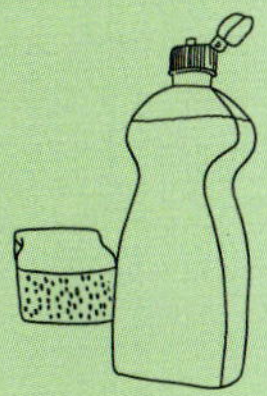

Most dishes washed in three minutes
42, by Taiyou Sugiura (JPN) in Minato, Tokyo, Japan, on 27 Sep 2024

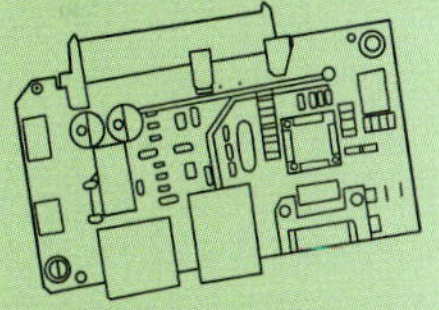

Most Raspberry Pis in parallel
750, by BitScope (AUS) and SICORP (USA) in New Mexico, USA, on 13 Nov 2017

First depiction of a Gorgon
700–660 BCE, on a terracotta *pithos* vase found in Thebes, Boeotia, Greece, in 1897

Heaviest praying mantis
Giant Asian mantises (*Hierodula membranacea*) are thought to be the heftiest of their kind; one well-fed female tipped the scales at 9 g (0.3 oz). Their green bodies are perfect camouflage when hunting prey among the foliage of tropical forests in south-east Asia.

Longest beak relative to body size
While there are birds with longer beaks overall – notably pelicans – the sword-billed hummingbird (*Ensifera ensifera*) stands out among all avifauna. At up to 10 cm (4 in) long, its bill is bigger than its body. It's evolved this way to access nectar in elongated trumpet-shaped flowers in the cloud forests of the Andes in South America.

Highest-grossing puppet movie
A 2011 revival of *The Muppets* (USA/JPN/UK) – starring lovable lime-green frog Kermit – earned $160.4 m (£100.9 m) globally, according to The Numbers. Created by puppeteer and filmmaker Jim Henson, Kermit and GWR share something in common: both turned 70 in 2025!

JAN 7 The **oldest competitive speed skater** is Iichi Marumo (JPN, b. 1 Apr 1929), aged 94 years 281 days when he took to the ice at an event in Yamagata, Japan, in 2024.

JAN 8 The **greatest rainfall in 24 hours** is 1,825 mm (71.8 in) – enough to cover an adult man! – which fell over the French island of Réunion in the Indian Ocean in 1966.

Editor's Letter

Welcome to the latest edition of the world's **biggest-selling annual book**. It marks the culmination of our year-long 70th anniversary celebrations – a year that has seen our record keepers approve 2,897 superlatives from 40,842 applications.

"How can I be part of it?" It's a question that we hear every day at GWR HQ. To help answer it, we've been focusing our attention on encouraging as many people as possible to "Be Part of It". The result, after assessing thousands of applications this year, is the book you now have in your hands.

There are more ways than ever to earn that much-coveted Guinness World Records certificate. You can start by reading this year's fully updated edition to find challenges that you think you could tackle. Be inspired by what you read here – and in this year's *GWR Gamer's Edition* and *Soccer Edition*, our sister books – and if you think you can do better, then get in touch. You can also check out what's happening on a daily basis via our website (**guinnessworldrecords.com**) and social-media accounts – see the back cover for a full list of where you can find us online, and follow the QR codes throughout the book for bonus content.

We've also been meeting wannabe record breakers at various book festivals, gaming conventions and live events across the globe, offering them a chance to attempt records in front of an official GWR Adjudicator. Indeed, our judges have been everywhere this year – on countless TV and radio shows, on the finish lines at some of the major marathons, including London, Sydney, Dubai and Berlin, and even in pixel form inside the record-breaking gaming platform Roblox, where you can now attempt official in-game challenges with encouragement from the GWR Coach. (You can take a side-quest to pp.188–89 for more gaming superlatives.)

We're so committed to helping you "Be Part of It" that we're even opening a dedicated entertainment venue where you can compete alongside – or against! – your friends and family. Guinness World Records London is a live experience inside The O2, the city's iconic dome on Greenwich Peninsula. There, you'll find more than 50 official

Longest career hosting a morning talk show (female)
In Jan 2026, TV presenter Kelly Ripa was recognized for her long service. She began fronting *Live* in Feb 2001, after an extensive search to replace former host Kathie Lee Gifford. Ripa currently fronts the show with her husband, Mark Consuelos, the fourth anchor with whom she has shared the desk.

Largest number made from LEGO® bricks
Bryce Martin, Erick Grady, Edward Woods and Rick Nyhan built a 15 x 5-ft "2025" out of plastic toy bricks at the Legacy Traditional School in San Antonio, Texas. Unveiled before the students on 7 Mar that year, the work used 42,752 pieces. It appeared alongside a 12,199-brick reproduction of the school's logo, which did not count towards the final total.

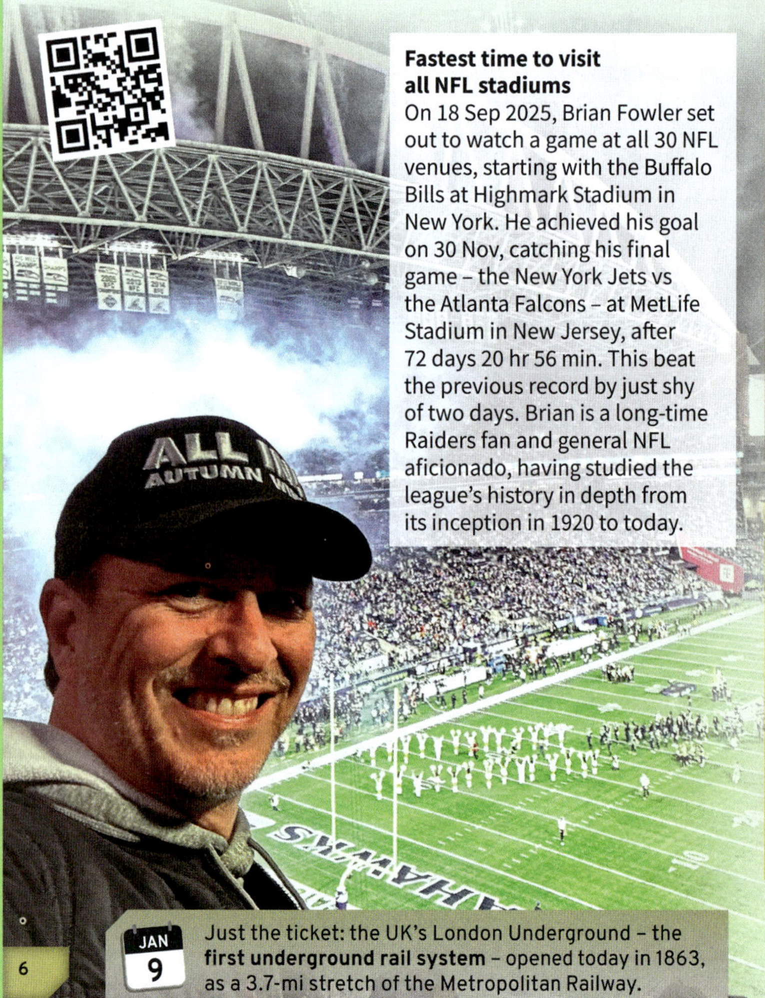

Fastest time to visit all NFL stadiums
On 18 Sep 2025, Brian Fowler set out to watch a game at all 30 NFL venues, starting with the Buffalo Bills at Highmark Stadium in New York. He achieved his goal on 30 Nov, catching his final game – the New York Jets vs the Atlanta Falcons – at MetLife Stadium in New Jersey, after 72 days 20 hr 56 min. This beat the previous record by just shy of two days. Brian is a long-time Raiders fan and general NFL aficionado, having studied the league's history in depth from its inception in 1920 to today.

Most hula-hoop rotations around the neck in 30 seconds
Sixth-grader Viha Gedia of Los Gatos, California, spun a hoop around her neck 128 times on 21 Mar 2025. That amounts to just over four rotations every second! Viha had been honing her hula-hoop skills for five years prior to the attempt.

Largest donation of toys in 24 hours
Californian charity Trina's Kids Foundation collected 141,262 toys on 13 Dec 2025 – enough to fill a football field! They were then distributed to underprivileged children for the holidays. This title perfectly encapsulates GWR's "Records for Good" initiative (scan the QR code to learn more).

JAN 9 Just the ticket: the UK's London Underground – the **first underground rail system** – opened today in 1863, as a 3.7-mi stretch of the Metropolitan Railway.

JAN 10 In 2017, Mads Pieler Kolding (DNK) struck a shuttlecock at 264.7 mph – the **fastest badminton hit in competition** – in Bengaluru, Karnataka, India.

Largest scale model of a city
Unveiled at the 1964 New York World's Fair, *The Panorama of the City of New York* spans 9,335 sq ft. It was built over a three-year period by model-making firm Raymond Lester & Associates and updated in 1992. The detailed diorama is now on show at the city's Queens Museum.

Largest chicken-wing-eating competition
Buffalo, New York, is famous for its chicken wings, and so made for the ideal setting for this record. The city collaborated with The Revelas Family Foundation to bring together 499 hot-headed participants in a speed-eating event to raise funds for teen mental-health research. Competitive eater George Chiger claimed the top prize, downing 36 spicy wings in just five minutes!

GWR challenges across six zones (see pp.12–13). If you think you've got what it takes to earn your place atop the leaderboards, then pay us a visit!

Until then, I hope you enjoy getting stuck into this year's book. Dotted throughout is a series of "Big Pictures", in which we take a magnifying glass to the inner workings of complex record objects and locations, such as the *International Space Station* (pp.116–17), the set of *Avatar 3* (pp.178–79) and an F1 pit stop (pp.200–01). Meanwhile, in our "Snapshot" features, 3D digital artist Joseph O'Neil illustrates what would happen if – among other scenarios – you went for a joyride in the **largest land vehicle** (pp.164–65) or let the **largest dinosaur** loose in Times Square (pp.38–39). Our layout artists at 55Design also take a striking visual approach to the Science & Technology chapter (pp.102–19).

We're proud to share with you the latest selection of GWR ICONS, among them wrestler/actor/activist John Cena (p.100), K-pop sensations BLACKPINK (p.40) and the 194-year-old Jonathan the tortoise, the **oldest-known land animal** (p.166). Finally, in our Kids Zone (pp.146–63), we induct eight more Young Achievers – inspiring record holders all under the age of 16, including a professional programmer, a World Surf League Championship competitor and a *two*-year-old snooker prodigy! See, you can never start too early if you want to be part of it!

Craig Glenday
Editor-in-Chief

Oldest competitive skateboarder (female)
World-champion boarder Judi Oyama (b. 22 Oct 1959) was still competing at the age of 66, and is due to represent Team USA at the World Skate Games in Paraguay in Oct 2026. A pro since the age of 17, her latest contest was the International Slalom Skateboarding Championship in Nov 2025.

Largest animatronic fish
Measuring 28 ft tall and 12 ft long, this majestic robotic seahorse was the focus of a reef-themed float created by The UPS Store for 2026's Pasadena Tournament of Roses® in California. The head-bobbing sculpture presided over a shoal of smaller seahorses and other fish. As per the event's rules, the float's decorations were all natural materials such as flowers and foliage. Seven months in the making, it won the parade's Director Award for best design.

JAN 11 A copy of 1963's *The Amazing Spider-Man* #1 sold for $1.38 m in Dallas, Texas, USA, in 2024. The **most expensive *Spider-Man* comic** initially cost 12 cents.

JAN 12 On this day in 2008, Merete Spilling Gjertsen (NOR, b. 8 Oct 1947) became the **oldest woman to ski to the South Pole**, aged 60 years 96 days.

US Collectors

Frog-related items
It's easy being green in Susan Burgos's California home, where she has 13,201 froggy antiques, decorations and accessories on display (see also p.97). Susan was the first person to claim this title since 2002, beating the previous record by nearly 3,000 items! GWR leaped at the chance to ask her about her amphibious assortment (see right).

1

When did you start your collection?
In 1983, I found a tiny tree frog in my kitchen. It stole my heart! It inspired me, and I bought my first item: a gold frog ring with emerald eyes.

Where do you find new pieces for your hoard?
Sometimes I come across them while travelling. I also look for them in various catalogues.

Do you have any favourites?
Well, one that springs to mind is an animated singing biker frog on a motorcycle that plays "Kokomo".

What is the greatest challenge as a collector?
Finding storage space! In the end, I bought a second home with a large garage so that I could house everything.

2

Slinkys
Susan Suazo owned a total of 1,054 spring-shaped toys as of the most recent count. Some are hung from the ceiling of her home in Los Lunas, New Mexico. No two Slinkys in Susan's collection are the same, with slight variations in colour, shape and size.

3

Heart-related items
Susan West of Idaho has been feeling the love for more than 40 years while building up her hoard of heart-shaped trinket boxes. The 1,560 caskets are a combination of gifts from friends or family and mementoes from Susan's own travels.

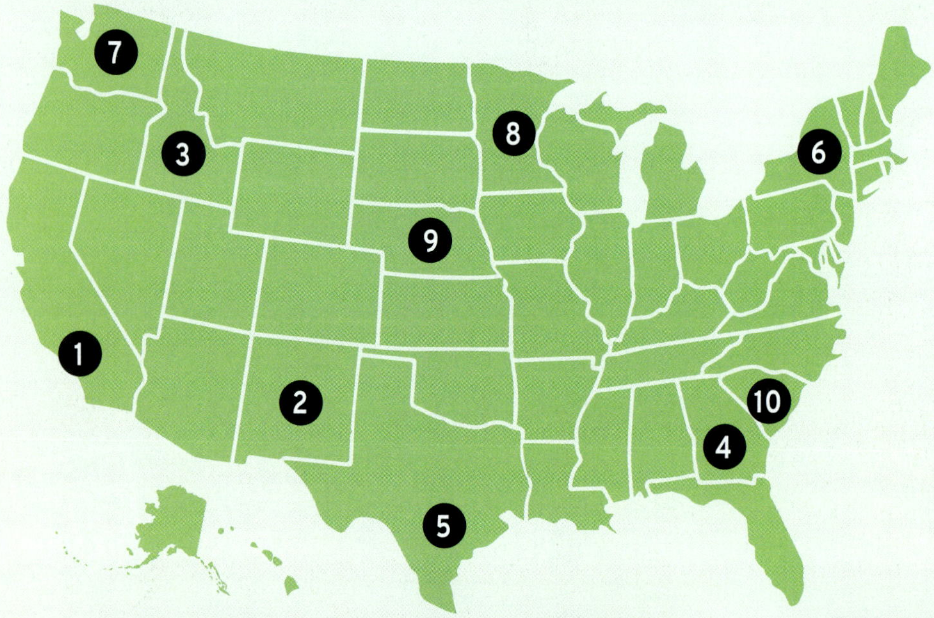

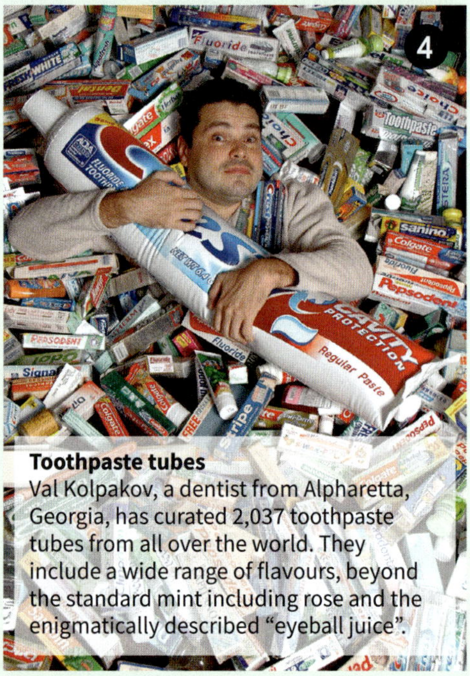

4

Toothpaste tubes
Val Kolpakov, a dentist from Alpharetta, Georgia, has curated 2,037 toothpaste tubes from all over the world. They include a wide range of flavours, beyond the standard mint including rose and the enigmatically described "eyeball juice".

JAN 13 Out of this world! Today in 2018, Jon Tannahill (AUS) hit the **highest score on *Space Invaders*** (218,870). He played on a vintage 1978 Taito arcade cabinet.

JAN 14 The **longest lightning storm** ever observed (by the *Cassini* orbiter) began on this day in 2009, on Saturn. It lasted 11 months, until 13 Dec. *Very* striking...

5

Coca-Cola memorabilia
Husband and wife Bardo and Olga Cuellar have an effervescent array of 7,099 mementoes relating to the classic beverage at their home in Humble, Texas. The couple have been amassing the keepsakes for 28 years, finally breaking the record in Aug 2025. Their most cherished item is a vintage 1939 Coca-Cola Original Westinghouse Ice Cooler.

6

Pizza boxes
New Yorker Scott Wiener has accrued 595 pizza boxes, all from pizzerias in his home state. The hoard comprises a mix of everyday and rare, limited-edition examples, many featuring pop-culture characters or celebrities. Scott's favourite box depicts George Clooney cooking at a pizza oven.

7

Converse shoes
Joshua Mueller's collection of Converse sneakers, which he's been stockpiling in Washington state since 1992, is 2,360 pairs strong and counting. Walking a mile in each would get him from New York to Florida and back again!

8

Snowmen
Karen Schmidt's Minnesota home is a winter wonderland, bursting with 5,127 snow-figure decorations that she has gathered over more than three decades. The frosty figurines come in many different forms and materials, and include a pink snowman that sings "Santa Baby".

Find out more
It's been a busy year here at GWR and we simply can't fit all the record-breaking action into *GWR 2027*… That's why we're offering you a treasure trove of extra bonus content – including videos and extended stories with record-holder profiles and back stories – on our YouTube channel and website **guinnessworldrecords.com/2027**. Look out for QR codes throughout the book.

9

***Muppets* memorabilia**
Rhett Safranek of Merna, Nebraska, owns 1,841 keepsakes relating to these popular puppets. He's been a devotee since being given a *Muppets* VHS tape when he was just two years old. His favourite item – and one of the rarest in his collection – is an Official Gonzo Master Replica figurine.

10

Buttons
South Carolina's Dalton Stevens has amassed 439,900 unique buttons. He's used them to customize everything from a 1981 Chevette and a guitar to even a coffin! Of the selection of heroic hoarders featured on these pages, Dalton boasts the biggest collection by far.

JAN 15 In 1885, Wilson Bentley (USA) captured the **first photograph of a snow crystal** with a glass-plate camera on his family's farm near Jericho, Vermont, USA.

JAN 16 Starting in 1949, Andrés Borrasé Sanou (CRI) was in charge of *Prensa Libre* for 58 years 349 days – the **longest career as publisher of the same newspaper**.

Device Downtime

From cellphones to laptops, our lives are now dominated by digital devices. But with many of us increasingly yearning for some analogue R&R as a break from all those screens, GWR offers a selection of real-world, hands-on records – ranging from arts and crafts to retro toys – to level up your next hobby…

LARGEST GINGERBREAD HOUSE RECIPE*

- ALL-PURPOSE FLOUR: 5,700 LB
- EGGS: 4,263
- BROWN SUGAR: 1,450 LB
- GRANULATED SUGAR: 550 LB
- CINNAMON: C. 300 LB
- EDIBLE GLUE: 20 GAL
- FONDANT: 20 LB

*MAIN INGREDIENTS

Bake gingerbread
Baking can be the perfect antidote to screen overload – and, what's more, you can pass on the good vibes by sharing some sweet treats with loved ones! To mark the 35th anniversary of Home Alone (USA, 1990) in 2025, Disney+ and Hulu joined forces to produce the **largest gingerbread house**. A replica of the McCallisters' home, it boasted an internal volume of 44,838 cu ft and featured two types of gingerbread tile: 800 dark-brown ones for the roof and shutters and 4,400 light-golden ones for the walls.

Play Simon
Simon is a vintage toy that has truly stood the test of time – it's also a great way to test your grey matter! Playing the conventional way is tricky enough, but Luke Banner added a new twist by memorizing the corresponding tones and colours to achieve the **most sequences completed in a game of Simon while blindfolded**. Luke completed 30 rounds, despite being unsighted – could you do better?

Draw with chalk
Embracing your artistic side is a great way to escape your screens, especially if you're working outdoors! In 2023, Preeti Gundapwar claimed the record for the **largest chalk street art by one artist** with her recreation of the northern lights (see pp.16–17), which spanned 2,438 sq ft. If you're looking to chalk up a similar record, then why not contact us and give it a go? The world is your canvas!

JAN 17 — In a cutting-edge act, Percy Selbit (UK, b. Percy Tibbles) staged the **first "person-sawn-in-half" illusion** at the Finsbury Park Empire in London, UK, today in 1921.

JAN 18 — The **first college basketball game** was fought between the universities of Iowa and Chicago (both USA) at Iowa City Armory in 1896. Chicago triumphed 15–12.

Get knitting
Needlecraft is enjoying a real resurgence, its blend of relaxation and concentration making it an ideal option for digital detox. Once you've got the knack of knitting or crocheting, it can be hard to stop – go on for long enough and you may even end up with a new world record! Take Daisy Ptak from California, who created the **longest crocheted scarf** (981 ft 9 in) in 2024. Now she just needs to find someone with a neck long enough to wear it!

Play Hungry Hungry Hippos
Originally a family favourite during the late 1970s and 1980s, this tabletop game sees players capture as many marbles as they can with chomping hippo heads. In 2025, the record for the **fastest time to clear a game of Hungry Hungry Hippos (team of two)** was broken twice. It first fell to YouTube comedians Chanse McCrary and Shayne Topp (of "Smosh" fame) in August with a time of 8.03 sec. However, serial record breaker David Rush and his son Peter improved on that mark in November, making a clean sweep in 5.80 sec.

Master origami
The ancient Japanese art of paper folding is a relaxing hobby but also demands precision and focus. When taken to record-breaking extremes, it involves some complicated logistics too. Fortunately, Paul Frasco and Shrikant Iyer had all this covered when they created the **largest origami dragon** in 2020. Constructed from a single massive sheet of paper over a period of 7 hr, their finished winged wonder measured more than 12 ft long and required 50 different folding stages. Thankfully, GWR also has many origami records on a much smaller scale!

Build with LEGO®
For a break from videogames, why not take a leaf out of Ian Roosma's book... and use plastic toy bricks to recreate your favourite virtual worlds? The **largest LEGO videogame map** is a reimagining of Hyrule from the popular series The Legend of Zelda (see pp.78–79) that comprises 24,718 bricks and includes 2,779 trees. The final diorama, which is now displayed on Roosma's wall, spans 2 x 7 ft.

When it comes to record breaking, nothing beats taking part! To help get you on the path to record-breaking glory, we've created a special online tool – the Record Selector – to pair wannabe record holders with the record titles best suited to their skills, interests and resources. Just follow the QR code to the right and start answering the simple questions. Alternatively, you can still look up existing titles the old-school way at **guinnessworldrecords.com**. Below, we walk you through the key stages on your journey to (hopefully!) becoming a GWR legend…

1

Select it!
Set up an account on the GWR website, then head to the Record Selector to be paired with a challenge that suits your skills.

2

Practise it!
Once you've chosen a record, we'll send over a detailed set of guidelines for your attempt. Read them carefully then get training.

3

Attempt it!
Once you've honed your skills, gather what you need to satisfy the guidelines – cameras, expert witnesses, stopwatches, etc. – and make your official attempt!

4

Prove it!
Next, send us your evidence and give us a few weeks to review it. We'll keep you in the loop regarding the progress of your claim.

5

Celebrate it!
Check your email for that all-important decision. If you're successful, then congratulations – you're now part of the GWR family, and can get the certificate to prove you're Officially Amazing!

JAN 19 In 1784, a "Monsieur Fontaine" (FRA) snuck on board a hot-air balloon as it took off in Lyon, France – an act that made him history's **first aeronautical stowaway**.

JAN 20 To get to the point: in 2023, Shailendra Kumar Dash of Sylhet, Bangladesh, made the **longest sewing needle** – 12 ft – the equivalent height of two adult men!

WHERE RECORD BREAKERS ARE MADE

Guinness World Records London

Test your skills, challenge your friends and break world records in this brand-new interactive attraction at The O2, London's iconic entertainment destination. See the book come to life with interactive exhibits and live record attempts (including your own!), and meet real-life GWR Coaches and Adjudicators.

GUINNESS WORLD RECORDS® LONDON

Have you got what it takes to be Officially Amazing? Do you have a special skill or talent that deserves a place in the record books? We think the answer is YES, and at **Guinness World Records London**, we're giving you the chance to prove it!

Guinness World Records London is an exciting new interactive adventure that lets you experience the thrill of record breaking live and up close… and maybe even walk away with a coveted GWR certificate. Located in the Entertainment District at The O2 on London's Greenwich Peninsula, this 2,300-m^2 (24,760-sq-ft) site features more than 50 official GWR challenges across six action-packed zones, where you can test your skills, compete against friends and family, and celebrate some extraordinary achievements.

The venue also includes interactive exhibits, themed food and drink, and a dedicated retail space offering record-inspired merchandise. So, why just read about record breakers when you can become one yourself?! Book now for **Guinness World Records London** – it's where record breakers are made!

Below: Get to the top of the leaderboard on any challenge and you could find yourself making an official attempt on the main stage in front of a crowd… and a real-life GWR Adjudicator! The stage will also host invited guests and celebrity appearances, so check the schedule for special events.

Right: In between challenges, head to the Explore zones, where we showcase a selection of our classic and unforgettable record holders. You'll also find interactive kiosks and sensory exhibits that let you feel, hear and even smell record breakers.

Above: When you're not attempting a record of your own, take a stroll along the GWR Walk of Fame and find out about the most famous and iconic record holders from the history of the book.

Below: Stay refreshed and keep your energy levels up by visiting the GWR restaurant, where you'll find all sorts of themed drinks and dishes.

*Images are mock-ups and are intended for illustrative purposes; the actual experience may differ. We expect **Guinness World Records London** to open Winter 2026. Timings subject to change.*

JAN 21 In 2018, Tonya and Kym Illman (both AUS) found the **oldest message in a bottle** at Wedge Island, Australia. It was sent 131 years 223 days previously, on 12 Jun 1886.

JAN 22 Lottie Williams (USA) was struck by fibreglass from a deorbiting Delta II rocket in Tulsa, Oklahoma, USA, in 1997, becoming the **first person hit by space junk**.

OFFICIAL ATTEMPT

At **Guinness World Records London**, the focus is on hands-on participation, so head to the Official Attempt stations found throughout the venue and have a go! Your RFID wristband will connect you automatically, and you'll receive all the instructions you need. Your band also keeps track of your results. How far can you progress up the leaderboard? Best in your group? Best of the day? Best in the world?! Let's find out…

Get up close to some genuine record-breaking artefacts, such as Alastair Moffatt's side-driving Mini Cooper (**tightest gap driven through on two wheels**), the **tallest electric toothbrush** and the **largest tape measure**!

Other exclusive exhibits include the dresses worn by the world's **tallest** and **shortest women** when they met for tea, the charred push bike used for the **longest full-body burn on a bicycle**, and the **loudest bike horn**!

You'll find **Guinness World Records London** in The O2's Entertainment District in Greenwich, London. Scan the QR code below now to start your record-breaking adventure and find out more, including how to go about reserving tickets.

JAN 23 Opened in 1997, the aptly named Tower of Terror at Dreamworld in Gold Coast, Queensland, Australia, was the **first rollercoaster to hit 100 mph** (160 km/h).

JAN 24 In 2015, Shawn Delierre (CAN) and Leo Au (CHN) played the **longest competitive squash match**, battling it out in Medicine Hat, Alberta, Canada, for 2 hr 50 min.

GWR Day 2025

Our annual celebration of record breaking last November inspired some extraordinary feats. Here we highlight just a few, including three records set atop The O2 in London – the site of GWR's upcoming entertainment venue. Thanks to everyone who made the latest GWR Day Officially Amazing!

HIGH-LEVEL ADJUDICATING
A windswept Will Munford tells us what it was like to adjudicate the GWR Day action on the roof of The O2.

What were the conditions like at the top of The O2?
Bleak. London is great for many things, but the weather isn't one of them! The gusts of wind were definitely the most challenging factor.

What practicalities had to be overcome on the day?
It took a big team to record and verify the measurements, and to get all the equipment to the top of The O2. I needed help for Josh's running-over-the-top record too, because I can't be in two places at once (unfortunately)!

Did any of the attempts surprise you?
All three did. I was knocked out by Jodie's strength and composure, Lucie's balance and explosiveness – despite the wind – and Josh's pace and stamina.

How did it feel to be part of this special event?
It was amazing! I witnessed feats never done before on top of one of the world's most iconic buildings. It's hard not to stop and think "Wow, I'm a lucky man."

Largest afro (female)
On 23 Oct 2025, Jessica Martinez's (USA) phenomenal 'fro secured her a GWR title in New York City, USA. She's shown here with GWR's Michael Empric, who presented Jessica with her official GWR certificate. The previous title holder had held the record for a considerable time; to see the amicable handing over of the crown, turn to p.42.

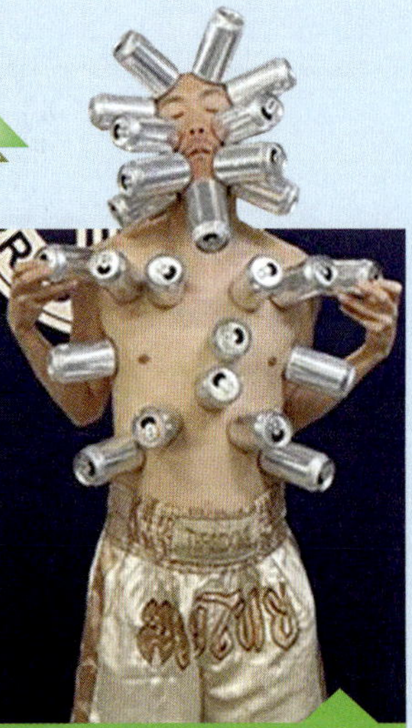

Most drink cans air suctioned on the body
Shunichi Kanno (JPN) attached 25 soda cans to himself without adhesive in Shibuya, Tokyo, Japan. His rehearsal didn't go according to plan, with cans refusing to stick, but he persevered and went on to smash his own record – last set in 2020 – by a count of five. All in all, it was a *can*-tastic performance!

Fastest ascent and descent of The O2 arena
Made in Chelsea star Josh Patterson took just 4 min 40.79 sec to cross The O2, an iconic landmark beside the River Thames in London, UK, on 4 Nov 2025 (**1**). This was Josh's fourth GWR title. On the same day, atop The O2's roof, *Gladiators* TV star Fury (aka Jodie Ounsley) achieved the **most weight moved by sandbag carry in one minute**, shifting 360 kg (794 lb) before her time ran out (**2**). Cirque du Soleil artist Lucie Colebeck (all UK) also executed the **most standing backwards somersaults by a woman in 30 seconds** – 17 (**3**).

JAN 25 The **longest unbeaten run in boxing** – 103 fights from 1911 to 1915 – ended when flyweight Jimmy "The Mighty Atom" Wilde (UK) was defeated by James "Tancy" Lee.

JAN 26 In 1924, Charles Jewtraw (USA) became the **first Winter Olympic gold medallist**, winning the 500 m speed-skating event in Chamonix, France.

Highest bicycle backflip
BMX freestyler Liu Haoran (CHN) celebrated GWR Day in style by performing a faultless 2.90-m-high (9-ft 6-in) reverse somersault on his bike in Dongguan, Guangdong, China. Liu has won many national and international contests, including four consecutive championships in the China BMX Freestyle League. He is seen as one of the biggest talents to enter the sport since it became an Olympic discipline in 2021.

Thirteen-year-old Liu's backflip shattered a record that had stood since two years before he was even born!

Most football sole touches on a moving quad bike in 30 seconds
Emirati serial record breaker Ammar Ahmed Alkhudhiri bounced a ball on the bottom of his feet 23 times while upside down on an ATV driven by his friend Abdulla Alhattawi. The attempt took place in Dubai, UAE, where Ammar is a three-time freestyle-football national champion.

Germany gets a kick out of GWR Day!
Feats of strength and dexterity dominated Germany's contributions to GWR Day 2025. Palina Glebova (above) executed the **most plastic bottles teed up and side kicked in one minute** – 12 – while Jens Gaude (right, both DEU) achieved the **most coconuts smashed by elbow** – 84 – in the same time. In all, eight new titles were set in Hamburg, resulting in some very happy new members of the GWR family (below)!

JAN 27 Extreme adventurer Sarah Hueniken (CAN) became the **first woman to ice-climb Niagara Falls,** on the US-Canada border, in the midwinter of 2015.

JAN 28 The **most bee stings survived** – 2,443 – were removed from Johannes Relleke (ZWE) near the Gwayi River in Zimbabwe (then Rhodesia) in 1962. *Ouch!*

GREEN PLANET

CONTENTS

In Inuit legend, auroras are the spirits playing a soccer game in the sky, hence their name for them: *aksarnirq* ("ball players").

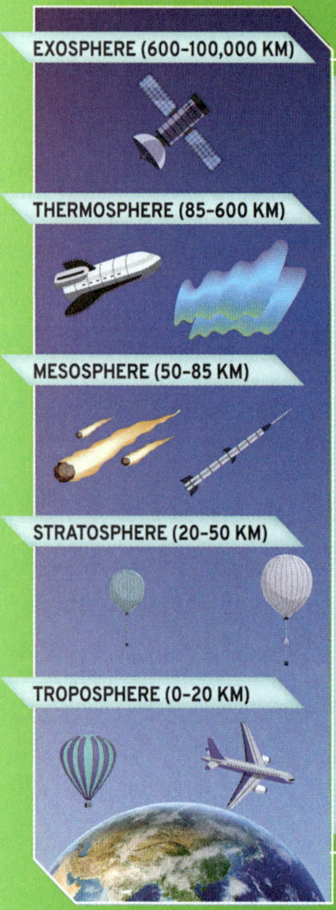

Earth's atmosphere is divided into five zones. The lowest starts at the planet's surface, while the highest peters out about a quarter of the way to the Moon, *c.* 100,000 km (62,000 mi) above us. We live in the troposphere, which is also where clouds form. Only specialized military aircraft and high-altitude balloons can reach the next layer, the stratosphere. Above that is the mesosphere, which looks like space, but still has enough air to cause fast-moving meteors to burn up as they pass through. The thermosphere – where the majority of auroras form – and the exosphere are what we'd think of as space, though there is still a trace of atmosphere there.

HIGHEST ATMOSPHERIC PHENOMENA

The aurora borealis and aurora australis, aka northern and southern lights, typically occur some 100 km (62 mi) above Earth's surface, but on rare occasions are seen as high as *c.* 800 km (500 mi). These ethereal illuminations are caused by charged particles emitted from the Sun interacting with Earth's magnetic field, and are usually more vibrant near our planet's poles. The main picture here was captured near the city of Yellowknife, in Canada's Northwest Territories.

Auroras appear in various colours including green, pink, yellow and purple, depending on the intensity of the solar particles and the gases present. Green is the most common shade for two key reasons: our eyes are more attuned to this part of the spectrum, and this is the colour naturally produced by atoms in oxygen-rich regions of the atmosphere where auroras most frequently play out.

Trees

Most massive plant
This autumnal vista in the Wasatch Mountains of Utah, USA, does not show a typical forest. The "trees" with yellow foliage are, in fact, a single network of quaking aspen (*Populus tremuloides*), comprising some 47,000 stems that share a single root system. Known as "Pando", this clonal organism covers 43 ha (106 acres) and weighs an estimated 6,000 tonnes (6,614 tons).

Oldest trees
These gnarled trees are bristlecone pines (*Pinus longaeva*), native to mountainous areas in the western USA. Dendrochronologists (tree-ring experts) have aged a living specimen in the White Mountains of California that started growing some 4,800 years ago. Another example – cut down in Nevada in 1963 – was estimated to have been *c.* 5,200 years old.

Shortest tree species
Growing in tundra across the Arctic, the woody-stemmed dwarf willow (*Salix herbacea*) rarely exceeds 6 cm (2.3 in) high. In its challenging habitat – with scarce rain, 24-hr darkness for half the year and, of course, freezing winds – staying close to the ground is key to this plant's survival.

Oldest extant tree species

The maidenhair (*Ginkgo biloba*) is considered a living fossil, as its ancestry dates back at least 270 million years, some 25 million years before the first dinosaurs. These Chinese native trees represent a transitional phase in plant evolution from ancient (e.g., ferns and cycads) to modern (e.g., conifers), possessing elements of both.

Tallest tree ever

There is much debate around this title as the key contenders all come from unverified 19th-century reports. Researchers agree, however, that it was most likely an Australian gum tree (*Eucalyptus*). Several examples from the state of Victoria were claimed to be in the 140–150-m (459–492-ft) range.

Of the 3 trillion trees on Earth today, a coast redwood (*Sequoia sempervirens*) in Redwood National Park in California, USA, takes the current **tallest** crown. As of 2019, "Hyperion" stood 116.07 m (380 ft 9 in) – this means it would loom about one-third taller than the US Capitol Building.

California also hosts the **tree with the largest volume**: "General Sherman", a giant sequoia (*Sequoiadendron giganteum*). The 83.6-m-tall (274-ft 3-in) tree comprises an estimated 1,591 m^3 (56,186 cu ft) of wood and bark; its trunk has enough lumber to construct 120 average-size houses!

Greatest circumference for a tree trunk

A majestic Montezuma cypress (*Taxodium mucronatum*), located at the centre of Santa María del Tule in Oaxaca, Mexico, measured 36.18 m (118 ft 8 in) around its base in 2005. "El Árbol del Tule" is 1,500–2,000 years old and much of the trunk's girth comes from its uneven, elliptical shape.

Largest tree canopy

Some tropical fig trees (*Ficus*) behave as "banyans" – i.e., producing prop roots that develop from branches into new trunks. Old trees can have thousands of these accessory trunks, enabling them to spread over vast areas. The largest is an Indian banyan (*F. benghalensis*), India's national tree, known as "Thimmamma Marrimanu", located in Anantapur, Andhra Pradesh; its crown covers 2.19 ha (5.41 acres) – enough to shade 52 basketball courts beneath its boughs.

Widest tree canopy (single trunk)

Excluding trees with multiple trunks (see above right), the broadest crown is the 60.4-m (198-ft 2-in) canopy of "Chamchuri", a rain tree (*Albizia saman*) located on the Thai Army cavalry grounds near Kanchanaburi. Another giant rain tree grows at the Gymkhana sports club in Chiang Mai, Thailand. The species is originally native to South and Central America.

Remotest tree

A solitary Sitka spruce (*Picea sitchensis*) on the subantarctic Campbell Island is c. 222 km (119.8 nautical mi) away from its nearest neighbour on the Auckland Islands. It is referred to as the "Ranfurly tree", named after a Governor of New Zealand, who may have planted it in 1901.

JAN 29 – The **longest curling throw** on record is 175.66 m (576 ft 4 in), unleashed by Eddie Kulbacki (CAN) on a frozen Park Lake in Neepawa, Manitoba, Canada, in 1989.

JAN 30 – In 2016, Levente Kovácsik and Norbert Ádám Szabó (both HUN) arrived in Antigua from Spain, becoming the **first team to kayak across an ocean**.

The forest is named after philanthropist John D Rockefeller Jr, who gave $2 m for redwood conservation in the late 1920s.

TALLEST FOREST

Part of Humboldt Redwoods State Park in north California, USA, the Rockefeller Forest – between Eel River and Bull Creek – contains the largest contiguous tract of old-growth coast redwoods (*Sequoia sempervirens*) on Earth. Across just 850 acres (344 ha), there are 130 trees that soar above 107 m (351 ft) – taller than the Statue of Liberty – averaging one such giant per 6.4 acres (2.6 ha). The area's loftiest titan is the 113.5-m (372-ft 4-in) "Stratosphere Giant", which is the world's fourth-tallest tree, just a couple of metres short of the outright record (see opposite).

JAN 31 Levelling up snack time, Hershey (USA) presented a 2,695-kg (5,943-lb) version of its REESE'S Take 5 – the **largest chocolate-nut bar** – today in 2020.

FEB 1 Italian telecoms giant TIM SpA choreographed the **most robots dancing simultaneously**, getting 1,372 Alpha 1S educational bots to boogie together in 2018.

Flowers

AALSMEER FLOWER AUCTION BY NUMBERS

43 million
cut flowers sold daily (and 4.8 million plants)

50+
countries shipped to

100
soccer fields that could fit into the site

35
special countdown clocks used for sales

50–60
years (oldest plants sold – bonsai trees)

Oldest flowering plant

The earliest-known plant with flowers (i.e., angiosperm) is *Florigerminis jurassica*, which has been dated to 164 million years old. The species was described in 2022 from a 4.2-cm-long (1.7-in) fossil discovered in Inner Mongolia, China. It consists of a stem, a leafy branch, a bulbous fruit and a tiny flower bud. This is presently the only recognized angiosperm from the Jurassic era, a time when flowerless plants like ferns and cycads were dominant.

Fastest flower opening

The petals of the bunchberry dogwood (*Cornus canadensis*) – a low-growing perennial found in North American spruce forests – can burst open in less than 0.5 milliseconds. That's 200 times quicker than the blink of an eye. Researchers uncovered this fleet floral phenomenon in May 2005 after scrutinizing high-speed video to learn more about how this species employs elastic energy to catapult its pollen.

Slowest plant to flower

The Queen of the Andes (*Puya raimondii*), native to high elevations in Bolivia and Peru, can take 80–150 years to bloom, after which it expires. It goes out in style, however, producing a massive flower spike (panicle) that can soar to 15 m (49 ft) tall; this also makes it the **largest bromeliad**.

Widest hibiscus flower
David Anchondo of Hobbs, New Mexico, USA, cultivated a variety of *Hibiscus moscheutos* aptly named "Pink Elephant" that spanned 30.48 cm (1 ft) – akin to a dinner plate – as confirmed on 29 Aug 2023. The humongous hibiscus is shown here with the proud gardener and his son, David Anchondo Jr.

Largest flower market
Aalsmeer Flower Auction in the Netherlands occupies a vast 99.9-ha (247-acre) warehouse – double the size of Vatican City, the **smallest country**. It has roots back to 1911 when local growers joined forces to command better prices. A global hub for trade in cut flowers, plants and bulbs, the auction turned over €5.3 bn (£4.4 bn; $5.5 bn) in 2024.

Highest flowering plants

On a 1955 expedition to Mount Kamet in Uttarakhand, India, N D Jayal – then director of the Himalayan Mountaineering Institute – documented two angiosperms blooming at *c.* 6,400 m (21,000 ft). These were *Ermania himalayensis*, a member of the cabbage family, and the alpine ranunculus (*Ranunculus trivedii*), a type of buttercup.

MOST FLOWERS ON A...

- **Chrysanthemum**: 4,351, grown by Yoshiteru Nomura (JPN), as counted on 4 Nov 2011.
- **Orchid (monopodial)**: 159, grown by Kevin Englisch (CAN), as counted on 21 Mar 2024.
- **Hellebore**: 66, grown by Anna Maclean (UK), as counted on 4 May 2006.

Largest single flower
Rafflesia (aka corpse flowers) are parasitic plants that dwell within forest vines in south-east Asia. When mature, a bud emerges from the host and unfurls into a huge, five-petalled bloom; the largest, at up to 111 cm (3 ft 7.7 in) across, belong to *R. arnoldii*. Their speckled, flesh-red petals and strong odour (akin to carrion) evolved to attract flies for pollination.

Largest family of flowering plants
Asteraceae (formerly Compositae) – better known as the daisy family – comprises more than 1,900 genera and some 32,000 species. Among them are many garden staples such as sunflowers, chrysanthemums and cosmos (pictured). Their closest rival is the orchid family (Orchidaceae) with an estimated 28,000 species.

FEB 2 — In 2020, the metropolitan area of Miami-Dade County in Florida, USA, staged the NFL's season finale for the 11th time: the **most Super Bowls hosted by a city**.

FEB 3 — On this day in 1966, the Soviet Union's robotic lander *Luna 9* successfully touched down on the lunar surface and captured the **first photos taken on the Moon**.

DID YOU KNOW?

For most of its life, the titan arum resembles a small tree. When not flowering (which can take up to a decade!), it is in its "vegetative stage". During this period, its underground tuber – the **heaviest corm**, at up to *c.* 150 kg (330 lb) – produces a stem with a single leaf blade. As this matures, the leaf divides into a series of branched leaflets, giving the plant a tree-like appearance.

TALLEST "BLOOM"

While not the world's **largest single flower** (see opposite), *Amorphophallus titanum* does take the crown if allowing for an entire flowering structure, botanically known as an inflorescence. In this species – endemic to rainforest in Sumatra, Indonesia – that comprises a towering spike (spadix) with hundreds of tiny flowers at its base, enveloped by a giant petal-like leaf (spathe). The largest on record stood 3.1 m (10 ft 2 in) tall, nurtured by Louis Ricciardiello (USA, right), as confirmed on 18 Jun 2010. Producing these floral structures is so energy-intensive that the titan arum only blooms once every seven to ten years, and even then the inflorescence lasts just a matter of days.

In bloom, *A. titanum* is infamous for its pungent aroma, likened to rotting meat and detectable up to 0.8 km (0.5 mi) away!

FEB 4 — Beth Neale (ZAF) and Miles Cloutier (CAN) locked lips for 4 min 6 sec – the **longest underwater kiss** – at the LUX* South Ari Atoll resort in the Maldives in 2023.

FEB 5 — *T-all* aboard! In 2018, the world's **shortest bus driver** – Frank Faeek Hachem (UK) – was confirmed to stand 136.2 cm (4 ft 5.6 in) in Chichester, West Sussex, UK.

Aquatic Plants & Algae

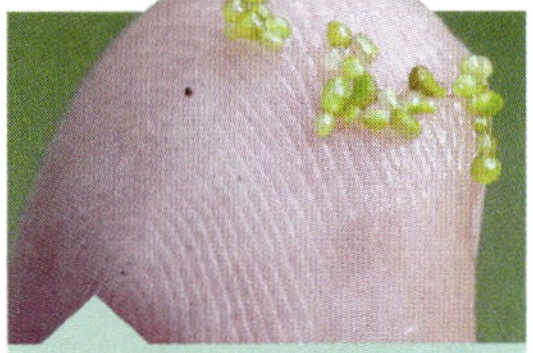

Smallest flowering plant
Watermeals (*Wolffia*) measure just 1 mm (0.04 in) across. Like duckweed – a close but slightly larger relative – they can be found floating in dense mats on the surface of stagnant ponds and swamps. Flowers, comprising one pistil and one stamen, sit within an inner cavity and bear the **smallest fruit**, weighing about the same as a grain of salt!

Despite sharing several similar traits – most notably the ability to photosynthesize (i.e., harness energy from sunlight) – algae such as seaweed, which range in scale from micrometres to metres, are not part of the kingdom of plants. Rather, they are placed into the diverse group of organisms known as protists, alongside the likes of amoebas and slime moulds.

Largest plant (by area)

In Shark Bay off Western Australia, there is a single colony of Poseidon's ribbon weed (*Posidonia australis*) that occupies *c.* 200 km² (77 sq mi) – enough to cover the entirety of Washington, DC. Based on area, this makes it the **largest organism** on the planet. The superlative seagrass field was spotlighted in a journal paper on 1 Jun 2022.

Sadly, ocean warming is putting habitats like Shark Bay at risk. An unprecedented marine heatwave in 2010–11 led to a seasonal loss of 1,310 km² (506 sq mi) of Western Australia's total marine meadows – the **largest seagrass decline**.

Largest single-celled organism

The fern-like green seaweed *Caulerpa taxifolia*, native to tropical waters of the Caribbean and the Indo-Pacific, regularly grows 20–60 cm (8 in–2 ft) long, and even up to 2.8 m (9 ft 2 in) in extreme cases. Yet, despite its size, each blade (frond) incredibly comprises just one cell. Like many seaweeds, it has evolved a range of structures including a stolon (stem) and root-like holdfasts that in both form and function imitate those of multicellular plants and algae.

In non-native regions – particularly in the Mediterranean Sea, where it was accidentally introduced in the 1990s – *C. taxifolia* has come to be called "killer algae" owing to its takeover of the ocean floor at the expense of other plants and organisms such as coral. It has even been included in the IUCN's *100 Worst Invasive Alien Species* list.

Deepest algae

Marine botanist husband-and-wife team Mark and Diane Littler (both USA) discovered an unknown species of crustose coralline algae on a seamount 295 m (968 ft) below the ocean surface off San Salvador, The Bahamas, in Oct 1984. Coralline algae is a type of red algae, which instead of green chlorophyll contains a reddish/pinkish light-absorbing pigment known as phycoerythrin. The specimen spotted by the Littlers managed to survive despite 99.9% of sunlight not reaching its depth on the seabed.

Largest macroalgal bloom

In recent years, vast agglomerations of *Sargassum* brown seaweed have formed in the tropical Atlantic, stretching from Mexico all the way to western Africa. The extent of what is known as the Great Atlantic Sargassum Belt (GASB) has been closely monitored by scientists at the Optical Oceanography Laboratory – part of the University of South Florida, USA.

The peak coverage of the GASB to date was in Jun 2022, with a monthly mean coverage of 6,989 km² (2,698 sq mi) – four times the size of Greater London, UK. This equated to a wet biomass of *c.* 23.3 million tonnes (25.7 million tons).

Fastest-growing seaweed
Giant kelp (*Macrocystis pyrifera*) can gain 50 cm (1 ft 7 in) of growth in a single day. Such speedy development contributes to it being the **largest seaweed**, with blades up to 60 m (197 ft) long. It grows near rocky coastlines (particularly in the Pacific Ocean), where it forms underwater forests that are havens for wildlife.

Fastest predatory plant
Southern bladderworts (*Utricularia australis*) can ensnare victims in just 5.2 milliseconds – 20 times quicker than we can blink! It hunts using modified leaves that resemble air-filled bags (i.e., bladders). If an insect or even tadpole swims too close, it can trigger a trapdoor on the leaf that sucks in water and the hapless creature with up to 2,800 *g* of acceleration! For the **fastest predatory plant on land**, turn over to the next page.

Largest lotus plantation
Guangchang County in Jiangxi, eastern China, is synonymous with the lotus (*Nelumbo nucifera*), where this aquatic plant has been cultivated for some 1,300 years since the Tang Dynasty. The area today has an annual yield of some 9,000 tonnes (9,920 tons) of dried seeds, for which there is culinary and medicinal demand. On 9 Jul 2016, GWR recognized one lotus paddy field in Guangchang that by itself covered 1.08 km² (0.4 sq mi).

FEB 6 — In 2015, master *jamón* cutter Noé Bonillo Ramos (ESP) ended the **longest marathon slicing meat** after 72 hr 13 min 8 sec at Les Grands d'Espagne in Paris, France.

FEB 7 — Testing a new spacesuit, NASA astronaut Bruce McCandless II (USA) performed the **first untethered spacewalk** from the Space Shuttle *Challenger* in 1984.

After measuring, La Rinconada park covered its record-setting lily pad in plaster in order to preserve it for posterity.

LARGEST LILY PAD

On 3 Feb 2012, Gaston Ribero (above right) – the owner of La Rinconada eco park in Santa Cruz de la Sierra, Bolivia – harvested a waterlily pad that spanned 3.2 m (10 ft 6 in). Its approximate surface area of 7.55 m^2 (81.3 sq ft) also makes it the **largest undivided leaf** on record. Though it wasn't known at the time, the pad belonged to a distinct species, which thanks to the joint efforts of Bolivian botany experts and the UK's Kew Gardens (see below) was formally classified as *Victoria boliviana* in 2022. In the wild, it's only known to exist in the Llanos de Moxos wetlands, located in the Beni region of north-east Bolivia.

Each year, several botanic gardens worldwide take part in the "Waterlily Weigh-Off", where they test how heavy a load their giant lily pads can support. In 2025, the top prize went to Bok Tower Gardens in Florida, USA, with a pad that bore 183 lb (83 kg) of various objects before sinking. Above is a shot at Royal Botanic Gardens, Kew, in London, UK, with botanical artist Lucy Smith, waterlily expert Carlos Magdalena and his then-six-year-old son Mateo, demonstrating the sturdiness of this floating foliage.

At the other end of the scale is the thermal waterlily (*Nymphaea thermarum*), the **smallest waterlily**, which has pads that span on average 15 mm (0.59 in) – more than 200 times smaller than the behemoth above. Its yellow flowers are about the size of a penny. This super-rare species is endemic to a single hot spring in Rwanda, and might now be extinct if it weren't for specimens in botanic collections.

FEB 8 Frank Divendal (NLD) never loses his place when reading... On this day in 2010, he received the title for the **largest collection of bookmarks** (103,009).

FEB 9 In 2012, Signal 1 Radio (UK) arranged for 41 couples to redeclare their love on a rollercoaster at Alton Towers – the **most vow renewals on a theme-park ride.**

Killer Plants

Largest Venus flytrap
On 7 Jun 2021, Jeremiah Harris (USA) revealed a Venus flytrap (*Dionaea muscipula*) with 6.1-cm-long (2.4-in) traps. Measured across the mid-rib, this cultivar – called "Alien" – has leaves more than double the typical size. Harris, founder of the Colorado Carnivorous Plant Society, bettered his previous record of 5 cm (1.96 in).

Most expensive carnivorous plant
A *Nepenthes veitchii* "Candy Dreams", so called for its bright stripes, was sold by Domonick Gravine of Tennessee, USA, to an anonymous buyer for $19,800 (£15,075) in Mar 2022. Vibrant colours and patterns, as well as nectar, are some of the tactics used by pitcher plants to lure prey into their fluid-filled pitfall traps.

DID YOU KNOW?

Deadly ricin has been used as a means of assassination. On 11 Sep 1978, Georgi Markov – an outspoken critic of the Communist regime in his native Bulgaria – died after a pinhead-sized micro-pellet containing ricin was fired into his leg via a weaponized umbrella in London, UK, four days earlier.

Oldest carnivorous plant fossil
In 2014, leaf fragments estimated to be 35–47 million years old were found to contain trapping organs similar to those present in today's flycatcher bush (genus *Roridula*). The fossilized specimens were preserved in amber recovered from a mine in Kaliningrad, Russia.

Largest carnivorous plant genus
In total, as of Oct 2025, there were nearly 900 known species of carnivorous plant across 19 genera. The most speciose genus is currently the sundews (*Drosera*), distinguished by their sticky leaves, with *c.* 259 documented species.

The **smallest carnivorous plant family** is Cephalotaceae, which contains only a single known species: the Albany pitcher plant (*Cephalotus follicularis*), which grows wild on the south-west coast of Western Australia.

Fastest terrestrial predatory plant
The pimpernel sundew (*Drosera glanduligera*) of southern Australia employs "snap tentacles" to capture small insects within 75 milliseconds, at accelerations of up to 7.98 m/s^2. The fast-moving appendages, powered by hydraulic pressure, catapult an unwitting bug on to shorter tentacles covered in a sticky glue-like substance. A bending motion of these glue tentacles then bears the victim towards the centre (rosette) of the sundew. Here, it is digested and its nutrients absorbed to supplement the often poor soil where these plants grow. For the **fastest predatory plant** overall, see p.22.

Deadliest plant
Based on human lives claimed, tobacco (*Nicotiana tabacum*) is the biggest plant serial killer, causing cancer, heart disease and many other conditions. According to 2025 World Health Organization data, more than 7 million people die prematurely each year from tobacco, commonly from smoking, with just under one-quarter of deaths being non-smokers passively exposed to tobacco fumes.

Most poisonous plant used for decorative arts
The vermillion seeds of the rosary pea (*Abrus precatorius*), aka jequirity beans, are widely used in jewellery and other handicrafts, particularly in southern Asia. This is despite the fact that they contain a lectin toxin called abrin which is similar to ricin (see left). Eating a single seed has been enough to be fatal; artisans who work with the beans have been poisoned just from accidental pinpricks.

Tallest poison ivy
Robert Fedrock (CAN) spotted a 20.75-m (68-ft) specimen of *Toxicodendron radicans* in Paris, Ontario, Canada, on 12 Mar 2023. Poison ivy contains a chemical cocktail known as urushiol, which on contact with skin can trigger an allergic reaction resulting in painful inflammation and blisters.

Lectins are a group of proteins that serve various functions in plants, such as defence against pests and pathogens. Many are harmless to humans in small quantities and when cooked properly, but some can be lethal. Estonian scientist Peter Hermann Stillmark identified the **first lectin** in 1888 when studying castor beans from *Ricinus communis* (left); now called ricin, it is one of the most toxic compounds known to humankind.

Largest cultivated pitcher trap
Robert and Diana Cantley (both UK) and the team at Borneo Exotics in Lindula, Sri Lanka, unveiled a prodigious pitcher with a volume of 2.986 litres (101 fl oz) on 16 Apr 2025. It was grown on a cultivar of the hybrid *Nepenthes sibuyanensis* x *merrilliana* that is provisionally designated *Nepenthes* "Titanic".

FEB 10 — Carlo Prisco (ITA) owns the **largest collection of *Assassin's Creed* memorabilia** – with 1,030 items of merch relating to the stealth games counted in 2019.

FEB 11 — Happy birthday to France's Lucile Randon, aka Sister André (b. 1904). She was the **oldest nun ever**, aged 118 years 340 days when she died on 17 Jan 2023.

Most dangerous plant stingers
One of the most notorious plants in the Alnwick collection – it's even kept in its own locked case! – is gympie-gympie (*Dendrocnide moroides*). Native to the rainforests of Australia, brushing against their leaves has been likened to being electrocuted; extensive contact can cause prolonged pain or even, in very rare cases, kill animals and possibly humans. Similar effects have been noted in the New Zealand tree nettle (*Urtica ferox*), aka *taraonga*.

MOST PLANT SPECIES IN A POISON GARDEN

The Alnwick Poison Garden in Northumberland, UK, was home to 97 toxic and narcotic species as of 2025. These include perennials such as foxgloves (*Digitalis purpurea*, **1**) and the Italian arum (*Arum italicum*, **2**), as well as trees (e.g., yew and laburnum) and climbing plants (e.g., ivy). The garden, opened in 2005, was a passion project of the Duchess of Northumberland, who said: "Rather than focusing solely on beautiful or exotic plants, I wanted a space that was thought-provoking, educational and slightly dangerous." In 2024, the Poison Garden welcomed some 110,000 visitors.

The potent aroma of some plants in the Alnwick Poison Garden causes around 100 people per year to faint or feel nauseous!

FEB 12 Today in 2024, a promo video for *Deadpool & Wolverine* (USA) logged 365 million views on YouTube, making it the **most watched movie trailer in 24 hours**.

FEB 13 Ray Macdonald and Rojjaporn Lertworawanich (both THA) hit 130.45 km/h (81.06 mph) in the **fastest tuk-tuk** at an airfield near Bangkok, Thailand, in 2020.

BIG PICTURE

Tardigrades

One of these micro critters might fit atop the tip of a needle, but don't let their diminutive size fool you: tardigrades are among the most robust life-forms on (and off!) Earth. By being able to endure radiation, extreme heat, decades in deep freeze and even the vacuum of outer space, they are a prime contender for the title of **hardiest animal**. Here, we examine the incredible anatomy of these resilient creatures – both inside and out.

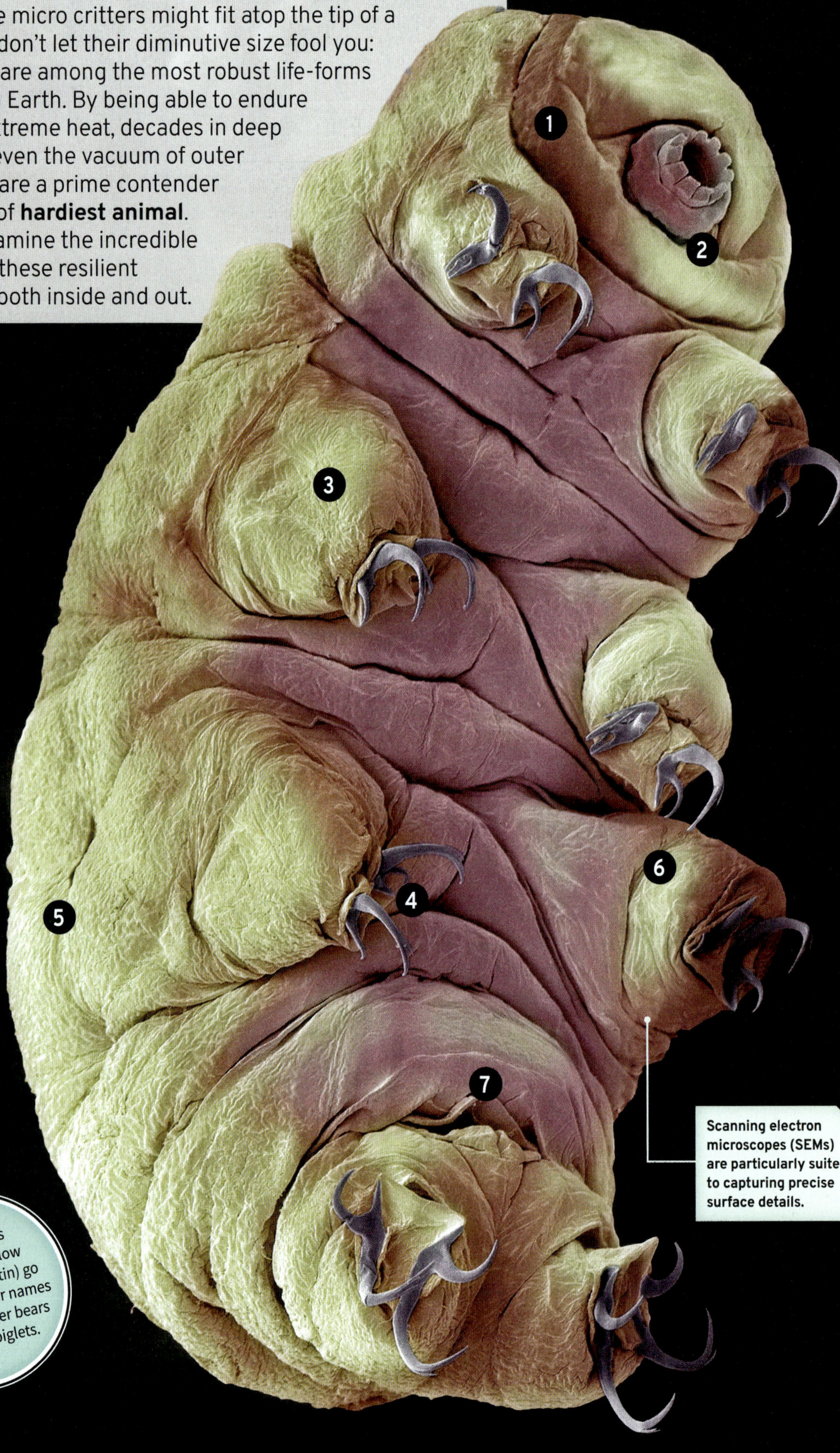

Scanning electron microscopes (SEMs) are particularly suited to capturing precise surface details.

Tardigrades (meaning "slow walkers" in Latin) go by several other names including water bears and moss piglets.

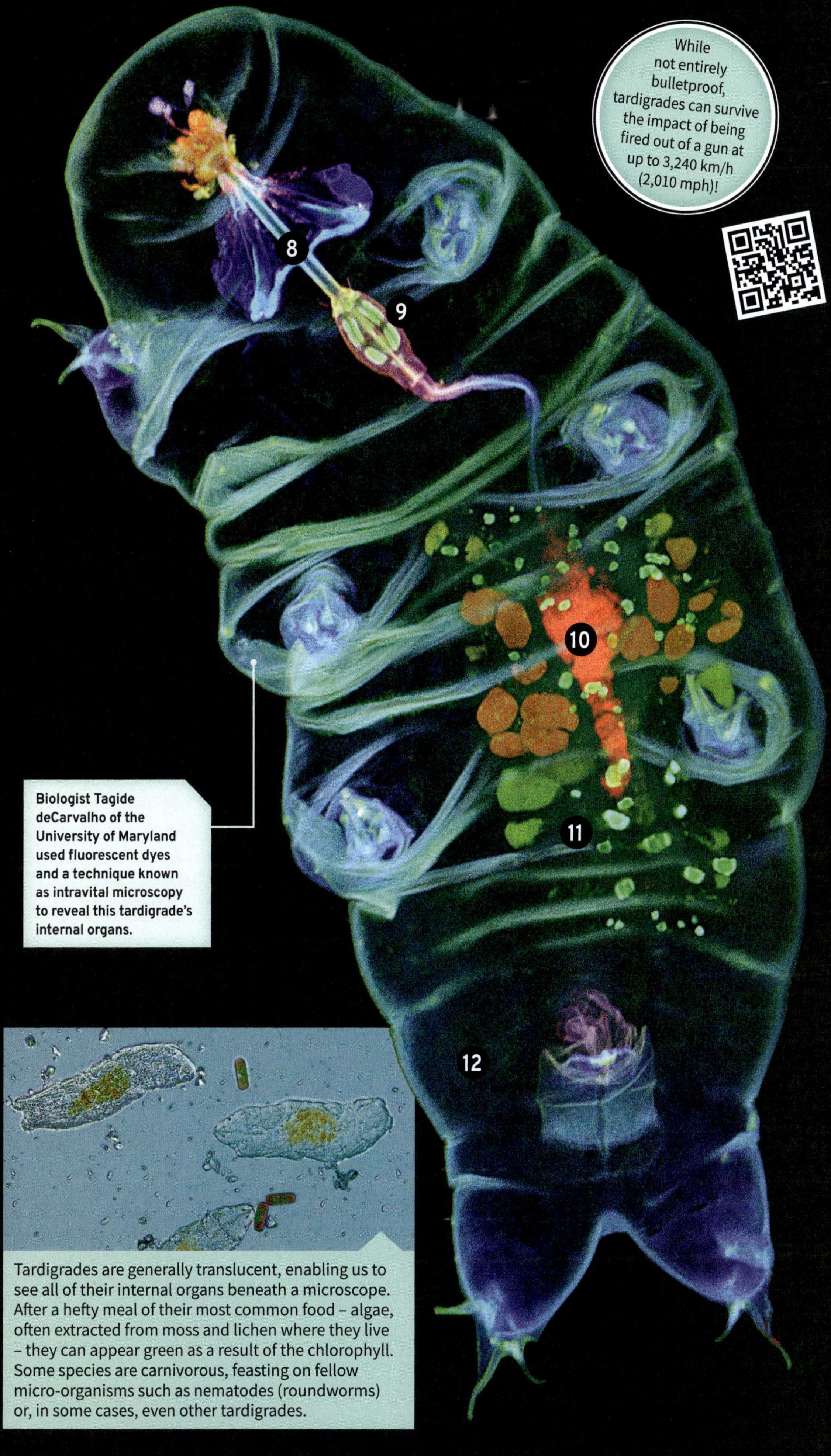

While not entirely bulletproof, tardigrades can survive the impact of being fired out of a gun at up to 3,240 km/h (2,010 mph)!

1: Tardigrades only have rudimentary vision: two tiny eyespots and a few sensory cells enable them to detect light levels, but they can't perceive shapes or colour.

2: A tubular mouth is part of the "buccopharyngeal apparatus" (see also **8** and **9**) that water bears use to eat.

3: Tardigrades are among the smallest animals to possess limbs, with four pairs of stubby legs. The rear set are oriented backwards and used more for gripping than propulsion.

4: Hook-like claws, which vary in form across the 1,000 or so species, help with movement and clinging to plant matter.

5: The outer skin – the cuticle – is shed at various stages of its life, enabling the water bear to grow over time.

6: In hostile conditions (e.g., extreme heat or cold), tardigrades can expel all body water, withdraw their legs and enter a ball-like "tun" state of suspended animation.

7: A feature shared with birds and reptiles, the cloaca is a multipurpose opening used for both reproduction and the expulsion of waste.

8: To feed, a pair of calcium-carbonate, spear-like "stylets" shoot out from the mouth to pierce plant/animal cells…

9: …at which point they use a powerful pharynx (throat muscles) to slurp out the juices from within the cells.

10: Here we can see the contents of the tardigrade's gut. It generally takes around 48 hr for algae to be digested.

11: Although not visible in this image, the gonad is positioned above the digestive system, producing either sperm (in males) or eggs (in females).

12: Water bears are filled with a fluid known as haemolymph, which acts like our blood, moving nutrients and waste products around the body.

Biologist Tagide deCarvalho of the University of Maryland used fluorescent dyes and a technique known as intravital microscopy to reveal this tardigrade's internal organs.

Tardigrades are generally translucent, enabling us to see all of their internal organs beneath a microscope. After a hefty meal of their most common food – algae, often extracted from moss and lichen where they live – they can appear green as a result of the chlorophyll. Some species are carnivorous, feasting on fellow micro-organisms such as nematodes (roundworms) or, in some cases, even other tardigrades.

Green Animals

Largest jewel beetle
Jewel beetles (Buprestidae) stand out among their kind thanks to their iridescent elytra (wing cases). Among the 15,500 or so species, the biggest are the metallic wood-borer *Euchroma giganteum* (pictured) of the Americas and *Megaloxantha bicolor* of Australia, both of which can reach 8 cm (3.1 in) long.

Heaviest parrot
Its flightless nature and ability to store sizeable reserves of body fat are two key factors that attribute to the superlative weight of the kākāpō (*Strigops habroptilus*). Males of this New Zealand native can tip the scales at 4 kg (8 lb 13 oz) – comparable to a pet cat. The mottled olive-green feathers of this bird are ideal for blending in among moss and ferns on the forest floor.

Heaviest snakes
In Feb 2024, the green anaconda – a large constrictor found mainly in the wetlands and rivers of South America – was taxonomically split into two: the southern (*Eunectes murinus*) and the northern (*E. akayima*). Fully grown, females of both species measure 3–5 m (9 ft 10 in–16 ft 4 in) from head to tail and typically weigh between 30 and 70 kg (66–154 lb).

Occasionally much larger individuals are sighted, reaching 7–8 m (22–26 ft) long with an estimated weight in excess of 300 kg (660 lb) – the same as four washing machines! It's likely that such hefty examples are pregnant or have recently consumed a substantial meal, such as a deer or tapir.

Shortest-lived reptile
Endemic to south-west Madagascar, the Labord's chameleon (*Furcifer labordi*) has a lifespan of just 4–5 months, with the shortest lives recorded in the most arid regions. Indeed, with an embryonic period of 8–9 months, this species spends more time in its egg than out, giving it the dubious honour of the **shortest-lived tetrapod** (four-limbed vertebrate) too.

Slowest mammal
With a top speed of 0.27 km/h (0.17 mph) in the jungle canopy, three-toed sloths (*Bradypus tridactylus*) of South America lead fairly sedentary lives. So much so that algae often grow on their shaggy fur, turning them green. It's a symbiotic relationship: the algae are given a damp home, while sloths gain camouflage and even a source of food.

Largest trogon
Shimmering emerald plumage, complemented by flashes of scarlet red, make the aptly named resplendent quetzal (*Pharomachrus mocinno*) instantly recognizable. It's found largely in the forests of Central America – in fact, it's the national bird of Guatemala – and is one of the most sought-after species on birdwatchers' wishlists. Males can attain lengths of over 1 m (3 ft 3 in), owing primarily to a pair of streamer-like tail plumes that emerge in the breeding season.

Largest grasshopper
With an extremely thin, stick-like body, the giant jumping stick grasshopper (*Proscopia gigantea*) typically measures up to 18 cm (7 in) long, though occasionally can slightly exceed this. It is native to Brazil and elsewhere in South America. There have been reports of a grasshopper from the border region of Malaysia and Thailand, said to measure up to 25 cm (10 in) long and be capable of leaping a distance of 15 ft (4.6 m), but such a species has yet to be formally identified.

Largest tree frog
Female white-lipped tree frogs (*Litoria infrafrenata*) can reach 14 cm (5.5 in) long from snout to vent and weigh up to 115 g (4 oz), akin to a small apple. The species is native to tropical rainforest in northern Australia, New Guinea and a few Indonesian islands. They are occasionally kept as pets, though a special "Kermit permit" is required to do so in Australia.

FEB 14 Happy Valentine's Day! At venues across Australia in 2008, matchmaker Fast Impressions (AUS) united 1,240 singletons for the **largest speed-dating event**.

FEB 15 In 2013, a meteor exploded over Chelyabinsk in central Russia. The **greatest measured impact event on Earth** was akin in scale to 500 kilotons of TNT.

LARGEST PEAFOWL
Peafowl (*Pavo*) are among the largest members of the pheasant family. They are famed for their iridescent plumage and elaborate tails with eyespots, which males go all out to display to attract a mate. Though perhaps less well-known than their bluer relations from India (*P. cristatus*), the biggest members of the clan are green peafowl (*P. muticus*) of south-east Asia. The males of this species attain a length of 3 m (9 ft 10 in) – up to 60% of which is tail – making them prime candidates for the longest birds on the planet today. A steeply declining population, largely driven by habitat loss, has resulted in green peafowl being listed as endangered since 2009.

Research indicates that the more eyespots (aka ocelli) in a peacock's tail train, the more appealing he is to females.

FEB 16 The **largest litter of goats** is seven kids, born to Fairywood MP Angelica, a Nigerian dwarf goat owned by Elizabeth Miller of Gilbert, Arizona, USA, in 2019.

FEB 17 On this day in 2012, Argentine body-modifier Axel Rosales added nine more metal studs to his face, securing the title for **most facial piercings** with 280.

Rocks & Gems

DID YOU KNOW?

All emeralds are green, but the shade of green varies. Emeralds are a form of beryl that are most commonly found in Colombia (see right), Zambia and Brazil. They owe their characteristic colour to trace elements of chromium and vanadium – levels of which determine the intensity of the greenness in each stone, with some leaning more towards blue and others more towards yellow.

Largest emerald producer
The country to export the greatest volume of gem-quality emeralds is Colombia, producing 55–60% of the world's total per annum. Another hotspot for these green gems is Zambia. Its Kagem mine complex, located in Copperbelt Province, by itself accounts for some 25% of global production (159,351 carats in 2024), making it the **largest emerald mine**.

Largest green diamond
At 40.7 carats, the "Dresden Green" is the biggest natural green-coloured diamond – a rare variant that owes its hue to irradiation. It is believed to originate from the Golconda mines in India. The jewel was acquired by Frederick Augustus II of Saxony in 1743 and mounted into a hat jewel with more than 400 white diamonds; it is still housed today at the Royal Palace in Dresden, Saxony, Germany.

100%

Most expensive emerald sold at auction
The 37-carat "Aga Khan Emerald" is the centrepiece of this diamond-bordered platinum-and-gold brooch. It fetched 7,765,000 Swiss francs ($8.83 m; £6.85 m) at Christie's in Geneva, Switzerland, on 12 Nov 2024. The Cartier jewel was commissioned by Prince Sadruddin Aga Khan in 1960 for his then wife, British socialite Nina Dyer.

Earliest emerald mine
Green gems began to be industrially dug at the so-called "Cleopatra Mines" in Egypt's Wadi Sikait valley, near the Red Sea, in at least the 1st century BCE. Demand for emeralds exploded under the Roman and Byzantine Empires (1st–6th centuries CE), who coveted the precious stones known then as *smaragdus*. For centuries, Wadi Sikait and its environs was the only known location to produce green beryl in the Mediterranean region.

Most emeralds on a necklace
Indian luxury jewellers Shiv Narayan created the Satlada Necklace mounted with 315 individual emeralds and 1,971 diamonds (also the **most diamonds on a necklace**), as confirmed on 10 May 2023. The seven-row solid-gold necklace took four months to assemble.

Most expensive green diamond sold at auction
Chow Tai Fook Jewellery paid an unprecedented HK$130,040,000 ($16.74 m; £11.45 m) for the 5.03-carat "Aurora Green", set in a gold and pink-diamond ring, at Christie's in Hong Kong, China, on 31 May 2016.

LARGEST...

Cut tsavorite garnet
Tsavorite was found by British geologist Campbell R Bridges in 1967 within what is now the Tsavo National Park, Kenya. One of the rarest forms of garnet – and prized for its vibrant green colour – the largest cut example was 325.13 carats, as assessed in Nov 2006. It was refined from a 185-g (6.5-oz) rough stone unearthed in Tanzania's Merelani Hills.

Another highly sought green garnet variant is demantoid (first found in Russia in 1851 and named after the old German word for "diamond" owing to its similar properties). The **largest cut demantoid** is 56.48 carats, as verified on 14 Nov 2025. It is owned by Hayrat Gems and Jewellery (UAE).

Malachite deposit
A widespread form of copper ore, malachite was among the earliest sources of green pigment, used in tomb paintings and as eye make-up in Egypt since 4000 BCE. The stone is widely associated with Russia, where a *c.* 70-tonne (77-ton) chunk was excavated at the Demidoff Mine in the 1830s.

But the largest deposit uncovered to date was in the 1890s at a Namibian site known as "Green Hill", aka the Tsumeb Mine, where more than 170 minerals have been catalogued. The Tsumeb malachite mass had approximate dimensions of 36 ft high, 130 ft wide and 590 ft deep (12 x 40 x 180 m).

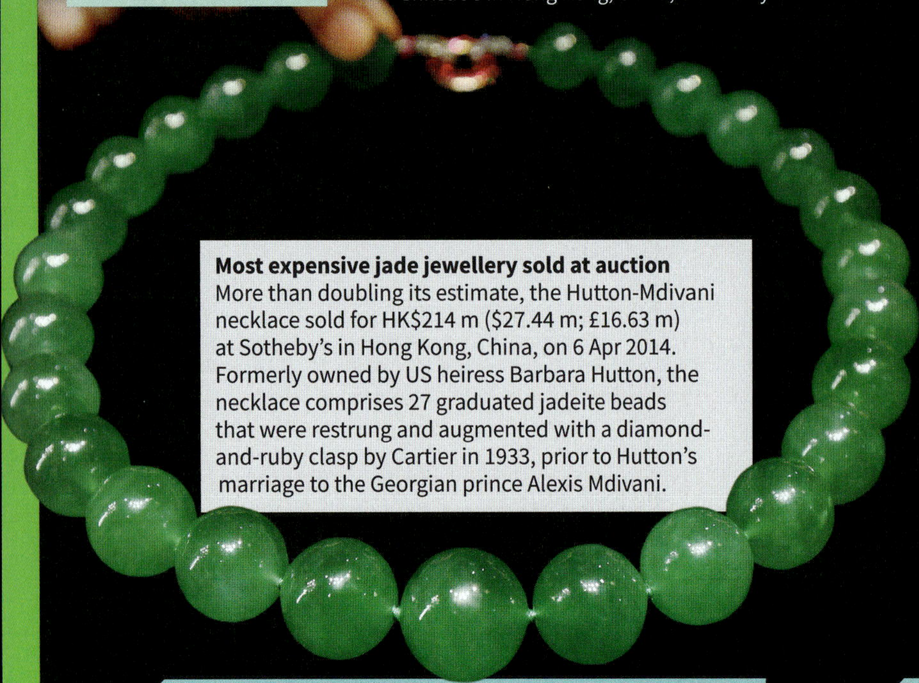

Most expensive jade jewellery sold at auction
More than doubling its estimate, the Hutton-Mdivani necklace sold for HK$214 m ($27.44 m; £16.63 m) at Sotheby's in Hong Kong, China, on 6 Apr 2014. Formerly owned by US heiress Barbara Hutton, the necklace comprises 27 graduated jadeite beads that were restrung and augmented with a diamond-and-ruby clasp by Cartier in 1933, prior to Hutton's marriage to the Georgian prince Alexis Mdivani.

First nuclear explosion
Ushering in the Atomic Era, the Trinity Test detonated a 25-kiloton plutonium implosion bomb in the Jornada del Muerto desert of New Mexico, USA, at 5.29 a.m. on 16 Jul 1945. The immense heat (*c.* 7,000°C or 12,600°F) caused some of the sandy soil at ground zero to melt and fuse into a green-coloured glassy substance, later dubbed trinitite or atomsite.

FEB 18 The **largest teapot**, standing 4.19 m (13 ft 9 in) tall and holding enough tea for *c.* 60,000 cups, was unveiled by Khadeer Tea (SAU) in Riyadh, Saudi Arabia, in 2023.

FEB 19 *Chop, chop!* Barber Konstantinos Koutoupis (GRC) snipped his way to glory in Athens, Greece, in 2017, giving a full trim in 47.17 sec – the **fastest haircut**.

LARGEST CUT PERIDOT

Peridots are a form of olivine, a green gem that occurs in volcanic areas and even occasionally in meteorites. Gaining their colour from iron content, their shade varies from lime and olive to a darker apple green. This prodigious specimen – unearthed in Myanmar and now owned by collector Yan Naing Soe (MMR) – tipped the scales at 769.03 carats when assessed on 16 Oct 2024. This makes it the same weight as an average pear. It was painstakingly carved, etched and polished into its egg-shaped form (see stages below) by master gem-cutter Victor Tuzlukov (RUS). Its 1,824 individual facets also make it the **most faceted peridot**.

Peridot – like malachite (see opposite) – is classed as an idiochromatic mineral that comes in a single intrinsic colour: green!

FEB 20 In 1935, Caroline Mikkelsen (DNK) became the **first woman on Antarctic land**, when she disembarked the M/S *Thorshavn* and set foot on the Tryne Islands.

FEB 21 Happy birthday to Jeanne Calment (FRA), the **oldest person ever** to have been authenticated. She passed away on 4 Aug 1997, aged 122 years 164 days.

Horticultural Heroes

ON THE RECORD

It took knowledge, dedication, hunger, passion, commitment, sacrifice, love and most importantly patience to achieve this record. And what we have gained is memories, legacy, tradition. Someday I will die, but the stories, they will live on – *Alex Babich, grower of the* ***tallest sunflower***

LONGEST...

Aubergine/eggplant

Veteran competitive grower Peter Glazebrook (UK) reaped two records at the latest CANNA UK National Giant Vegetables Championship, held in Malvern, Worcestershire, UK, on 26–28 Sep 2025. His eggplant (*Solanum melongena*) measured in at 49 cm (1 ft 7.3 in). Also recognized was his **tallest runner bean plant**, with a full extent of 8.006 m (26 ft 3.2 in) – about the height of a two-storey house.

Two months later, on 12 Nov, it was confirmed that Glazebrook had cultivated the **tallest broad bean plant** too, topping 3.80 m (12 ft 5.6 in). Poignantly, this was his 30th GWR title since he'd earned his first 30 years earlier.

Sweet pepper

Seasoned growers Kevin, Gareth and Jamie Fortey of Cwmbran, Gwent, UK, had a 26.7-cm-long (10.5-in) paprika-style red pepper (*Capsicum annuum*) ratified at the Malvern Autumn Show in Sep 2025. The family improved on their own record with a 30.4-cm (11.97-in) example on 10 Nov 2025.

Radish

"King of the Longs" Joe Atherton (UK) added yet another title to his cornucopia of root-veg records with a phenomenal daikon (*Raphanus raphanistrum* var. *longipinnatus*) at the 2025 UK National Giant Vegetables Championship. At 7.848 m (25 ft 8.9 in) end to end, the radish was big enough to span a FIFA-certified soccer goal, with some root to spare.

HEAVIEST...

Tomatillo

Rolf Böhland (DEU) grew a cooking apple-sized husk tomato (*Physalis philadelphica*) that registered 236 g (8.32 oz) at the Central German GPC Weigh-in Championship in Unterwellenborn, Thuringia, Germany, on 6 Sep 2025. This is seven times weightier than a typical tomatillo.

It surpassed the record of British gardener Graham Barratt, who presented a 198-g (6.98-oz) specimen just two weeks earlier on 22 Aug. Barratt, who enjoyed a bumper season in 2025, does retain a number of other titles set that year, though:

- **Heaviest luffa**: 2.82 kg (6 lb 3.5 oz)
- **Longest luffa**: 1.699 m (5 ft 6.8 in)
- **Tallest luffa plant**: 11.672 m (38 ft 3.5 in)
- **Longest pea pod**: 18 cm (7 in).

Heaviest aubergine/eggplant
This title was broken twice in 2025. First to claim it was Erik Gunstrom (above) of Pennsylvania, USA, who presented a 3.969-kg (8-lb 12-oz) eggplant on 19 Aug. Just a few weeks later on 12 Sep, Martin Truttmann (CHE) made history with an uber aubergine of the Aswad variety that tipped the scales at 5.078 kg (11 lb 3 oz) and had a circumference of 80 cm (2 ft 7.5 in).

Pomelo/pummelo

On 27 Jan 2023, Kazuki Maeda (JPN) presented a 26-cm-wide (10.2-in) pomelo (*Citrus maxima*) that weighed 5.528 kg (12 lb 2.9 oz) in Yatsushiro, Kumamoto, Japan. It bettered his 2021 record for this grapefruit-like fruit of 5.386 kg (11 lb 13.9 oz).

Celeriac

Chris Marriott (UK) claimed this title for the second time in 2025 with an 8.01-kg (17-lb 10.5-oz) *Apium graveolens* var. *rapaceum*, assessed at the Malvern Autumn Show in Sep.

Cantaloupe melon

Green-fingered teen Llorenç Soler Adrover (ESP) had a 31.446-kg (69-lb 5.2-oz) cantaloupe (*Cucumis melo*) confirmed at a competition in Villanueva de la Serena, Spain, on 28 Aug 2023. It was heavier than a golden retriever dog.

Marrow

This record came very close to being toppled by Mark Baggs in 2025 (see **longest marrow**, opposite). But his best effort fell *c.* 5 kg (11 lb) short of the 116.4-kg (256-lb 9.8-oz) mark laid down by Vincent Sjodin (UK) on 23 Sep 2021.

Tallest sunflower
Breaking a decade-old record, Alex Babich (USA, b. UKR) grew a humongous *Helianthus* (dubbed "Clover") in his backyard in Fort Wayne, Indiana, USA, that towered 10.90 m (35 ft 9 in) high. He credits the feat to his whole family, who aptly live by the motto: "Plant a seed. Water with love. Watch hope grow."

Heaviest tomato
Dan Sutherland of Walla Walla, Washington, USA, is the undisputed king of titanic tomatoes (*Solanum lycopersicum*). He lost his crown in 2022, but came back with a vengeance in 2025 to break the record *four* times! His largest fruit of the season – all of which were of the "Domingo" variety – weighed in at 7.661 kg (16 lb 14.2 oz) on 19 Jul, which is heftier than most bowling balls!

FEB 22 — In 2003, Shoaib Akhtar (PAK) unleashed the **fastest delivery of a cricket ball** – 161.3 km/h (100.23 mph) – during a World Cup match in Cape Town, South Africa.

FEB 23 — Mark Evans (UK) has had the name of his daughter, Lucy, inked 667 times over his body – the **most tattoos of the same name** – as verified in Wrexham in 2022.

GARDEN GIANTS HARVESTED IN 2025

1. **Longest marrow**	1.454 m (4 ft 9 in)	Mark Baggs (UK)
2. **Heaviest sweet potato**	43.2 kg (95 lb 3.8 oz)	Beni Meier (CHE)
3. **Heaviest pumpkin**	1,278.8 kg (2,819 lb 4 oz)	Ian and Stuart Paton (both UK)
4. **Heaviest gooseberry**	65.59 g (2.31 oz)	Graeme Watson (UK)
5. **Heaviest peach**	828.5 g (1 lb 13 oz)	Henry Chiles (USA)

Correct as of 24 Feb 2026

The Paton twins' giant gourd is also the **largest pumpkin by circumference** at 649.8 cm (21 ft 3.8 in) around.

FEB 24 Leo, a thrifty cocker spaniel owned by Emily Anderson (UK), deposited the **most coins into a piggy bank by a dog in one minute** (23) in Aberdeen, UK, in 2023.

FEB 25 The **fastest short-track 1,000 m (female)** was run in 2 min 30.94 sec by Maria Mutola of Mozambique at an indoor event in Stockholm, Sweden, in 1999.

Nurturing Nature

Largest seed bank/vault

Seed banks are robust, high-tech facilities designed to both research the genetics of plants and safeguard their future. The precious organic collections are protected from all manner of threats including fire, flooding and even bombs! The largest example, with more than 2.4 billion seeds, taken from *c.* 40,000 species, is the Millennium Seed Bank at Wakehurst in West Sussex, UK, which is managed by Royal Botanic Gardens, Kew.

Most trees planted by a team in one hour

As part of a nationwide drive to regreen India, the Government of Assam's Forest Department coordinated a 60-min planting frenzy on 15 Sep 2023. Civil servants, local citizens and the military turned out to dig holes for 331,929 saplings. Assam's eventual goal is to plant 10 million trees.

MILLENNIUM SEED BANK IN NUMBERS

190
Countries/territories seeds originate from

-20°C
Temperature of the seed stores

10 years
Period at which seed viability is tested

12 hr
Maximum shift length in the vault owing to the low 15% humidity

Smallest urban park

Despite having existed since 1988, a pint-sized park measuring just 0.24 m^2 (2.58 sq ft) – smaller than a typical manhole cover – was officially designated by authorities in Nagaizumi, Shizuoka, Japan, on 25 Dec 2024. It features planting, a flower-etched plaque and a rock topped with a wooden seat, just big enough for a single occupant.

At 2,004 km^2 (773.7 sq mi), the **largest urban park** is Chugach State Park, within the administrative boundaries of Anchorage in Alaska, USA. Established on 6 Aug 1970, Chugach is around 10 times bigger than the city itself.

Largest rooftop garden

Atop the 15-building government headquarters of Sejong in South Korea lies a 79,194-m^2 (852,437-sq-ft) urban oasis, as verified on 29 Jan 2016. It boasts more than a million plants, including fruit trees, herbs and vine-covered pergolas, all connected via 33 km (20.5 mi) of paths. As well as bringing some natural respite for workers, an up-to-1-m (3-ft 3-in) layer of soil acts as an effective insulator, helping to keep heat inside in the winter and out in the summer.

Most people planting trees simultaneously

The campus of Babasaheb Bhimrao Ambedkar University in Lucknow, Uttar Pradesh, India, was made a bit greener when 2,055 people all planted a tree there on 9 Jul 2025. The mass planting was overseen by the Government of Uttar Pradesh's Environment, Forest and Climate Change Department and Uttar Pradesh Forest Corporation.

Most trees planted by an individual in 24 hours

Working at an average rate of one tree every 3.75 sec, 22-year-old silviculturalist Antoine Moses (CAN) bedded in a veritable forest of 23,060 saplings near the town of High Level in Alberta, Canada, on 17–18 Jul 2021. For added motivation, his friend and fellow tree planter Kilty Elliott went for the record on the same day, himself logging 18,500, for a combined total of 41,560 between them.

Both contenders surpassed the previous record of 15,170 – set by Ken Chaplin (also a Canadian) in 2001. After the epic "plantathon", Moses reflected: "I smiled all the way through and said 'thank you' 500 times. What we do together is so incredibly fulfilling."

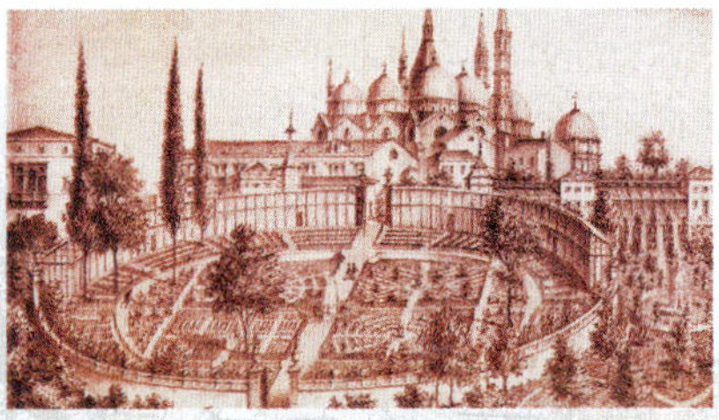

Oldest botanical garden (one site)

Italy's Orto Botanico was founded by the University of Padua in 1545, initially focusing on medicinal plants. Nearly five centuries on, it survives with much of its original layout (above): a moated circular garden (representing the world) containing a grid of flowerbeds. The UNESCO World Heritage Site attracts some 180,000 visitors every year, who tour the gardens and a museum that was added in 2023. It is also still an active centre for botanical research.

FEB 26 In 2008, after a month of building by the townsfolk of Bethel, Maine, USA, the **tallest snowman** (technically, snow-woman) topped out at 37.21 m (122 ft 1 in).

FEB 27 Ernest and Barbara Kellogg of Virginia, USA, shelled out $675,000 (£442,847) at auction for "Snowmass Matrix" in 2010, making him the **most expensive alpaca**.

LARGEST PERMANENT HEDGE MAZE
Opened in Sep 2017, the Yancheng Dafeng Dream Maze in Jiangsu, China, is spread over 35,596.74 m^2 (383,160.1 sq ft), which is the equivalent area of five soccer pitches! It comprises a series of interconnected mazes, planted around a central observation tower. The main section takes the form of a stag, with the other smaller mazes laid out in geometric shapes. The 9.45 km (5.87 mi) of walkways also represents the **largest path network in a hedge maze**. Strolling the entire route (dead-ends and all) would be equivalent to walking Paris' Champs-Élysées five times, or just over three lengths of the National Mall in Washington, DC.

The living walls of Yancheng's "Labyrinth of Dreams" are made from some 100,000 Chinese juniper shrubs (*Juniperus chinensis*).

FEB 28 To mark 2009's World Sword Swallowers' Day, Natasha Veruschka (USA) took on the **longest sword swallowed**, ingesting a 58-cm (1-ft 11-in) blade. *Gulp!*

MAR 1 Flying a biplane, ace aviator Kingsley Just (AUS) executed the **most consecutive aircraft rolls** – 987 – in the sky over Lethbridge, Victoria, Australia, in 2014.

GREEN PLANET

Round-Up

Largest plastic-bottle tree sculpture
Caroline Chaptini (LBN, above), in partnership with the Municipality of Amioun, created a 21.06-m-tall (69-ft) sculpture dubbed "Cedar of Hope", as confirmed in Koura, Lebanon, on 23 Nov 2025. Schools and universities countrywide collected 452,000 plastic bottles for the project, which were later sold for recycling. The funds were donated to the nation's Kids First cancer charity.

The cedar of Lebanon (*Cedrus libani*) is a historic national symbol that takes pride of place on the country's flag, adopted in 1943.

Oldest poisonous-plant flower fossils
In 1986, two fossilized blooms from the extinct species *Strychnos electri*, dated to 20–30 million years ago, were unearthed in an amber mine in the Dominican Republic. Certain *Strychnos* species contain toxic compounds such as strychnine (once widely used as rat poison) and toxiferine. The latter has traditionally been used in hunting-arrow toxins known as "curares".

More recently, the **oldest poisoned arrows** were uncovered by archaeologists working at the Umhlatuzana Rock Shelter in KwaZulu-Natal, South Africa. News of the discovery of these small flint arrowheads, which are 60,000 years old and bear traces of the toxic succulent *Boophone disticha*, was published in Jan 2026.

Oldest vine
The vineyards of Zogang County – a mountainous region in Tibet, China – are home to more than 60 centenarian grapevines. The oldest among them is a 416-year-old specimen that was verified by GWR on 21 Sep 2025. It stands 8 m (26 ft 2 in) tall, with a girth at ground level of 209 cm (6 ft 10 in). Most cultivated vines rarely exceed 50 years, so those that survive beyond a century are exceptional.

Oldest deer in captivity
A Rocky Mountain elk (*Cervus canadensis nelsoni*) named Beauty (b. 2 Jun 1998) passed away aged 27 years 158 days on 7 Nov 2025. The dearly departed deer was cared for by Lloyd Dancsok and his family in Esterhazy, Saskatchewan, Canada, for more than a quarter of a century.

Fastest-growing tree fern
Two fern species can grow as much as 0.5 m (1 ft 7 in) per year: the Norfolk tree fern (*Sphaeropteris excelsa*) and the closely related black tree fern (*S. medullaris*). Both are native to Australasian islands in the South Pacific.

Heaviest squash
Joe Jutras (USA) presented a 2,200-lb (997.9-kg) squash (*Cucurbita maxima*) at an official Great Pumpkin Commonwealth event in Warren, Rhode Island, USA, on 11 Oct 2025. That makes the gargantuan gourd around twice as heavy as a concert grand piano!

Highest-pitched sound by an animal
The male *Supersonus aequoreus* (a species of katydid, or bush cricket) can emit a 150-kHz squeak to attract females. To do so, it scrapes parts of its forewings together, while the right forewing is set against its back to create a resonance chamber. The species is native to rainforest on two Colombian islands.

MAR 2 — In 2019, British Naturism signed up 195 recruits to bare all on the Grand National rollercoaster in Blackpool, UK – the **most naked people on a theme-park ride**.

MAR 3 — Measuring 772 micrometres (0.03 in) across, the **thickest human-hair strand** was plucked from the beard of Pakistan's Muhammad Umair Khan in 2021.

Longest time to hug a tree
Between 8 and 11 Dec 2025, Truphena Muthoni (KEN) embraced a tree for 72 hr in Nairobi, Kenya, improving on her own record. A committed environmental activist and founder of the "Hug the Earth" initiative, Truphena told GWR: "If one person can stay connected for 72 hr, then surely humanity can learn to protect what still sustains us."

Largest display of bonsai trees
On 14 Jun 2025, a garden of 10,836 miniature trees was presented by His Holiness Dr Sri Ganapathy Sachchidananda Swamiji of the Avadhoota Datta Peetham ashram (both IND) in Mysuru, Karnataka, India. The diminutive forest comprises more than 250 tree species, which Dr Swamiji cares for using traditional Japanese techniques.

TALLEST...

- **Artichoke plant**: Nathan Garnett (UK) cultivated a 3.29-m (10-ft 9-in) cardoon (aka artichoke thistle, *Cynara cardunculus*), as verified in Rayleigh, Essex, UK, on 1 Jul 2025.
- **Pepper plant**: James Abraham (IND) nurtured a 5.5-m-tall (18-ft 1-in) *Capsicum*, as confirmed in Mallapally, Kerala, India, on 7 May 2025.
- **Okra plant**: Risim Rongpi (IND) grew an okra (*Abelmoschus esculentus*) that stood 8.2 m (26 ft 10 in) when measured in Diphu, Karbi Anglong, Assam, India, on 29 Mar 2025.

Largest multi-species spider web
A web spanning 106 m² (1,141 sq ft) was discovered in Sulfur Cave, on the Albania-Greece border, and formally documented on 17 Oct 2025. What made it so remarkable, other than its scale, is that it was co-built by two different species: some 69,000 domestic house spiders (*Tegenaria domestica*) and more than 42,000 common sheet weavers (*Prinerigone vagans*). The structure consists of thousands of individual funnel-shaped webs linked together like a patchwork quilt.

Longest wild snake specimen
In late 2025, a giant female reticulated python (*Malayopython reticulatus*) was found in Maros Regency, Sulawesi, Indonesia. It is believed to be the longest wild snake to be formally measured: evidence seen by GWR confirms a length of 7.22 m (23 ft 8 in), as of 18 Jan 2026. The python was assessed by Diaz Nugraha (a wildlife guide and licensed snake handler) and Radu Frentiu (an explorer and nature photographer, above). It is now in the care of Budi Purwanto (left), a conservationist striving to protect Sulawesi's serpents.

Largest squash mosaic
On 10 Oct 2025, Sunnyfields Farm unveiled a 212-m² (2,281-sq-ft) Halloween-themed organic portrait in Southampton, Hampshire, UK. The tennis-court-sized mosaic depicted the rock star Ozzy Osbourne, aka "The Prince of Darkness", who had passed away in July that year. His widow, Sharon, and children, Kelly and Jack, even paid the farm a visit to survey the humongous homage.

The Ozzy mosaic beat Sunnyfields' own record from 2023, inspired by Tim Burton's 1993 movie *The Nightmare Before Christmas*.

MAR 4 Since this day in 1989, the **highest indoor high jump** title has belonged to Javier Sotomayor (CUB), after he leapt to 2.43 m (7 ft 11.66 in) in Budapest, Hungary.

MAR 5 To launch *Gran Turismo 7* in 2022, Sony PlayStation MEA (UAE) choreographed 265 moving vehicles into the *GT7* logo – the **largest synchronized car dance**.

SNAPSHOT

Largest Dinosaur

Movies love to imagine prehistoric predators rampaging through modern cities – usually with a ferocious *T. rex* leading the charge. But what if, instead of fearsome hunters, the placid, plant-eating **largest land animal ever** was allowed to roam in New York's Times Square?

The heart of New York City, Times Square is a bustling intersection that sees up to 330,000 visitors each day. It's famed for its soaring skyscrapers, eye-catching adverts and street performers – less so for nature… Indeed, the animals most likely to be spotted here are pigeons. That said, given that all modern birds are descended from dinosaurs, anyone who's been to this landmark has already strolled among *T. rex*'s living relatives. But how would the biggest beast to ever walk Earth have fitted in among the teeming crowds of Times Square?

Although various species vie for the title of **largest dinosaur**, one thing's for sure: it would have been a sauropod (Sauropoda). This group of huge herbivores – typified by *Brontosaurus* ("thunder lizard") – all had long necks, pillar-like legs and slender tails. One sauropod subset took "giant" to a whole new level: the titanosaurs, which included the likes of *Patagotitan* and *Argentinosaurus*.

Extrapolations based on (admittedly limited) fossilized leg bones and vertebrae of titanosaurs indicate that they may have towered up to 20 m (65 ft) tall, stretched as long as two bowling lanes and weighed in excess of 100 tonnes (110 tons).

This is more than three times the height of today's **tallest animal** – the giraffe (*Giraffa*) – and some 20 times heftier than African bush elephants (*Loxodonta africana*), which by weight are now the **largest land animals** (5.5 tonnes; 6 tons).

Some scientists have even posited that so-called "super sauropods" may have rivalled the **largest animal ever**: blue whales (*Balaenoptera musculus*), which can weigh 190 tonnes (209 tons).

Quibbles over maximum sauropod size will continue to rumble on among palaeontologists. But if one *did* land in the centre of the Big Apple and start strolling along Seventh Avenue, it's safe to say that tourists, pigeons and yellow taxi drivers alike are all going to make way for this jumbo jaywalker!

Consuming some 120 kg (265 lb) of foliage a day, a titanosaur would likely feel more at home in New York's Central Park!

As well as acting as a counterweight balance, sauropods' long tails may have been used to communicate and even for self-defence.

MAR 6 The **heaviest elephant bar deadlift (female)** is 291 kg (641 lb), by Tamara Walcott (USA) in Ohio, USA, in 2022.

MAR 7 In 2012, after 105 hr of Hindi film song karaoke, India's Sunil Waghmare called time on the **longest singing marathon**.

MAR 8 Peter Boyd (UK) created the **largest stamp mosaic** – 270.5 m^2 (2,912 sq ft) – using *c.* 528,000 stamps in 2017.

MAR 9 The **most leaves on a clivia** (aka bush lily) is 79, grown by Qian Ruixin of Harbin, Heilongjiang, China, in 2025.

ICON BLACKPINK

In the early 2010s, Jisoo, Jennie, Rosé and Lisa devoted their lives to becoming K-pop idols. And by the decade's end, after countless hours in the studio and on the road, all their hard work had paid off. During their teenage years, the girls met as trainees of YG Entertainment, a Korean agency known for coaching and championing some of the biggest names in the K-pop industry. They each spent four to six strenuous years in training until the time came for their debut in 2016.

With their catchy pop hits, the quartet quickly gained fans (better known as "Blinks") who, on 26–27 Jun 2020, helped them to secure the title for the **most viewed YouTube video in 24 hours** (now held by the BTS hit "Butter"), by watching the video for "How You Like That" 86.3 million times.

Their second LP – *BORN PINK* – made them the **first female K-pop group to reach No.1 on the UK** and **US albums charts** in 2022. As of 1 Apr 2026, they were also the **most viewed** and **most subscribed band on YouTube** (41.756 billion and 100 million, respectively). With plenty of K-pop milestones under their belt, nearly a decade of consistent success on streaming services and more than 30 sold-out stadium shows on their latest world tour, their status as the current most successful girl group is surely now affirmed.

As YG Entertainment trainees, the girls lived together in a boarding-school environment and adhered to a demanding schedule of dance and vocal lessons, with only one rest day every fortnight. Each month, they would be required to showcase their progress – on their own and in a group – in front of the company's producers and sometimes even the CEO.

VITAL STATISTICS

Name	BLACKPINK
Members	Jisoo (KOR) Jennie (KOR) Rosé (NZ/KOR) Lisa (THA)
Debut	2016
Current GWR titles	Multiple, including **most streamed female group on Spotify** – 16.94 bn, as of 1 Apr 2026
Accolades	Honorary members of the Order of the British Empire; *TIME* magazine's Entertainer of the Year 2022

In Jul 2022, BLACKPINK transformed themselves into virtual avatars and staged a free concert within Tencent Games' battle-royale shooter, *PUBG Mobile* (2018), in which they launched their single "Ready for Love". Off the back of this, they became the **first winners of the Best Metaverse Performance at the MTV Video Music Awards** on 28 Aug 2022.

In Jul 2025, BLACKPINK began their *DEADLINE* tour and debuted "JUMP", their first single in three years.

For “Blinks”, the concert-day fun starts long before the band take to the stage, as they unite outside the venues to practise dance routines wielding trademark heart-shaped light sticks (aka “hammerbongs”). Glow sticks have become a key part of K-pop gigs, with most bands having their own branded wands that light up in time to their music.

In recognition of their work as COP26 advocates, BLACKPINK became the first K-pop band to be awarded honorary MBEs at Buckingham Palace in London, UK, on 22 Nov 2023. His Majesty King Charles III presented them with this esteemed honour after they called on their fans to get involved with the 2021 UN Climate Change Conference.

BLACKPINK have not only enjoyed phenomenal success as a group, but more recently as solo artists too. On 28 Aug 2022, Lisa (above) became the **first solo K-pop winner at the MTV Video Music Awards** (for the single “LALISA”), and on 26 Jan 2025, Rosé’s No.1 hit “APT.”, with US singer Bruno Mars (below), became the **fastest K-pop track to reach 1 billion streams on Spotify**, just 100 days after its release.

Discover all of GWR’s incredible ICONS at **guinnessworldrecords.com/records/icons**

HUMANS

CONTENTS

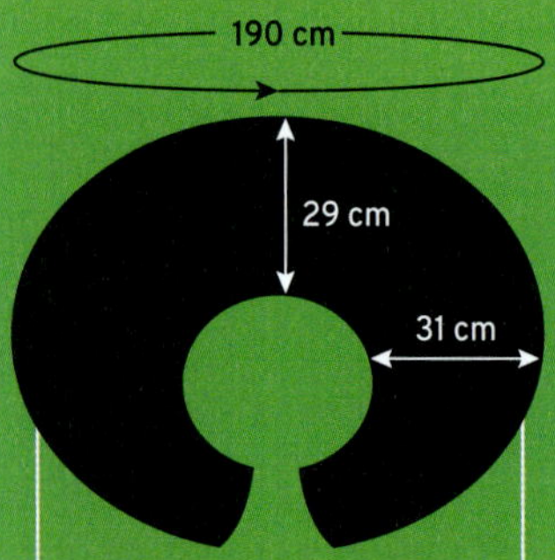

There isn't a universal way to measure an afro hairstyle. GWR bases it on three key metrics: height (from the scalp to the highest point); width (from just above the ear to the widest point); and circumference (measuring all the way around with a soft tape). All three dimensions must be surpassed in order to claim the title. Above, see how Jess's afro measured up.

"Meeting Aevin is just such a joy. I feel like she is the same online as she is in person – a lot of personality," Jess told GWR.

LARGEST AFRO

On Guinness World Records Day 2025 (20 Nov), a new *hair*-oic member of the GWR family was revealed in New York City, USA. Jess Martinez (USA, sitting on the right in main picture) has cultivated an afro with a circumference of 190 cm (6 ft 2.8 in).

During her 15-year reign as the big hair queen, former holder Aevin Dugas (sat opposite) campaigned to encourage others to embrace their natural hair; she was recognized as a GWR ICON in 2025. Aevin is happy to relinquish the title, saying: "It's not a competition, it's literally all love." She attended our photoshoot to pass over the crown to her successor.

Oldest...

Married couple ever
By 4 Nov 2025, Lyle and Eleanor Gittens (both USA) had a combined age of 216 years 132 days. The husband and wife – who now live in Miami, Florida, USA – first met in 1941 while students at Clark Atlanta University in Georgia, and wed in June the following year. Theirs is also the **longest marriage for a living couple**: 83 years 153 days.

Man
Former farmer João Marinho Neto (b. 5 Oct 1912) of Apuiarés, Ceará, Brazil, was aged 113 years 178 days, as verified by LongeviQuest on 1 Apr 2026. He attributes his long life to his close-knit family, which includes 22 grandchildren and 15 great-grandchildren.

OLDEST PEOPLE BY CONTINENT

North America
Naomi Whitehead (USA): 115 yr 187 dy

South America
Yolanda Beltrão de Azevedo (BRA): 115 yr 78 dy

Asia
Shigeko Kagawa (JPN): 114 yr 308 dy

Oceania
Aileen Kars (NZ): 112 yr 201 dy

Africa
Hélène Malfuson (TUN/FRA): 111 yr 276 dy

Validated ages by LongeviQuest; as of 1 Apr 2026

Plumber
Still the owner of his own company aged 94 years 127 days on 4 Jun 2025, Roger Lighthart (USA, b. 28 Jan 1931) has been fixing leaky pipes and broken boilers in the Greater Los Angeles area in California, USA, since 1954.

Weekly newspaper columnist
Canada's Al Donohue (b. 20 Jun 1929) has written an op-ed for weekly Ontarian journal *The Eganville Leader* since 2012, after several of his letters to the editor proved popular with the publication's readers. He was still penning his column aged 96 years 129 days on 27 Oct 2025.

Nun
Sister Francis Piscatella (USA, b. 20 Apr 1913) of East Williston in New York, USA, was 112 years 346 days old on 1 Apr 2026, as ratified by LongeviQuest. She has belonged to the Sisters of St Dominic of Amityville since 1931.

Tenor opera singer
Veteran performer Yasuo Harada (JPN, b. 31 May 1931) was 94 years 99 days old when he assumed the role of Lieutenant Pinkerton in *Madama Butterfly* in Higashi, Hiroshima, Japan, on 7 Sep 2025. Across a 70-year-plus career, Harada has appeared on stage in numerous concerts and recitals, as well as releasing CDs and DVDs of his operatic work.

Gaming streamer
Yang Binglin (CHN, b. 10 Dec 1935) – better known by his persona "Gaming Grandpa" – was still active online aged 89 years 253 days on 20 Aug 2025. Through his gameplay videos (which lately have focused on titles such as *Assassin's Creed Shadows*), he hopes to inspire a healthy life balance between work and play.

Hockey player
Octogenarian Linda Sinrod (USA, b. 21 Sep 1940) hung up her skates for the last time on 7 Apr 2025, aged 84 years 198 days, after playing a "bittersweet" final league game in Virginia, USA. The former college figure skater, who first took up ice hockey in her 30s, advised: "I would tell others that you are never too old to start playing. I actually quit when I was 45 thinking I was too old, but came back to playing at age 67."

Competitive croquet player
Having only first picked up a mallet at the age of 95, Jean Farguson (UK, b. 10 Sep 1926) has gone on to compete for Lodsworth Croquet Club in West Sussex, UK. At her most recent match on 3 Aug 2025, she was 98 years 327 days old.

Mount Fuji climber
Kokichi Akuzawa (JPN, b. 14 Jun 1923) was 102 years 52 days old when he summitted this iconic 3,776-m (12,389-ft) peak in Shizuoka, Japan, on 5 Aug 2025.

Competitive rower
On 18 Aug 2024, the Frankfurt Long Distance Regatta in Germany welcomed a 97-year 268-day-old entrant in the form of Walter Wagner (DEU, b. 24 Nov 1926).

Living person
Ethel Caterham (UK, b. 21 Aug 1909) was aged 116 years 223 days on 1 Apr 2026, as validated by supercentenarian experts at LongeviQuest. When she first claimed this prestigious title in 2025, Caterham received a rather special visitor – King Charles III – to congratulate her in person (left). While Caterham is Europe's most senior citizen, the oldest validated individuals (all of whom are women) from the other five continents are listed left.

MAR 10 How low can *you* go? The **lowest limbo skating over 25 m** is 16 cm (6.29 in), achieved by Takshvi Vaghani (IND) in Ahmedabad, Gujarat, India, in 2024.

MAR 11 In 2023, Takuya Iwamoto (JPN) really racked up his air miles by jumping on the **most scheduled flights in one week** – 84 – with the attempt ending on this date.

1

2

Carlos set his latest record by reaching the summit of Manaslu in Nepal; he aims to climb all 14 of the planet's 8,000-m peaks.

AGELESS ADVENTURERS: OLDEST TO...

Record	Age	Name & Date of Birth
1. **Complete an IRONMAN® 140.6 triathlon (female)**	80 yr 69 dy on 11 Oct 2025	Natalie Grabow (USA, b. 3 Aug 1945)
2. **Climb an 8,000-m mountain**	86 yr 233 dy on 26 Sep 2025	Carlos Soria Fontán (ESP, b. 5 Feb 1939)
3. **Climb El Capitan (female)**	70 yr on 23 Sep 2021	Dierdre Wolownick (USA, b. 23 Sep 1951)
4. **Scuba dive as a married couple (aggregate age)**	173 yr 18 dy on 31 Aug 2025	Minoru (b. 1 Nov 1936) and Mitsuko Amano (b. 12 Jun 1941; both JPN)
5. **Visit the North Pole**	95 yr 236 dy on 10 Aug 2025	Richard Eitel (USA, b. 17 Dec 1929)

3

Dierdre is the mother of record-breaking free-solo climber Alex Honnold; they climbed El Cap in California, USA, together in 2017.

5

4

MAR 12 In Lucca, Italy, the **first World Sudoku Championship** ended on this day in 2006. Czechia's Jana Tylová was the number-puzzle contest's inaugural victor.

MAR 13 Community charity Kiwanis Club of Little Havana amassed 119,986 people in Florida, USA, to come together and form the **longest conga line** in 1988.

Meet the Tallest Man

Sizing up Sultan

The world's **tallest living person** is Sultan Kösen of Türkiye, with a standing height of 251 cm (8 ft 2.8 in) when last measured officially by GWR back in 2011. But has he grown taller over the past 15 years? Or shrunk? To find out, we caught up with Sultan during his recent trip to London while filming a documentary for the UK's Channel 4. GWR Editor-in-Chief Craig Glenday and adjudicator Will Munford took the opportunity to re-measure him, using a ladder and a tape measure but also, for the first time ever, a 3D body scanner. Has the world's loftiest lad lost or gained any centimetres?

Dr Jack Ashby takes hundreds of images of Sultan from every angle using a handheld scanner. He then stitches them together to build a 3D digital model that can be processed and measured by computer.

Height taken from data captured in the 3D scan

SULTAN WAS VISITING LONDON TO FILM THE WORLD'S TALLEST MAN: THE NEXT CHAPTER – THE SEQUEL TO A DOCUMENTARY MADE BY WILD DREAM FILMS. A TEAM FROM GWR PAID A VISIT TO THE SET TO SAY "HI" AND HAVE SULTAN RE-MEASURED.

"Measuring people as tall as Sultan is a real challenge," explains GWR adjudicator Will, "because the medical device normally used to assess height – a stadiometer – doesn't go high enough!" Instead, Sultan's stature is ascertained by placing him flat against a wall, marking his standing height and measuring this with a steel tape. On this visit, a secondary assessment was made by Dr Jack Ashby of the Sport, Health and Performance Enhancement (SHAPE) Research Centre at Nottingham Trent University, UK. He used a wireless Artec Leo scanner (top right) to create a digital model of Sultan accurate to 0.1 mm, or 4,000ths of an inch.

Sultan and Craig find time to pop into the famous Hamleys toy store on London's Regent Street to sign books.

Sultan shows off the world's **largest hands** – 28.5 cm (11.22 in) from the wrist to the tip of the middle finger.

MAR 14 Dirk Leonhardt of Germany completed the **longest ice triathlon** today in 2022, skating, cycling and running on a frozen track in Frankfurt for 165.16 km (102.63 mi).

MAR 15 In 2016, fashion designer Emma Sandham-King (UK) unveiled the **first three-piece suit designed for a horse** – a tweed outfit complete with shirt, tie and cap.

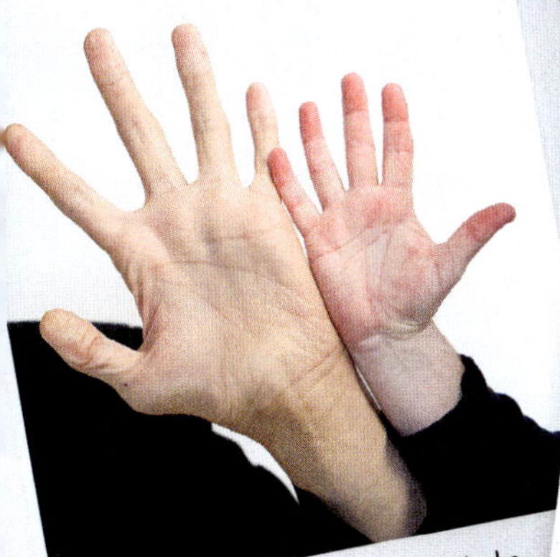

Documentary filmmaker Stuart Clarke compares his average-sized hand to Sultan's. No contest!

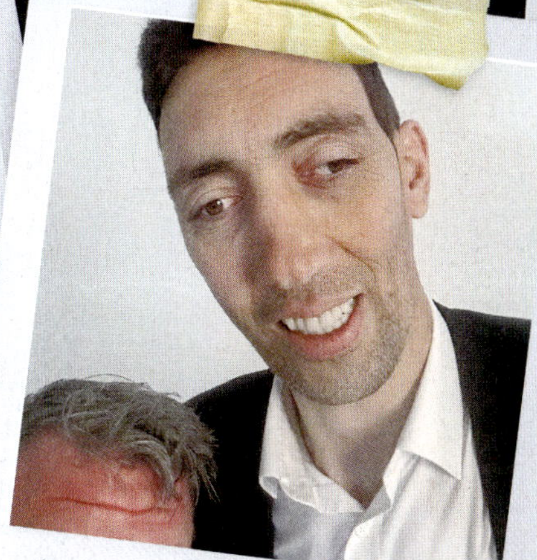

As Craig discovered, taking a selfie with Sultan is never easy – especially with a height difference of 80 cm (2 ft 7 in)!

THE RESULTS

After a day of measuring and scanning, Sultan's current height was confirmed:

- Tape (average) .... 250 cm ... (8 ft 2.4 in)
- 3D scan .... 249.1 cm ...... (8 ft 2 in)
- Final average ...... 249.55 cm ... (8 ft 2.2 in)

This small reduction in height – of just 1.45 cm (0.6 in) – leaves us in no doubt that Sultan is still the world's **tallest living man** and **person**. "It's important for GWR to keep tabs on Sultan's height," concluded Craig, "but it's also a lovely opportunity to just spend some time catching up with this living legend. There's never a dull moment when you spend a day in Sultan's life!"

MAR 16 Following heart surgery in Rome, Italy, in 2009, Armando Porcelli (ITA, b. 9 Oct 1914) became the **oldest triple-bypass patient**, aged 94 years 158 days.

MAR 17 The **largest gathering of leprechauns** saw 1,263 people fill the streets of Bandon in County Cork, Ireland, as part of the town's 2012 St Patrick's Day celebrations.

Family Matters

Most albino siblings
Albinism is a congenital condition that causes the body to produce little to no melanin – the pigment that lends colour to our hair, eyes and skin. Pakistan's Aslam Parvez and Shameem Akhtar, who both have albinism, have six children who inherited the same trait: Muqadas Bibi, Musarat Begum, Mohammed Rafi, Naseem Akhtar, Ghulam Ali and Haider Ali (all UK).

Oldest adoptee (female)
Mary Banks Smith (b. 5 Mar 1939, right) was aged 76 years 96 days when she officially became the adopted daughter of Muriel Banks Clayton (both USA) in Dallas, Texas, USA, on 9 Jun 2015. Clayton (b. 22 Jul 1922) was 92 years 322 days old on the same day, making her the **oldest adoptive parent**.

DID YOU KNOW?

Twinning rates have risen by one-third since the 1980s. A 2021 study indicated that the number of twins being born globally has increased from nine to 12 in every 1,000 deliveries, though this varies across countries. The **highest twinning rate** overall is in Côte d'Ivoire in West Africa: 24.9 per 1,000 births.

Oldest human embyro (successful pregnancy)
After several years of trying to conceive naturally, Lindsey and Tim Pierce (both USA) decided to adopt an embryo; they were matched with one that was produced via IVF in 1994 and then stored on ice by the genetic parents. When Thaddeus Daniel Pierce was born in London, Ohio, USA, on 26 Jul 2025, he was in a sense already aged 31 years 56 days old – making him only a couple of years younger than his parents! As Lindsey commented after her son's arrival: "It's like something out of a sci-fi movie."

Most centenarian siblings
Sheila Burns (née Clarke) of County Galway, Ireland, turned 100 on 7 Jan 2017 to become the sixth of 13 siblings in the Clarke clan to reach the milestone. She joined four brothers – Joseph, Charles, Patrick and James – and sister Margaret in the centenarian club. Their mother, Margaret, also surpassed 100. The odds of seven people in a 15-person family exceeding 100 years old are in the order of one in 12 sextillion (i.e., 12 followed by 21 zeroes!). All six siblings, most recently Sheila in 2021, have now passed away. In addition, four other Clarke children – Mary, John, Hubert and Sarah – made it into their ninth decade, helping the clan to also claim **most siblings to exceed 90 years old**.

Oldest adoptee (male)
William "Bill" Stains (USA, b. 13 Jan 1946) was adopted by Jessica and Ryan Fiscus at the Orphan Court in Enola, Pennsylvania, USA, aged 74 years 304 days on 12 Nov 2020. The former baseball umpire officiated at many of Ryan's games when growing up (indeed, to this day, Bill still goes by "Coach"); the two stayed in touch over the years and their families grew close, leading to the unorthodox adoption.

Most family members to graduate from one university
As of Jul 2022, an unprecedented 44 members from across three generations of the Wuensche family (USA) had received a diploma from Texas Tech University in Lubbock, Texas, USA. The first to do so was Francis Wuensche Holden in 1953. On top of this, 14 of their spouses have also studied there.

The same record but to graduate in the **same academic year**, meanwhile, is seven. This was achieved by mother Martina Hülser (DEU) and six of her children – Michelle (ITA), Sarah, Daniela, Emanuel, Christina and Eliah Bardelli (all DEU), who collectively concluded their degrees at Italy's University of Urbino in 2020.

Most premature quadruplets
The Bryant quads – Lainey, Kali, Lennon and Koen – were born 115 days early at the UAB Hospital in Birmingham, Alabama, USA, on 31 May 2024. They're pictured above a year later with their proud parents, Rebecca and Lavareis Bryant (both USA), and two of their elder siblings. Rebecca reflected: "To see them struggle and fight so hard… but now they're home, and we get to do their first birthday and think about outfits and smash cakes!"

The Bryant quads broke an almost 30-year record held by the Tepper family (AUS), with quads that were born 104 days early in 1997.

MAR 18 With one strike, taekwondo expert Ali Bahçetepe (TUR) secured the title for the **most concrete blocks broken in a single stack** (37) in Menteşe, Türkiye, in 2015.

MAR 19 The **fastest kiteboarding speed** is 36.07 mph (58.04 km/h), logged by Steve Smith and Project SWIFT (both UK) on the beach at Hayling Island, UK, in 2015.

On turning one, "Nash Potato" received 70 new outfits, toys and (with doctors' dispensation) cake with extra whipped cream!

MOST PREMATURE BABY

Weighing just 285 g (10 oz) – lighter than a grapefruit – Nash Keen was born on 5 Jul 2024, 133 days ahead of his due date, at University of Iowa Health Care in Iowa City, USA. Right, his mom Mollie holds Nash for the very first time, three weeks after his delivery. "He was so tiny, I could barely even feel him on my chest," she recalled. "I was very nervous… but the moment he was placed on my chest, all my nerves disappeared – it felt like pure relief and love all at once." Described by his parents, Randall and Mollie (below), as "pure joy in a tiny package", Nash celebrated his first birthday on 5 Jul 2025.

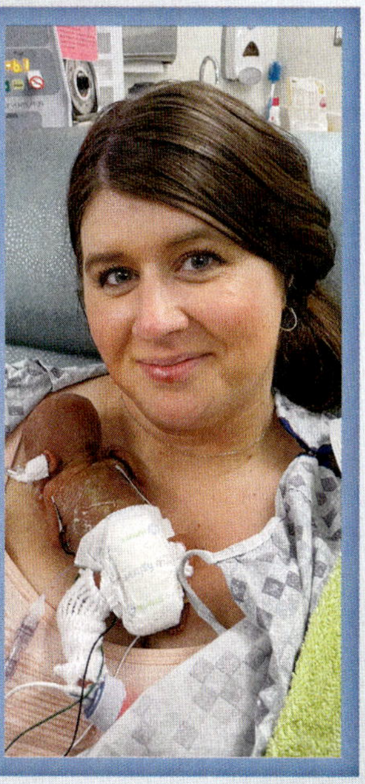

ON THE RECORD

"He's still just a little boy, our sweet, silly, strong Nash, and while the world may see a miracle or a record breaker, we see our son who loves snuggles, silly sounds and blowing raspberries. We're happy to share his light, but we also work hard to keep his life grounded in love, normalcy and joy"
– Mollie Keen

MAR 20 In 2023, Australian strongman Troy Conley-Magnusson turned more than heads in Sydney by setting the **fastest time to rotate a Ferris wheel by hand**: 16 min 55 sec.

MAR 21 Over the course of 10 hr in 2015, university student Rajveer Meena (IND) recalled 70,000 digits – the **most Pi decimal places memorized** – in Vellore, India.

Body Beautiful

First prosthetic tattoo arm
Made in 2016, the earliest tattoo-gun arm was created by artist and engineer Jean-Louis Gonzal and worn by J C Sheitan Tenet (above, both FRA) in Lyon, France. The lightweight prosthesis uses parts from a vintage mechanical typewriter and a gramophone, and boasts a distinctive "dieselpunk" aesthetic.

Oldest figurative tattoos
Two naturally mummified individuals dated to 3351–3017 BCE bear the inked images of a sheep, a bull and motifs shaped like the letters "S" and "L". The Gebelein mummies – named after the ancient Egyptian site where they were found – are housed in the archive of the British Museum in London, UK.

One of the mummies is the **oldest tattooed woman**. The letter-shaped marks described above appear on her upper arm and shoulder.

Longest-running tattoo convention
The Richmond Tattoo & Arts Convention in Virginia, USA, celebrated its 37th year in 2025. Inaugurated in 1988, the weekend-long event sees around 200 internationally recognized tattooists demonstrating their work, alongside art showcases, educational sessions and performance art.

Most Marvel comic-book-character tattoos
Lifelong Marvel fan Tom Radford (UK) is embellished with 63 tats of comic-book icons, as verified in Hull, East Yorkshire, UK, on 13 Dec 2025. Working with artist Andy Walker, he has spent some 350 hr under the needle, and invested around £18,000 ($24,000) in his superhero skin salute.

Longest tattoo session
On 2 Feb 2025, Darren "Sraw" Arellano (USA) completed a 64-hr 30-min inking marathon in Denver, Colorado, USA. He improved on the previous record by almost 3 hr.

Most signatures tattooed on the body
Funky Matas (aka Jorge Matas, USA) has adorned himself with 273 signatures, as confirmed in Miami, Florida, USA, on 13 Aug 2025. His back is covered with the autographs of friends, family, well-known tattoo artists and a string of celebrities, including martial-arts movie star Jackie Chan (left).

Most tattoos of landmarks
James O'Connor's body is decorated with 17 must-see sites, as verified in Salem, Massachusetts, USA, on 21 Sep 2025. All the images show landmarks in the US city of Boston, including the Bunker Hill Monument and the Tobin Bridge. James was supported by Renee Mandrake and Witch City Ink (all USA).

Most tattoos of the same band
Such is Tom M Engelbrecht's (NOR) devotion to rock group Metallica that he has had himself inked with 72 designs of them, as verified in Bergen, Vestland, Norway, on 13 Dec 2024. Tom's etchings include every member since 1983, along with lyrics and even the notes of "Fade to Black". He began with a half sleeve in 2010 and isn't done yet!

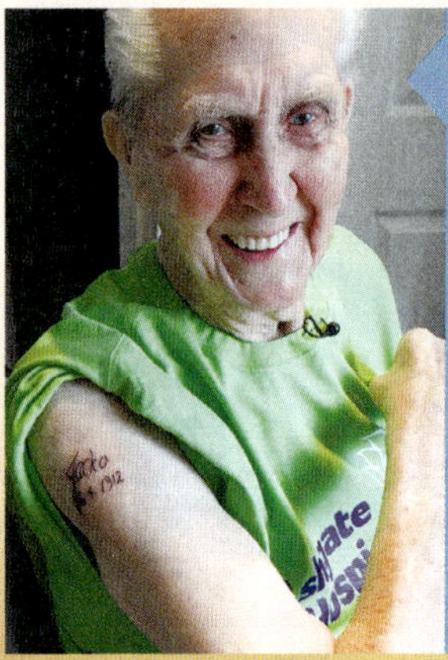

Oldest person to receive their first tattoo
Jack Reynolds (UK, 1912–2020) was tattooed with his nickname ("Jocko") and birth date on 6 Apr 2016 – his 104th birthday – in Chesterfield, UK. For the next three years, the young-at-heart OAP marked each birthday with a GWR title, including the **oldest person to ride a zip wire** in 2018.

MOST TATTOOS BY DESIGN

Batman
12, by Costas Moutsios (GRC) in Athens, Greece, as of 30 Jan 2024

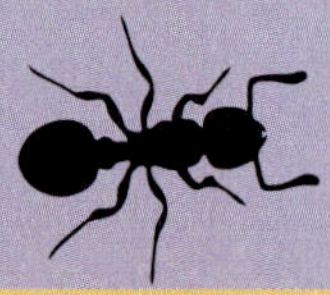

Insects
864, by Michael Amoia (USA) in New York City, USA, as of 28 Oct 2021

Skulls
376, by Charles "Chuck" Helmke (USA) in Melbourne, Florida, USA, as of 3 Dec 2016

Feathers
216, by Charlotte Guttenberg (USA) in Melbourne, Florida, USA, as of 3 Dec 2016

MAR 22 In 1997, Sadir Kattan (AUS) threw the **smallest returning boomerang** – just 48 mm (1.8 in) long and 45 mm (1.7 in) wide – at a contest in Melbourne, Victoria, Australia.

MAR 23 After 20 years of collecting, Kadri Prekaj had the **largest collection of axes**, as verified on this day in 2023. The 1,023 choppers are on show at his home in Pejë, Kosovo.

MOST TATTOOED TWINS
Aline Galiano and Alena Hahnle (both DEU) – aka the Petunia Twins – have an average bodily tattoo coverage of 70%, as confirmed in Los Angeles, California, USA, on 11 Oct 2025. The sisters had their first tattoos on the same day when they were aged 17: a bow-tie motif on the upper arm to symbolize their close connection. The following year, the duo started to do tattooing themselves and now have their own professional studio – Petunia Twins Ink, in LA. They've already started covering older tattoos with heavy blackouts, and their aim is to reach 99% coverage.

The twins' fave tats are on their foreheads: a feminine mandala for each of them, with the same design but different colours.

MAR 24 In 1988, Mellissa Sanders (USA) ended 516 days of elevated self-confinement, started in Indianapolis, USA, in Oct 1986: the **longest time pole sitting in a shack.**

MAR 25 Speed-chewer Anthony Falzon of Sliema, Malta, claimed the **most marshmallows eaten in one minute** (25) in 2013, demolishing the previous mark of 17.

Most Body Mods

The adornment of the body is as old as humanity. Ancient Egyptians pierced ears, while indigenous Amazonians stretched and bejewelled their lips to show status. In Africa and Oceania, tattoos signified bravery, belonging and beauty – a practice adopted and spread by sailors worldwide in the 18th century. Today, people continue to use piercings, ink and implants to express identity, and none more so than Neska Fuerzina and Rolf Buchholz. As the **most modified people** on the planet, they have reinvented themselves through a combination of art, culture, rebellion… and quite a bit of pain!

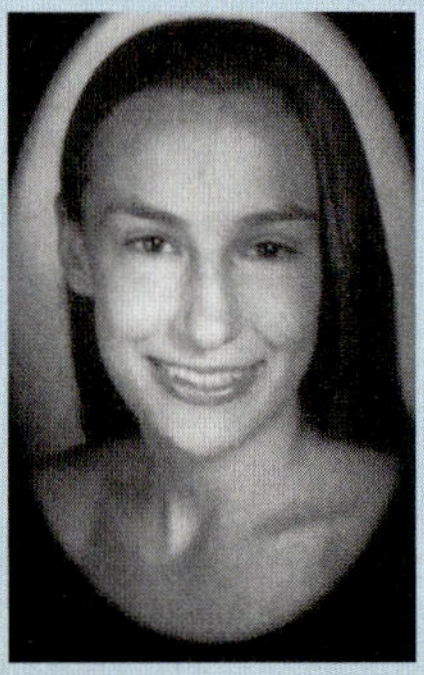

Most modified woman
Neska, an army veteran from Connecticut, USA, began her body-mod journey aged 21 with a small tattoo on her left hip. (She's pictured here at 17 years old.) Today, her tattoos adorn 99.98% of her body – also making her the **most tattooed woman ever** – and are enhanced with a further 109 body alterations.

Most modified man
A former IT professional, Rolf Buchholz (DEU) had undergone a total of 516 body mods as of the last official count in Dortmund, Germany, on 16 Dec 2012, although he has since added more. Rolf only had his first piercing and tattoo at the age of 40, but has made up for lost time since then!

1: Neska has a permanently furrowed brow – but the result of a ridged implant, rather than constant worries!

2: Custom bio-wires run along her temples. These segmented implants are also used in medical applications.

3: Neska gives tattoo artists "a lot of creative freedom – once I've found one whose style I'm comfortable with".

4: She has also had some body parts reshaped, such as her ears (conch recontouring).

5: Neska's body is a living and ever-changing canvas. "In terms of my body being covered, it's still hard to imagine a set ending."

6: Her arms are textured with dermal sculpting and a range of subdermal implants.

7: On her ribs, Neska has a pair of spider implants, while a flaming phoenix tattoo rises majestically from her hip.

8: "I think my most famous body modifications are my horn implants," says Rolf of his trademark silicone peaks.

9: Above his tattooed eyeballs, Rolf boasts upwards of 30 eyebrow piercings.

10: There are approximately 170 piercings on Rolf's face alone, including 111 that border and stud his lips.

11: Alongside a selection of smaller flesh tunnels, Rolf's ears are stretched with a quartet of larger expanders.

12: Rolf's tattoo tapestry covers some 90% of his body. "My most painful modification was my palm tattoo," he says.

13: His forearms and wrists are studded with a variety of subdermal implants.

14: Magnetic fingertips on his right hand allow Rolf to attach small metal objects to his digits – a neat party trick!

Round-Up

Largest 24-hour online cultural-awareness lesson
On 15–16 Sep 2025, a total of 1,382 people took part in a celebration of natural Afro hair while also learning about hair discrimination, equality and empowerment. The enlightening seminar was led by World Afro Day, an annual awareness campaign established by Michelle De Leon (both UK) in 2017.

Oldest personal trainer
Jack White (USA, b. 6 Aug 1938) was still hosting one-to-one fitness sessions as of his 87th birthday in 2025. Based in Scottsdale, Arizona, USA, the OAP trainer told GWR that he wanted to demonstrate to his grandchildren how to set and achieve goals.

He sounds a good match for Henry Young (AUS, b. 26 Sep 1923) – the **oldest competitive tennis player**. Henry was 102 years 15 days old when he took part in the ITF World Tennis Masters Tour World Championship in Bol, Croatia, on 11 Oct 2025.

Largest gathering of centenarians
Care provider My Guardian (AUS) arranged a special lunch for 150 guests who were all aged over 100 years old in Sydney, New South Wales, Australia, on 23 Oct 2025. The eldest attendee at the banquet was 109. In a heartfelt speech, My Guardian's founder, Jad Haber, said: "Today is more than a record; it's a call to action for all Australians to recognize and celebrate our elders as the living pillars of our nation."

Longest natural beard locks
Untrimmed for 10 years, Rudolf Martino's (USA) dreadlocked beard measured 1.06 m (3 ft 6 in) in Birmingham, Alabama, USA, on 5 Aug 2025. Rudolf decided to grow it to complement his locked hair.

Oldest person with a milk tooth
Most of us will have lost all of our baby teeth (aka deciduous teeth) by our early teens. But Cornelius O'Neill (IRL, b. 8 Jul 1933) retained two of them at the age of 91 years 253 days, as confirmed in Dublin, Ireland, on 18 Mar 2025.

The **female** record is held by Marian Stordahl (USA, b. 11 Feb 1928), who still had her last milk tooth aged 95 years 138 days as verified in Marquette, Michigan, USA, on 29 Jun 2025.

Longest tongue
Nick Stoeberl (USA) had a 10.1-cm (3.9-in) licker when measured in Salinas, California, USA, on 27 Nov 2012. It's so long, he's even painted with it!

Tallest wig
Helen Williams (NGA) crafted a 15.37-m-tall (50-ft 5-in) wig – more than three storeys high! – as verified in Lagos, Nigeria, on 27 Sep 2025. Aptly, she told GWR that she sees "no limits in life, only new heights to reach".

The professional hairpiece maker also holds GWR titles for the **widest** – 3.65 m (11 ft 11 in) – and **longest wig** – 351.2 m (1,152 ft 3 in).

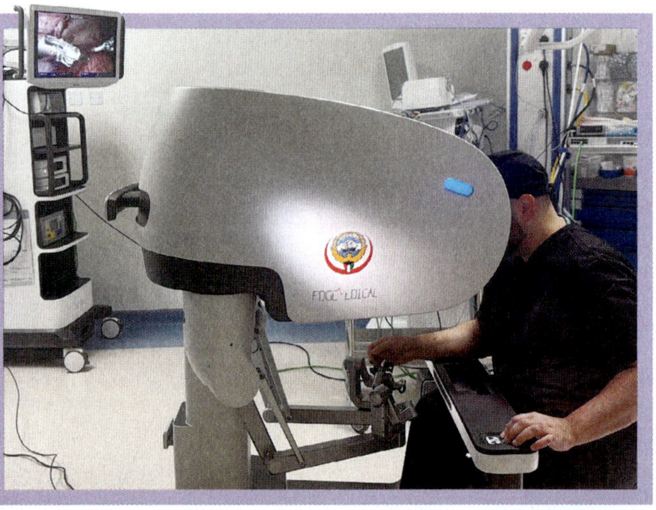

Greatest distance between surgeon and patient
On 23 Sep 2025, surgeons in Kuwait and Brazil carried out two robotic telesurgery hernia operations across 12,034 km (7,478 mi) – one each way. The network had an average latency of just 199 milliseconds. The procedure was facilitated by Jaber Al-Ahmad Hospital, Zain Group and The Kuwait Foundation for the Advancement of Sciences (all KWT) and SCOLLA Collaborative (BRA).

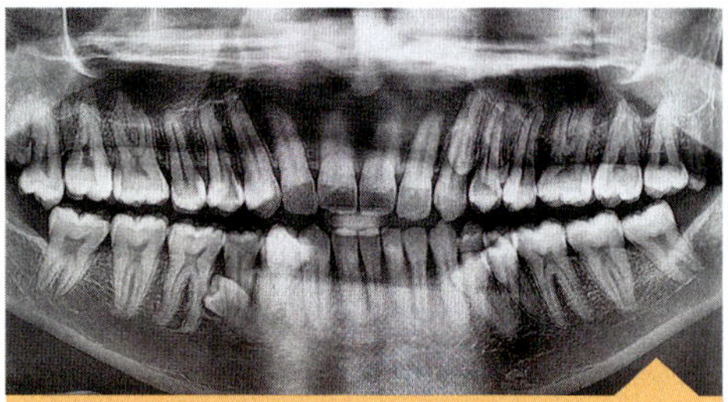

Most teeth
Prathab Muniandy's (MYS) mouth has 42 teeth (10 more than standard), as verified in Klang, Selangor, Malaysia, on 28 Dec 2023. An X-ray also revealed two extra ones yet to emerge.

The **female** record for hyperdontia – 38 – goes to Kalpana Balan (IND), as counted on 24 Jun 2023 in Thanjavur, Tamil Nadu, India.

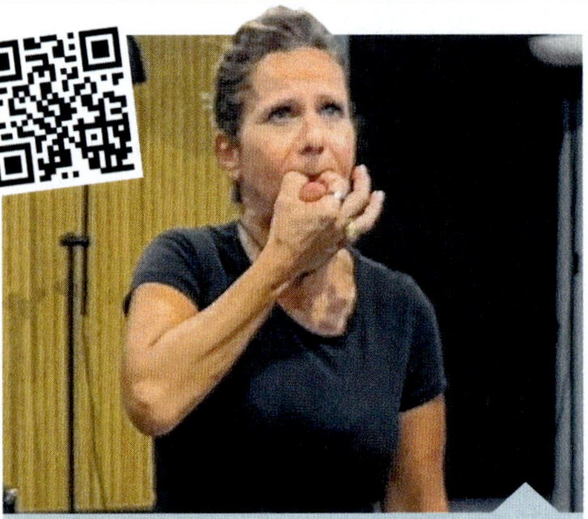

Loudest whistle
Female: Virginie Agop Boyadjian (LBN) unleashed a piercing 116.7-dB whistle in Dubai, UAE, on 27 Nov 2025.
Male: On 7 Jul 2014, Luca Zocchi (ITA) emitted a 125-dB whistle – louder than a drag-car race – at a music school in Varese, Italy. This tied with Marco Ferrera's (USA) feat of 5 Mar 2004.

Most rhinestones on the body
Make-up artist Holly Murray (UK) joined the *glitter*-ati by adorning herself with 74,880 rhinestones for *Lo Show dei Record* in Milan, Italy, on 16 Jan 2025. Her sparkling feat more than doubled the previous total.

On 21 Apr 2026, Holly donned the **most layers of liquid latex make-up applied to the face** – 125 – in 2 hr 20 min, at GWR's HQ in London, UK. Find out more about her flexible facial on our *What's The Record?* podcast.

MAR 26 Tom Schaar (USA) completed the **first skateboard 1080** (a dizzying three full rotations while airborne) in Tehachapi, California, USA, on this day in 2012.

MAR 27 *The Power of the Dog* (NZ/UK, 2021) earned the **most Oscar nominations for a film with a female director** (12) for New Zealander Jane Campion in 2022.

Most tattooed person (multiple layers)
As of 4 Feb 2026, the most tattooed individual in terms of multi-layered inking is Ephemeral Remy (aka Jeremy "Remy" Schofield, CAN). Since 2005, the former chef has had at least 90% of his body's surface area covered and re-covered in up to 40 layers of tattoo ink, with some regions filled in more than 100 times! Remy continues to have his "never-ending" artwork revised in up to three sessions per week.

The **widest tongue** is 8.88 cm (3.49 in) – broader than a cricket ball – and belongs to Brian Thompson (USA), as confirmed in La Cañada, California, USA, on 30 Jul 2018.

Largest mouth gape (female)
Susan Morgan (UK) can stretch her jaws 8.10 cm (3.19 in) apart, as verified in Durham, UK, on 27 Jul 2025. She applied for the title after seeing the former holder on ITV's *This Morning*. "She placed several items in her mouth," Susan told GWR, "and each time I thought, 'I can do that!'"

Isaac Johnson (USA) holds the **overall** title, with a 10.19-cm (4.01-in) gape – expansive enough to accommodate a baseball – as verified in Milan, Italy, on 22 Feb 2022.

Most birthday candles in the beard
Joel Strasser (USA) packed his facial fuzz with 613 cake candles in Nampa, Idaho, USA, on 30 Aug 2025. The serial beard stuffer has many related GWR titles, including those for **pencils** (456), **chopsticks** (520) and **golf tees** (607).

Oldest first-time grandfather
Aged 91 years 209 days, Charles Smith (AUS, b. 1 Feb 1934) became a grandpa to Isla Smith in Brisbane, Queensland, Australia, on 29 Aug 2025. He was 55 years old when he had his only son (Ashley) in 1989, and Ashley's wife, Hanna, gave birth to Isla.

Remy (left) joins GWR ICON Lucky Diamond Rich (AUS/NZ) – the **most tattooed person (total coverage)** – as the ultimate in skin embellishment. But whereas Remy's title is based on the amount of tattooing done over cumulative layers, Lucky's record is based on the percentage of the body tattooed. He has an *ink*-redible 100% coverage, the result of more than 1,000 hr under the needle. Lucky began with a full set of colourful designs from across the world. Next, he had a 100% covering of black ink, including his eyelids, the skin between the toes, down into the ears, and even his gums. He followed that with white designs over the black and coloured designs on top! Discover the **most tattooed woman** on p.52.

To date, Remy has spent nearly 2,000 hr being tattooed. Only parts of his face, palms and soles remain untouched.

Largest conch flesh tunnels
Body-mod devotee Nero Daikokudo (JPN) has two 3.8-cm-wide (1.4-in) rings fitted in his upper ears, as confirmed in Suita, Osaka, Japan, on 21 May 2025. Nero, who also has a striking tattoo body suit, describes himself as an artist, model and "cultural icon in progress" on Instagram.

MAR 28 Inventor Henri Fabre (FRA) achieved the **first take-off from water in an aircraft** in 1910. His floatplane – *Le Canard* ("The Duck") – flew for *c*. 1,650 ft (500 m).

MAR 29 Gaber Kahlwai Gaber Ali (EGY) really turned things around on this day in 2015. He performed the **most cartwheels in one minute** – 67 – in Giza, Egypt.

SNAPSHOT

Tallest Christmas Tree

One way to fully appreciate the immensity of the world's **tallest-ever Christmas tree** is to relocate it next to one of the world's most visited monuments. We've done just that – erecting it alongside the iconic *Christ the Redeemer* statue overlooking Rio de Janeiro in Brazil.

In Nov 1950, Northgate Mall in Seattle, Washington, USA, unveiled a festive showstopper that earned global attention: a 212-ft-tall (64.6-m) Douglas fir (*Pseudotsuga menziesii*), recognized at the time as the world's **tallest cut Christmas tree** (left).

The sheer scale of the project would be apparent to anyone trying to recreate it today, especially atop the 710-m-high (2,329-ft) Mount Corcovado in Rio. A tree of this size would weigh *c.* 23 tonnes (50,700 lb) and need a specially prepared logging truck for transport. Befitting its celebrity status, the Seattle fir was given a full escort detail to guide it along the city's narrow streets, so just imagine how challenging it would be negotiating the tight twists and turns of the road through Rio's Tijuca National Park!

There's not a lot of room at the peak of Corcovado, so the existing platform would need extending. It's a bit blustery up there, too, so to anchor the tree in place, you'd need an even more elaborate system of industrial-strength cables than was used in the Seattle mall parking lot.

As with the original record breaker, a team of workers equipped with climbing gear would need to scale the massive trunk to hang strings of ornaments and bulbs, creating a dazzling light show – a colourful beacon that would be visible for many kilometres off the Atlantic coast.

Given the Herculean effort needed to erect and decorate this most ambitious of festive spectacles, it's little wonder that the record hasn't been surpassed in more than 75 years.

The Seattle tree was lit with 3,600 bulbs, needing a dedicated electrical generator. It was also topped with two red beacons to warn passing aircraft!

The **tallest bedded (living) Christmas tree** is a 44.7-m-tall (147-ft) giant redwood (*Sequoiadendron giganteum*) that was planted in the 1860s at the Cragside estate in Northumberland, UK. The tree's lights – more than 1,300 of them – were first switched on during a ceremony organized by the UK's National Trust on 5 Dec 2025.

At 38 m (125 ft) tall (including pedestal), *Christ the Redeemer* – known locally as *Cristo Redentor* – is 40% shorter than the colossal Christmas tree. The soapstone-clad Art Deco statue was constructed between 1922 and 1931. In 2007, it was designated as one of the New Seven Wonders of the World.

To recreate the denser look of a traditional Christmas tree, extra branches were harvested from the same forest and attached to the 287-year-old trunk.

MAR 30 In 1992, Disney's *Beauty and the Beast* (USA) became the **first animated film nominated for the Best Picture Oscar**.

MAR 31 Born this day in 1928, Gordie Howe (CAN) became the **oldest NHL player** in 1980, aged 52 years 11 days.

APR 1 The **first internet radio show** – *Geek of the Week*, produced by Internet Talk Radio (USA) – debuted today in 1993.

APR 2 The **most wedding flower girls** (253) saw Charlene Pearson and Leon Watts (both AUS) marry in Hita, Japan, in 2017.

ICON Christina Koch

On 1 Apr 2026, NASA's Artemis II mission rose into the sky over Florida, USA, carrying astronauts to the Moon for the first time in more than 50 years. For Christina Koch (USA), the flight was the latest superlative feat to add to an already record-rich career.

The Michigan-born electrical engineer decided early on that she wanted to be an astronaut. As a kid, Christina followed NASA's Space Shuttle missions and attended the prestigious Space Camp programme in Huntsville, Alabama. After university, she trained at the NASA Academy before working as a researcher in support of the *Juno* space probe and at the Amundsen-Scott South Pole Station in Antarctica. She completed her astronaut training in 2015.

From 14 Mar 2019 to 6 Feb 2020, she notched up the **longest continuous time in space by a female astronaut** – 328 days 13 hr 58 min – as a flight engineer on the *International Space Station* (*ISS*; below). During her space sojourn, she also took part in the **first all-female spacewalk** (below right).

As part of the Artemis II crew, Christina added three more records to her tally, becoming the **first woman to leave low-Earth orbit**, and breaking the **women's altitude record** on her way to the crew's new mark for the **greatest distance from Earth** – an astonishing 406,771 km (252,756 mi)!

Above, Christina with her Artemis II crewmates on board *Integrity*: mission specialist Jeremy Hansen (top), pilot Victor Glover (bottom) and commander Reid Wiseman (right). Also pictured is the mission's mascot and "zero-g indicator", Rise. The launch of the Artemis II's massive SLS rocket on 1 Apr (below) was watched live by more than 18 million people around the world.

Aboard the *Integrity* spacecraft, the crew of Artemis II became the first humans to see the whole Earth since the Apollo Program ended in 1972. Speaking about the experience after their return to Earth on 10 Apr, Christina said, "When we saw tiny Earth [...] what struck me wasn't necessarily just Earth. It was all the blackness around it. Earth was just this lifeboat hanging undisturbingly in the universe."

On 6 Apr 2026, the crews of Artemis II and China's *Tiangong* space station were briefly the **farthest separated humans ever**, at 419,581 km (260,714 mi).

VITAL STATISTICS	
Name	Christina Hammock Koch
Birthplace	Grand Rapids, Michigan, USA
Birth date	29 Jan 1979
Current GWR titles	Multiple, including **longest continuous time in space by a female astronaut** – 328 days 13 hr 58 min

Christina completed more than 200 investigations during her epic 328-day stint on board the *ISS*. She also tested the station's BioFabrication Facility, a 3D bioprinter designed to print human tissues in microgravity. NASA studied how extended spaceflight was affecting Christina, both physically and mentally, generating invaluable information for future deep-space missions.

On 18 Oct 2019, at 11:32 UTC, Christina and her long-time training partner Jessica Meir left the *ISS*. They spent the next 7 hr 23 min in the vacuum of space, replacing parts of the station's electrical system. At 18:55 they re-entered the craft, having made history with the **first all-female spacewalk**. It was one of six spacewalks Christina carried out during this mission, giving her a grand total of 42 hr 15 min outside the *ISS*. This meant that she went from a spacewalk rookie to an expert, whose cumulative time is behind only veteran astronauts Peggy Whitson and Sunita Williams – the latter having recorded the **most spacewalk time (female)**, with 62 hr 6 min.

Discover all of GWR's incredible ICONS at guinnessworldrecords.com/records/icons

RECORDOLOGY

CONTENTS

Around 90% of this miniature marvel is made from original Fiat Panda parts, including the lights, wheels, seats (there's a tiny one in the rear, which would fit a child) and windows. Andrea debuted his record-breaking ride at the "Panda a Pandino" Fiat festival, held at Visconti Castle in Lombardy, Italy, in Jun 2025. The event celebrated the 45th anniversary of this much-loved Fiat model.

"It all started in our junkyard, but above all, with a crazy idea," Andrea reflects. "A year of cutting, welding, mistakes and laughter."

NARROWEST DRIVEABLE CAR

Parking's never a problem for Andrea Marazzi (ITA)! His super-slimline Fiat Panda is just 50.2 cm (1 ft 7.7 in) wide, as verified in Bagnolo Cremasco, Lombardy, Italy, on 21 Jun 2025. A trained mechanic, Andrea set himself the challenge of building this unique vehicle (aided by a small team) to give new life to a 1993 Panda that was to be demolished at his family's scrapyard. His "Flat Fiat" has an electric motor powered by two 12-volt batteries and is fully driveable. The car, which is a third of the width of a standard Panda, can reach a modest speed of 15 km/h (9.3 mph) and travel for *c.* 25 km (15.5 mi) on a single charge. It's not road-legal, though, so Andrea only takes it for a spin at fairs and shows.

Serial Record Breakers

For some people, the thrill of setting a world record becomes an irresistible addiction. Here, we showcase some of our most prolific record breakers – an elite group who, between them, are the proud owners of more than 700 GWR certificates.

Lim Kai Yi (MYS)
The youngest member of this group, Lim broke his first record, **fastest solve of a 4 x 5 Klotski puzzle**, on 23 Jan 2021 when he was just 16. After setting a flurry of puzzle records, he turned his fast fingers to other challenges, including **fastest time to sort 30 coloured soft toys** (pictured), which he broke at his college in Penang, Malaysia, on 15 Nov 2024.

Christian Roberto López Rodríguez (ESP)
Christian started breaking records in 2017, inspired by a childhood love of GWR and a desire to prove that diabetes doesn't have to hold anyone back. He specializes in the same sort of offbeat athleticism as Ashrita Furman (see opposite), with titles such as **fastest mile in high heels** (6 min 10 sec) and **fastest 100 m hopping on one leg** (15.17 sec).

Silvio Sabba (ITA)
Personal trainer Silvio got his start in 2011, before going on a record-breaking record-breaking spree in 2012 that saw him make 120 successful applications in a year. His superlative poise earned him titles such as **longest time on a balance board** (2 hr 36 min), but he has since diversified into many other areas. Silvio's son Cristian (right) has also got in on the act, earning four GWR titles with his dad.

In Nov 2024, Silvio dusted off his motorbike racing licence to claim the title **most people jumped from a low ramp** (43).

APR 3 — In 2021, Tracey Nicol-Lewis's (UK) **largest collection of *Harry Potter* memorabilia** reached 5,284 items. A truly *wand*-erful hoard!

APR 4 — Chinese feline Bao Zi achieved the **fastest 10 m on a skateboard by a cat**, finishing in a time of just 12.85 sec.

Leah Shutkever (UK)
The top-ranking serial record breakers are all men, but one woman has made it into the top 20. Britain's leading speed-eater, Leah holds 25 GWR titles, including **fastest time to eat a burrito**, which she achieved in 32.35 sec in Feb 2022. If we include research-based (rather than applied-for) records, Taylor Swift's 90+ titles get her into the top five.

Ashrita Furman (USA)
Since making his debut with **most star jumps** on 14 Aug 1979, Ashrita has become GWR's **most prolific record breaker**, with 850 applications accepted. From his base in the Jamaica neighbourhood of Queens, New York, Ashrita has tried his hand at everything from pogo-sticking up skyscrapers to speed-eating lemons, but specializes in quirky athletic feats such as **fastest mile on a space hopper** (13 min) and **fastest half-marathon balancing a milk bottle on the head** (2 hr 33 min). At his peak in 2018, Ashrita held 233 records simultaneously – the all-time **most GWR titles by an individual**. Despite having retired from the record-breaking game, he still holds 146 active GWR titles.

David Rush (USA)
David began his rapid rise through the record ranks on 2 Jan 2015 with **longest time juggling three objects blindfolded**. As well as juggling, he holds many titles for balancing, such as **greatest distance walked with a bicycle on the chin** (168.76 m, or 553 ft 8 in) and **longest time balancing a ladder on the chin** (19 min 11 sec). His record tally surpassed Ashrita's in 2023, and as of 4 Dec 2025, he holds the **most GWR titles (current)** with 193.

APR 5 — Shipwrecked Poon Lim (CHN) was finally rescued in 1943 after having endured the **longest survival alone on a liferaft**: 133 days.

APR 6 — In 1896, a hop, skip and jump of 13.71 m (45 ft) was enough to make James Connolly (USA) the **first modern Olympic champion.**

Collectors

Black Panther memorabilia
Tyesha Elam (USA) has amassed 2,546 *Marvel*-lous mementoes of Wakanda's superpowered king T'Challa, as verified in Houston, Texas, USA, on 3 Apr 2025. Following the passing of Chadwick Boseman – who played the title role in *Black Panther* (USA, 2018) – from cancer in 2020, Tyesha resolved to use her record to mark his legacy and promote cancer screenings.

Teenage Mutant Ninja Turtles memorabilia
Cowabunga, dude! As of 8 Feb 2025, Dave Fawcett (CAN) had 2,195 objects related to the "heroes in a half shell", which he keeps in Hamilton, Ontario, Canada. As a child, Dave insisted that all his birthday parties (and presents) were *TMNT*-themed. His favourite pieces include a soft-head Donatello (the techy turtle), which was a Christmas present in 1988 and his very first *TMNT* toy.

TRASH TALK
Alexander Smoljanovic opened the lid on his wheelie wonderful collection for GWR.

When did you start collecting?
In 2003, a neighbour who worked for the local disposal service gave me four miniature bins that a sales rep had gifted her. I moved on to real ones in 2008, when my aunt gave me a yellow 120-litre wheelie bin.

What do friends and family think of your collection?
They all understand my hobby and support me. If anyone doesn't understand me, I explain: "It's like a stamp collection – different shapes, colours and sizes… just larger."

Which is the most unusual bin in your collection?
I have a special wheelie bin with a divider inside so that you can dispose of two different kinds of waste in the same bin. It's called the "MEKAM" system and was invented by Rolf Schiller in the 1980s. It saves space, money and resources.

Lastly, what does it mean to you to have a GWR title?
It's the first world record for my hometown, Wanzleben; I'm very grateful and proud of it!

Jellycat toys
Hope Roberts (UK) owned 877 unique plushies as of the latest count in Bedford, UK, on 3 Dec 2025. She bought her first Jellycat, a small white rabbit with a pink bow, for just 20 pence in a charity shop and rapidly grew her hoard, attracting tens of thousands of fans on TikTok and Instagram along the way.

Crocheted items
As of 4 Aug 2024, Chandralekha Kulangareth (aka Chandralekha Umesh, IND) had collected 1,358 yarn-crafted keepsakes, which she stores in Kannur, Kerala, India.

Socks
Jim Donovan (USA) boasted 1,531 pairs of socks, as verified in Philadelphia, Pennsylvania, USA, on 8 Dec 2025. The former CBS news anchor regaled viewers with his taste for wacky footwear; in response, they sent him new pairs in their droves. "This record is as much theirs as it is mine," Jim admitted.

Finger puppets
Salacnib "Sonny" Molina (USA) possessed 2,978 miniature puppets, as verified in Woodstock, Illinois, USA, on 7 Jun 2025. It's part of an eclectic variety of record-breaking hoards accrued by this seasoned collector, including **salt and pepper sachets** (594 matching pairs) and **Pringles tubes** (1,262).

Deadpool memorabilia
Gareth Pahliney (ZAF) had accumulated 4,250 items based on the wisecracking Marvel superhero, as of the most recent count in Lansdowne, Virginia, USA, on 3 Dec 2025. Maximum effort!

Dog-related items
As of 15 Mar 2025, Rosa, Marià, Nuri, Enric, Miquel and Teresa Gabarró (all ESP) had rounded up 5,025 canine curiosities, which are housed in Terrassa, Barcelona, Spain. The collection was started by the siblings' late parents, and includes doggy figurines, lighters, clocks and magnets.

Cameras
As of 6 Apr 2025, Dr Arcot Vasantha Rao Arun (IND) had 5,707 vintage cameras on display in his museum in Chennai, Tamil Nadu, India. His collection began in 1997, with a twin-lens camera that he snapped up at a flea market.

Waste bins
Improving on his own record, trash-can titan Alexander Smoljanovic (DEU) had 270 dustbins as of 31 Oct 2025. He keeps his cumbersome collection in three garages in Wanzleben-Börde, Germany. Alexander particularly prizes purple, gold, silver or transparent models. One of his most beloved bins is a purple 360-litre (95-gal) example that a contact arranged to be transported to him from the UK.

APR 7 An epic grooming session by Texas Hearing and Service Dogs (USA) in 2012 generated the **heaviest ball of dog hair** – a furry mass that weighed 201 lb (91.17 kg).

APR 8 You call *that* a knife? In 2016, the Bowie Chamber of Commerce in Texas, USA, produced the **largest Bowie knife**, which boasted a 20-ft 6-in-long (6.24-m) blade.

ON THE RECORD

Family and friends are very supportive of my collection. For my birthdays and Christmas I always get ponies as gifts and they all keep an eye out for ponies when they're shopping. For my 40th birthday, my cousin made me a My Little Pony cake!
– *Miranda Worby*

My Little Pony began as a toy line by US firm Hasbro in 1981. Since then, it has gone on to encompass comic books, movies and TV series.

MY LITTLE PONY (MLP) MEMORABILIA

As of 13 Jul 2025, Miranda Worby (UK) had accrued 4,550 unique MLP mementoes in Lowestoft, Suffolk, UK. Miranda was given a pink pony called Snowflake when she was just three years old, but only started collecting in earnest in 1997 with the rise of online trading. She has travelled more than two hours to pick up particularly rare items for her hallowed herd.

"My Little Pony was my favourite toy growing up," Miranda told GWR. "I wanted a real horse, but had to settle for the toys!" Her most common model is "G1 Sundance", of which she has 25 different variants.

APR 9 French inventor Édouard-Léon Scott de Martinville sang a snippet of a folk song into his wax-cylinder recorder in 1860, creating the **first recording of a human voice**.

APR 10 Happy birthday to Sean Keaney (UK), who entered the world in 1990 with the **most teeth for a newborn** – a superlative set of 12 deciduous pearly whites.

Work Hard, Play Hard

A MONOPOLY ON MONOPOLY
Neil Scallan (below) gets a new Monopoly set every few days. He reveals what it's like to grow a record-breaking collection.

Can you recall one of your most memorable experiences buying a set?
The Norwich City FC shop had a 5-ft [1.5-m] square board on their wall and I won it on eBay. When Norwich played QPR in London, I had to go [there] to pick it up. [After collecting it], I paid for my parking and then I couldn't locate my car so I was walking around for over an hour with the 5-ft board and hundreds of QPR fans around.

The board is now at my parents' house and they use it to block the sun coming through their front window!

Do you have a favourite set?
I love the Hong Kong handover set from 1998. I also like the Kinder Surprise German edition – it's very colourful.

Roughly, how much have you spent on your collection?
Maybe £250,000 [$337,000], but my biggest headache is paying more than a grand per month on storage. I would rather spend that money on more games.

Do you buy duplicates?
If I see a set and I can't remember if I have it, I'll buy it because I'd rather have two than none.

Which sets are you still searching for?
I'm looking for the Brunei edition (a new country for Monopoly) and the Cronulla Sharks [rugby team] edition.

First female chess grandmaster (GM)
After 16 years as the Women's World Chess Champion, Nona Gaprindashvili (GEO) was awarded GM status at the 23rd Chess Olympiad in Buenos Aires, Argentina, in Oct 1978.

Fastest time to solve a 3x3x3 rotating puzzle cube
Nine-year-old Teodor Zajder (POL) became the first person to break the sub-3-sec barrier with a 2.76-sec solve at the GLS Big Cubes Gdańsk 2026 event in Poland on 8 Feb.

Young cubers are currently dominating the **3x3x3** titles: the **average** record (i.e., the best of five solves) was claimed by eight-year-old Xuanyi Geng (CHN) – 3.84 sec – at the Beijing Winter 2026 event in China on 11 Jan.

Longest duration juggling three balls while performing a headstand
An inverted José Valencia (COL) kept three balls in constant rotation for 5 min 14 sec in Turku, Finland, on 15 Jun 2025. Nine months prior to this, on 22 Sep 2024, the circus performer claimed the **five-ball** variation of this record, keeping the balls aloft for 45 sec while balanced on his head.

Fastest sport-stacking 3-3-3 stack (female)
On 26 Oct 2025, Sama Basaw (CHN) stacked and unstacked nine cups in three separate piles in 1.463 sec. The record was broken at the World Sport Stacking Association 2025 Asian Sport Stacking Championships in Dalian, Liaoning, China.

Fastest time to build the LEGO® Star Wars Millennium Falcon microfighter
Lifelong LEGO fan Nikolay Fomin (CZE) constructed a 94-piece replica of this iconic sci-fi starship in 1 min 38.34 sec in Prague, Czechia, on 26 Jan 2024.

Largest collection of completed jigsaw puzzles
Khloud Abo Zayda of St Paul, Minnesota, USA, set down the last piece of her 2,453rd jigsaw on 25 Oct 2024. The puzzle fanatic had to start her collection over from scratch after moving to the USA from Jordan.

Youngest female player to defeat a grandmaster in a chess tournament
Aged 10 years 156 days, Bodhana Sivanandan (UK, b. 7 Mar 2015) beat 60-year-old GM Pete Wells in the final round of the 2025 British Chess Championship in Liverpool, UK, on 10 Aug. That day, she also became the **youngest Woman International Master**.

Gukesh Dommaraju (IND, b. 29 May 2006; inset) also made history as the **youngest chess world champion**, aged 18 years 197 days in Singapore on 12 Dec 2024.

Fastest time to arrange a chess set blindfolded
Despite his vision being obstructed, Jeyakirithik Jeyakumar (IND) correctly positioned 32 pieces on a chess board in 30.63 sec in Chennai, Tamil Nadu, India, on 16 Jan 2026.

Most yo-yo tricks in one minute
Naoshi Terasawa, aka "Performer NAOKI" (JPN), executed 52 different tricks in Nagaizumi, Shizuoka, Japan, on 9 Sep 2025. The previous record (51) had stood for 21 years. On the same day, NAOKI achieved the **most pinwheel yo-yo tricks in 30 seconds** – 136.

Largest collection of Monopoly boardgame memorabilia
For the last decade, Neil Scallan (UK) has monopolized this GWR title, breaking his original record of 1,677 on three occasions. As of 9 Oct 2024, Scallan's stash in the West London suburb of Hayes stood at 4,379. "I never thought I would get this high a number," he told GWR. "I promise my girlfriend that I will stop, but it's been 25 years and so much fun. I wonder what will be my 4,500th set...?"

APR 11 On this day in 2021, competitive speed-eater Leah Shutkever (UK) recorded the **fastest time to eat a hot dog with no hands:** 18.15 sec.

APR 12 In 2025, Paweł Durakiewicz (POL) finished Norway's Frozen Lake Marathon in 4 hr 57 min 54 sec without footwear: the **fastest barefoot marathon on ice/snow.**

THE BIGGER, THE BETTER! SUPERSIZED SETS

Largest...	Dimensions	Record holder(s)
1. **Jenga***	L: 2.4 m (8 ft) W: 2.4 m H: 3.7 m (12 ft 2.25 in)	Archie Lyons and Caterpillar Inc. (both USA)
2. **Snakes and ladders**	95.63 m² (1,029.35 sq ft)	Global Village (UAE)
3. **Cornhole**	L: 19.58 m (64 ft 3 in) W: 9.80 m (32 ft 2 in) H (highest point): 3.11 m (10 ft 2.4 in)	Goodyear Tire & Rubber Company (USA)
4. **Mahjong** △	L: 1 m (3 ft 3.4 in) W: 0.75 m (2 ft 5.5 in) H: 0.5 m (1 ft 7.7 in)	Shenzhen Longhua Uniworld (CHN)

*Correct as of 25 Mar 2026. *Dimensions for the complete nine-level tower made from 27 blocks. △ Dimensions for one of the 136 tiles.*

Mahjong is a tile-based game that originated in 19th-century China. The symbols on the tiles reflect strategy, luck and prosperity.

APR 13 When Leandro Reis (USA) achieved the **largest collection of airline tags** – 692 – in 2024, he surpassed the previous mark of 637, which had stood for 20 years!

APR 14 Since Susanne Baird (UK) depilated 40 pairs of legs in Edinburgh, UK, in 2008, the **most legs waxed in one hour** record has remained unbroken.

Super Skills

Highest drop into a temporary quarter pipe
On 25 Sep 2025, six-time vert skateboard world champion Sandro Dias (BRA) dropped 60.33 m (197 ft 11 in) into a quarter pipe at the Centro Administrativo Fernando Ferrari in Porto Alegre, Brazil. The attempt took place on a special ramp with seven platforms at different heights, designed to progressively test the limits of the sport. During the feat, Sandro also achieved the **fastest speed skateboarding on a quarter pipe** – 103.8 km/h (64.4 mph).

Most cannonball juggling catches in 30 seconds
British extreme juggler Daniel Teplitski caught a trio of cannonballs – each weighing 7 kg (15 lb 6 oz) – 43 times in Birmingham, UK, on 10 Dec 2025. He comes from a circus family: his dad was a "power juggler" too, and when Daniel was aged eight, he asked his father to show him the ropes. The rest is GWR history!

Most Risley spins of a person in 30 seconds
Named after the 19th-century acrobat "Professor Risley" (aka Richard Risley Carlisle), this act sees a performer rotate a partner on the soles of the feet. Robel Mezgebe Weldemikael and Meareg Hishe Mehari (both ETH) executed 38 Risley spins in San Francisco, California, USA, on 20 Nov 2025.

Farthest forward-flip pogo-stick jump
On 19 Jun 2025, Henry Cabelus (USA) bounced 6.75 m (22 ft 2 in) on a pogo stick, during which he flipped head over heels, in Pittsburgh, Pennsylvania, USA. The mid-air manoeuvre was achieved at the Pogopalooza festival.

Farthest reverse ramp jump by car
Sultan Muhammad Khan (PAK) performed a 37.1-m (121-ft 8-in) retrograde ramp jump in Quetta, Pakistan, on 13 Dec 2025. A professional stuntman, Sultan drove a standard 2,500-cc Toyota Mark X. On the same day, he also set the **fastest mile driven in reverse** – 58.12 sec.

Highest unassisted martial-arts 360° spin kick
On 22 Nov 2025, Carlos Jaen (VEN) executed a full mid-air turn at a height of 2.23 m (7 ft 3 in), followed by a kick, in Valencia, Carabobo, Venezuela. The move is common to martial arts such as taekwondo and kickboxing.

Longest tennis rally between two moving cars
Tennis pros Jamie Murray and Laura Robson (both UK) conducted a 101-stroke rally while atop two separate cars on 23 Jun 2025. They could have kept going, but ran out of runway! The feat was part of the Lexus Served at Speed campaign at Duxford Airfield near Cambridge, UK.

Farthest trampoline slam dunk
Daniel Schmidt (DEU) flew 10.3 m (33 ft 9 in) off a trampoline to slam-dunk a basketball for *Guinness World Records – die Große Show der Weltrekorde* in Munich, Germany, on 29 Aug 2025. Daniel's acrobatic delivery prompted viewers to vote him their favourite performer of the night.

Longest basketball shot while blindfolded
On 31 Jul 2025, an unsighted Osman Gürcü (TUR) hooped a basketball from 24 m (78 ft 8 in) away in Denizli, Türkiye. Osman's many other GWR titles involving pinpoint accuracy include the **longest bull's-eye in darts** – 8 m (26 ft 2 in).

Most consecutive 1980 spins in snowboarding
Multiple Olympic medallist Su Yiming (CHN) deftly performed two jumps in which he rotated five-and-a-half times in the air in Saas-Fee, Valais, Switzerland, on 7 Oct 2025. The first back-to-back 1980 ever, the acrobatic attempt saw the snowboarder deliver a backside 1980 with a melon grab, then follow with a switch-stance 1980 with a tail grab.

Most flaming concrete blocks broken in 30 seconds
On 6 Nov 2025, Narayanan N (IND) surpassed his own record of 29 by smashing a total of 37 blazing concrete slabs on the set of *India's Got Talent* in Mumbai, Maharashtra, India.

Most consecutive inside loops in a glider
Pilots Jan Carboch and Michal Vorlíček (both CZE) executed 62 airborne loops in the skies above Kolín, Czechia, on 3 Oct 2025. It took them 10 min to complete the set, once they had reached a suitable altitude.

Most drifting revolutions in a hand-controlled car in one minute
On 19 Jul 2025, Christina Vithoulkas (AUS) completed 11 sliding rotations in 60 sec in Melbourne, Victoria, Australia. She has T5 paraplegia after a motocross accident, and says that drifting gives her the same rush as motorbike jumps. Christina – who drives a modified automatic car, using hand controls instead of a footbrake and clutch – dressed as TV's Ali G on the day (right)!

In motor racing, a drifting revolution allows drivers to take a more direct line through a corner while maintaining their speed.

APR 15 In 2023, Pongo the piglet performed the **most tricks by a pig in one minute** (15) – from sitting down to raising a trotter – with help from his owner Iris Brun (ITA) in Italy.

APR 16 Barry Nelson (USA), born on this day in 1917, was the **first on-screen James Bond**. He portrayed the suave spy in a CBS broadcast of *Casino Royale* in Oct 1954.

Quincy has won Gold and Silver Clown awards for hand balancing at the International Circus Festival of Monte-Carlo.

LONGEST DURATION ON A ROLLA BOLLA WHILE BALANCING A PERSON ON THE HEAD

Rubel Medini (ITA) supported Quincy Azzario (ESP) while astride a balance board for 34.88 sec in Copenhagen, Denmark, on 23 Oct 2025. A performer since the age of 14, Rubel's other circus-related GWR titles include the **tallest stack of platforms balanced on a rolla bolla**, poising himself atop a precarious tower of 11 boards in Benidorm, Spain, on 20 Sep 2021. The dynamic duo are members of The Circus Arts Conservatory in Sarasota, Florida, USA.

APR 17 Don't let Con Damouras (AUS) lay the table… In 2005, he racked up the **most plates smashed in 30 seconds** (86) in Sydney, New South Wales, Australia.

APR 18 Is it a bird? Is it a plane? No, it's Superman! Published on this day in 1938, *Action Comics* #1 saw the debut of the "Man of Steel" – the **first superhero with superpowers**.

Super Strength

Pushing the boundaries
Alex Goulding's (UK) specialist skills have earned him a string of GWR titles. They include **one minute** records for the **most 180 push-ups** – 29 – and the **most push-ups to planks** – 84. Alex has also notched up the **most plyometric push-ups** – 19 – in which he propels himself into the air on to raised platforms on either side of his body.

Heaviest weight held in an abdominal plank
On 25 Dec 2025, Yaser Zeyad (JOR) supported a tractor tyre weighing 185.05 kg (407 lb 15 oz) while performing a front-plank pose in Zarqa, Jordan.

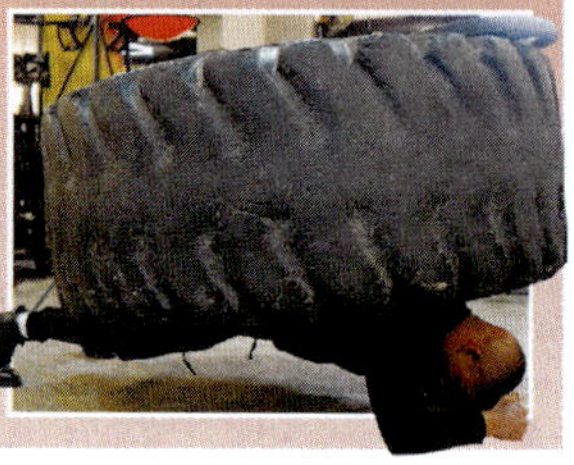

On the same day, Yaser earned himself another Christmas present with a GWR title for the **heaviest Samson's chair** – holding a weight of 358.40 kg (790 lb 2 oz) while squatting against a wall.

Heaviest tyre flip
On 9 Nov 2025, Xiao Yang (CHN) overturned a 628-kg (1,384-lb 8-oz) tyre in Guangzhou, Guangdong, China. That's similar to the weight of an adult Holstein-Friesian cow, or the equivalent of Xiao lifting six times his own body weight.

Most push-ups in one hour with a 60-lb pack
On 9 Nov 2025, Rohtash Choudhary (IND) completed a punishing 822 push-ups while bearing a weight of 60 lb (27.2 kg) at the JLN Stadium in New Delhi, India.

Heaviest deadlift with one finger
Egmond Molina (ABW) lifted 159 kg (350 lb 8 oz) with his middle finger in Seroe Colorado, Aruba, on 29 Jan 2026. Earlier that month, he had also hauled a 9,860-kg (21,737-lb) bus for 20 m (65 ft) – the **heaviest vehicle pulled by the neck**.

Longest time to hold a person and motorcycle by the teeth while suspended upside down
An inverted Leonardo Costache held a motorbike and rider by the teeth for 21.17 sec on 11 Mar 2026. The Romanian strongman's other titles include **heaviest weight held with the teeth while suspended upside down** – 192.84 kg (425 lb 2 oz) – on 10 Nov 2025. His compatriot and duo partner, Vita Morondel, set the **women's** record – 90.90 kg (200 lb 6 oz) – on 5 Sep 2025. All the feats took place in Bucharest, Romania.

Most squats in three minutes (female)
On 9 Aug 2025, Mari Davtyan (ARM) performed 170 squats in Talin, Aragatsotn, Armenia. On 22 Aug, she also notched up the **one minute** record – 84 squats.

Most consecutive squats
Reza Mohammadi (IRN) logged 1,100 squats in Tehran, Iran, on 24 May 2025. It took him 27 min, with only 2-sec pauses between repetitions.

Heaviest weight balanced in a headstand (female)
Hema Varshini Jeyaraj (IND) supported a 50.9-kg (112-lb 3-oz) barbell on her upper arms while performing a headstand in Tiruppur, Tamil Nadu, India, on 13 Jul 2025.

Most pull-ups in one hour (female)
Police officer Jade Henderson (AUS) carried out 733 pull-ups in Gold Coast, Australia, on 22 Aug 2025. On 13 Dec, Paula Gorlo (POL) nailed the **one minute** title – 45 – breaking the previous record by one pull-up, in Fasty, Poland.

Longest time holding the human-flag position on a flying helicopter
On 16 Nov 2025, Samer Madi (LBN) supported himself for 21 sec while hanging from a frame on the side of a chopper. The attempt took place over René Mouawad Airport in the Akkar Governorate of Lebanon. "This record is more than just a personal victory," Samer reflected afterwards. "It's a message that with dedication and passion, we can push the limits of what the human body can do."

Heaviest deadlift (II2)
GWR's II impairment categories are reserved for people with intellectual challenges. Kyle Landi (CAN) lives with Down Syndrome, but his condition hasn't limited his ambition. On 29 Jan 2026, he deadlifted a 117.38-kg (258-lb 12-oz) barbell in Burlington, Ontario, Canada. A seasoned bodybuilder and motivational speaker, Kyle's other II2 GWR titles include **one minute** records for the **most weight deadlifted** – 1,044.07 kg (2,301 lb 12 oz) – **most pull-ups** (23) and **most chin-ups** (15).

APR 19 — First held in 1897, the Boston Marathon is the **oldest continuously run marathon**. The inaugural race was won by John J McDermott (USA) in 2 hr 55 min 10 sec.

APR 20 — In 2012, to mark the centenary of their home stadium, Fenway Park, 32,904 Boston Red Sox fans raised a glass in Massachusetts, USA – the **largest toast at one venue**.

MOST FOOT-JUGGLING SPINS OF A TABLE IN 30 SECONDS

On 3 Dec 2025, circus artist Emma Phillips (NZ) flipped a table over 77 times with her feet in London, UK. To hone her skills, Emma trained for more than three years at the elite Beijing International Arts and Wuqiao Acrobatics schools, and is one of the few Western artistes to practise Chinese-style foot juggling. Uniquely, she also combines umbrella and table juggling in her performances – an extremely difficult skill to master, given the disparity in their weight and bulk.

"I'm from a small town in New Zealand," Emma says, "but when I saw Cirque du Soleil, that just sort of sparked something inside me."

APR 21 Overseen by Dr Chung Sung Min (KOR) and Dentium Co. (IND), 1,136 people brushed up on their toothcare skills in the **largest dentistry lesson** in Delhi, India, in 2024.

APR 22 In 2002, Lars Clausen (USA) embarked on the **longest unicycle journey** – 14,686.82 km (9,125.97 mi). He crossed the USA twice, finishing on 12 Nov that year.

Super Endurance

Most tandem parachute jumps in 24 hours
Couple Sven Jseppi and Heather McLay (both USA) performed 108 skydives together above Manteo, North Carolina, USA, on 22 Sep 2025. The pair were airborne for around 16 hr in all. Afterwards, Sven paid tribute to their huge support crew, but especially Heather, who "let me spin us back to the ground like a Tasmanian devil and she didn't get sick".

Greatest simulated distance on a fan bike in one hour
Jonathan Zweig (USA) rode the equivalent of 44.28 km (27.51 mi) in 60 min on a static cycle on 29 Aug 2025. The pertinacious cyclist used the event as a fundraiser for the cancer charity Cure Leukaemia, from his garage in Newport Beach, California, USA.

Most consecutive days to run an ultramarathon distance
Shannon-Leigh Litt (NZ) had run at least 50 km (31 mi) for 800 successive days, as of 11 Mar 2026. She started her challenge on 1 Jan 2024, having initially aimed for "just" 200 days! The ultramarathon queen is shown above after her 800th run.

The **male** record is held by the UK's Sam King, who racked up 80 ultra runs between 27 Sep and 15 Dec 2025, breaking the previous record by a count of 20. Sam ran to raise funds for the charity Headway UK, which supports victims of brain injuries.

Fastest Antarctic Ice Marathon
This annual event sees runners complete a 42.1-km (26.2-mi) course while battling an average windchill temperature of -20°C (-4°F). On 14 Dec 2022, Seán Tobin (IRL) finished the arduous race in a time of 2 hr 53 min 33 sec.

In Jan 2026, GWR was saddened to hear of the death of US runner Liesl Muehlhauser, who had achieved the **women's** title – 3 hr 29 min 16 sec – on 13 Dec 2024.

Fastest 100 m wakeboarding while lit on fire
Having donned multiple fire-resistant racing suits, Italian stuntman Niccolò Fava was set alight, then wakeboarded 100 m in just 10 sec in Abu Dhabi, UAE, on 5 May 2025.

Later that day, the cool-headed Niccolò went on to achieve the **greatest distance wakeboarding while on fire** – 285 m (935 ft).

Longest duration full-body contact with ice (female)
Maria Bodaj (POL) remained immersed up to her neck in an ice box for 3 hr 33 min 33 sec in Bąkowo, Gdańsk, Poland, on 28 Jun 2025. Impressively, Maria was the first woman to break the three-and-a-half-hour mark.

On the same day, her compatriot Damian Kasprzyk achieved the **male** title – a bone-numbing 5 hr 1 min 33 sec, nearly an hour longer than the previous record!

Longest time breath held voluntarily underwater
On 14 Jun 2025, freediver Vitomir Maričić (HRV) remained submerged for 29 min 3 sec on one breath in a pool in Opatija, Croatia. "The mental fight was horrible!" he admitted later. "I don't know how I managed, but I'm sure glad I did!"

Greatest distance pulling a rickshaw in 24 hours
Yuji "Gump" Suzuki (JPN) carried a passenger for 129.73 km (80.61 mi) in a human-drawn cart at Ajinomoto Stadium in Chofu, Tokyo, Japan, on 4–5 Dec 2025.

Most consecutive handstand push-ups
On 16 Apr 2025, Mohammed Alikrawiy (IRQ) executed 68 vertical push-ups in a row while maintaining a handstand in Al-Najaf, Iraq.

Longest basketball marathon
A team from MOST: Men Opposing Sex Trafficking (USA) hit the basketball court for a straight 121 hr 3 min 20 sec in Fairburn, Georgia, USA, from 16 to 21 Mar 2025. The attempt raised more than $300,000 (£231,200) to support the organization, which the previous year had undertaken the **longest softball marathon** – 120 hr 59 min.

APR 23 — In 2005, the **first YouTube video** – "Me at the Zoo" – was uploaded by company co-founder Jawed Karim (USA, b. DEU). It has notched up more than 384 million views.

APR 24 — Born in 1896, Charlie Rivel (ESP, b. Josep Andreu Lasserre) enjoyed the **longest career as a clown**, raising smiles for 82 years between 1899 and 1981.

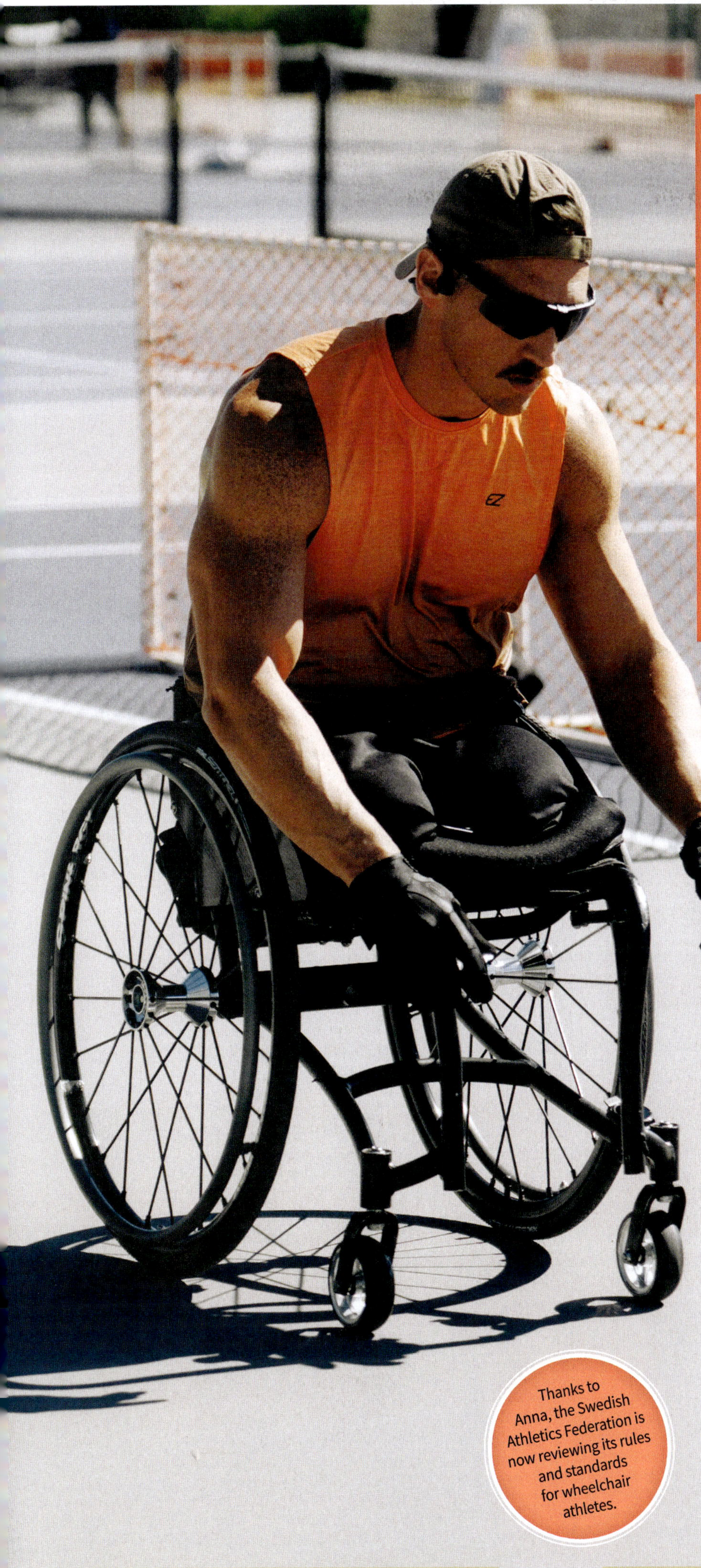

GREATEST DISTANCE BY WHEELCHAIR IN 24 HOURS

Michael Egan (USA) propelled himself for 245.2 km (152.37 mi) – enough to have got him from Paris, France, to Brussels, Belgium – on 10 Nov 2025. The Marine Corps vet completed 720 laps at Morgan's Sports Complex in San Antonio, Texas, USA. "We all experience adversity in our life," he told GWR, "and we are faced with a choice of whether that pain is destructive or transformative. This record is to commemorate the choice I made and hopefully encourage others to do the same."

ON THE RECORD

"If there is something you are passionate about or a goal you've been putting off saying you'll do it one day, hold yourself accountable to it. There is no better time than today"
– Michael Egan

Greatest distance by wheelchair in 24 hours (female)

On 26 Apr 2025, Anna Louise Svensson (SWE) covered a total of 164.88 km (102.45 mi) in her wheelchair in Växjö, Sweden. She achieved the feat as a competitor in Växjö's VXO Ultrafest, but had to gain permission from the Swedish Athletics Federation before being allowed to compete in this ultramarathon.

Thanks to Anna, the Swedish Athletics Federation is now reviewing its rules and standards for wheelchair athletes.

APR 25 In 1960, the USS *Triton* SSRN 586 completed the **first submarine circumnavigation**, having embarked on its epic round-the-world trip on 24 Feb.

APR 26 On this day in 2019, Tumen-Ulzii Zandraa (MNG) registered the **largest collection of chess sets** – 438 boards – in Ulaanbaatar, Mongolia. Check mate!

Yoga

DID YOU KNOW?

There are 84 traditional yoga *asanas*. Deriving from the Sanskrit word for "seat", *asana* refers to the different body positions practised in yoga. Many of the poses are named after things from nature such as animals (e.g., Simhasana – "Lion") and plants (e.g., Padmasana – "Lotus").

Most people performing the chair pose simultaneously
To mark the International Day of Yoga on 21 Jun 2025, over 1,000 pliable participants from the Akshar Yoga Kendraa school came together in Bengaluru, Karnataka, India, to take part in a series of record attempts, arranged by the World Yoga Organisation and Shree Mahaprabhu Jagannath Sangh (all IND). The crowd performed various *asanas*, including the **chair pose** (1,695 people). They also claimed titles for the **most people performing the...**

- **Warrior II**: 1,634 (see **4**, opposite)
- **Downward-facing dog**: 864
- **Mermaid**: 863
- **Eagle**: 522.

Youngest yoga instructor
Pratyaksh Vijay (IND, b. 22 Dec 2017) was introduced to yoga when he was four years old, and after a few months he knew that it was his calling. Before he'd even started regular school, Pratyaksh had completed a 200-hour teacher-training course, and on 24 Nov 2023, at the age of just 5 years 337 days, he began teaching in Kota, Rajasthan, India. The bendy boy wonder told GWR: "I want to spread the knowledge of ancient yoga to the whole world so everyone can enjoy a healthy and tension-free life."

Coincidentally, the **female** record is also 5 years 337 days. It was set by Phoenix Giselle Hicks (USA, b. 20 Jul 2019; see p.154) in Houston, Texas, USA, on 22 Jun 2025.

Longest time to hold the womb pose
8 hr 34 min 11 sec, by Yash Moradiya (IND) on 25 Oct 2022

Fastest time to solve a rotating puzzle cube while in the bridge position
Keeping his hips in the air and his feet on the floor, prolific record breaker Lim Kai Yi (MYS) unscrambled a 3x3x3 cube in 27.84 sec in Butterworth, Penang, Malaysia, on 15 Nov 2024. This feat came two years after he set the **scorpion position** version of this title (23 sec) on 13 Oct 2022.

LONGEST TIME TO HOLD THE...

Yoganidrasana pose
On 20 Jul 2025, Sona Ramesh (IND) lay on her back with her legs crossed behind her head for 31 min 41 sec in Tiruppur, Tamil Nadu, India. This is also known as the yogic sleep pose.

Most viewers for a yoga livestream on YouTube
Saurabh Bothra (IND) guided 246,252 yogis through an hour-long exercise class in Nagpur, Maharashtra, India, on 12 Jan 2024. During the COVID-19 lockdown, Bothra co-founded HaBuild, a habit-building platform that offers daily yoga classes online. He began with just three students, but now has 14.8 million members and 3 million YouTube subscribers.

Later that day, Sona's twin sister, Sonia, achieved the **longest Dwi Pada Sirsasana pose** – 32 min 2 sec. Similar to the Yoganidrasana *asana*, Sonia's feet were crossed behind her head, yet she had to remain sitting upright.

Bhunamanasana pose
Smita Kumari (IND) sat on the floor with her legs stretched out to the sides, her fingers holding her feet and her chin touching the ground for 2 hr 33 min 37 sec in Ahmedabad, Gujarat, India, on 17 Feb 2025.

Bridge pose
José Andrés Montiel León (ECU) spent 1 hr 25 min 16 sec in the bridge position in Guayaquil, Ecuador, on 9 Nov 2024. This *asana* required him to lie down with the soles of his feet on the floor and his hips in the air, creating a straight line from his knees to his chest.

Firefly pose
With his legs extended forward and his entire weight resting on his hands, contortionist Oyindamola Kolawole (USA) remained elevated on his palms for 8 min 52 sec in Atlanta, Georgia, USA, on 29 Dec 2024.

Rooster pose
While studying for a degree in Naturopathy and Yogic Science, Dhanraj S Shetty (IND) held himself aloft in a cross-legged position for 13 min 41.28 sec in Bengaluru, Karnataka, India, on 15 Jun 2024. He surpassed the previous record by nearly eight minutes.

Most nationalities in a yoga lesson
On 23 Jan 2024, the Emirates Group (UAE) celebrated the diversity of their workers with a desert-based yoga class in Dubai, UAE. Employees from 144 different countries took part, hailing from as far and wide as Chile and Mongolia. The lesson was steered by Emirates Group staff with prior yoga training and attendees were given biodegradable cork mats to ensure it was a zero-waste event.

APR 27 In 1908, the Olympic Games in London, UK, opened with the **first Parade of Nations**, which saw all the athletic teams enter the stadium behind their national flags.

APR 28 In 2015, the Wooden Spoon Society (UK) played the **most northerly rugby match** at 78° latitude – then the site of the magnetic North Pole – in Nunavut, Canada.

STRETCHING THE LIMITS! YOGA EN MASSE		
Record title	**Total people**	**Organizer**
1. **Largest yoga lesson**	300,105	Ayush Department, Government of Andhra Pradesh (IND)
2. **Most people performing the cobra pose in multiple venues**	1,596	Lokmat Campus Club, Pravin Masalewale and C M International School (all IND)
3. **Largest rhythmic yoga lesson**	289	Jack Tattersall and Yoga Drum (both UK)
4. **Most people performing the Warrior II pose**	1,634	Akshar Yoga Kendraa, World Yoga Organisation and Shree Mahaprabhu Jagannath Sangh (all IND)
5. **Largest yoga class on paddleboards**	305	Raphaela Schäufele (DEU)

Correct as of 27 Apr 2026

APR 29 Clement X (ITA, b. Emilio Altieri) became the **oldest elected pope** in 1670, aged 79 years 290 days. He held the position until his death just six years later.

APR 30 On this day in 1967, the **first images of Earth from the Moon** were captured by the *Surveyor 3* robotic lander, an unmanned US spacecraft equipped with a TV camera.

Food & Drink

Largest scotch egg
Oli Paterson and Phoenix Ross (both UK, left to right) made a supersized scotch egg weighing 7.81 kg (17 lb 3.48 oz) in Enfield, London, UK, on 17 Jun 2025. To claim the title, their titanic take on this classic British dish had to stay intact when sliced. See a few key stats about the superlative snack below.

INGREDIENTS AND NUTRITIONAL VALUES

7 kg
Sausage meat

1.8 kg
Single ostrich egg

20 litres
Oil

20,000
Calories

1,500 g
Protein

Largest pizza party
Taste of New Haven (USA) hosted a get-together for 4,525 pizza fans in Connecticut, USA, on 12 Sep 2025. The city of New Haven is regarded as the "pizza capital of the United States" and each year stages a street party to celebrate.

Most freshly cooked hamburgers sold in eight hours
A total of 5,995 fresh hamburgers were assembled at the Burger Show (ECU) in Guayaquil, Ecuador, on 26 Jul 2025. The event, sponsored by food-production company Bimbo, attracted over 50,000 attendees, including local celebrities such as Andy Buesa and Mar Rendón.

Largest mojito cocktail
Havana Restaurant & Cocktail Lounge in Niagara Falls, Ontario, Canada, served up an XXL 4,500-litre (1,188-gal) mojito – enough to fill 30 bathtubs – on 7 Sep 2024. The drink, which took two hours to prepare, consisted of 90 kg (198 lb) of mint, 400 litres (105 gal) of both lime juice and syrup, 600 litres (158 gal) of rum, 1,020 litres (269 gal) of soda and 2,400 kg (5,291 lb) of crushed ice. The colossal cocktail was distributed to the public, with money from each sale donated to a local children's charity.

Most expensive cup of coffee
Made with a variant of one of the world's rarest coffee beans – Hacienda La Esmeralda from Panama – a hand-brewed V60 filter coffee sold for 2,500 AED ($680; £501) at Roasters Speciality Coffee House in Dubai, UAE, on 13 Sep 2025.

Tallest stack of pancakes
To mark their 50th birthday on 19 Aug 2025, Australian restaurant Pancakes On The Rocks stacked 230 of their signature snacks to a record-breaking height of 108.3 cm (3 ft 6.6 in) in Sydney, New South Wales. The tower was built by the eatery's operations manager, Arnaud Feige.

Largest tray liner
On 26 Nov 2025, McDonald's in Tokyo, Japan, revealed a 9.6-m² (103-sq-ft) replica of a fast-food paper tray cover – some 80 times bigger than the object that inspired it. The liner depicted their signature fries and was displayed at Shimokitazawa's Mikan Shimokita complex, alongside paintings of other popular menu items such as the Big Mac.

Most ice-cream scoops balanced on a cone
Gökhan Şahin (TUR), who makes ice cream for the Turkish café chain Kahve Dünyası, carefully stacked 132 scoops of gelato on a regular wafer cone in Istanbul, Türkiye, on 18 Jul 2025.

Largest nut brittle
On 16 Oct 2025, a smorgasbord of 228 chefs from Sorsogon Province in the Philippines prepared 144.16 m² (1,551 sq ft) of praline – enough to cover two-and-a-half cricket pitches. Weighing in at 3,208.5 kg (7,073 lb 8 oz), the sweet snack contained local produce, such as pili nuts and *sangkaka* (sugar candy).

Largest cookery lesson (multiple venues)
Spearheaded by celebrity chef Jamie Oliver (pictured), a total of 10,515 people from all over the world took part in a virtual culinary class on 1 Jul 2025. The livestream, organized by Jamie's Ministry of Food Foundation and Wonde (both UK), taught viewers how to make fresh pasta with tomato sauce in 30 minutes.

MAY 1 To celebrate May Day 2010, the **tallest maypole** was erected in Eicherloh, Germany. The blue-and-white mast stood 57.08 m (187 ft 3 in) tall.

MAY 2 In 1952, the **first jet-powered commercial aircraft** – the British de Havilland Comet, operated by BOAC – flew from London, UK, to Johannesburg, South Africa.

THINNEST SANDWICH SLICED BY HAND

On 7 Oct 2025, "Six Pack Chef" (aka Wallace Wong, CAN) visited GWR HQ in London, UK, and added six new GWR titles to his collection. For starters, he cut and assembled a wafer-thin sandwich with a thickness of just 5.12 mm (0.2 in)!

Next, the speedy slicer secured the **fastest time to fillet a 12-lb fish** (see left; 1 min 17.85 sec), the **most zucchini slices in 30 seconds** (111) and the **most button mushroom slices in 30 seconds** (109). Wallace also set the **blindfolded** versions of the **zucchini** (right) and **mushroom** titles – 131 and 120 slices, respectively – surprisingly chopping *more* of the vegetables than when he could see!

Wallace's slim sandwich was made from Japanese milk bread and filled with slices of cucumber and tomato.

MAY 3 In 1994, the Mandai Night Safari in Singapore waited for sunset before opening its doors to the public, becoming the world's **first nocturnal zoo**.

MAY 4 Mali's Halima Cissé and husband Abdelkader Arby became proud parents of nine babies (nonuplets) – the **most children at a single birth to survive** – in 2021.

Largest *Zelda* Collection

Constantine "Coz" Adams (USA) has loved Nintendo's *The Legend of Zelda* series since receiving his first game – *Link's Awakening* for the Game Boy – as a nine-year-old in 1993. After many years of collecting videogame-related items, in 2012 Constantine decided to narrow his focus to just his favourites, building the **largest collection of *The Legend of Zelda* memorabilia**. In the basement of his home in Fairfax, Virginia, USA, he had a total of 3,918 unique items as of 19 Jul 2025.

Coz also collects items related to his other childhood favourites, including the *Metroid* and *Final Fantasy* franchises.

1: These Amiibo figurines inspired Constantine to start building up his *Zelda* collection. A quest to acquire every Amiibo reintroduced him to the characters and stories of the series, and he started collecting everything *Zelda*-related he could find.

2: This case holds a coveted full set of *Zelda*-themed game-watches. These simple wristwatch LCD games were produced by American toy company Nelsonic in 1989.

3: Early merchandise, like this tabletop pinball machine from 1989, relied heavily on official artwork drawn by Nintendo illustrators such as Katsuya Terada and Yōichi Kotabe. This was because the original in-game sprite of Link was only 16 pixels tall!

4: The Official *Legend of Zelda* board game was published by Milton Bradley in 1988. Unusually, it was a unique game with tabletop-RPG-style dice-based combat, rather than a simple *Zelda*-themed version of an existing game. Mint-condition examples like this are extremely rare.

5: These posters (just two of the dozens in Constantine's collection) were made to promote the first 3D entry in the series, 1998's *Ocarina of Time*. This time-travelling epic remains the **most critically acclaimed game ever**, with a Metacritic score of 99.

6: This mask is a reproduction of the world-ending magical item that drives the story of cult-classic series entry *Majora's Mask* (2000).

7: It took more than two years of searching for Constantine to track down the last of these action figures, made by Epoch in 2002.

8: This limited-edition Nintendo DS console is decorated with the Hylian Crest – the coat of arms used by Princess Zelda's family.

9: Constantine made this rupee-filled chest himself (which means it doesn't count towards his collection total). On opening, it lights up and plays the chest-discovery music from *Ocarina of Time*.

Amazing Pets

Highest bar jump by a guinea pig

Tempted with some tasty lettuce offered by her 13-year-old owner, Zoe Hearn (USA), guinea pig Cora leapt over a 26.67-cm (10.5-in) hurdle on 22 Oct 2025. This improved on the previous record of 24 cm (9.4 in), set in 2023. The pair from San Francisco, California, USA, had been in training for this attempt for a few years.

Oldest cockatiel

On 10 Jan 2026, the Reicher family of Northbrook, Illinois, USA, celebrated the 33rd birthday of their beloved Sonny. He's described by his mom, Janet, as a "great companion"; she ascribes his longevity to good nutrition (including pasta and vegetables), cleanliness and lots of socialization.

OLDEST...

Sibling cats
Billie and Buffy (both UK): 44 years 54 days combined

Rabbit
Herbie (UK): 15 years 82 days

Llama
"King's Alice in Wonderland" (USA): 29 years 174 days

Chicken
Gertie (USA): 15 years 100 days

Horse
Fancy (USA): 37 years 329 days

All above set in 2025

Longest ears on a donkey

A rescue donkey named Hope has ears with an average length of 40.2 cm (1 ft 3 in) – almost the same size as this book when open! – as confirmed in Byron, Georgia, USA, on 22 Dec 2025. She is now cared for by Hannah Frost (USA), who believes this accolade could help shine a spotlight on often-overlooked donkeys, as well as raising the profile of the endangered mammoth jackstock breed in particular.

Most high-fives by a cat in one minute

Not leaving her owner Emily Lakin (UK) hanging, rescue cat Misty Pearl *paw*-formed 40 high-five tricks – that's one every 1.5 sec – in Highcliffe, Dorset, UK, on 5 May 2025.

Most followed pig on Instagram

Limelight-hogging Merlin (@merlinthepig) had a staggering 1.1 million Insta fans as of 26 Feb 2026. The Vietnamese potbelly lives with Mina Alali (USA) – who adopted him in 2022 – in Sacramento, California, USA. Their most popular posts revolve around Merlin using his snout to push buttons with recorded messages that express his mood and needs.

Most basketball slam dunks by a dog in 30 seconds

Guided by multi-record-setting dog trainer Olga Jones (UK), Bonnie the springer spaniel caught and dunked 10 balls into a hoop in Reading, Berkshire, UK, on 14 Dec 2025. Later, on 23 Apr 2026, Jones also claimed the **one minute** record with her border collie Simba, who managed to net 17.

Tallest residential cat-scratching post

Will Powers commissioned sculptor Arend Smith (both USA) to create a 4.9-m-tall (16-ft 1-in) lifelike tree just for the felines in his house in Farmington Hills, Michigan, USA. Complete with branches, textured bark and bracket fungi, the prodigious play tower – measured on 18 Jun 2025 – is apt given that this is the home of the world's **tallest cat**: Fenrir, a savannah who stood 47.83 cm (1 ft 6.8 in) to the shoulder in 2021.

Most dogs riding on a paddleboard

"Doggy paddle" took on a new meaning at the UK Dog Surfing Championships organized by SHAKA SURF at Branksome Chine in Dorset, UK, on 27 Jul 2025. With their humans close at hand, a total of 12 pooches rode the waves together on a single board (below). At the same event, two human-dog pairs achieved the **fastest 50 m on a paddleboard** with a time of 32 sec: Gigi with Matthew Jenkins and Boo with Ben Gray (all UK).

Longest tongue on a dog

Ozzy – a cross between a French mastiff and a bullmastiff – has the competition licked with his 19.89-cm (7.83-in) tongue, measured on 12 Sep 2025. His owner, Angela Pick of Oklahoma City, USA, told GWR that his tongue has always lolled out to one side since he was a puppy, though added: "It's funny, he doesn't really lick a whole lot!"

MAY 5 Stuntman Derek Lea (UK) cleared 57.2 m (187 ft 8 in) – the **longest ramp jump by a car towing a caravan** – at Bentwaters Parks in Suffolk, UK, in 2004.

MAY 6 On this day in 2021, Su Chung-Tai (CHN) achieved the **most bounces of a soap bubble** – 424 – on his hand before it popped in Taipei, Taiwan, China.

HIGH HORSES & PINT-SIZED PONIES

GWR has recently welcomed two new equine stars into its ranks of amazing animals, each at the extreme end of the same spectrum.

First over the line was Pumuckel from Breckerfeld, Germany, who was confirmed as the **shortest horse** on 16 Aug 2025. At just 52.6 cm (1 ft 8.7 in) to the withers (i.e., the shoulder blades), he's surpassed in height by a typical golden retriever. The bijou Shetland pony has been owned by Carola Weidemann (DEU, right) since he was five months old, and now plays an important role as a therapy animal.

A few months later, a four-year-old shire horse by the name of Hugo claimed the loftier title of **tallest horse** in Towcester, Northamptonshire, UK. When assessed on 28 Mar 2026, the giant – described by his owner, Lisa Masters (UK, below), as "a big softie, like an oversized dog" – measured 199 cm (6 ft 6.3 in) to the withers. Surprisingly, Lisa told GWR that Hugo's parents were fairly average in stature, so his rapid growth rate was somewhat unexpected!

Carola regularly takes Pumuckel to visit schools, nursing homes and hospices to bring some joy to everyone's day!

As well as unlimited hay and two buckets of hard feed per day, Hugo is also quite partial to a banana as a treat!

MAY 7 Veteran actress Dame Judi Dench (UK, b. 9 Dec 1934) became the **oldest *Vogue* cover model**, aged 85 years 150 days when the issue launched today in 2020.

MAY 8 Marcello Ferri of Italy raised 985.8 kg (2,173 lb 5 oz) with just his middle finger in 2023: the **most weight lifted by dumbbell rows in one minute (one finger)**.

Lucky Charms

Most leaves on a clover

Four-leaf examples of the typically three-leaved *Trifolium repens* are a mutation seen in one in every *c.* 10,000 clovers. They have been regarded as lucky talismans for millennia (learn more below). So, how fortunate must Yoshiharu Watanabe (JPN) have been when, on 2 Aug 2023, he discovered a *63-leaf* clover in Nasushiobara, Tochigi, Japan?

In an effort to reduce damage to the natural environment, GWR no longer monitors records for **most four-leaf clovers collected**. However, there is currently an open category for **most four-leaf clovers *identified* in one hour**, which is awaiting its inaugural holder. Best of luck!

Largest collection of *maneki-neko* (beckoning cats)

The Maneki-Neko Museum in Seto, Aichi, Japan, houses 5,460 waving feline figurines that for centuries have been associated with prosperity in Japanese culture. Often positioned in shop or restaurant windows, a beckoning left arm is thought to usher in customers, while the right arm is said to attract money; two waving arms covers both bases!

Largest human four-leaf clover

Casino operator Galaxy Entertainment Group (CHN) arranged 1,068 of its staff into this iconic good-luck symbol in Macau, China, on 29 Aug 2016. Rare four-leaf clovers have been warding off evil spirits since ancient times, popularized by the Celtic druids. Later adopted by Christianity – e.g., Eve is said to have picked one as a memento when departing the Garden of Eden – the quatrefoil foliage has come to signify four virtues: hope, faith, love and grace.

Largest fuzzy dice

On 11 Nov 2011, tourism officials in Las Vegas, Nevada, USA, presented a pair of 1.22-m (4-ft) fluffy dice at the city's famous welcome sign. While now most often seen dangling on car rearview mirrors, the original "lucky dice" emerged in the 1940s among WWII fighter pilots. They would add gambling ephemera to their planes' cockpits for good luck prior to missions.

Largest horseshoe

Abhishek Mazumder (IND) oversaw the production of a 2.47-m-tall (8-ft 1-in) steel horseshoe – almost 1 ft (30 cm) taller than the **tallest horse ever** (a Shire gelding named Sampson). It was commissioned to mark the centenary of the Mahalaxmi Race Course in Mumbai, India, in 2016.

Meanwhile, the **largest collection of horseshoes** (of a regular size) is 13,855, amassed by Petru Costin (MDA) for his museum in Ialoveni, Moldova, as verified on 4 Jul 2021.

Largest *omamori*

Traditionally pocket-sized, *omamori* are silk purses containing prayers and good wishes offered as charms at Shinto temples and shrines in Japan. Games developer Atlus (JPN) created a supersized 2.6 x 1.9-m (8-ft 6-in x 6-ft 2-in) version to mark their first-ever festival on 7 Jun 2024. It was adorned with Atlus's snowman mascot, Jack Frost.

Largest human rainbow

Fortune favoured Polytechnic University of the Philippines on 18 Sep 2004 when they assembled a crowd of 30,365 in Manila to form this auspicious meteorological phenomenon. Rainbows are synonymous with hope and, as some would have it, pots of gold. The treasure at the end of this one was a GWR title that has since stood for more than two decades.

Largest collection of ladybird-related items
Sheri Cummings of Lake in the Hills, Illinois, USA, is dotty for ladybugs, with a 6,047-piece-strong collection to prove it as of 28 Feb 2022. These beetles are often seen as a favourable omen, perhaps because as natural pest controllers they tend to be conducive to a bountiful harvest.

LUCKY NUMBERS

7
Considered a mystical, auspicious number in ancient Mesopotamia, and still by many cultures to this day

8
In East Asia, the word for "eight" sounds very similar to "prosper"

9
Linked to good fortune in Norse mythology

13
While often considered *un*lucky, in Italy the phrase *fare tredici* ("make thirteen") roughly translates as "to hit the jackpot"

39
Interpreted as a divine message, particularly in Catholic countries

MAY 9 In 1984, the Chicago White Sox and the Milwaukee Brewers played the **longest baseball match** (8 hr 6 min). The White Sox won 7–6 in the 25th innings.

MAY 10 The **largest porcelain doll**, measuring 1.72 m (5 ft 7.7 in) tall, was unveiled in Jingdezhen, Jiangxi, China, in 2018. It was made by Wang Chu and Deng Jiaqi (both CHN).

LARGEST DALA HORSE SCULPTURE
This unmissable equine landmark, which stands 13 m (42 ft 7 in) tall and 12.8 m (42 ft) long, has welcomed visitors to the city of Avesta in Dalarna, Sweden, since 13 Dec 1989. The concrete sculpture was built by Skanska Teknikk and decorated by painting contractor Miljönären Måleri (both SWE), with restoration work undertaken in 2019. Dala horses are traditional wooden toys, produced in the region since the 17th century. They come in a range of sizes and patterns (see above), and are cherished by locals and tourists alike as a symbol of good fortune and Swedish identity.

A marker next to the giant Dala horse logs the former record height attained by Swedish pole vaulter Armand Duplantis (see p.208).

MAY 11 In honour of St Brendan, 463 people got into the habit in 2013 at Ardfert Central National School (IRL) in County Kerry for the **most people dressed as monks**.

MAY 12 In 2014, daredevil Johnny Strange (UK) hauled a 677.8-kg (1,494-lb) Cessna 172P plane in Essex, UK. This is the **heaviest weight pulled by pierced ears**.

Crazy Contests

UNSTUNG HERO
Lucy Dermody (UK) on her triumph at the 2025 World Stinging Nettle Eating Championship (see opposite)

Tell us a bit about yourself.
I'm originally from Taunton [in Somerset] but currently live in Bridport, 20 minutes away from the Bottle Inn. I've just completed a two-year apprenticeship in viticulture and now work full time at a local vineyard in Dorset.

Have you long planned to take part in this contest or was it spur of the moment?
I'd heard through friends that the nettle-eating competition was coming up and I thought I'd give it a go! I'd never eaten a nettle before the day of the competition.

How did you find the experience?
It was easier than I was expecting it to be. I used a rolling technique, which I think helped, though by the end my mouth was a bit numb and my hands were tingling!

What was it like to win?
It was a bit of a surprise to be honest! My favourite part was later telling my family, who all found it hilarious.

Most wins of the World Bog Snorkelling Championships
Despite retiring in 2023, teacher Neil Rutter (UK) was drawn back by the "bog bug" and secured his sixth trophy on 24 Aug 2025. Playing out in 180-ft-long (55-m) water-filled trenches in the Waen Rhydd peat bog near Llanwrtyd Wells, Powys, UK, the **longest-running bog-snorkelling competition** has been attracting mud-loving swimmers since 1985.

If one outlandish sport weren't enough, Llanwrtyd Wells has also hosted the Man versus Horse Marathon since 1980. The **longest-running human vs horse race** pits runners against equestrians to cover a 21-mi (34-km) mixed-terrain course. For only the fifth time, two legs won out in 2025, with Dewi Griffiths crossing the finish line almost 12 min ahead of his equine rival, Gweni (ridden by Gabi Morley).

Longest-running annual sauna marathon
Established in Estonia in 2007, the Otepää European Sauna Marathon held its 14th edition in 2025; in total, 200 teams of four took part, representing 18 countries. Racers must call at the most saunas in five hours, with extra points for stops at ice holes and hot tubs.

Most wins of the World's Ugliest Dog Contest
A rare African sand dog named Chi Chi was declared "top dog" at this unconventional US canine beauty pageant seven times between 1978 and 1991. The 2025 victor of the Californian event was Petunia, a two-year-old hairless English-French bulldog (pictured above with her owner, Shannon Nyman).

Most wins of the Wife Carrying World Championships
Taisto Miettinen has claimed eight titles at this wacky race: six bearing Kristiina Haapanen in 2009–13 and 2017 (a record for **most wins by a woman**), then two more with Katja Kovanen (all FIN) in 2022–23. The top prize at the competition – staged in Sonkajärvi, Finland – is the equivalent weight of the winning female partner in beer.

Most wins of the Nathan's Hot Dog Eating Contest
This Fourth-of-July institution at Coney Island in New York City, USA, requires gobbling as many hot dogs as possible in 10 min. In 2025, the wiener winners were veterans Joey Chestnut and – in the **women's** category – Miki Sudo (both USA). Their victory tallies now sit at 17 and 11, respectively.

Largest hole-digging championship
An army of 1,452 shovellers gathered for the All-National Hole Digging Competition at Narita Dream Farm in Chiba, Japan, on 2 Feb 2020. Teams of six fought to excavate the deepest hole in 30 min, with the winners walking away with the hallowed Golden Shovel and 100,000 yen.

Largest frozen-hair competition
The biggest "pool" of competitors ever registered at the Takhini Hot Springs Hair Freezing Contest in Whitehorse, Yukon, Canada, is 288 on 1 Apr 2020. To win, entrants must allow the subzero air to freeze their wet locks into the most innovative and comical 'dos!

Longest-running finger-wrestling contest
Since 1959, the Bavarian Finger Wrestling Championships, held annually near Munich, Germany, see entrants haul rivals across a table using just a leather band wrapped around each contestant's middle finger. The pasttime, known as *Fingerhakeln*, has roots to at least the 1800s, and perhaps once helped resolve tavern disputes.

MAY 13 Professional parkour athlete Lorenz Wetscher (AUT) executed the **farthest sideways jump from a standing start** – 2.83 m (9 ft 3 in) – in Tyrol, Austria, in 2023.

MAY 14 In 2005, the 319.2-m-long (1,047-ft) aircraft carrier USS *America* became the **largest ship scuttled**. It was intentionally sunk after target practice off Virginia, USA.

The origins of competitive nettle eating date back to 1986, when Dorset farmer Alex Williams presented a stinging nettle that was 15 ft 6 in (4.72 m) long and wagered that if anyone could present a longer example, he would eat it. When a holidaying couple from the USA produced a 16-ft-long (4.88-m) nettle, Williams kept his promise – and the rest is history.

MOST STINGING NETTLES EATEN IN ONE HOUR (FEMALE)

Representatives from GWR were in attendance at the 2025 World Stinging Nettle Eating Championship, which, after a few years' hiatus, returned to the Bottle Inn in Marshwood, near Bridport, Dorset, UK, on 21 Jun. Among the female entrants, Lucy Dermody (UK, below) claimed a record by chomping her way through 68 ft (20.73 m) of nettles (*Urtica dioica*). That year's male winner was Michael Hobbs (inset above), who consumed 74 ft (22.56 m) of the ferocious foliage.

The nettles are picked the day before and cut into 2-ft (60-cm) lengths. All the leaves must be eaten; the stems are then counted.

MAY 15 The **first game show** was a quiz aired on CKCL Radio in Canada in 1935; hosted by Roy Ward Dickinson (UK), it was titled *Professor Dick and His Question Box*.

MAY 16 The **first Oscars ceremony** rolled out the red carpet in Los Angeles, California, USA, on this day in 1929. The Best Picture gong went to silent drama *Wings* (1927).

RECORDOLOGY

Slime

Most people slimed in relay in three minutes
A gutsy group of 73 kids, parents and TV stars successfully poured gunge over each other on the set of *Saturday Mash-Up!* in Glasgow, UK, on 13 Jul 2024. Host Kia Pegg (right) was the first to be slimed, followed shortly after by Apollo, Dynamite, Sabre and Viper from the sports entertainment show *Gladiators* (BBC).

Most people slimed in three minutes
Leyland Playscheme – an annual children's holiday camp held in Lancashire, UK – reserve Thursdays for "messy" activities, and you can't get much messier than attempting a slime world record! On 7 Aug 2019, entertainer Aaron Hobin (UK) poured buckets of gunk over 100 attendees.

Largest slime
Chemists from Fachverband der Chemischen Industrie Österreichs (AUT) filled a pool with 10,350 kg (22,817 lb 14 oz) of white gloop at a trade fair in Tulln, Austria, on 14 Jun 2018.

Footage from the attempt was later used in an advert, showing ski jumper Thomas Morgenstern running through the slime with local children.

Most people slimed simultaneously
A mass gunging with 3,026 participants took place at Nickelodeon SLIMEFEST in Sydney, New South Wales, Australia, on 15 Sep 2012.

The **online** version of this title stands at 195, and was set by the Nickelodeon Kids' Choice Awards (USA) on 13 Mar 2021. The ceremony took place virtually due to the COVID-19 pandemic, requiring viewers to self-slime at home. For more slimy shenanigans by Nickelodeon, see opposite and below.

When preparing slime, it goes without saying that things can get messy! Take extra care if younger kids are involved.

Most people slimed at an awards show
Since 2003, Nickelodeon (USA) has secured multiple GWR titles with its trademark green goo. At the 35th Kids' Choice Awards in California, USA, 1,000 celebrities and guests were showered in their signature slime – including hosts Miranda Cosgrove and Rob Gronkowski (above) and rapper Jack Harlow (below) – on 9 Apr 2022.

Most people making slime simultaneously
To celebrate Community Friendship Day as part of their Fourth-of-July weekend activities, 933 citizens of Carson in California, USA, assembled to make Star-Spangled-Banner-themed slime with red, white and blue dyes and glitters on 1 Jul 2018.

Greatest distance to stretch homemade slime in 30 seconds
TV presenter Luke Franks (UK) extended a lump of slime for 5.19 m (17 ft) on the set of *Scrambled!* (CITV, 2014–21) in Goudhurst, Kent, UK, on 12 Nov 2018.

The **under-16s** version of this title recently surpassed the adult record, at 8.72 m (28 ft 7.3 in). It was achieved by 10-year-old Freya Evans of Bodelwyddan, Clwyd, UK, on 7 Jul 2024.

Largest slime-making lesson
The Centre des sciences de Montréal (CAN) taught 491 people how to make slime in Quebec, Canada, on 19 Jun 2022. Discover how you can below!

HOW TO MAKE SLIME

INGREDIENTS + EQUIPMENT

100 ML (3.4 FL OZ) OF PVA GLUE
FOUR TEASPOONS OF CONTACT LENS SOLUTION (MUST CONTAIN BORIC ACID)
ONE TEASPOON OF BICARBONATE OF SODA
FOOD COLOURING (OPTIONAL)
GLITTER (OPTIONAL)
BOWL
SPOON

1. Squirt the PVA glue into a bowl.
2. Add the contact lens solution. If you'd like to make your slime more exciting, you can add some food colouring and/or glitter at this stage.
3. Add the bicarbonate of soda.
4. Mix the ingredients together with a spoon until the slime has a gooey consistency.
5. Scoop the slime out of the bowl once you're happy with it.
6. Visit the GWR website to find out what records you can attempt with your slime.

Slime is what is known as a "non-Newtonian fluid" – a substance that can be both a solid and a liquid depending on how it's handled. It can remain in compact clumps when pulled apart quickly, yet appear runny when stretched gently. Other non-Newtonian fluids include ketchup, custard and honey.

Most people slimed in 24 hours
Nickelodeon Australia unleashed more of the brand's infamous green gunge on 3,309 concertgoers at SLIMEFEST in Sydney, New South Wales, on 26 Sep 2014. For both the matinee and evening shows, presenter Luke Ryan (below) was in charge of the supersized slime cannon, and young musicians such as Sabrina Carpenter (inset right), Cody Simpson and Justice Crew went on to entertain the gunk-covered audience.

MAY 17 The **most rabbits pulled out of a magician's hat** is 300, by Walter Rolfo and Piero Ustignani (both ITA) in 2008.

MAY 18 In 1998, Ginette Harrison (UK) became the **first woman to climb Kangchenjunga** in the Himalayas.

MAY 19 Julian Mittermaier (DEU) covered 674.18 m (2,211 ft) – the **longest slackline walk over water** – in 2017.

MAY 20 The **fastest sheep to hand-knitted jumper** is 4 hr 45 min 53 sec, set by Team Groenewoud (NLD/DEU) in 2017.

Teetering Towers

Tallest bowling-ball tower
Two people share the record for stacking 10 bowling balls without adhesives or supports: Dave Kremer (USA) in Los Angeles, California, USA, on 19 Nov 1998, and Shen Xiaoshi (CHN, above) in Beijing, China, on 8 Jan 2016. The final towers had to stand stably for at least five seconds.

Tallest human pyramid in motion

Forming a self-supporting pile of people is no easy task, as evidenced by the fact it took more than four decades for the outright **tallest human pyramid** record to tumble (see opposite). But imagine throwing the element of movement into the mix… Thirty members of the NSA Roller Gymnastics Team (USA) embraced this challenge in 1985, forming a four-level stack that roller-skated 47.2 m (155 ft) in eight seconds in Philadelphia, Pennsylvania, USA.

Also pushing the boat out on their "people steeple" were the 65 divers who formed the **largest underwater human pyramid**. MCM Communication and Ammara Siriphong (both THA) organized the scuba enthusiasts into formation on the seabed off the island of Koh Kradan, Thailand, on 11 Nov 2023.

Fastest time to build a 30-level Jenga tower

Prolific speed puzzler Lim Kai Yi (MYS) assembled a classic Jenga set in just 2 min 8 sec in Butterworth, Malaysia, on 16 Dec 2022.

The equivalent record for an **under-16 team of two** is 5 min 35 sec, built by sisters Dhakshana and Sana Kaarthick (IND/USA) in Morrisville, North Carolina, USA, on 17 Dec 2023.

Most Jenga Giant blocks on one vertical Jenga Giant block

Tian Rui (CHN) created a tower with 918 extra-large wooden blocks on a single upturned block in Qingdao, Shandong, China, on 14 Apr 2025. The final structure, comprising 47 storeys, measured 1.56 m (5 ft 1 in) tall and had to be handled with great care as it weighed around 113 kg (249 lb)! As you'll see below, Tian's skills don't stop at balancing blocks…

Tallest house of cards (eight hours)

Tian Rui (CHN), aka the "Card Architect", built a 62-floor pyramid in Qingdao, Shandong, China, on 30 Mar 2025. It was the first of three house-of-card titles that the steady-handed stacker would claim in 2025, including the **one hour** record (32 levels) on 2 Apr and the outright **tallest house of cards** – arranged in the traditional pyramidal shape – which topped out at 2.91 m (9 ft 6 in) on 29 Apr.

Most Jenga blocks on one vertical Jenga block

On 24 Jul 2025, Abbetjes Meindert de Boer (CAN) built a 4,881-piece Jenga tower perched precariously on just a single upright block. He used bricks from more than 90 Jenga sets, and took six hours to smash the existing record of 3,149 that was achieved by Tian Rui (see below) on 3 Apr 2025. In doing so, Abbetjes reclaimed a record title he'd previously set in 2024 with 3,132 blocks.

Tallest playing-card structure

Since 1992, architect-turned-professional card stacker Bryan Berg (USA) has continued to raise the bar for monumental playing-card builds. The tallest he has created to date stood 7.86 m (25 ft 9 in) – almost as high as two double-decker buses – and was built from 1,100 decks of cards at the state fair in Dallas, Texas, USA, on 16 Oct 2007.

TALLEST STACK OF…

- **Cars**: 10.725 m (35 ft 2 in), by Chery New Energy Automobile Co in Wuhu, Anhui, China, on 22 Sep 2023.
- **Tyres**: 7.98 m (26 ft 2 in), by S&S Tire at their headquarters in Lexington, Kentucky, USA, on 17 Aug 2024.
- **Chairs**: 5.205 m (17 ft), by Jay Ehsan (UK) in Manchester, UK, on 22 Apr 2021.
- **Sugar cubes**: 2.08 m (6 ft 10 in), by Camille Courgeon (FRA) in Blanquefort, France, on 1 Jul 2013.
- **Macarons**: 2.07 m (6 ft 9 in), by the Vocational School of Visionary Arts in Tokyo, Japan, on 22–23 Aug 2014.
- **Glass bottles**: 1.90 m (6 ft 3 in), by Silvio Sabba (ITA) in Rodano, Milan, Italy, on 16 Feb 2017.
- **Poppadoms**: 1.72 m (5 ft 7 in), by Tipu Rahman (UK) at the Tamarind restaurant in Northampton, UK, on 11 Oct 2012.

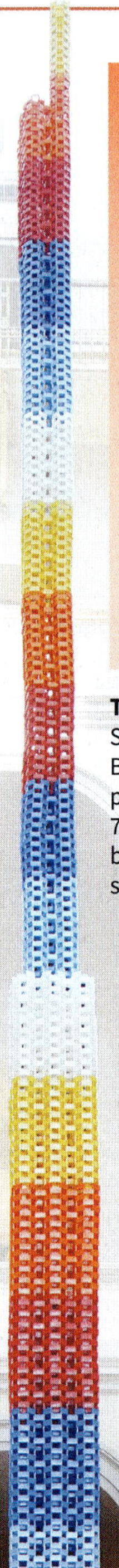

Tallest domino structure
In 2024, YouTuber and domino artist Lily Hevesh (USA, standing third in from the right) assembled a crack team of builders hailing from the USA, Germany, Belgium and the Netherlands. Over six days (8–13 Jul), the squad constructed a 10.13-m (33-ft 2-in) domino tower – the same height as a telephone pole – at the National Building Museum in Washington, DC, USA.

MAY 21 In 2011, Latvia's Normunds Pakulis organized the **most people playing checkers underwater** – a total of 88 – in a swimming pool in Riga.

MAY 22 The All Blacks' Michael Jones (NZ) recorded the **first Rugby World Cup try**, against Italy, at Eden Park in Auckland, New Zealand, on this day in 1987.

The boy at the very top of the tower wore a helmet and harness tied to a crane, so he was caught when the pyramid collapsed.

TALLEST HUMAN PYRAMID

Acrobatic history was made on 4 Sep 2025 when members of the Kokan Nagar Govinda Pathak sports club, supported by the Sanskruti Yuva Pratishthan Trust (both IND), formed a 10-tier tower in Thane, Maharashtra, India. The pyramid reached 14.73 m (48 ft 3 in) during the Hindu Festival of Dahi Handi ("Curd Pot"); a key part of this celebration sees teams clamber on top of each other in a bid to shatter a suspended earthenware vessel filled with yoghurt.

DID YOU KNOW?

Until now, no human pyramid has exceeded nine levels. This was first achieved in 1981 by Colla Vella dels Xiquets de Valls in Catalonia, Spain – where performers known as *castellers* form towers at festivals. This was later matched by Pratap Sarnaik and the Jai Jawan Govinda Pathak team (both IND), also in the city of Thane, in 2012.

ON THE RECORD

"This extraordinary feat symbolized not only unmatched physical endurance and balance but also showcased the spirit of teamwork, discipline and Maharashtra's age-old Govinda tradition. The 10-tier pyramid stood as a living monument of courage and unity – *a member of Kokan Nagar Govinda Pathak*"

MAY 23 The **oldest independent railway company**, Ffestiniog Railway, was founded in Wales, UK, in 1832, by an act of Parliament. It is still operating today.

MAY 24 In 2014, Blosom – the **tallest cow ever** – measured 190 cm (6 ft 2.8 in) from the hoof to the withers in Orangeville, Illinois, USA.

Circus Acts

The activities on these pages are strictly for professionals only – don't try them at home!

Most helicopter spins on aerial silks
Cirque du Soleil acrobat Mizuki Shinagawa (JPN) executed 20 helicopter spins on the set of GWR's Italian TV show, *Lo Show dei Record*, on 14 Feb 2025. This skill involves wrapping a suspended length of silk around the legs and waist, then letting it unravel, spinning the performer down to the ground.

Highest static trapeze act
Skydiver and circus artist Marlene Kiepke (DEU) decided to combine her passions by doing a trapeze routine while hanging beneath a hot-air balloon at an altitude of 3,261 m (10,698 ft). The attempt took place over Rheine-Eschendorf, Germany, on 5 Sep 2023. Kiepke even worked in the **highest silks performance**, descending from the trapeze on a broad ribbon of fabric before parachuting back down to Earth.

Most pumpkins cut with a swallowed chainsaw-pommel sword in one minute
On 28 Jan 2025, Jelly Boy, aka Eric Broomfield (USA), took to the *Lo Show dei Record* stage with a circus prop of his own design – a sword with a chainsaw instead of a handle. He proceeded to ingest the sword and use the running chainsaw sticking out of his mouth to rapidly carve 17 pumpkins.

Most hula hoops spun simultaneously
Australian hoop performer Marawa the Amazing (aka Marawa Ibrahim) has held this record for more than 10 years, having raised the bar to a seemingly unbeatable 200 hoops on 25 Nov 2015.

Greatest distance on a giraffe unicycle while juggling three objects
Young clown Rusbelin Junior (COL) covered 83.14 m (272 ft 9 in) on a 3-m-tall (9-ft 10-in) unicycle, keeping a trio of clubs in the air the whole time. This feat was filmed in Milan, Italy, for *Lo Show dei Record* on 19 Feb 2025. The 12-year-old Rusbelin has been performing with his father's circus since the age of three.

Most knives thrown around two people in one minute
On 8 Feb 2024, *Got Talent* star Alfredo Silva (BRA) precisely threw 41 knives around two human targets on the set of *Lo Show dei Record*. To make things more challenging, his assistants were standing on either side of a wooden board that was mounted on a spinning platform.

The **most knives thrown around a human target in one minute** has been held by master of the impalement arts "The Great Throwdini", aka David Adamovich (USA), since 2007. On 26 Dec, he hurled 102 blades around target girl Tina Nagy in Freeport, New York, USA.

Most flames blown in full-body burn in one minute
On 17 Aug 2025, French firefighter Jonathan Vero blew 89 plumes of fire from his mouth while he himself was alight in Oignies, Hauts-de-France. This is the seventh GWR title for the stunt performer, whose other full-body-burn records include the **fastest 100 m sprint on fire** (17 sec), **greatest distance run on fire** (272 m; 892 ft) and **most jumping jacks on fire** (50).

Most hula hoops spun on stilts
Amazi (aka Mariam Olayiwola; UK) kept 27 hoops rotating while balanced on a pair of stilts during a GWR event in London, UK, on 10 Mar 2025. Amazi is the current leader of the record-breaking hoop troupe The Majorettes, which was founded by Marawa the Amazing (see left) in 2012.

Most bounce forward-somersaults with an exercise ball in one minute
Fitness influencer Merle Loosen (DEU) discovered the art of bouncy-ball gymnastics while browsing social media in 2023 and thought it looked like fun. On 29 Aug 2025, she managed 41 exercise-ball-assisted front flips on the set of *Guinness World Records – die Große Show der Weltrekorde* in Munich, Germany.

MAY 25 — Eco group Oceanum Liberandum (PRT) assembled 274 litter-picking divers at their **largest underwater clean-up** off Sesimbra, Portugal, in 2024.

MAY 26 — According to the World Flying Disc Federation, the **longest time aloft for a flying disc** is 16.72 sec, thrown by Don Cain (USA) in Pennsylvania, USA, in 1984.

DANIELLA D'VILLE'S DAREDEVIL FEATS

On 17 Sep 2025, GWR joined British circus star Daniella D'Ville for a day of record breaking at The Phoenix Arts Club in London, UK. The multi-talented Daniella started with the **tightest frying-pan roll**, crumpling the metal pan into a tube with a circumference of 18 cm (7 in) – about the thickness of a roll of cling film. She then moved on to whip tricks, achieving the **most flowers cut with an overhead whip crack in 30 seconds** (19). Next, Daniella was hoisted into the rafters to attempt the **fastest suspended straitjacket escape**, managing to wriggle out in just 7.07 sec! Finally, the versatile performer turned her hand to the sideshow staple "human blockhead" trick, claiming the **most nails hammered into the nose in one minute**, driving in 15 nails.

Daniella earned her first GWR title in 2012 by having eight concrete blocks smashed on her stomach while lying on a bed of nails.

MAY 27 On this day in 2016, radio DJ Frank van der Lende (NLD) watched his 21st live gig in the Netherlands: the **most music concerts attended in one week**.

MAY 28 Jenny Doan (AUS) set the **most stairs climbed while hula hooping** (10,241) in 2022 by scaling a staircase at Denver Union Station in Colorado, USA, multiple times.

Adaptive Adventurers

SAILING SOLO

Craig Wood (below), who sustained severe injuries while serving in Afghanistan resulting in the loss of both his legs and his left forearm, made history in 2025 by becoming the first triple amputee to sail across an ocean singlehanded.

Have you always sailed?
My dad taught me when I was a child and it grew naturally from there. He also kept my hobby alive when I was injured by directing me towards Paralympic sailing.

What triggered the idea to attempt a trans-Pacific journey by yourself?
I'd been sailing around the world for the last eight years and so my skill and experience had been building along the way. I felt like giving back to charity and sailing was a platform that suited my skills.

Any highlights on the voyage?
Seeing whales as I left Mexico, sailing under a full moon with bioluminescence behind me, and seeing a lunar rainbow.

What would you like people to take from this?
Don't waste your life saying you can't do things you've never tried because you're too scared to try. Find out what you can't do by trying everything for yourself and you'll discover so many possibilities open up.

First blind woman to run a marathon on each continent
On 23–30 Jan 2017, visually impaired runner Sinead Kane (IRL) took part in the World Marathon Challenge, which comprises seven 42.1-km (26.2-mi) races on all seven continents within seven days. Kane started in Antarctica and ended in Australia, with her fastest time (4:24:39) logged during the second race in Chile.

First amputee to climb Everest
After two failed ascents in 1989 and 1995, Tom Whittaker (UK) topped the world's **highest mountain** (aka Sagarmāthā or Chomolungma) on 27 May 1998. His right foot had been amputated in 1979 after a car accident.

Everest's **first double-amputee climber** was Mark Inglis (NZ), who lost both legs beneath the knee to frostbite in 1982. He summitted via the north side on 15 May 2006.

The **first female amputee** to achieve this milestone, on 21 May 2013, was former top-flight volleyball player Arunima Sinha (IND), who lost a leg after a violent robbery in 2011.

Hari Budha Magar (NPL) became the **first double above-knee amputee to climb Everest (LA3)** on 19 May 2023. It was part of a wider mission that would see Magar tackle seven of the highest peaks on Earth (see pp.144–45.)

Shortest wing walker
Canadian John Ferguson, who has achondroplasia and stands 1.24 m (4 ft 1 in) tall, took to the skies above the UK strapped atop a biplane on 17 Sep 2025. The social-media star is keen to pursue more adrenaline-fuelled records, though confessed that he may need to run them by his mom first!

Fastest swim of the North Channel (MP3)
On 16 Aug 2025, Jeremias Mateo Castillo (ESP) swam from Northern Ireland to Scotland, UK, in 12 hr 3 min 33 sec. It was part of his Oceans Seven quest, a septet of channel crossings he has pursued since a climbing accident in 2015 that caused multiple bone and neurological injuries. He'd already logged MP3 speed records for the **English Channel** (11 hr 30 min in 2024) and the **Strait of Gibraltar** (3 hr 53 min in 2022).

Most ultramarathons completed in a non-racing wheelchair in one week
Serial record breaker Lexi Chambers (UK), who lives with complex regional pain syndrome, which led to a below-knee amputation in 2019, undertook six gruelling 50-km (31-mi) races across the UK from 10 to 16 Aug 2025. One of these, completed in 5 hr 12 min on 13 Aug, also represents the **fastest ultramarathon in a non-racing wheelchair**. The ex-army nurse wanted to show what can be achieved using everyday equipment.

First solo ocean crossing by a triple amputee
Craig Wood (UK) pulled into Hiroshima Harbour in Japan on 24 Jun 2025, having departed from Puerto Vallarta in Mexico on 25 Mar. The unprecedented traverse of the Pacific was completed on board his catamaran *Sirius II*. After his 90-day odyssey, the British Army veteran said: "I'm exhausted – but so proud to complete an expedition that many thought impossible."

First disabled person to ski solo and unsupported to the South Pole
In 2014, British Army soldier Jonny Huntington suffered a stroke that resulted in paralysis down his left side. His rehabilitation introduced him to Nordic skiing, which became a passion (he now even competes for Team GB). This new vocation was pushed to the limit between 21 Nov 2024 and 6 Jan 2025, when after hauling a 110-kg (242-lb) sled for over 911 km (566 mi), he ended the **longest solo and unsupported Antarctic ski expedition (CIH)** at the South Pole.

MAY 29 Edmund Hillary (NZ) and Tenzing Norgay (IND/Tibet) completed the **first ascent of Everest**, reaching the summit of the world's **highest mountain** in 1953.

MAY 30 In 2013, Andrew Sleeth of Mike's Golf Carts took to the links in Georgia, USA, driving the **longest golf cart**. The behemoth buggy measured 9.62 m (31 ft 6.7 in).

Head online for a full guide to GWR's range of impairment categories.

GREATEST DISTANCE SWAM WITH FINS AND SWIM AIDS (AA3)

In six-and-a-half hours on 21 Aug 2025, Kerry-Lee Gockel (AUS) circumnavigated Great Keppel Island (aka Wop-pa) in Queensland, Australia. The 20.4-km (12.7-mi) swim was ratified by the Keppel Islands Swimming Association. Known as the "Wingless Warrior", Gockel was born without arms owing to congenital amelia. She developed a passion for open-water swimming and has continued to push her maximum distance, with this being double her previous longest effort. She was accompanied on the journey by Joep Buijs (in pink swim cap, below), who provided assistance with food and drink whenever Gockel paused for a rest break.

The previous year, Gockel completed a relay swim around Great Keppel Island with her husband, each covering half of the route.

ON THE RECORD

"It's very cool to be part of open-water swimming history. A big thank you to everyone who made this possible. This record means more than that to me, though. It's throwing down the gauntlet to another wingless warrior. If you think you can't do hard things because of what you don't have, think again. You can do things people *with* arms can't do"

MAY 31 Australian Minnie Munro walked down the aisle at the age of 102 to become the **oldest bride** on this day in 1991. The groom, Dudley Reid, was a mere 83.

JUN 1 The Gotthard Base Tunnel opened between Erstfeld and Bodio in Switzerland in 2016. The 57-km (35.4-mi) transport link remains the **longest rail tunnel**.

Extreme Explorers

Fastest sand-skiing speed
Mahé Freydier (FRA) hit 121 km/h (75 mph) on the Toro Mata dune in Acarí, Peru, on 25 Sep 2025. In doing so, the sand-ski speedster smashed the previous record of 92 km/h (57 mph), which had remained unbroken for 15 years.

DID YOU KNOW?

Sand skiing is a modern sport with much older roots. For centuries, desert peoples have used planks (sometimes coated in oils or animal fat) to glide across sand. In the early 1900s, pioneers such as France's Marie Marvingt experimented with aluminium skis to ride Saharan dunes. Today's popular sand-ski sites range from the Namib Desert in southern Africa to the giant dune known as Monte Kaolino, a mining spoil heap in Germany that hosts the annual SandSpirit sandboarding contest.

First woman to climb the 8,000ers without supplementary oxygen
On 23 Sep 2025, He Jing (CHN) reached the summit of Manaslu – the world's eighth-highest peak – in the Nepalese Himalayas. This marked the last in her series of ascents of all 14 mountains over 8,000 m (24,246 ft), a feat made all the more impressive given that she didn't use bottled oxygen.

Oldest man to climb Mount Kilimanjaro
On 20 Jul 2017, Fred Distelhorst (USA, b. 21 Jan 1929) topped Africa's highest mountain (5,895 m; 19,340 ft) aged 88 years 180 days. He made the four-day ascent in a group that included his granddaughter, Ellen Edgerton, and local guides.

Fastest unsupported crossing of the Himalayas by bicycle
Avisek Tunga (IND) took just 20 days 15 hr 56 min to cycle across the Himalayan mountain range, finishing on 13 Oct 2025. He covered 3,569 km (2,218 mi) altogether, at an average speed of 7.20 km/h (4.47 mph).

Fastest cumulative time to swim the Oceans Seven
Elite swimmer Andreas Waschburger (DEU) crossed seven of the most testing waterways around the world in a total time of 49 hr 37 min 45 sec. He began with the English Channel on 8 Sep 2023 and ended with the North Channel, between Northern Ireland and Scotland, UK, on 4 Sep 2025.

Longest journey by motor scooter
On 17 Aug 2024, Gustavo Vasconcelos de Queiroz finished his epic 27,830-km (17,292-mi) ride on a Honda ADV150 in Prudhoe Bay, Alaska, USA. The journey took four months, taking him from his native Brazil, to the southern tip of South America, and ending in the northernmost state in North America.

First woman to row across the Atlantic from Europe to South America (mainland to mainland)
Zara Lachlan (UK) completed her row from Lagos in Portugal to Cayenne in French Guiana on 1 Feb 2025. She rowed at least 17 hr per day on the 97-day odyssey in her monohull *Avandra*. The feat also made Lachlan (b. 2 Apr 2003) the **youngest woman to row across any ocean solo**. She was aged 21 years 208 days on departure.

Highest-altitude skysurf jump
On 10 Nov 2025, Olga Naumova (BLR) leaped from a helicopter flying at 6,384 m (20,945 ft) above Syangboche, Nepal. After freefalling, she skysurfed then parachuted down with her board. She hoped that her remarkable feat would "inspire girls around the world not to be scared to be bold and to dream big".

Longest ice swim
Krzysztof Gajewski (POL) improved on his own record by swimming 6.025 km (3.74 mi) in 1 hr 52 min 52 sec in a lake at Kopalnia Wrocław near Paniowice, Poland, on 13 Dec 2025.

The **women's** record was also shattered in 2025. Bárbara Hernández Huerta (CHL) covered 3.84 km (2.39 mi) in 1 hr 6 min 15 sec in the Canal Señoret in Puerto Natales, Magallanes, Chile, on 30 Aug 2025. All ice swims must take place in water with a temperature below 5°C (41°F), with only a standard costume, cap and goggles permitted, as per the rules of the International Ice Swimming Association.

Fastest circumnavigation by car
The record for the **first and fastest man and woman to have circumnavigated the Earth by car** covering six continents under the rules applicable in 1989 and 1991 embracing more than an equator's length of driving (24,901 road miles; 40,075 km), is held by Saloo Choudhury and his wife Neena Choudhury (both India). The journey took 69 days 19 hours 5 minutes from 9 September to 17 November 1989. The couple drove a 1989 Hindustan "Contessa Classic" starting and finishing in Delhi, India.

Among other hazards, Lachlan had to row around a pod of orcas and was bitten by a barracuda! On the plus side, she got to swim with dolphins.

JUN 2 In 2013, a 3,486-strong group honed their core strength for 45 min in the **largest pilates class**. The mass tone-up was organized by Türkiye's Denizli Municipality.

JUN 3 The **largest ruby** tipped the scales at 21.955 kg (48 lb 6.4 oz) when weighed in 2009 in Bangalore, India. The colossal corundum is owned by Rajiv Golcha (IND).

Kerepakupai Merú is the **tallest waterfall**, with a drop of 979 m (3,212 ft). Its local Pemón name means "waterfall of the deepest place".

HIGHEST HIGHLINE OVER A WATERFALL

On 21–23 Oct 2025, six extreme adventurers with a head for heights crossed a 148-m-long (485-ft) slackline from the top of Auyán Tepui in Venezuela at a height of 1,008 m (3,307 ft) above the base of Kerepakupai Merú (aka Angel Falls). The fearless sextet are: Lukas Irmler (who led the expedition), Jens Decke (left), Valentin Rapp (above), Antonia Rüede-Passul, Karl Schrader (all DEU) and Rafael Bridi (BRA). The crossing came after an arduous six-day trek through the jungle, supported by indigenous Pemón Kamarakoto guides. In their honour, the line was named "Amanöm", meaning "the most beautiful" in the Pemón language.

ON THE RECORD

"Finally, I have the answer to the question 'Which is the most beautiful line I've ever walked?' This line has everything I am searching for: a crazy exposure and an unmatched height, a stunning landscape and a wild adventure to even get there"
– Lukas Irmler

JUN 4 — In 1924, the USA's Ford Model T became the **first car to sell 10 million units.** At its peak, up to 40% of all automobiles sold in the USA were "Tin Lizzies".

JUN 5 — Christian Roberto López Rodríguez (ESP) likes to use reverse thinking. In 2022, he ran the **fastest 100 m backwards** (13.17 sec) in Cabañas de la Sagra, Spain.

Round-Up

Most decimal digits memorized underwater
Memory master Christian Schäfer (DEU) recalled an 87-digit-long number, which he studied while submerged in a pool in London, UK, on 8 Apr 2026. Christian's record-smashing recall has helped earn him multiple GWR titles (see also p.190).

Most people dressed as dinosaurs
On 11 Apr 2026, a terrorizing pack of 682 cosplay *T. rexes* took over the campus of the University of Calgary in Alberta, Canada. The event was part of activities to mark the college's 60th anniversary – the institution's mascot is Rex O'Saurus.

Longest line of lasagnes
Lidl served up 1,215 layered pasta dishes at its Belenenses store in Lisbon, Portugal, on 20 Jul 2025. They included 195 kg (430 lb) of bolognese sauce!

Fastest time to visit all Major League Baseball (MLB) stadiums
In just 25 days – from 20 Aug to 13 Sep 2025 – baseball-loving Jepssy Beltré Santana (DOM) watched a game at all 30 MLB venues. He travelled between them by public transport and on foot.

Most expensive trading card sold at auction
On 16 Feb 2026, a "Pikachu Illustrator" card owned by WWE star Logan Paul (USA, left) sold for $16,492,000 (£12.07 m) online via Goldin Auctions. Designed by Atsuko Nishida (JPN) – who is widely credited as Pikachu's creator – it was one of only 39 cards released as a prize in a 1998 illustration contest, and was never originally put on sale.

Largest polar-bear dip
On 13 Dec 2025, a group of 3,134 cold-water enthusiasts braved the chilly sea at Ølberg beach in Sola, Norway. Organized by local swimming group Badeglede (NOR), the bracing dip drew participants from around the world. Each person had to stand in waist-deep water with a maximum temperature of 10°C (50°F) for at least one minute.

Largest tape measure
Ali Spagnola (right), Davis DeWitt and Tyler Reece (all USA) made this XXL tape measure in North Hollywood, California, USA. It was 87 cm (2 ft 10 in) tall and 56 cm (1 ft 10 in) wide, with a 76.2-m-long (250-ft) tape, as ratified on 14 Mar 2026. Filmed for Ali's YouTube channel, the build included devising a custom mobile app to control the deployment of the tape.

Most elbow air flares in one minute
"Amin Drillz" (aka Amin Mohammadian, AUT) rotated on his upper arms 61 times in Berlin, Germany, on 20 Jun 2024. The month before, he had achieved the **most elbow spins in one minute** – 64 – pivoting on one elbow while propelling himself with his other hand.

Most cans kicked off a person's head in one minute (under 16s)
Kickboxer Orell Herzog (DEU) struck 31 cans from the well-protected head of an assistant in Hamburg, Germany, on 18 Nov 2025. Orell was just 11 years old when he achieved this feat to mark GWR Day (see pp.14–15).

Largest game of catch (baseball/softball)
A total of 1,179 pairs teamed up for a mass catching session organized by the Yogi Berra Museum & Learning Center in Little Falls, New Jersey, USA, on 21 Sep 2025. The attempt celebrated the the 100th anniversary of the baseball legend's birth.

Fastest ascent of Mount Kilimanjaro (CIH)
After 5 days 6 hr 50 min, Jayashree Vijay Mohan (IND) topped Kilimanjaro – Africa's biggest peak – in Tanzania. A stroke had left Jayashree paralysed on her left side. She took on this challenge "not just for myself, but for every [stroke] survivor who has ever been told to 'slow down' or 'settle'."

JUN 6 Richard Hollingshead (USA) opened the **first drive-in cinema** today in 1933 in Camden, New Jersey. The car-bound cinephiles saw *Wives Beware*, a 1932 comedy.

JUN 7 Brazilian star Pelé's 1970 FIFA World Cup winner's medal fetched £346,000 ($498,994) at auction on this day in 2016, becoming the **most expensive soccer medal**.

Fastest garden shed
Brian Cade (UK) hit a speed of 198.65 km/h (123.43 mph) in a shed-shaped vehicle in York, UK, on 11 Oct 2025. A self-confessed "petrol head", Brian built it around a TVR chassis, basing the design on a motorized shed that he'd seen in a children's book.

Largest collection of frog-related items
Susan Burgos (USA) has amassed 13,201 froggy favourites, as confirmed in Camarillo, California, USA, on 12 Jan 2026. Her hoard encompasses a wide range of items, including jewellery, Christmas ornaments, toys and antiques. One of her most treasured keepsakes is a 1.8-m-tall (6-ft) metal leaping frog, which enlivens the pool area in her back yard.

Fastest speed on a tandem motorcycle
Rider Jack Frost and passenger Paul Milbourn (both UK) clocked 377.7 km/h (234.7 mph) across 1 mi (1.6 km) from a standing start at Elvington Airfield in Yorkshire, UK, on 23 Mar 2025. The result was ratified by the UK & International Timing Association.

Most ascents of Everest in a single season
Tashi Gyalzen Sherpa (NPL) summitted Everest (8,848.8 m; 29,031 ft), Earth's **highest mountain**, four times – on 9, 14, 19 and 23 May 2025 – all from the Nepalese (south) side.

Fastest 100 km pushing a wheelchair
On 5 Apr 2025, Simon Clavreuil pushed Amélie Folny (both FRA) a distance of 100 km (62 mi) in 9 hr 50 min 35 sec in Crevin, France. Having secured a GWR title, the duo have now set their sights on completing an IRONMAN® challenge!

Fastest swim around St Helena (female)
Croatian marathon swimmer Dina Levačić circled *c.* 45 km (28 mi) around this remote South Atlantic island in 17 hr 13 min 28 sec on 26 Feb 2026. "I knew it would be tough, but it was tougher than expected," she admitted. Levačić is the first person to swim this route. Open Water Africa and the World Open Water Swimming Association ratified her feat.

Longest marathon crocheting
Chidinma Modupe Okafor (NGA) crocheted for 100 hr 50 min in Lagos, Nigeria, from 4 to 8 Dec 2025. She created a range of yarn wearables and art, from a large Timberland-style boot to a tapestry based on aspects of Nigerian culture.

Largest soccer-ball sentence
On 6 Sep 2025, the call to action "Rise up L.A." was spelled out with 1,461 footballs in Los Angeles, California, USA. The attempt, organized by PNC Bank (USA), sought to inspire locals in the wake of devastating wildfires in the area.

Most people snorkelling simultaneously
A group of 305 snorkellers took to the waters at Siyam World, Maldives, on 5 Dec 2025. The event was arranged by Freedive Maldives and Siyam World Maldives (both MDV) to highlight reef conservation in the region.

Most standing backwards somersaults in 30 seconds
On 18 Feb 2026, gymnast Fred Blijden (NLD) executed 22 reverse flips from a standing position in Best, Eindhoven, Netherlands. Fred improved on the previous record by a count of three. For the **women's** record, see p.14.

Highest-altitude vehicle light drawing
The lights of two Honda cars produced the remarkable image above, at an elevation of 4,160.15 m (13,649 ft), on 18 Feb 2025. Its dramatic setting is the Pamir Plateau in Kashgar Prefecture, Xinjiang Uygur Autonomous Region, China. The Dongfeng Honda S7 team, ZhiHu, Wang Sibo and Xinxing She (all CHN) collaborated on creating the long-exposure depiction of a snake in the shape of the Chinese character for "blessing".

JUN 8 – Batting sensation Mithali Raj (IND) retired in 2022 having notched up the **most runs in an international cricket career (female)** – 10,868 – across all formats.

JUN 9 – Happy birthday Kwek Yu Xuan (SGP)! Born prematurely in 2020 at Singapore's National University Hospital, she weighed a mere 212 g (7.48 oz) – the **lightest birth**.

SNAPSHOT

Tallest Iceberg

More than two-thirds of Earth's freshwater is locked away in glaciers and ice sheets. When chunks break off, or "calve", from these icy slabs, they become ocean-borne icebergs. Some of these glacial fragments are less than a metre wide. Others are considerably larger...

Icebergs are commonly classified into two main shapes. "Tabular" icebergs are flat-topped, steep-sided slabs. They're found mainly in Antarctic regions – unsurprisingly, given that the Antarctic Ice Sheet is home to 90% of the world's glacial ice. These frozen titans typically form when a section of ice shelf (a large expanse of Antarctic sea ice) breaks away, creating a large, flat, floating island of ice.

In contrast, "non-tabular" icebergs are generally smaller and far more irregular in form. They include a variety of shapes, from domed and wedge-like structures to the dramatic pinnacles that most people would instinctively associate with icebergs.

To convey some idea of the extraordinary scale of these huge icy structures, we've sailed two of the largest recorded icebergs to Sydney Harbour, perilously close to the iconic Opera House. This Australian architectural marvel tops out at 67 m (219 ft), yet is dwarfed by the ice.

Just behind the building is the **tallest non-tabular iceberg**, which rose some 167 m (550 ft) above the water – the equivalent of a 55-storey building. It was spotted off western Greenland by Commander Robertson Dinsmore of the ice breaker USCGC *Eastwind* in Mar 1957. The International Ice Patrol considers any iceberg standing 75 m (246 ft) above the water to be "very large", so this one certainly qualified!

The gargantuan iceberg looming in the distance is the **largest iceberg ever** to be accurately measured. B-15 (see more right) is one of several Antarctic monoliths to have soared *c.* 200 m (650 ft) above the waterline.

Of course, any such ice giants would present a formidable threat to anything in their path. Given which, it's probably just as well that the Sydney Opera House remains safely on land in warmer climes! Quite how safe remains to be seen, however, as melting ice is now contributing to a global sea-level rise of around 4.5 mm (0.1 in) per year.

B-15, which calved from Antarctica's Ross Ice Shelf in Mar 2000, was the **largest iceberg ever**. Using satellite imagery, NASA calculated its size to be 300 x 40 km (186 x 25 mi), giving a surface area of around 11,000 km^2 (4,250 sq mi). That makes this tabular giant about the same size as Jamaica! The picture above was taken the following year, and shows the northern edge of its frozen expanse.

Incredibly, there is an even larger contender for this title. On 12 Nov 1956, the crew of the USS *Glacier* sighted a tabular iceberg estimated at more than 31,000 km^2 (12,000 sq mi) in area, floating some 240 km (150 mi) west of Scott Island in the Southern Ocean. But given that the crew did not have the advantage of satellite photography back then, its size is purely an approximation.

Icebergs appear blue because their thickly packed, bubble-free ice reflects blue wavelengths while absorbing red light.

Danish architect Jørn Utzon took inspiration from the shape of sea shells – not icebergs – when planning his radical design for Sydney's famous performing-arts venue, which formally opened in 1973. But despite its relatively modest size, this Australian landmark packs a lot of cultural clout: it has been designated a UNESCO World Heritage Site, and earned Utzon the renowned Pritzker Architecture Prize. When the Sydney Symphony Orchestra is playing there, the temperature must be kept at 22.5°C (72.5°F) so that instruments stay in tune – something they might struggle to maintain if the Opera House were ever to find itself in more frigid waters like these!

JUN 10 In 1981, Kathleen Saville became the **first woman to row the Atlantic**, with Curtis Saville (both USA) in *Excalibur*.

JUN 11 Sweden beat Estonia 6–2 in the **first FIFA World Cup qualifying match** on this day in 1933.

JUN 12 Lareesa Guttery (AUS) tore through the **most bikini waxes in four hours** (262) in Perth, Western Australia, in 2004.

JUN 13 Akis Petretzikis (GRC) prepped the **most hamburgers in one hour** (3,378) in Thessaloniki, Greece, in 2019.

ICON John Cena

Growing up, John Cena (USA) would watch wrestlers in awe and craft his own world championship belts from cardboard when playing with his brothers. He has since swapped those handmade replicas for the real deal… an unprecedented 17 times. In the hope of becoming a bodybuilder, John moved from his quiet hometown in Massachusetts to Los Angeles in 1999. Despite his degree in exercise physiology and kinesiology, his job applications were mostly rejected. So, John enrolled at Ultimate Pro Wrestling's Ultimate University, where he created his first wrestling persona: "The Prototype".

In 2001, John signed a development contract with the World Wrestling Federation (now WWE), and within a year he was promoted to their main roster (see below). Soon after, he adopted a new persona and fans loved it; as the "Doctor of Thuganomics", he would rap his trash talk, and wear oversized chains and a backwards cap.

John went on to overcome many obstacles (as well as opponents!). He became one of the WWE's longest-serving wrestlers, with over 23 years under his belt by the time he retired in Dec 2025. And although John is no longer competing in the ring, it is clear from his commitment to his fans and his burgeoning acting CV that "the champ is here" to stay.

VITAL STATISTICS

Name	John Felix Anthony Cena
Birthplace	West Newbury, Massachusetts, USA
Birth date	23 Apr 1977
Current GWR titles	Multiple, including **most WWE Championship titles (male)** – 17, as of 13 Dec 2025
WWE matches	1,476 (won 1,138)
Notable Cena firsts	• Album: *You Can't See Me* (2005) • Movie: *The Marine* (USA, 2006) • Book: *Elbow Grease* (2018)

In 2002, Kurt Angle (above left) – the **first Olympic champion to compete in WWE** – dared a rookie to face him in the ring. Aged 25, John stepped up and made his WWE debut. When Kurt asked him to state the one quality that made him worthy of a fight, John replied "ruthless aggression" and threw the first punch. John ultimately lost to Kurt, but there's no denying he made an "impactful" first impression.

Throughout his WWE career, John demonstrated superhero-like strength by performing his signature "Attitude Adjustment" move (above). He debuted this takedown manoeuvre in 2003 when he raised the 350-lb (158.8-kg) "Rikishi" over his shoulders and hurled him headfirst on to his back. John is also known for the "You Can't See Me" taunt (below), which originated as a dare from one of his younger siblings.

John's passion for the sport was sparked by his dad, John Joseph Cena, who worked as a Chaotic Wrestling ring announcer.

In recent years, John has established himself as a Hollywood star – following a similar path to fellow wrestler-actor Dwayne "The Rock" Johnson (see opposite). Focusing on comedy and action, John has starred in movies such as *The Suicide Squad* (USA, 2021) and *Heads of State* (USA, 2025) with Idris Elba (right). He even cameoed in Greta Gerwig's *Barbie* (USA, 2023) – the **highest-grossing film by a female director** ($1.447 bn; £1.101 bn) – as a merman with curly locks.

John won his 17th world championship after beating Cody Rhodes at WrestleMania 41 in Las Vegas, Nevada, USA, on 20 Apr 2025. He made wrestling history by claiming the **most WWE Championship titles (male)** outright; he'd previously shared it with Ric Flair – WWE's first two-time Hall of Famer – who earned his 16 titles between 1981 and 2000.

John hasn't just fulfilled his own dreams; he's made those of others come true too, having granted the **most Make-A-Wish Foundation wishes** – 650, as of 19 Jul 2022. To celebrate John's 500th wish in 2015, WWE presented the charity with a $1-m cheque and reasserted their ongoing commitment to bringing joy to critically ill children.

John was seen as a "good guy" for the majority of his WWE career, embodying the mantra "hustle, loyalty, respect". But on 1 Mar 2025, he became a "heel" (an unruly villain character) by turning on his respected rival, Cody Rhodes (above, on mat). He was instructed to do so by "The Rock" (aka "The Final Boss"; above left). This storyline shocked fans and resulted in another record for John: the **longest WWE face run before turning heel** – 22 years 247 days.

Discover all of GWR's incredible ICONS at **guinnessworldrecords.com/records/icons**

SCIENCE & TECHNOLOGY

CONTENTS

The observatory
The NSF–DOE Vera C Rubin Observatory is located near the peak of Cerro Pachón in central Chile. The facility is jointly funded by the National Science Foundation and the Department of Energy's Office of Science (both USA). It is named for American astronomer Vera Rubin (1928–2016), whose investigations into the rotation rates of galaxies provided the first strong evidence for the existence of dark matter.

Rubin's LSST Camera, mounted vertically in the observatory's primary telescope

LARGEST DIGITAL CAMERA

On 23 Jun 2025, the Vera C Rubin Observatory revealed the first images taken with its 3-tonne (6,600-lb), 3,200-megapixel camera. Each picture covers 9.6° of the night sky (roughly the width of the dipper in the Big Dipper, aka the Plough) at a resolution that would need 400 ultra-high-definition screens to display at full size. The image above is a snippet of a test picture, showing the detail captured in just 1.5° of sky.

Over the next 10 years, the observatory will carry out the Legacy Survey of Space and Time (LSST), mapping the southern sky every few days. This project will improve our understanding of dark matter, find new asteroids and comets, spot supernovas and possibly even locate the theorized – but not yet found – "Planet Nine" at the edge of our Solar System, beyond Pluto.

SCIENCE & TECHNOLOGY

Space Toilets

By the time it made its first flight on 7 May 1992, on board the Space Shuttle *Endeavour*, the toilet known as the "EDO WCS" had cost NASA a staggering $30 m (£16.4 m), making it the **most expensive toilet** ever made. Why does something as simple as a toilet become so complex when you go to space?

THE DEVELOPMENT OF THE EDO WCS (THE ACRONYMS STAND FOR "EXTENDED DURATION ORBITER" AND "WASTE COLLECTION SYSTEM") BEGAN IN 1984 AS AN UPGRADE TO THE EXISTING SHUTTLE TOILET.

How does a space toilet work?

On Earth, humans have the luxury (though it may not always feel like that) of being continually pulled down by gravity. This means, among many other things, that when we go to the toilet, we can count on gravity to separate us from our waste.

In a weightless environment, this doesn't work. One NASA scientist described the process of defecating in zero-g as "like taking your toilet at home, bolting it to the ceiling and trying to use it there".

Space toilets rely on air suction. They have fans that pull air from the cabin, and this powerful current sucks urine and poop into the machine. Once everything is contained, the toilet has to separate liquids, solids and air, then hygienically dispose of the waste and return the air – sanitized and filtered – back to the cabin. It also must be compact, light and, crucially, extremely reliable.

1. Urine funnel
There are several different designs and sizes of this fitting, and each astronaut has their own individually fitted one.

2. Pre-treatment pump
Urine is quite corrosive and can damage machinery. This component adds a neutralizing chemical to the stream before it hits the separators.

3. Fan separators
These combine a powerful fan with a centrifuge that separates liquid and air. The urine is either purified and recycled into drinking water or vented into space, while the air is pushed back out through the filters.

4. Fecal bag
This holds solid waste and vomit, but allows air and small particles through.

5. Waste container
This drum can be sealed and replaced when full, and the used ones jettisoned to burn up on re-entry.

6. Compactor
A stick with a metal disc on the end. You put the lid on the bag, then squash it down flat to get the air out.

NASA TRIED MAKING AN AUTOMATIC PISTON SYSTEM TO SQUASH DOWN THE WASTE BAGS, BUT IT WEIGHED TOO MUCH AND DIDN'T WORK VERY WELL. OFTEN THE SIMPLEST ANSWER IS THE BEST ONE.

JUN 14 The USA has made the **most changes to a national flag** – 26 – since its adoption on this day in 1777. A star has been added every time a state joined the Union.

JUN 15 Brazil and North Korea played the **coldest soccer FIFA World Cup match** – with an on-pitch temperature of -1°C (30.2°F) – in Johannesburg, South Africa, in 2010.

The Universal Waste Management System

The present-day descendant of the toilet that launched on *Endeavour* is NASA's Universal Waste Management System, or UWMS. This was installed on the *International Space Station* in 2022 and is also in the Orion capsule built for the Artemis Moon missions. It is the **most powerful space toilet**, drawing in air at 7.5 litres per second, and is also significantly smaller and lighter than the Shuttle WCS.

The trade-off is that the UWMS, or at least early versions of it, proved to be uncomfortably loud – astronauts reportedly took to wearing earplugs during tests in 2021. This picture shows the UWMS running in an anechoic chamber in 2022, while engineers tried to work out how to tame its 75-dB motor whine.

Cleaning the ISS toilet is a day-long job

Boldly going

During the Apollo missions of the 1960s, NASA astronauts had to use what was called the "Fecal Containment System" (or FCS). Although it sounds hi-tech, the FCS was little more than a clear-plastic bag held in place down there with double-sided tape. Using the FCS required a lot of manual handling of things people prefer not to manually handle, and was difficult to use without "substances" escaping. After the bag was filled, the user had to inject an antibacterial solution and knead the (still warm) bag until it was mixed in. The whole process was so unpleasant that Apollo astronauts typically ate less than half their food to keep toilet visits to a minimum.

05 13 29 44	CDR	Oh - Who did it?
05 13 29 46	CMP	Who did what?
05 13 29 47	LMP	What?
05 13 29 49	CDR	Who did it? (Laughter)
05 13 29 51	LMP	Where did that come from?
05 13 29 52	CDR	Give me a napkin quick. There's a turd floating through the air.

~~CONFIDENTIAL~~

THE LIMITATIONS OF THE FCS WERE DEMONSTRATED BY THE APOLLO 10 "LOOSE POOP INCIDENT" IN 1969, WHICH WAS IMMORTALIZED IN THE OFFICIAL MISSION TRANSCRIPT.

Proper Potty Protocol

Using the toilet in space isn't as simple as checking the seat's down. Here's the astronaut training checklist for the WCS.

1. Put toe restraints down in the locked position
2. Check **VACUUM VENT LINE** is set to **OPEN**
3. Place new bag in the WCS Coffee Can
4. Set **MODE** position switch to **COMMODE/MANUAL/EMU**
5. Unstow urinal hose from Velcro strap, install personal urinal funnel
6. Check airflow
7. Check **WCS POWER** light is ON
8. Pull up **COMMODE CONTROL** lever, wait 15 seconds
9. Push **COMMODE CONTROL** lever to the **FWD** position
10. Move thigh restraints into place, ensure proper seal on seat
11. Urinate/defecate, placing all used tissues/wipes in the WCS Coffee Can **!NOT IN COMMODE!**
12. Pull **COMMODE CONTROL** lever back, push down
13. Remove and clean urinal funnel, clean seat as required
14. Close trash bag, remove from Coffee Can
15. Place used trash bag in WCS trash module
16. Stow hose in cradle
17. Set **MODE** position switch to **AUTO**
18. Check **WCS POWER** light turns off ~30 seconds after hose stowage

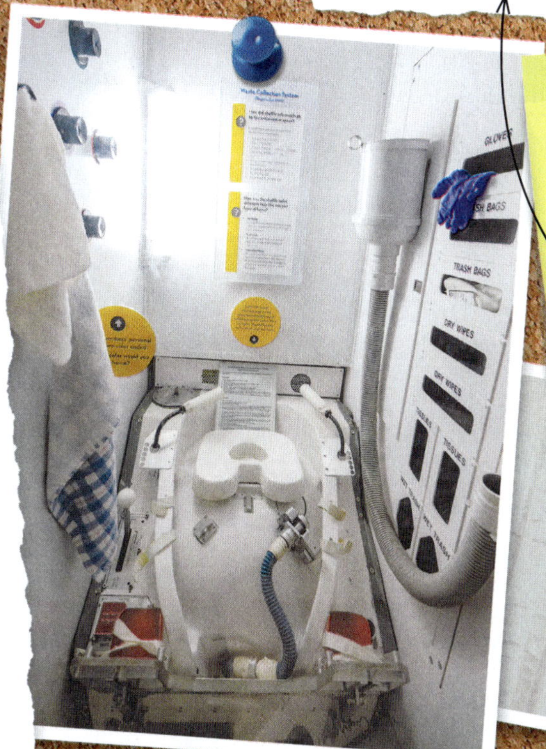

JUN 16 Signed on this day in 1373, the **oldest treaty still in force** is the Anglo-Portuguese Treaty of Alliance, making Portugal the UK's oldest ally.

JUN 17 Seasoned speed eater André Ortolf (DEU) downed the **most mashed potato eaten in 30 seconds** – 598 g (1 lb 5 oz) – in Augsburg, Germany, in 2016.

Rockets

The **largest single-chamber rocket engine** ever built was the Rocketdyne F-1, which carried the Apollo astronauts to the Moon in 1969. Here, we look at the workings of these massive motors, and explain how they could accelerate a 3,238-tonne (3,569-ton) rocket to twice the speed of a rifle bullet.

How rockets work

Rocket engines rely on a particular type of chemistry, whereby a combustible fuel reacts with a second chemical (an oxidizer) that causes it to burn and release lots of heat (an exothermic reaction). This heat expands the gases created by the chemical reaction within the enclosed combustion chamber. The gases are forced out of the open bottom of the engine at high speed. Newton's laws of motion tell us that the gas moving in one direction will push the rocket in the opposite direction.

This is the same principle as used in jet engines, but with one crucial difference: in a jet engine, the oxidizer that reacts with the fuel is air pulled in from outside. In a rocket, the oxidizer is typically pure oxygen carried in separate tanks. Using oxygen makes the reaction much more violent, and so generates much more thrust. It also means that rocket engines work in the vacuum of space.

TO KEEP THE F-1 GOING, ITS PUMPS HAD TO PULL 976 LITRES (257 GAL) OF RP-1 FUEL (HIGHLY REFINED KEROSENE) AND 1,565 LITRES (413 GAL) OF LIQUID OXYGEN INTO THE COMBUSTION CHAMBER EVERY SECOND!

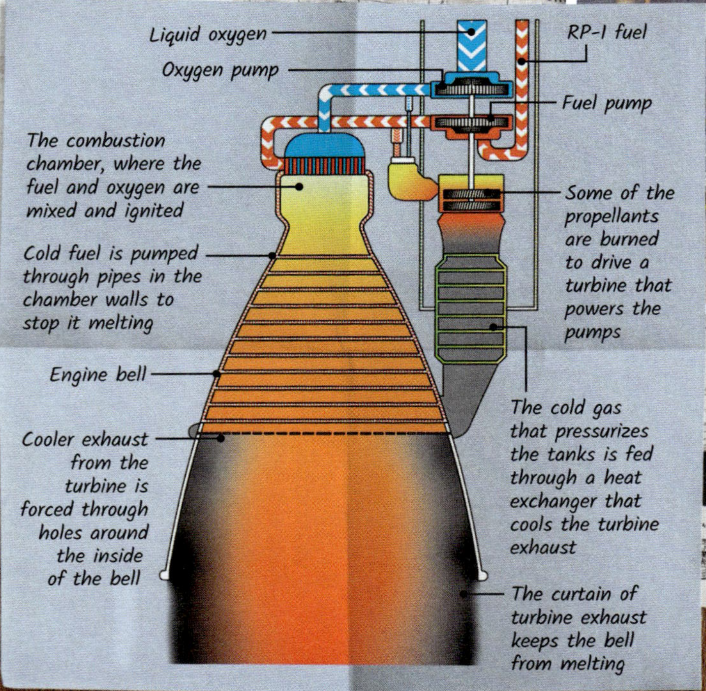

The Saturn V rocket that launched the **first crewed mission to the surface of the Moon** used five Rocketdyne F-1 engines in its first stage. Each one generated 6,770 kilonewtons (1,522,000 pounds-force) of thrust – that's the same power as 10 modern airliners running at full throttle.

SATURN V

-SPEC-

FIRST FLIGHT	9 NOV 1967
HEIGHT	111 M (364 FT)
MASS	3,238 TONNES (3,569 TONS)
PAYLOAD TO ORBIT	140 TONNES (154 TONS)

Fuelling the fire

In their quest to squeeze the most power possible out of their engines, rocket scientists have taken risks with some really nasty chemicals over the years. Here are some of the things that have been tried as propellants:

Ethanethiol
CH_3CH_2SH
Smells so bad that just a drop in an Olympic swimming pool would make the whole thing stink. Rocket tests using it in the 1950s reeked so badly of rotting meat that they attracted vultures and clouds of flies.

Dimethylhydrazine
$H_2NN(CH_3)_2$
Called "devil venom" by Soviet engineers, this fuel ignites on contact with its oxidizer, red-fuming nitric acid. Unfortunately it also ignites on contact with most metals, clothing and skin. Plus, it's a deadly poison.

Chlorine trifluoride
ClF_3
An oxidizer that causes nearly everything to ignite. It can set fire to sand, asbestos and glass, and turns into clouds of acid when extinguished. In theory it's poisonous, but it is hard to consume without catching fire.

Modern rockets

The Rocketdyne F-1 has never been surpassed in size – in part because the technology used in rockets has changed. Many modern engines run at much higher pressures and with what are called "closed-cycle" designs that feed the unburned exhaust gases from the gas-generator turbines into the main chamber. They're smaller and more efficient. The present-day **most powerful rocket** – the SpaceX Starship (below) – uses 33 smaller engines, rather than the five very big ones that powered the Saturn V.

STARSHIP

This dark band isn't part of the engine, it's the bottom of the "curtain" of cool, smoky exhaust from the gas-generator motor

The shockwave produced by a Saturn V launch reached 203 decibels. That means it was loud enough to make your ears hurt even at a distance of 1.6 km (1 mi)

ROCKET DESIGNERS USE MULTIPLE DISPOSABLE "STAGES" BECAUSE IT ENABLES THEM TO DROP HEAVY TANKS ONCE THEY'RE EMPTY. WITHOUT STAGING, AROUND 90% OF THE ROCKET'S MASS WOULD HAVE TO BE JUST FUEL AND OXYGEN.

JUN 18 In 2020, a storm produced the **longest-lasting lightning flash** – 17.1 sec – over Argentina and Uruguay.

JUN 19 Nirvana singer Kurt Cobain's Martin D-18E sold for $6 m (£4.8 m) in 2020, the **most expensive guitar at auction**.

JUN 20 In 2015, the **largest mashed-potato serving** (1,198 kg; 2,641 lb) was made in East Binghamton, New York, USA.

JUN 21 In 1931, Germany's "Rail Zeppelin" hit 230 km/h (143 mph) near Berlin – the **fastest propeller-driven train**.

Drone Displays

On 28 Sep 2024, more than 1,000 drones took to the sky over Mansfield in Texas, USA. The drones, operated by Sky Elements, formed into a 121-m-tall (397-ft) flaming phoenix to claim the **largest pyrotechnic drone display**. Here we take a look at the technology behind this fiery spectacle.

USING PYROTECHNICS LIKE FIREWORKS MEANS BEING OBSESSIVELY CAUTIOUS ABOUT SAFETY. IF THE CONNECTION BETWEEN THE CONTROL STATION AND THE FIRING TRIGGER IS INTERRUPTED FOR EVEN A MOMENT, THE SYSTEM DISARMS ITSELF.

THE **LARGEST DRONE DISPLAY** OVERALL INVOLVED A STAGGERING 22,580 MULTIROTORS OVER HEFEI, ANHUI, CHINA, ON 5 FEB 2026. THE ANIMATIONS AND IMAGES WERE CREATED BY GUANGDONG EHANG EGRET MEDIA TECHNOLOGY (CHN).

The phoenix – which even flapped its wings – was the climax of a 12-min display that played out over a local baseball field. The drones formed into various animated creatures before 1,164 of them ignited their pyrotechnics for the fiery finale. This wasn't Sky Elements' first rodeo when it comes to GWR titles. Since breaking their debut record in 2023, the team at the Texas-based company have earned 14 titles, including the **longest drone animation** (30 min) and the **most drone shows performed by different pilots in 24 hours** (25).

The drones in an aerial display are not individually controlled by human pilots. Instead, Sky Elements designed and animated the display using specialized modelling software, which can convert the shapes into detailed flight paths for each individual drone. During the display, the computer control systems are monitored by a pair of drone pilots, who can command the drones to land or change course in case of problems.

JUN 22 In 2015, Patrick Wills (USA) sank a total of three aces at the Laurel Hill Golf Club in Lorton, Virginia, USA – the **most holes-in-one in a single golf round**.

JUN 23 Ship's cook Robert Morris (UK) left the merchant navy in 1969 after 16 years' service, claiming the **most ships worked on over a career** (50).

SETTING UP

Once the display is finalized, the arduous work of getting everything ready begins. For the record attempt, 1,200 drones had to be charged, inspected and tested, their communications settings configured, and their pyrotechnic units installed and armed. Even with all those checks, seven drones encountered problems and safely grounded themselves, and 29 did not fire their pyrotechnics within the time limit and so weren't counted.

Precise positioning
In addition to the drones' built-in GPS, the formation flying of these shows relies on a system called RTK (real-time kinematic) GPS for positioning the drones. This adds a fixed base station in a precisely surveyed location in the display area. By comparing its known position with its GPS fix, the base station can continuously calculate the amount of error in the satellite signal. This real-time error adjustment is then beamed to the drones so they can correct their own GPS fixes. RTK systems are accurate to within 10 cm (4 in).

Specialized hardware
All Sky Elements pyro drones are based on the ubiquitous IFO (identifiable flying object) quadrotor, which is made by UVify in South Korea and used by drone-display companies worldwide. These machines were developed from UVify's racing drones, and have a similar emphasis on power, manoeuvrability and precision.

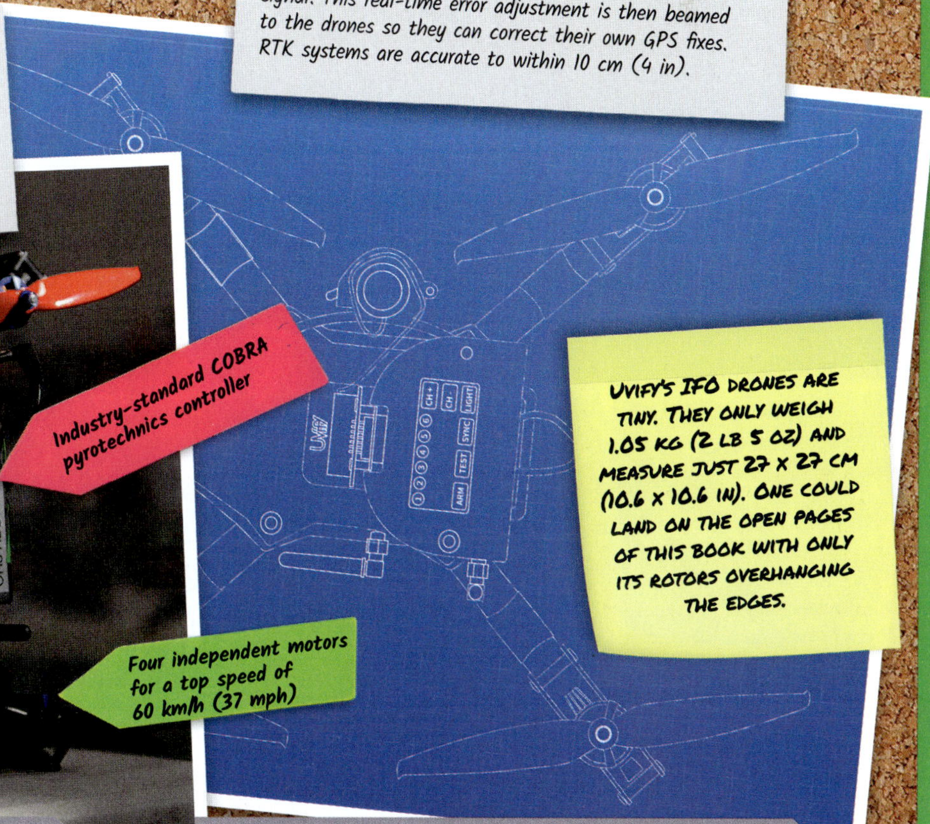

UVIFY'S IFO DRONES ARE TINY. THEY ONLY WEIGH 1.05 KG (2 LB 5 OZ) AND MEASURE JUST 27 X 27 CM (10.6 X 10.6 IN). ONE COULD LAND ON THE OPEN PAGES OF THIS BOOK WITH ONLY ITS ROTORS OVERHANGING THE EDGES.

JUN 24 Drew McQuiston (USA) hopped around a track in 7 min 40 sec to set the **fastest mile on a pogo stick** in Pittsburgh, Pennsylvania, USA, in 2017.

JUN 25 In 1999, Kurt Osburn (USA) undertook a 4,569-km (2,839-mi) road trip with a difference across the USA – in the form of the **longest bicycle wheelie**.

Tokamaks

On 4 Sep 2024, GWR adjudicators travelled to Naka in Ibaraki, Japan, to verify the **largest operational tokamak**. This colossal contraption, called the JT-60SA, is the latest iteration in a 70-year quest to deliver near-unlimited power by harnessing nuclear fusion – the process that drives the Sun.

THE WORD TOKAMAK IS DERIVED FROM THE RUSSIAN PHRASE TOROIDAL'NAYA KAMERA MAGNITNYMI KATUSHKI ("TOROIDAL CHAMBER WITH MAGNETIC COILS"), AND WAS COINED IN THE 1950S BY SCIENTIST IGOR GOLOVIN.

What is fusion?
Nuclear fusion is the process of combining two light atomic nuclei into one heavier nucleus, which releases energy. Conventional nuclear power stations utilize the opposite process, called nuclear fission. This is where energy is generated by heavy and unstable elements spontaneously breaking apart.

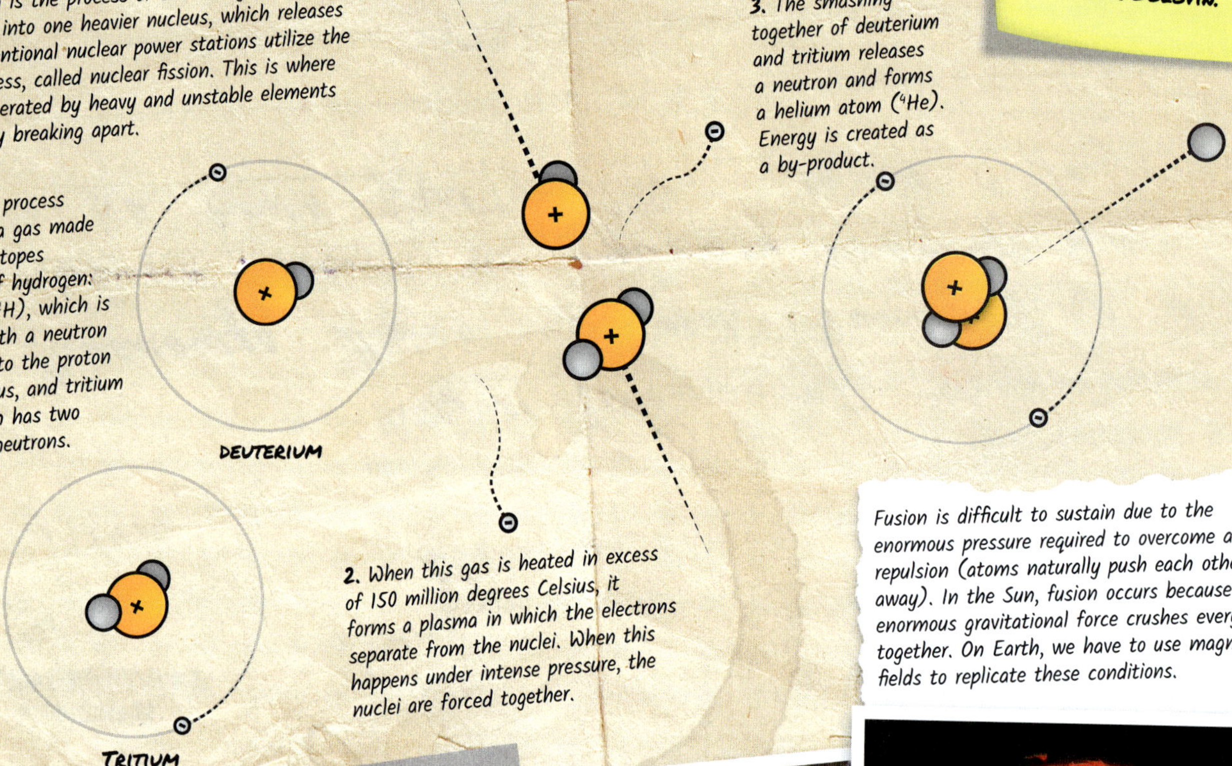

1. The fusion process begins with a gas made from two isotopes (variants) of hydrogen: deuterium (^2H), which is hydrogen with a neutron in addition to the proton in its nucleus, and tritium (^3H), which has two additional neutrons.

2. When this gas is heated in excess of 150 million degrees Celsius, it forms a plasma in which the electrons separate from the nuclei. When this happens under intense pressure, the nuclei are forced together.

3. The smashing together of deuterium and tritium releases a neutron and forms a helium atom (^4He). Energy is created as a by-product.

Fusion is difficult to sustain due to the enormous pressure required to overcome atomic repulsion (atoms naturally push each other away). In the Sun, fusion occurs because its enormous gravitational force crushes everything together. On Earth, we have to use magnetic fields to replicate these conditions.

JT-60SA

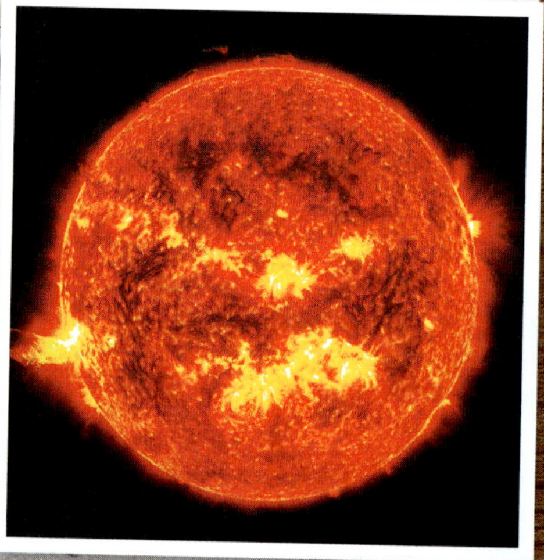

The JT-60SA (Japan Torus-60, Super Advanced) was built as part of an international megaproject called ITER (International Thermonuclear Experimental Reactor). The 2,500-tonne (2,755-ton) machine can hold a total plasma volume of 160 m³ (5,650 cu ft). This is 60% larger than the previous record holder – the Joint European Torus in Oxfordshire, UK – but less than a quarter of the size of the still-under-construction ITER tokamak in France. Its operators at Japan's National Institutes for Quantum Science and Technology will use it as a development vehicle for ITER, as well as for optimizing the design of reactors built after ITER.

JUN 26 *The World is Yours*, the **first colour TV show**, was broadcast in the USA in 1951. Only a handful of prototype televisions could pick it up at the time.

JUN 27 Cherokee Community High School's class of 1929 achieved the **longest-running class reunion** with their 77th annual meeting in Kansas, USA, in 2006.

How does a tokamak work?
The ultimate goal of the tens of thousands of engineers and scientists working on projects like the JT-60SA and ITER is a device capable of sustaining a fusion reaction and harvesting the energy it creates to generate power. To do so, the device must be able to withstand incredible pressures and temperatures without destroying itself. Tokamaks do this by using powerful magnetic fields to hold the searingly hot plasma away from the metal chamber walls.

PLASMA INSIDE

Deuterium and tritium are pumped into a toroid (doughnut-shaped) vacuum chamber, then heated to millions of degrees using a combination of two electromagnetic heating systems that use tuned microwave energy. This causes the gas to break down into plasma. Crucially, plasma is electrically charged, which means it can be manipulated with magnets.

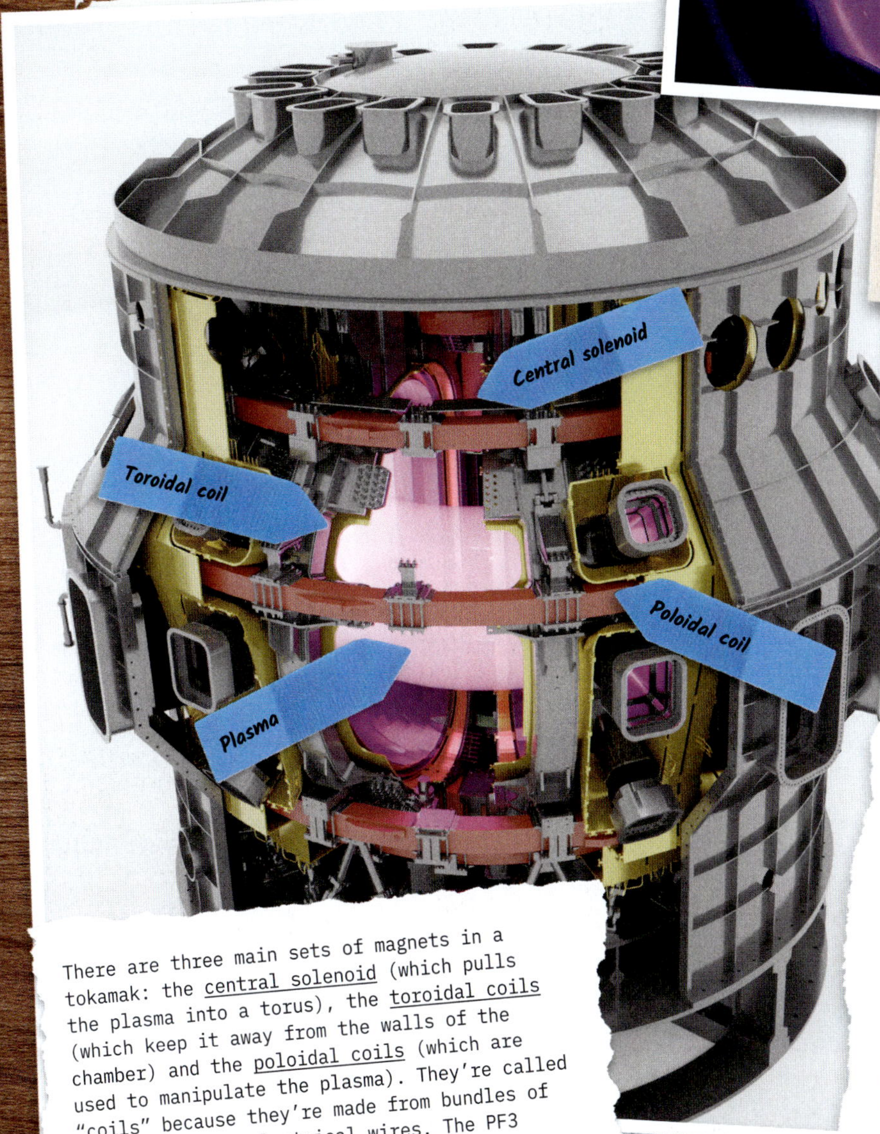

There are three main sets of magnets in a tokamak: the central solenoid (which pulls the plasma into a torus), the toroidal coils (which keep it away from the walls of the chamber) and the poloidal coils (which are used to manipulate the plasma). They're called "coils" because they're made from bundles of superconducting electrical wires. The PF3 coil (see below) contains 12.8 km (7.9 mi) of niobium-titanium cabling.

Vacuum vessel
This is a strong double-walled steel chamber. During operation, a mixture of water and boron is pumped through the void to cool it and absorb neutron radiation.

Plasma
The JT-60SA and ITER are both designed to form the plasma into an inverted teardrop shape, which channels waste particles down towards the divertor.

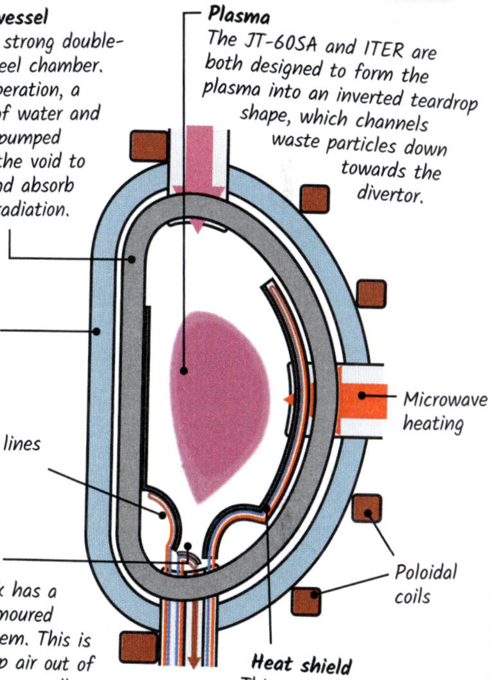

Divertor
The tokamak has a tungsten-armoured exhaust system. This is used to pump air out of the chamber, as well as aiding regulation of the plasma temperature and extraction of waste particles.

Heat shield
This prevents the plasma from damaging the vacuum chamber. In ITER, it will be replaced by a lining of beryllium plates called the "blanket". These will absorb the kinetic energy of the escaping neutrons, converting it into heat.

The next step
The JT-60SA's record is expected to fall in 2030 to the massive ITER tokamak currently being built in Cadarache, France. In Jun 2024, its primary contractor, Fusion for Energy, celebrated the completion of the last of the tokamak's poloidal field coils, which include the 389-tonne (428-ton) PF3 (left), the ***largest superconducting magnet*** *ever built.*

JUN 28 In 1997, Mimrelunds Tösen, a black-and-white bunny owned by Tine Hygom (DNK), executed the **highest jump by a rabbit** by clearing a 99-cm (3-ft 3-in) bar.

JUN 29 In 2012, on the set of *Guinness World Records Gone Wild!*, Thomas Gartin (USA) inserted \$3.50 nasally – the **most US quarters held in the nose.**

Solar Racing

Since 1987, the Bridgestone World Solar Challenge has sent teams of engineers on a 3,000-km (1,860-mi) race across Australia using only the power of the Sun. In 2025, the Delft Solar Team (NLD) triumphed for the eighth time, extending their record for the **most wins**. Here, we look at the tech behind their success…

Meet Nuna

The Delft Solar Team (then called the Nuon Solar Team) claimed their first victory in 2001. Their car (shown below) was called Nuna, and every subsequent generation of the team's vehicles has shared this name. Each race brings with it updated regulations, and so Nuna is redesigned from scratch every time.

Built for the 2025 race, Nuna 13 (right) is a compact "catamaran" design, with 6 m² (65 sq ft) of solar panels (a third less than the original Nuna). The panels are mounted on a thin "deck" that connects the hulls surrounding the wheels on either side.

NUNA 13

Refined aerodynamics, efficient power systems and low-friction mechanical components enable Nuna 13 to cruise for up to 300 km (186 mi) without sunlight, despite having a battery around 5% of the size of the battery in a typical plug-in electric car.

Non-emergency braking is handled by reversing the connection between the wheels and the motor – a process called regenerative braking. Instead of the motor driving the wheels, the wheels spin the rotors in the motor, which converts their kinetic energy back into electricity and slows the car down.

The key innovation for Nuna 13 was the addition of its "swordfins" – one built into the back of the cockpit, and another that could be added to the opposite side as needed. These improved the stability of the car, but could also automatically adjust their angle to act as sails, giving a small speed boost in crosswinds.

Race to the Sun

The Bridgestone World Solar Challenge was first held in 1987, and has taken place biannually since 1999. The entrants are required to make the 3,021-km (1,877-mi) trip from Darwin, Northern Territory, to Adelaide, South Australia, under just the power from their vehicle's on-board solar panels.

The competing teams are typically based at universities (Delft Solar Team's members are students at the Delft University of Technology in the Netherlands), and the event serves as both a showcase of the latest technology and a proving ground for the engineers of tomorrow.

The inaugural winner was Sunraycer (below), an experimental General Motors concept car, which finished in 44 hr 54 min.

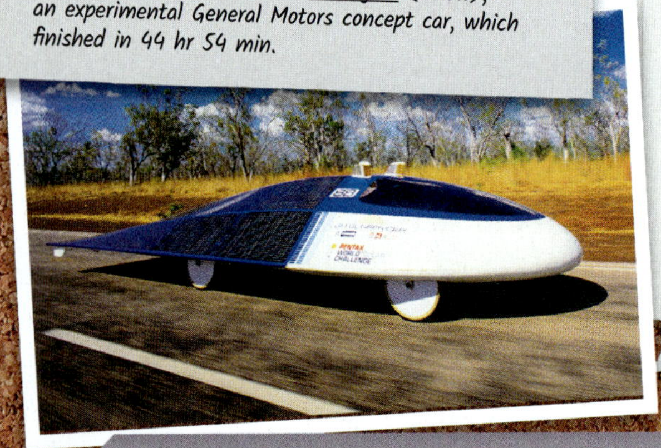

BRIDGESTONE WORLD SOLAR CHALLENGE

JUN 30 On this day in 1988, a bike teetered around the track at the Jago Sports Club in Indonesia. To this day, its 19 riders still represent the **most people on a bicycle**.

JUL 1 The **highest railway station** opened in 2006. The Qingzang Railway's stop in Tanggula – a town in Tibet, China – lies at an altitude of 5,068 m (16,627 ft).

How do solar panels work?
Solar panels rely on a principle called the "photoelectric effect", whereby some materials release electrons when they absorb energy from sunlight. The movement of these electrons creates an electric current.

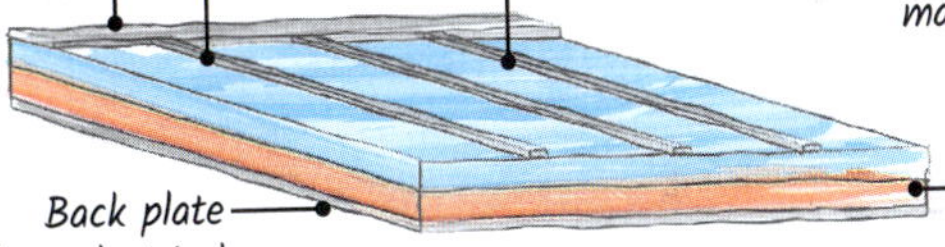

Basic solar cell

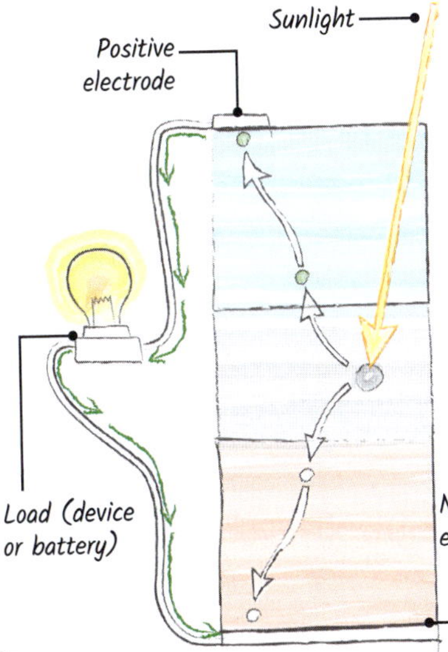

Solar panels are made using a sandwich of silicon-based semiconductor layers. The layers use two materials: N-type silicon, which is grown with impurities (called dopants) that increase the number of free electrons, and P-type silicon, which is doped with elements that have fewer free electrons and so create "holes" that attract free electrons.

N-TYPE

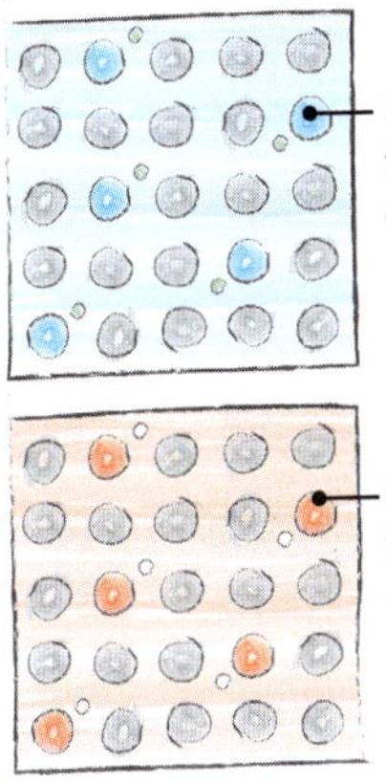

P-TYPE

When bonded together, an area forms around the join called the "depletion region". Here, the free electrons in the N-type region migrate towards the holes in the P-type region, and holes migrate towards the N-type layer, leaving an area with no free electrons or holes.

Depletion region

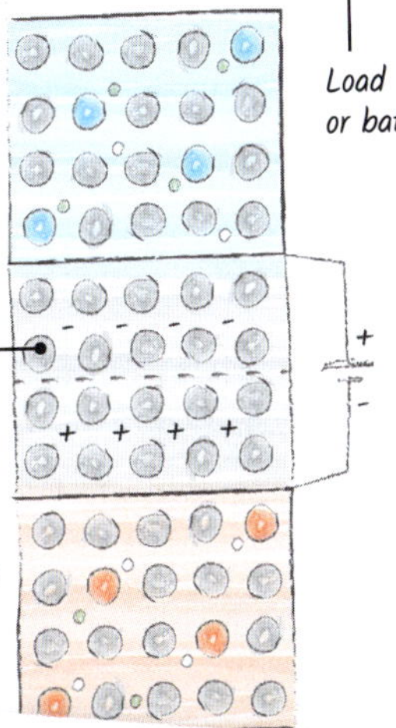

An electric field forms as a result of the depletion layer, and this blocks further movement of electrons and holes.

When the solar panel is connected in a circuit, the energy absorbed from sunlight is enough to overcome the barrier of the electric field. This allows electrons to flow around the circuit, creating a current that can power devices and charge batteries.

CHALLENGER CLASS

IN ADDITION TO THE "CHALLENGER CLASS" THAT *NUNA 13* RACES IN, THERE ARE ALSO "CRUISER CLASS" CARS, WHICH HAVE TO MORE CLOSELY RESEMBLE CONVENTIONAL CARS. THEY'RE AWARDED POINTS FOR SPEED, BUT ALSO PASSENGER CAPACITY AND LUGGAGE SPACE.

Early in the morning, the light from the Sun is too weak to provide full power to the car (the race takes place in August, but that's late winter in the southern hemisphere). The team therefore start each day by charging the car's on-board battery using the solar panels. To get the most power from the low-angle morning sunlight, and so to get on the road as soon as possible, Nuna 13's solar panel is designed to pivot up so it can be pointed toward the Sun.

RULES AND REGULATIONS
The Bridgestone World Solar Challenge has strict rules to ensure fairness and keep the participants safe. For the 2025 race, Challenger-class vehicles could be no more than 5.8 m (19 ft) long and 2.3 m (7 ft 6.5 in) wide, with at least three wheels. The on-board battery was limited to 3 kilowatt-hours (by comparison, the battery pack on a Nissan Leaf holds up to 75 kW/h) and had to be sealed in tamper-proof packaging to prevent secret non-solar charging.

The driver had to be seated inside a reinforced safety cell, with a five-point racing harness and space for a crash helmet. Teams had to demonstrate that the driver could get out in less than 15 sec.

JUL 2 In 2002, adventurer Steve Fossett (USA) touched down in Queensland, Australia, completing the **first solo circumnavigation by balloon.**

JUL 3 The **oldest vegetarian restaurant**, Haus Hiltl, opened its doors in Zurich, Switzerland, in 1898. It is currently run by the fourth generation of the Hiltl family.

Loudest Sound Ever

On 27 Aug 1883, the volcanic island of Krakatoa was blasted apart by a colossal eruption, generating the **loudest sound** in history. Measured from 160 km (100 mi) away, the volume of this blast was 180 decibels (dB). But what does that mean, and how does it compare to other loud sounds?

BEFORE

Where is Krakatoa?
The island of Krakatoa is located in the Sunda Strait – a narrow channel that runs between Sumatra and Java in what is now Indonesia. Before the explosion it measured 9 x 5 km (5.6 x 3.1 mi). During its 1883 eruption, the island was almost completely destroyed, with an estimated 25 km³ (6 cu mi) of rock and earth being blasted to powder and dispersed in the atmosphere. This map shows the approximate area that the explosion – which may have been as loud as 310 dB at its source – could be heard.

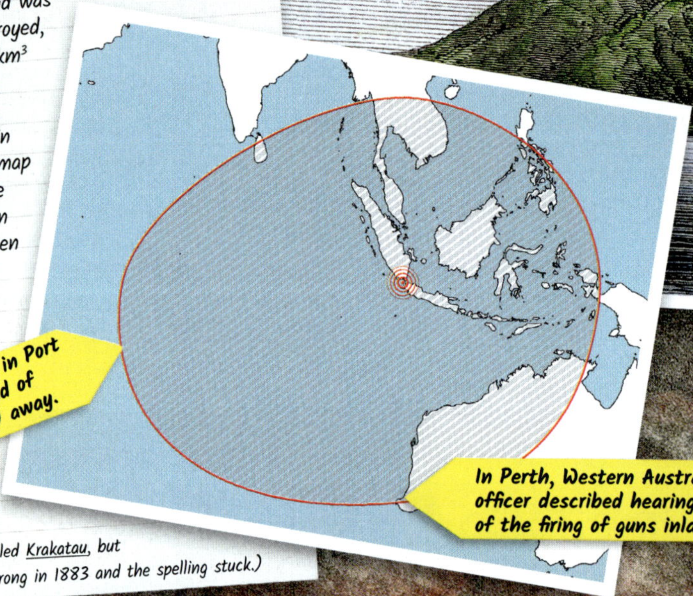

People heard the explosion here, in Port Mathurin on the Mauritian island of Rodrigues, 4,782 km (2,971 mi) away.

In Perth, Western Australia, a navy officer described hearing "sounds as of the firing of guns inland".

(The island is actually called Krakatau, but reporters got the name wrong in 1883 and the spelling stuck.)

THE AUDIBLE COMPONENT OF THE SHOCKWAVE FADED OUT AFTER AROUND 5,000 KM (3,100 MI), BUT THE INFRASOUND (WITH A PITCH BELOW THE RANGE OF HUMAN HEARING) WAS DETECTED BY SCIENTIFIC INSTRUMENTS ALL OVER THE WORLD.

Deafening roar
Survivors from the area around the Sunda Strait lost their hearing as a result of the blast. That close, the volume would have exceeded 194 dB, which is the threshold at which the amplitude of a sound-pressure wave (see opposite) becomes greater than atmospheric pressure. The delicate membranes of their ear drums would have literally ruptured by the extreme force of more than twice standard atmospheric pressure. Beyond 194 dB, pressure waves behave differently – more like a shockwave or sonic boom than sound.

This illustration was based on testimony from someone who witnessed the earlier stages of the 1883 eruption.

AFTER

JUL 4 The **largest gathering of people with the same birthday** – 228 – celebrated jointly in 2012, at an event organized by Stichting Apenheul (NLD) in Apeldoorn, Netherlands.

JUL 5 A pedalling pooch named Norman executed the **fastest 30 m on a bicycle by a dog** – 55.41 sec – in Los Angeles, USA, in 2014. His owner was Karen Cobb (USA).

What is sound?
What we hear as sound is created by our ear drums resonating with pressure waves moving through the air. These waves slosh molecules back and forth, creating high-pressure crests and low-pressure troughs that spread out from their source. The pressure difference between crests and troughs is called the amplitude of the wave, which we hear as volume, while the gap between crests is the wavelength (or frequency), which determines the pitch.

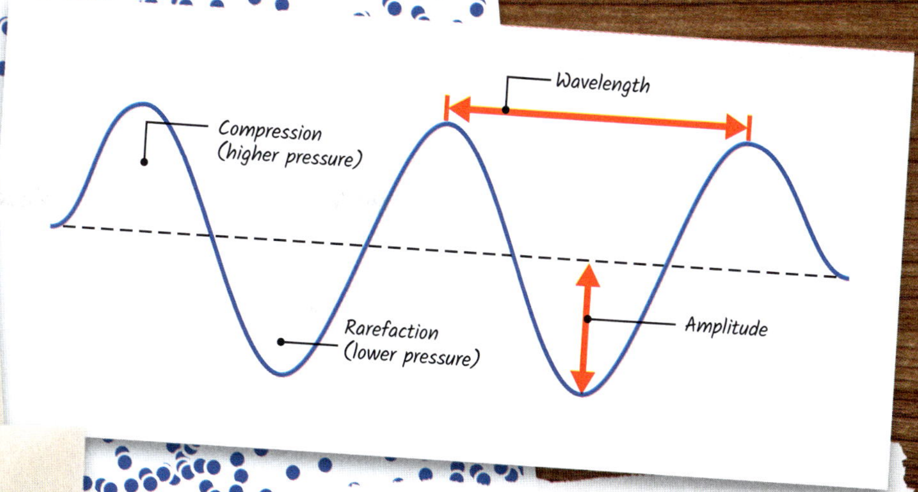

Decoding decibels
The decibel (dB) is calculated from the difference between a measured sound wave and a reference pressure. The reference pressure is 20 micropascals (μPa) – which is the smallest wave that humans can hear. A measured sound wave of 20 μPa, therefore, would have a volume of 0 dB. From there it increases on what's called a logarithmic scale, meaning the difference between the two values is written as a logarithm (or power of 10). This compresses the massive range of amplitudes we can hear into a scale of 0 to 194 dB, but it also means that it doesn't scale how you might expect.

Measuring sound isn't straightforward because our perception of volume doesn't scale evenly with the amplitude of sound waves. An increase in amplitude from 6.3 million to 8.9 million μPa looks like it should be a lot, but that's only the difference between 110 and 113 dB, which would be a barely perceptible change to most people. In addition, human hearing is sensitive to particular frequencies – a high-pitched sound will seem much louder than a low-pitched one. When professionals measure sound, they typically use a "weighting", which accounts for this variation. Most of GWR's "loudest" titles use "A-weighting", usually written as dB(A), which is configured to closely imitate how we hear sound.

Krakatoa in context
As it radiates from its source, the intensity of a sound rapidly diminishes. This is because the energy of the initial sound is dispersed over an ever-growing volume of air. Here are a range of common (and not-so-common) sounds that show the range that is covered by the decibel scale.

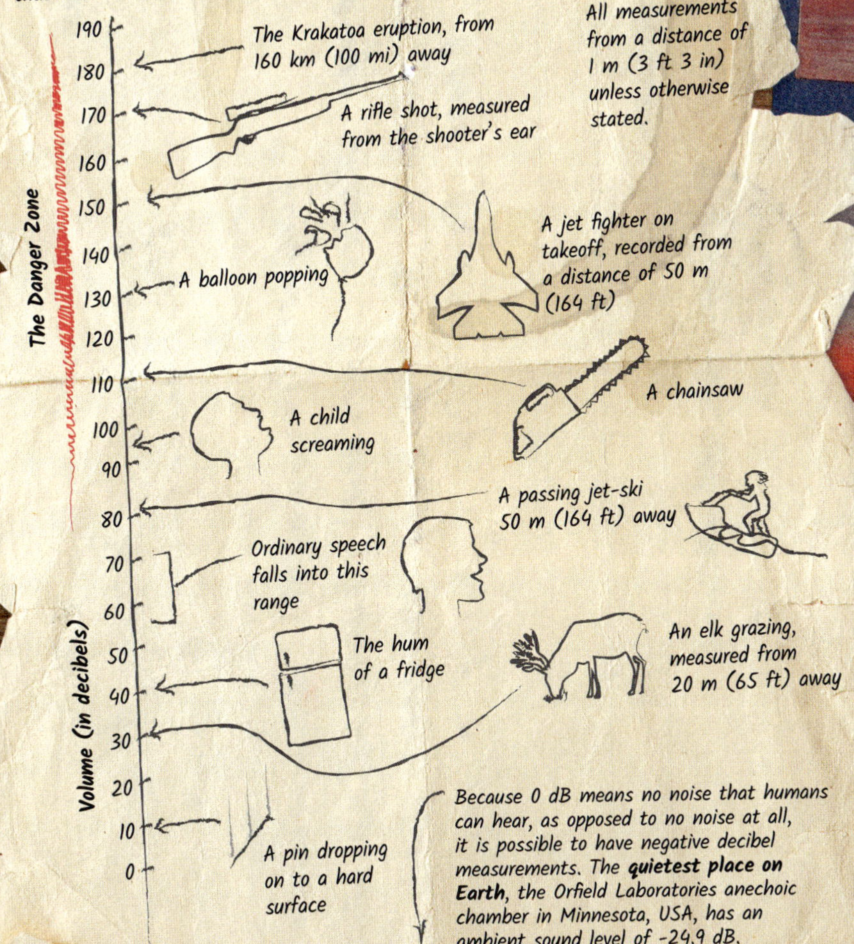

All measurements from a distance of 1 m (3 ft 3 in) unless otherwise stated.

Because 0 dB means no noise that humans can hear, as opposed to no noise at all, it is possible to have negative decibel measurements. The ***quietest place on Earth***, the Orfield Laboratories anechoic chamber in Minnesota, USA, has an ambient sound level of -24.9 dB.

The eruption caused weeks of wildly colourful sunsets all around the world.

BIG PICTURE

Inside the *ISS*

The *International Space Station* (*ISS*) is humanity's **longest-lasting outpost in space**, having been continuously occupied for 25 years as of 2 Nov 2025. Here, veteran NASA astronaut and multiple record holder Sunita Williams (USA) relaxes amid the clutter of a quarter-century of work and life on the station.

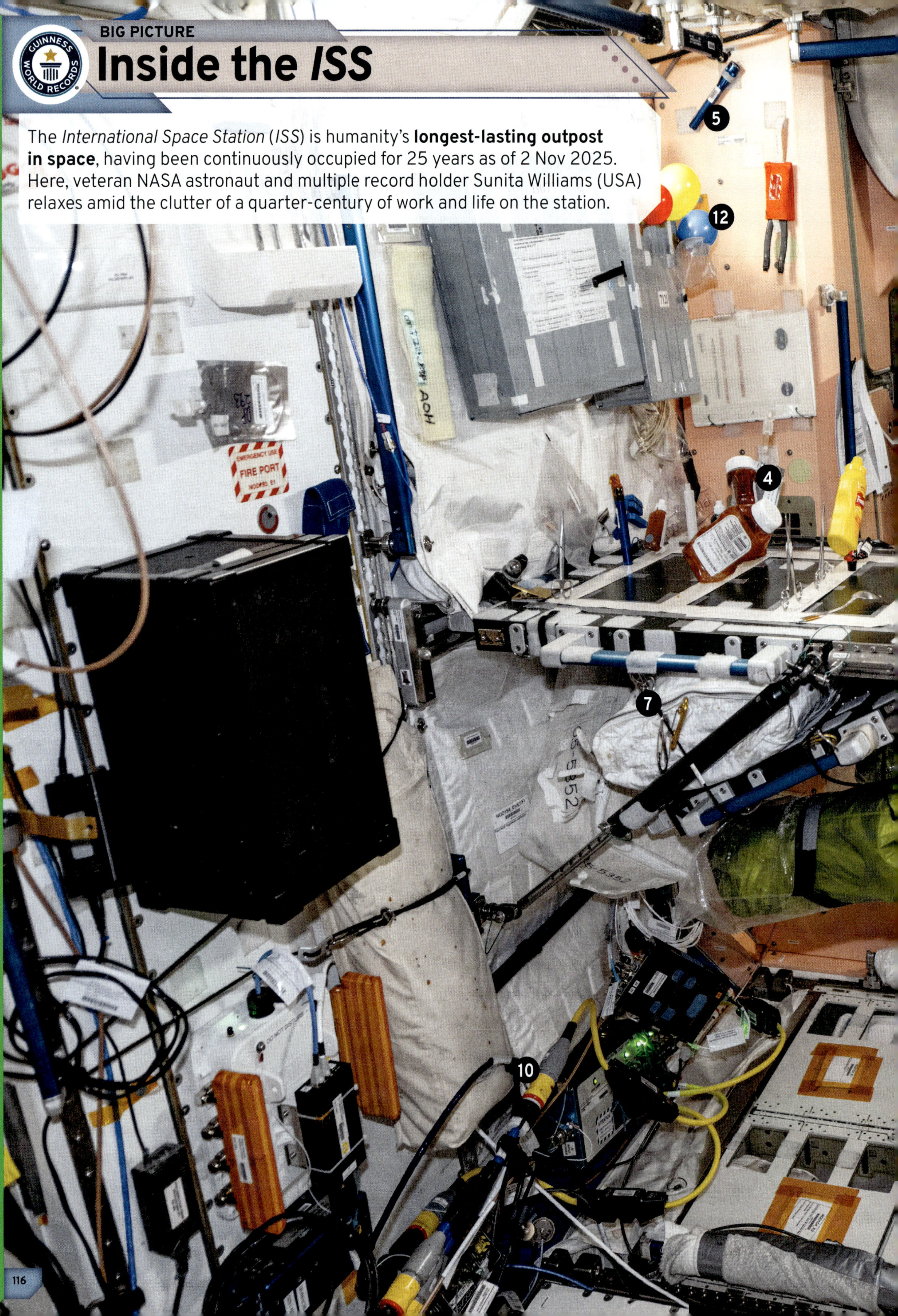

1: Sunita is in the space station's galley, located in the *Unity* node, where the crew typically eat their meals.

2: The *Unity* node connects the NASA/ESA/JAXA side of the station with the Russian modules. The area behind Sunita is the storage-bag-filled Pressurized Mating Adaptor – which connects *Unity*'s square hatches to the *Zarya* module's round hatches.

3: These blue grab-bars allow the crew to get around in zero-g. To keep herself from floating away, Sunita has hooked her feet under a bar.

4: Living in zero-g causes people's sinuses to swell up, so they lose much of their sense of smell and taste. As a result, astronauts use a lot of condiments and hot sauces.

5: The *ISS* is covered in hook-and-loop fastening tape (or Velcro®), which is used to secure many items in place.

6: Things that aren't covered with those fuzzy strips are often stuck down with orange Kapton adhesive tape. This doesn't obscure labels or leave residue.

7: Anything that can't be stuck down is clipped in place with climbing carabiners.

8: The crew go through a lot of wet wipes, as they can't easily wash with water.

9: Every hatch has an emergency checklist for closing it in the event of a pressurization failure.

10: *Unity* is criss-crossed by 216 sets of pipes for gas and liquid, as well as 9.6 km (6 mi) of electrical cabling. Most of it is behind the wall panels.

11: Although it doesn't mean much in zero-g, the *ISS*'s modules all have a standardized "floor" and "ceiling". This makes things less confusing for the crew. In *Unity*, the "floor" is made up of large storage lockers.

12: As the main gathering place for the *ISS* crew, the *Unity* node often hosts social events like birthdays, hence these party balloons!

In Jan 2025, Sunita Williams became the **oldest woman to complete a spacewalk**, aged 59 years 133 days.

Round-Up

Longest journey by fungus boat
On 5 Aug 2025, maritime mycologist Sam Shoemaker (USA) paddled a fungus canoe 42.4 km (26.3 mi) across the Catalina Channel in California, USA. His vessel was cultured from the mycelium (thread-like root system) of *Ganoderma polychromum* – a tough bracket fungus that grows on trees in the coastal forests of California.

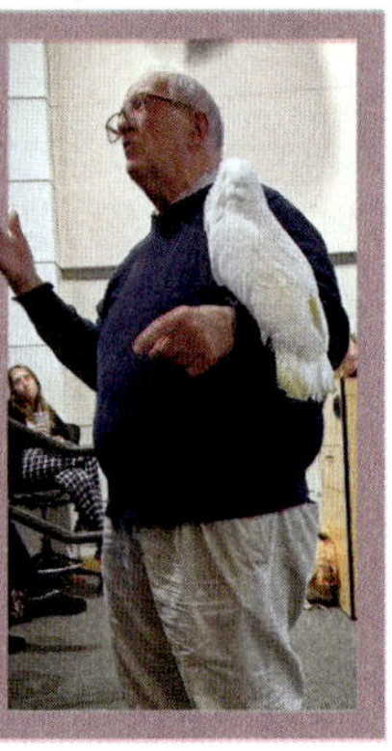

Longest career as a science teacher
Kenneth Savage (USA) wrapped up his last day of teaching on 16 Jun 2025. His final lesson took place at Westbrook High School in Connecticut, USA – the same school (and the same classroom!) where he taught his first lesson 54 years 289 days earlier.

Fastest robot to solve a 4x4x4 puzzle cube
British brothers Matthew (pictured) and Thomas Pidden built a puzzle-solving machine that conquered a 4x4x4 cube in 45.3 sec on 12 May 2025. Matthew wrote code to handle image recognition and solving algorithms as a university project, while Thomas designed the hardware.

Fastest drift by an electric car
On 29 Oct 2025, stunt driver Jason Ye (CHN) pulled off probably the most dramatic drive ever seen in the staid surroundings of the Chinese Ministry of Transport Highway Test Ground in Beijing. After getting up to speed in a Guangzhou Automobile Group Hyptec SSR, Ye slid through the measurement gates at a 38° angle and a speed of 213.52 km/h (132.68 mph).

Sweariest robot
In 2025, a Hello Robot Stretch at the University of Oregon was taught three profanities as part of a study into human attitudes towards robot collaborators. Researchers Naomi Fitter, Madison Shippy and Brian Zhang found that human study participants were more forgiving of a robot's errors (dropping things, knocking them over) if it cursed in apparent frustration afterwards.

Fastest DNA sequencing technique
On 15 Sep 2025, a team from the Broad Institute, Roche Sequencing Solutions and the Boston Children's Hospital (all USA) sequenced the genome of a young patient in just 3 hr 58 min 59 sec. For context, the **first human genome sequence** (completed in 2007) took more than a decade to compile.

Longest badminton rally by a robot
Playing against a human opponent, the XA1 wheeled robot successfully returned 1,452 hits in Shaoxing, Zhejiang, China, on 22 Dec 2025. The robot was developed by Zhejiang Shenchen Kaidong Technology (CHN), who intend to market it as a training aid for competitive players.

First fully autonomous passenger ferry
The *Olympia Dream Seto*, a 500-passenger ferry operated by Ryobi Ferry (JPN), began making independent voyages in Dec 2025. The ship had been retrofitted with level-4 autonomous navigation systems, which allow it to sail with minimal human oversight in the congested waters of Japan's Seto Inland Sea.

First wheelchair user in space
European Space Agency engineer Michaela Benthaus (DEU) crossed the Kármán line on board Blue Origin's New Shepard spacecraft on 20 Dec 2025. Benthaus had wanted to be an astronaut since her sci-fi-obsessed childhood, but suffered a major setback in 2018 when she was left paralysed by a mountain-biking accident.

Highest point on Venus
Following a 2025 review of existing mapping data by researcher Jim Singh (AUS), the tallest peak on the surface of our closest planetary neighbour has been identified as one of a cluster of mountains provisionally named the "Western Pinnacles", in the Maxwell Montes region of the Ishtar Terra plateau. The highest of these rises 10,690 m (35,072 ft) above the mean planetary radius.

First solid-state freezer
In the Jan 2026 issue of *Nature*, a team from the Hong Kong University of Science and Technology (CHN) revealed what they called an "elastocaloric freezing device". This was a small prototype freezer that used a heat-exchanger made from a nickel-titanium shape-memory alloy. When compressed, this alloy heats up, but it then rapidly cools when relaxed. The device

Highest bridge
The deck of the Huajiang Grand Canyon Bridge in Guizhou, China, is 626 m (2,053 ft) high at the point where it passes over the Beipan River. The crossing, which opened in Sep 2025, has a 1,420-m (4,658-ft) main span and an integrated bungee-jump platform for the bravest visitors.

JUL 8 — Students at Nokomis Regional High School in Maine, USA, finished the **longest canoe** on this day in 2006. It took 32 people to paddle the 45.4-m (149-ft) boat.

JUL 9 — In 2019, Rob Scallon and Sweetwater Sound built the **largest effects pedalboard** in Fort Wayne, Indiana, USA. Rob played his guitar through 319 effects pedals.

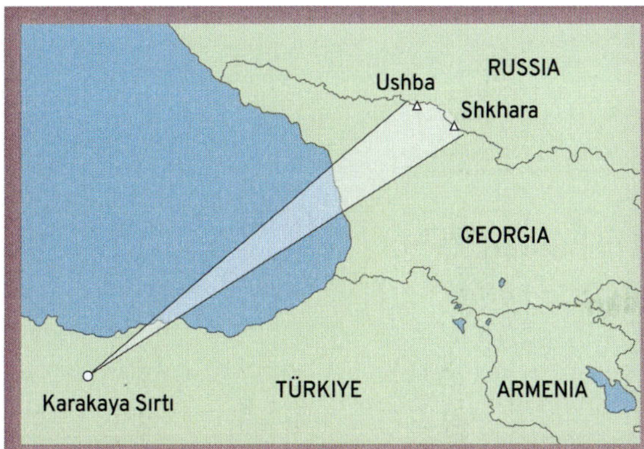

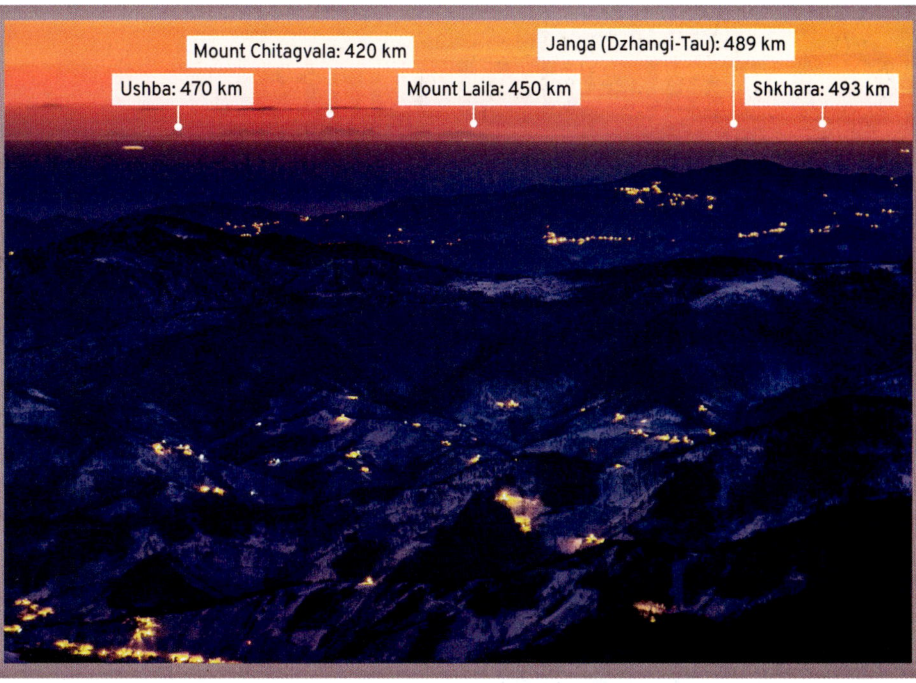

Longest line of sight on Earth
Slovakian photographer Richard Jezik snapped this panorama from a freezing-cold mountaintop in Giresun Province, Türkiye, on 15 Dec 2024. Having set up his camera in the dark, he waited until dawn for the perfect atmospheric conditions. The peaks of the Caucasus Mountains are visible above the Black Sea horizon. On the far right is the 5,203-m (17,070-ft) summit of Shkhara, a mountain located 493.07 km (306.37 mi) away on the Russia–Georgia border.

froze 20 ml (0.67 fl oz) of water in two hours by transferring energy from the heating part of the cycle to an external heat-sink.

Highest drop of an uncased smartphone
To show off the new Honor Magic8 Lite, Honor International (UAE) dropped their flagship smartphone from a height of 6.13 m (20 ft 1.3 in) on to a tiled floor in Dubai, UAE. The phone was tested afterwards and confirmed to have survived its plunge intact and remained fully functional.

Farthest aircraft pull with a cordless drill
On 17 Mar 2025, an Airbus A380 was pulled 1.43 m (4 ft 8.3 in) across its hangar in Munich, Germany, using a Parkside drill hooked up to a winch-and-pulley mechanism. The stunt was a collaboration between Lidl and Lufthansa Airlines (both DEU).

Most spacecraft docked to a space station
Between 27 Nov and 9 Dec 2025, the *International Space Station* (*ISS*) hosted a record eight visiting spacecraft – meaning there was a vehicle at every one of the *ISS*'s docking/berthing ports. On the Russian side, the total included Soyuz MS-27 and MS-28, as well as cargo ships Progress 92 and 93. On the NASA-operated side, the ports were occupied by Crew Dragon *Endeavour* along with cargo ships Dragon C211, Cygnus NG-23 and HTV-X1.

Most public toilets in a pedestrian zone
Each year, as many as 2 million Hajj pilgrims descend on the Muslim holy city of Mecca in Saudi Arabia. The challenge of keeping so many visitors safe and comfortable has inspired many superlative public-works projects in recent years.

The latest of these to break ground is a pedestrianized walkway adjacent to the Muzdalifah plain, where pilgrims spend their second night in the city. This facility, which was built by the Kidana Development Company (SAU) in 2025, includes 1,613 toilets as well as the **most charging stations** (232), the **most mist sprayers** (322) and the **largest marquee complex**, which shades an area of 226 ha (558 acres) – about two-thirds the size of Central Park in New York – from the Arabian sun. As a side-effect of all these initiatives, Mecca has the **most public toilets per capita**, with one for every 20 people.

Longest journey walked by humanoid robot
Between 10 and 13 Nov 2025, AgiBot A2, an android built by AgiBot Innovation (CHN), hiked from Jinji Lake in Suzhou to The Bund in downtown Shanghai – a distance of 106.28 km (66.04 mi). The robot made the 56-hr trek autonomously, though AgiBot did need human helpers for its 15 battery swaps and to shelter it from a heavy downpour.

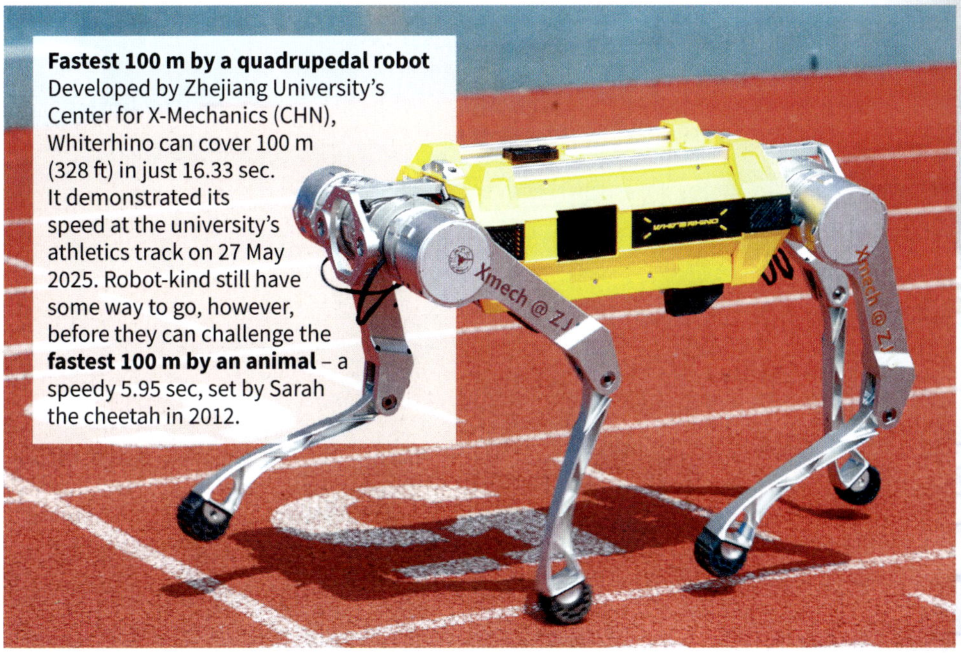

Fastest 100 m by a quadrupedal robot
Developed by Zhejiang University's Center for X-Mechanics (CHN), Whiterhino can cover 100 m (328 ft) in just 16.33 sec. It demonstrated its speed at the university's athletics track on 27 May 2025. Robot-kind still have some way to go, however, before they can challenge the **fastest 100 m by an animal** – a speedy 5.95 sec, set by Sarah the cheetah in 2012.

JUL 10 The **heaviest robot** – a 197-tonne (217-ton) self-driving locomotive called AutoHaul – transported its first load of ore in Pilbara, Western Australia, on this day in 2018.

JUL 11 At the 1999 British Ferret Racing Championships, Warhol claimed the title of **fastest ferret**, blitzing the 10-m (32-ft 9-in) tube race in 12.59 sec.

SNAPSHOT

Tallest Mountain

The **highest point on Earth**, Mount Everest stands as a symbol of lofty human ambition. But this giant is humbled by a long-dead volcano on Mars whose vast, effortless rise across the horizon shatters our sense of scale.

Olympus Mons is both the **tallest volcano** and **tallest mountain** in the Solar System, and its size is almost impossible to imagine. To help you appreciate just how enormous it is, we've visualized it here looming over Everest – the **highest mountain on Earth**. "Mount Olympus" lies in a depression on the Martian surface and rises over 25 km (15 mi) – nearly three times higher than Everest. And its base is just as astonishing – it's more than 20 times wider than it is high and would cover much of the country of France (inset). You could walk up its gentle slope for days without ever seeing the summit.

This shallow rise is what makes Olympus Mons so different from Earth's mountains. Instead of jagged peaks, it spreads out like a giant shield, hence its designation as a "shield volcano". On Earth, the movement of tectonic plates breaks up mountains and volcanoes, limiting how tall they can grow. But Mars doesn't have active plate tectonics, so lava from repeated eruptions kept piling up in the same place for millions of years.

Lower gravity on the Red Planet has also played a huge role. There, surface gravity is just 38% as strong as it is on Earth. With less downward force holding it back, the mountain was able to rise higher and spread wider than anything possible on Earth. Despite this, summitting Olympus Mons might actually prove easier than Everest, given its gentle incline. That is, of course, if you can survive the Martian dust storms, solar radiation, freezing temperatures and virtually airless atmosphere!

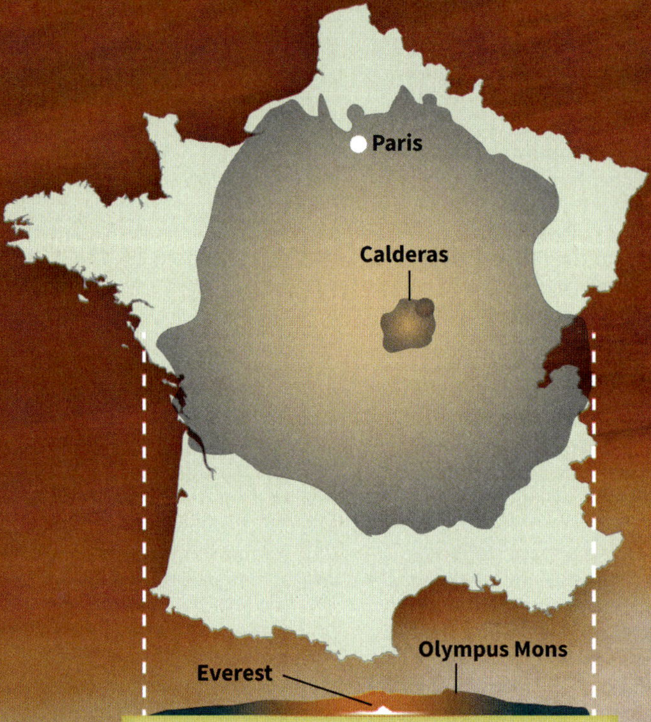

Olympus Mons is roughly 600 km (370 mi) at its widest point – comparable with central France – and has a footprint of *c.* 300,000 km² (120,000 sq mi). In the centre of the mountain are a series of calderas (collapsed impact craters) forming a depression that's 3.2 km (2 mi) deep and 80 km (50 mi) wide.

Mars is named after the Roman god of war. But the study of Martian geography is known as "areography", from Ares, the Greek god of war.

JUL 12 Did you hear the one about the **largest audience for a comedian**? In 2008, Germany's Mario Barth (DEU) drew 67,733 fans to the Olympiastadion in Berlin.

JUL 13 In 2012, Nick Nicora (USA) served up a 39,746.8-litre (10,499-gal) margarita – the **largest cocktail** – in Sacramento, California, USA. *Hic!*

JUL 14 Arne Lindström (NOR) sculled between England and France in 3 hr 35 min in 1994, the **fastest row across the English Channel by an individual.**

JUL 15 Look sharp! The **greatest distance to throw a spear** is 258.63 m (848 ft 6.5 in), by David Engvall (USA) at Aurora, Colorado, USA, on this day in 1995.

ICON Hilda Baci

Self-belief can take you beyond your limits, enabling you to scale heights you never deemed possible and even motivating others to do the same. Step forward Nigeria's Hilda Baci...

In 2023, this singular chef, restaurateur and internet sensation undertook the **longest cooking marathon** (see below right), cheered on by thousands of onlookers. She made it clear that this wasn't just for her, but to "put Nigerian cuisine on the map" and "to inspire young African women to chase their dreams". Hilda's feat provided food for thought, and ushered in a wave of enthusiasm for record breaking; within two months, GWR had received more than 1,500 new applications from Nigerians. As she knows, every record attempt is also an opportunity to hone a host of empowering (and even career-defining) talents.

Hilda started young, helping out at her mother's restaurant in Abuja while still at primary school. "I always got so many tips because I used to memorize the whole menu and I was very sharp-mouthed!" she recalls. She launched the catering business Hilda's Kitchen (now known as My Food by Hilda), becoming a professional chef in 2020. Thanks to her dynamic social-media presence, she now has millions of online followers, and has also secured another GWR title (see below).

Finally, this inspirational ICON has some invaluable advice for *GWR* readers. "Consistency beats talent. Systems beat hustle. And humility keeps you growing," she told us. "Excellence is not a one-time performance – it's discipline repeated consistently."

VITAL STATISTICS

Name	Hilda Baci (b. Hilda Effiong Bassey)
Birthplace	Akwa Ibom, Nigeria
Birth date	20 Sep 1995
Current GWR titles	**Largest serving of rice; largest serving of Nigerian-style jollof rice**
Accolades	The Future Awards Africa Young Person of the Year (2023)

As their T-shirts make clear, Hilda's mother, Lynda Ndukwe, has long been her most important supporter. Lynda, who owns the Calabar Pot restaurant in Gudu District, Abuja, says that she was "shaking" when Hilda told her of her ambitions to make the **largest serving of Nigerian-style jollof rice**. "That pot was like my office!" she joked. "Even the cover... people could not carry it. They had to bring in cranes to lift it!"

ON THE RECORD

"If my journey gave someone else the courage to attempt something bold, then that means more to me than the title itself. Records can be broken – that's their nature. But inspiration, the ripple effect of belief, is what truly lasts"
– *Hilda Baci*

On 12 Sep 2025, Hilda and brand Gino Nigeria created the **largest serving of Nigerian-style jollof rice** – 8,780 kg (19,356 lb 9 oz) – in Victoria Island, Lagos, Nigeria. The XXL-sized helping of this dish included 4,000 kg (8,820 lb) of basmati rice, 164 kg (361 lb 8 oz) of fresh goat meat and some 600 kg (1,322 lb) of Hilda's own jollof pepper mix. More than 16,600 portions were shared out after. An exultant Hilda described the experience as "nine hours of fire, passion and teamwork".

Discover all of GWR's incredible ICONS at **guinnessworldrecords.com/records/icons**

Hilda's pictured with two of her GWR certificates. When she's not breaking records, she's running her own restaurant, My Food by Hilda. The multi-talented chef also starred as the host of Nigerian TV's *Dine on a Budget* and won 2021's "Jollof Face-off" contest against a Ghanaian chef.

Hilda completed the **longest cooking marathon by an individual** – a stamina-sapping 93 hr 11 min – in Lekki, Lagos, between 11 and 15 May 2023. Her epic "cook-a-thon" was followed by millions of fans in Nigeria and the wider world via a live stream. Her legions of admirers even crashed GWR's website while seeking updates! This highly competitive record has been broken twice since then. The current holder is Evette Quoibia (AUS, b. LBR), with a time of 140 hr 11 min – more than five days – ending on 25 Feb 2024.

HISTORY

CONTENTS

The mock battle is just one part of a broader cycle of religious plays performed during the four-day event. It begins with a liturgical drama that tells the story of the martyrdom of St John the Baptist (1). Following this, another group stages a medieval romance about Emperor Charlemagne and the legendary Twelve Peers of France (2). Finally, the great armies of the Turks and the Christians meet in battle (3) – a performance in which dozens of volunteers deliver pre-written speeches and dialogues that narrate the story of the centuries-long conflict between Christian Europe and the Muslim Ottoman Empire.

LARGEST HISTORICAL RE-ENACTMENT

On 31 Aug 2025, the streets of Zacatecas in central Mexico were filled by 17,601 costumed re-enactors, each taking the role of a soldier in the army of either the Holy League or the Ottoman Empire. After the parade, the two armies clashed in an hours-long fantastical retelling of the 1571 Battle of Lepanto. This colossal confrontation forms the finale of a multi-day cultural festival known as the Morismas de Bracho, which has been staged every year since at least 1835.

As battle re-enactments go, the Morismas de Bracho is not very accurate (if nothing else, Lepanto was a naval battle). It is, rather, a mixture of historical events and a tradition of religious public theatre that has its origins in medieval Spain. The Battle of Lepanto, as restaged every year in Zacatecas, is a morality play and a Christian fable, drawing on the history of the Spanish *reconquista* as well as the Christian conversion of Mexico.

This picture shows the climactic battle between "King Felipe" (left) and "The Moorish King" (aka "King Selim"; right).

Museums

Largest collection of ventriloquist dummies
The Vent Haven Museum in Fort Mitchell, Kentucky, USA, hosted 1,145 talking puppets as of 29 Sep 2025. Believed to be the only museum dedicated to the art of ventriloquism ("belly speaking"), its roots date to 1937 when its founder – W S Berger – began to amass paraphernalia related to this field.

Most museums visited in 24 hours
Culture-vulture pals Johnny Cruz Buckingham, Michael Osborne Bedient II, Casey Felz and Jonathan Chen (all USA) dashed across London, UK, on 15–16 Aug 2025, calling at 49 institutions. They stayed long enough to take a selfie in each; above, top to bottom, is: Japan House, the Natural History Museum and The National Gallery. They beat the previous mark by seven.

CURIOUS CURIOS

Largest kite museum
Weifang World Kite Museum
• Weifang, Shandong, China
• **Area**: 8,100 m² (87,190 sq ft)
• **Exhibits**: 1,300

Largest espionage museum
International Spy Museum
• Washington, DC, USA
• **Area**: 9,750 m² (104,950 sq ft)
• **Catalogued items**: 9,281

Largest fragrance museum
Xuelei Fragrance Museum
• Guangzhou, Guangdong, China
• **Area**: 9,500 m² (102,260 sq ft)
• **Scent stations**: 300

Oldest museum
Within the Tower of London complex – built at the heart of the English capital by William the Conqueror in the 11th century – sits the Royal Armouries Museum. It has been exhibiting militaria stored at the royal fortress to elite visitors since at least the late 15th century. But in 1660, with the restoration of King Charles II, entry was expanded to a wider audience, albeit still with an entry fee. Its most enduring display is the "Line of Kings", an exhibit that showcases the arms and armour of generations of English monarchs. Each king's equipment is borne by a mannequin atop or beside an elaborately carved wooden horse.

Most museums (country)
According to data gathered by UNESCO, there were some 104,000 museums globally in 2021. The lion's share of these were in the USA, which is home to 33,082, including institutions devoted to topics as eclectic as barbed wire, potatoes and espionage (see left). This puts the USA far ahead of Germany and Japan, with a total of 6,741 and 5,738 edifying attractions, respectively.

The country with the **most museums per capita** depends on criteria. Based on number of museums per million citizens, the Pacific island nation of Niue's sub-2,000 citizens means that, despite only having one museum, it statistically speaking has a ratio of *c.* 625 museums per million people – in the unlikely event it experienced a 500-fold population boom, that is! Among non-microstates that tend to skew per capita data, the record goes to Sweden. The country's 10.6 million citizens have a choice of 1,600 museums – that's 151 permanent exhibitions per million inhabitants.

Largest museum collection (total items)
Part of the USA's Smithsonian Institution, which is spread across multiple sites, New York City's American Museum of Natural History boasts a mind-boggling archive of 33,430,000 specimens and artefacts. Nearly 70% of these sit within its Invertebrate section, predominantly made up of preserved ants, bees/wasps, beetles and moths.

Highest museum in a building
Reaching up to 426.8 m (1,400 ft), the Makkah Clock Tower Museum occupies the top four floors of the Abraj Al Bait tower in Mecca, Saudi Arabia. Established in 2019, it takes visitors on a tour across the history of horology, exploring time through the lens of science, technology and art.

The impressive edifice in which the museum is housed is a multiple record holder in its own right. Not only is it the world's **tallest clock tower**, topping out at 601 m (1,972 ft) overall, but it also bears the **largest clock face**: a 43-m-wide (141-ft) example located on its outer façade.

Most visited museum (current)
Located within China's Forbidden City in Beijing, The Palace Museum attracted 17 million people (three times the population of Norway) in 2024, according to the latest *Global Attractions Attendance Report*, published by TEA/AECOM in Oct 2025. A custodian to some 1.8 million items, including vast collections of ceramics, textiles, jade and bronzework, The Palace Museum offers a unique window into China's lavish imperial past.

JUL 16 In 1935, the **first parking meters** were installed in Oklahoma City, USA. The Park-o-Meter was invented by newspaper editor Carlton Cole Magee (USA).

JUL 17 Garry Turner (UK) clipped the **most clothes pegs on the face** for a TV show in Istanbul, Türkiye, in 2013. He fitted 161 pegs between his jawline and hairline.

LARGEST ARCHAEOLOGICAL MUSEUM

Two decades after building work commenced in 2005, the Grand Egyptian Museum (GEM) fully opened to huge fanfare (above) on 1 Nov 2025. The site covers some 470,000 m^2 (5 million sq ft), with an internal 81,000-m^2 (871,900-sq-ft) floor area – akin to about 11 soccer fields. It was designed by Irish architects Heneghan Peng, with construction overseen by BESIX (BEL) and Orascom (EGY). Its 100,000 or so artefacts are displayed across 12 galleries, and an 11-m-tall (36-ft) statue of Ramesses II (right) greets visitors in the main foyer.

The GEM's exhibits cover all 30 key periods of ancient Egypt, from the predynastic to the Greco-Roman eras (*c.* 5000 BCE to *c.* 400 CE).

One of the most-hyped areas of the GEM is its Tutankhamun Gallery. This is the first time that the entire contents from the tomb of the "Boy King" (see pp.130–31) will have been on display together. Comprising 5,398 objects, including his iconic gold coffin (above) in which his mummified body was laid to rest, it is by far the **largest ancient Egyptian burial hoard**.

JUL 18 In 2012, See's Candies of California, USA, unveiled the **largest lollipop**. The chocolate-flavoured treat weighed a hippopotamus-sized 3,176.5 kg (7,003 lb)!

JUL 19 NASA astronaut Michael Collins (USA) took the **first selfie in space** in 1966, turning his camera around while orbiting Earth in the cramped *Gemini 10* capsule.

Archaeology

HAIHUN HOARD HIGHLIGHTS

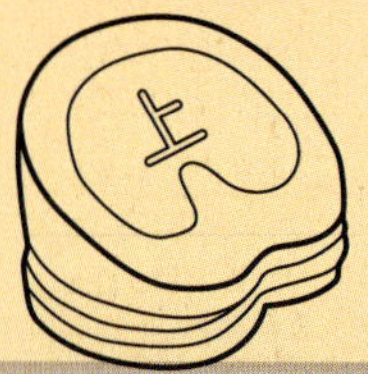

Gold ingot
These hoof-shaped ingots, each weighing as much as 250 g (8.8 oz), were traditionally given as diplomatic gifts.

Goose lamp
The tomb contains thousands of finely made bronze items, including bowls, sculptures and goose-shaped lamps.

Ceremonial bell
Liu He was buried with texts and religious items that provide insight into the practices of Han-Dynasty Confucianism.

Largest hoard of gold coins
On 9 Sep 1993, a large number of Roman *aurei* were found by metal detectorists looking over fresh construction spoil in the city of Trier, Rhineland-Palatinate, Germany. The coins had been buried beneath the floor of a Roman cellar, probably in around 196 CE. The Trier Hoard comprises 2,518 solid-gold coins with a combined weight of 18.5 kg (41 lb). A few larger hoards of gold coins have been found in the past – including an enormous cache of *aurei* discovered in Brescello, Italy, in 1616 – but these finds were not catalogued and the coins were melted down.

Largest archaeological archive
Maintained by the London Museum in the UK, the London Archaeological Archive and Research Centre holds detailed reports and finds (uncovered items) from excavations in and around the British capital. As of 29 Jan 2026, the facility had information on 14,063 excavations. The earliest records are from the 1830s, and new reports are added every month as builders break ground on new projects in the ancient city.

Oldest animal cemetery
In Jan 2021, Polish archaeologists Marta Osypińska and Piotr Osypiński published a paper on a cluster of animal burials in the ancient Egyptian port of Berenike. The site held the remains of 536 cats, 32 dogs and some other animals, including several small monkeys and a juvenile baboon, all dating from the 1st and 2nd centuries CE. The graves were deep and the animals laid out with care – arranged as if sleeping, or wrapped in fabric shrouds. Some were buried with mementoes such as decorated collars or toys.

Highest-altitude archaeological site
Llullaillaco is a 6,736-m-high (22,100-ft) dormant volcano on the border between northern Chile and Argentina. In Mar 1999, archaeologists Johan Reinhard (USA) and Constanza Ceruti (ARG) led an expedition to the summit, where they discovered an Inca ceremonial site. Amid the ruins were the mummified remains of three children, believed to have been left as sacrifices around 1500 CE. Although they never knew it, these children, and the priests that likely accompanied them, held the record for the **highest altitude reached by humans** for approximately 300 years.

Oldest worked wooden object
Found by a geologist walking on the foreshore near Clacton-on-Sea in Essex, UK, in 1911, the Clacton Spear is a 38.7-cm (1-ft 3-in) shaft of yew. Its finder assumed it was a bit of antler because it was unearthed from 420,000-year-old sediment. On closer inspection it was revealed to be a weapon that had been sharpened with flint tools. In Jan 2026, archaeologists in Greece uncovered what may be an even older object – a 430,000-year-old wooden pickaxe made by Neanderthals.

Largest coin hoard
In Mar 2011, archaeologists in Jiangxi, China, received a tip-off about some Han-Dynasty objects that had been dug up by farmers near the village of Guanxi, some 40 km (25 mi) north of Nanchang. Their preliminary excavation revealed a monumental tomb complex and started what has become a years-long archaeological megaproject. They had found the tomb of Liu He (*c.* 92–58 BCE), Marquis of Haihun – an aristocrat who was briefly emperor of China. In 2016, excavators uncovered a treasury chamber containing 5 million bronze *wu zhu* coins (inset), a trove that dwarfs the 150,000-silver-coin Brussels Hoard, which previously held the record.

The main excavation campaign at Guanxi ended in 2018, but the process of cataloguing the tomb's contents will continue for many years. A large modern museum and conservation facility has been constructed nearby to support work on the site, and to showcase the remarkable objects that have been found (see left).

JUL 20 Musician and sound engineer Idem Abasifreke (NGA) ended his **longest whistling marathon** – 40 hr 1 min 2 sec – at Beatisblaak Studio in Lagos, Nigeria, in 2025.

JUL 21 In 2007, glassmaker Xaver Hofmeister (DEU) produced the **tallest mouth-blown vase** in Germany. At 3.56 m (11 ft 8 in), it was akin to a stack of 17 stein glasses!

LARGEST COMMUNITY ARCHAEOLOGY PROJECT

Between 2005 and 2018, the Currently Occupied Rural Settlements project (CORS) recruited a total of 15,066 volunteers to excavate 2,511 test pits around the UK.

The project was created to solve a problem that has long troubled archaeologists: ancient settlements are usually hidden under modern ones, making excavations difficult. It worked by having a team of archaeologists engage with local community groups, supervising a few days of digging and the analysis of the finds uncovered. CORS trenches were limited to 1-x-1-m pits, visible in these pictures of a selection of CORS volunteer excavators.

Historians are still studying the data assembled by the project. One clear trend is the impact of the Black Death, with late-14th-century finds being scarce or entirely absent in many places.

CORS was led by Carenza Lewis, who helped develop this "big dig" approach to archaeology while working on the TV show *Time Team*.

JUL 22 Pioneering pilot Wiley Post (USA) completed the **first solo around-the-world flight** when his Lockheed Vega – the *Winnie Mae* – landed back in New York City in 1933.

JUL 23 Serial record breaker Ashrita Furman (USA) hopped up 1,899 steps in 57 min 51 sec to claim the **fastest pogo-stick ascent of the CN Tower** in 1999.

BIG PICTURE

Tutankhamun's Tomb

On 26 Nov 1922, British archaeologist Howard Carter chipped away the ancient plaster that was sealing a door beneath the Valley of the Kings, near Luxor in Egypt. On the other side he saw "wonderful things" – the tomb of the Pharaoh Tutankhamun (*c.* 1341–1323 BCE), which had lain untouched for thousands of years. Although robbers had broken in soon after the teenage king's death, throwing the tomb into disarray, they are thought to have been caught in the act and the tomb resealed with its treasures largely intact. Carter and his assistants catalogued a total of 5,398 items, making it the **largest ancient Egyptian burial hoard**.

Wonderful things

The main image across these pages is a modern reproduction of the tomb's antechamber at the time of its discovery, looking through a viewport in the southern wall. The picture below shows the real thing, taken in 1922 by photographer Harry Burton, looking towards the southern wall. Visible on the left is the wreckage of two ceremonial chariots, piled up in a corner after being damaged in the robbery.

The tomb's full contents went on display together for the first time in 2025 at the Grand Egyptian Museum in Giza (see p.127).

1: The antechamber is dominated by three gilded wooden couches. This one is carved in the likeness of the god Ammit, the crocodile-headed devourer of the souls of the unjust dead.

2: The second couch is carved to resemble Mehet-Weret, the celestial cow and creation goddess of the sky.

3: The lion-headed couch has a frame carved into two stylized lionesses that represent the goddess Mehit. The animal heads on each couch had inlaid crystal eyes.

4: This wooden head and torso, made to Tutankhamun's measurements, is thought to be part of the **oldest surviving mannequin** (or dress form). In the actual tomb, it was stored in another chamber next to a chest of clothing.

5: The entrance to the burial chamber was flanked by a pair of identical statues, both thought to be depictions of Tutankhamun himself.

6: The shrine that constituted the outermost layer of Tutankhamun's coffin can be seen through the doorway. Inside this was another smaller shrine, with two more inside that. Within the innermost shrine was a coffin, containing another coffin and finally the young pharaoh's famous golden sarcophagus.

7: This round-topped chest, made from white-painted wood and ebony, held clothing ranging from embroidered robes to linen underwear.

8: These egg-shaped wooden boxes contained the remnants of cooked ducks and other fine foods.

9: The central couch had a simple white-painted bed and some other furniture piled haphazardly on top.

10: The wooden chests atop and around the lion-headed couch contained a variety of treasures, including ornately carved hunting bows, a large scarab beetle carved from the mineral lapis lazuli and a solid-gold ceremonial sceptre.

Record-Breaking Romans

Tallest Roman aqueduct
The Pont du Gard was built between 40 and 60 CE to carry an aqueduct (water channel) across the Gardon valley in southern France. In the middle of its span, this massive stone bridge rises 48.8 m (160 ft) above the valley floor. It was originally part of a 50-km-long (31-mi) watercourse designed to serve the city of Nemausus (present-day Nîmes).

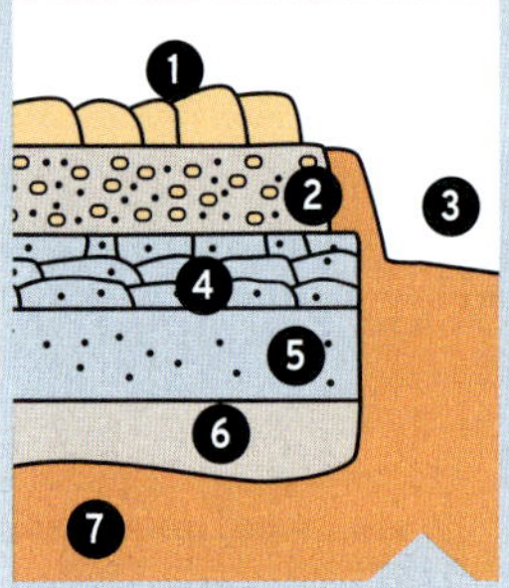

Structure of a Roman road
Routeways such as the Via Appia (see right) incorporated four main courses, in layers. Drainage ditches ran alongside.
1: Large stone slabs (*summum dorsum*), bordered by a kerb. Reserved for the most important roads
2: Crushed stone, gravel and sand in cement (*nucleus*)
3: Drainage ditch
4: Cement mortar containing gravel (*rudus*)
5: Crushed rock (*statumen*)
6: Packed dry earth or sand
7: Levelled ground

Longest-lasting empire
For almost 1,500 years, the Roman Empire dominated Europe and beyond. Most historians agree that its inception dates to 27 BCE, when the Roman politician Octavian overthrew the Roman Republic to become Emperor Augustus. Rome fell to Germanic invaders in 476 CE, but its ensuing "Eastern" (or Byzantine) empire, based at Constantinople (now Istanbul), is widely regarded as a continuation of the original Roman one. It wasn't until the fall of that city to Ottoman (Turkish) forces in 1453 CE that the empire ended.

First monumental dome
The 21.55-m-wide (70-ft 8-in) Temple of Mercury at Baiae near Naples, Italy, is believed to have been constructed in the 1st century BCE. Made from packed tufa rubble, it was actually a city baths, rather than a temple. The dome is unusual for being pierced by both an upper oculus – an opening to the sky – and four windows, and inspired later Roman domes such as the Pantheon (see right).

Largest Roman mosaic
In 2010, archaeologists uncovered a contiguous mosaic measuring 1,050 m^2 (11,302 sq ft) in Antakya, Türkiye. The tiled flooring was laid down for a palatial Roman villa in the 4th century CE, and includes both detailed representational art and elaborate geometric patterns.

Oldest road surface still in use
Stretches of the Via Appia (Appian Way) in Italy date from its original construction in 312 BCE. The road formed the main link between Rome and Brindisi in south-east Italy and is named after Appius Claudius Caecus, a Roman censor who initiated construction. Today, the Appian Way follows a later course defined by Pope Pius VI, but parts of the old road (Via Appia Antica) are still in use. In the area of Velletri, it is possible to drive on the original Roman-paved surface, interspersed with block paving and tarmac refurbishment.

Largest masonry dome
The concrete roof of the Pantheon in Rome measures 43.3 m (142 ft) across, wider than any dome built only of masonry (i.e., unreinforced stone or brick). Constructed by the emperor Hadrian in 118–128 CE, it rises 22 m (71 ft) above its base and out-spans the famous domes of the great Italian cathedrals of Florence (Santa Maria del Fiore) and Rome (St Peter's), as well as that of St Paul's in London, UK.

Largest hacksilver hoard
During the declining years of the Roman Empire, provincial officials began using chopped-up decorative silverware – fine items that would once have graced the tables of the Roman aristocracy – as a sort of currency known as "hacksilver". On 12 May 1919, archaeologists at Traprain Law – the site of an ancient hillfort in Lothian, UK – uncovered a cache of hacksilver weighing 23.94 kg (52 lb 12.8 oz). It is thought to have been a diplomatic payment sent by Roman officials to a British tribe.

Largest ancient stadium
The Circus Maximus in Rome, Italy, could house 255,000 spectators in three tiers of seating. This concrete, marble and stone structure measured 610 m (2,000 ft) long and 198 m (650 ft) wide, and reached its greatest size under Emperor Trajan in 103 CE. It was used for chariot races, athletics, gladiator combat, animal hunts and processions. The last recorded race here took place in 550 CE.

JUL 24 Aerobatic pilot Joann Osterud (CAN) completed the **longest inverted flight** in 1991. She flew upside down for 4 hr 38 min over British Columbia, Canada.

JUL 25 Sushi Kirimon launched the **most expensive sushi** in Osaka, Japan, in 2023. The dish, called "Kiwami Omakase", costs ¥350,000 ($2,475; £1,927).

LONGEST CONTINUALLY EXCAVATED ARCHAEOLOGICAL SITE

Located south of Naples in Italy, the Roman city of Pompeii was buried under 4–6 m (13–20 ft) of volcanic ash and pumice in 79 CE, when Mount Vesuvius erupted. The city lay undisturbed and forgotten for centuries, though from the 16th century onwards, some artefacts and structures were unearthed. In 1748, a full-scale excavation began in earnest under the auspices of the Bourbon King Charles III of Spain, who commandeered many artefacts for his personal collection. The project has been ongoing to some degree ever since, uncovering fascinating glimpses of Roman day-to-day life such as bathhouses, ordinary homes and street-corner cafés (right).

The city's identity was finally confirmed in 1763, with the discovery of inscriptions reading "res publica Pompeianorum" ("state of the Pompeians").

JUL 26 In 1980, Joe Bowen (USA) teetered into Bowen, Kentucky, at the end of the **longest journey on stilts**. He'd started 4,804 km (2,985 mi) away in Los Angeles.

JUL 27 Mario Villagrán (ECU, b. 3 Jan 1956) became the **oldest K2 climber** in 2023, topping the 8,611-m (28,251-ft) mountain in Pakistan aged 67 years 205 days.

Bygone Sports

Longest-running cheese-rolling race

The annual tradition of chasing a wheel of Double Gloucester cheese down the steep slopes of Cooper's Hill in Gloucestershire, UK, was first recorded in 1836. Participants hurl themselves down the hill in the hope of catching the runaway cheese, or at least tumbling across the line first.

Discorso
SOPRA IL GIVOCO
DEL CALCIO
FIORENTINO
Del Puro Accademico Alterato.
Al Sereniss. Gran Duca di Toscana Suo Signore.
IN FIRENZE
Nella Stamperia de' Giunti, 1580.

According to de' Bardi's rulebook, each team should consist of 27 men: three *datori indietro* (goalkeepers), four *datori avanti* (full-backs), five *sconciatori* (blockers) and 15 *innanzi* or *corridori* (runners). Games take place on a 100 x 50-m (328 x 164-ft) pitch with goals that run the full width at either end.

Oldest football rulebook

Italian renaissance polymath Giovanni de' Bardi published *Discorso Sopra il Giuoco del Calcio Fiorentino* in 1580. It lays out, in detail, the rules of the sport today known as Calcio Storico Fiorentino, an early form of football that had been played in Italy since the Middle Ages. The version of the game he described was contested each year in the Piazza Santa Croce in Florence, Italy. It died out in the late 17th century but made a comeback in the 1930s.

Oldest football

In the 1970s, a small grey leather ball, roughly 16 cm (6.3 in) in diameter, was found tucked behind some wooden panelling at Stirling Castle in Scotland, UK. This ball has been dated to around 1540–70, a time when it is known that the ancestors of today's rugby and association football were popular with the men and women of the Scottish royal court.

Largest ball-game field

The town of St Columb Major in Cornwall, UK, is home to an ancient Shrovetide football game (see opposite) called the St Columb Hurling. Victory is secured either by throwing the ball into one of two stone troughs in the town, or by running the ball across the parish boundaries. The second of these scoring methods means that technically the entire parish – an area of around 20 sq mi (52 km²) – serves as the playing field.

Largest whistling archery tournament

The tradition of whistling archery, or *Xiang Jian*, stretches back at least 1,500 years in Tibet, China. It sees archers replace the metal tips of their arrows with carved wooden whistles that are fired into padded leather targets. On 29 Sep 2024, the Linzhi Whistling Archery Association held a tournament with 300 competitors in Linzhi, Tibet, China.

Oldest air race

The Gordon Bennett Cup has been the premier event in the world of ballooning for 120 years. Named for its founder, a Gilded-Age newspaper owner, the race challenges aeronauts to fly lifting-gas balloons as far as possible from the start line. It is not uncommon for entrants to cover more than 1,000 km (620 mi), which posed a major problem for the organizers in the years before radios were commonplace. The winners of the 1910 race, for example, came down in the Canadian wilderness and had to trek cross-country for 10 days before they could get word to race officials.

First auto-polo match

Billed as "America's Most Dangerous Sport!", auto polo was – as its name suggests – a variation on polo, played with cars instead of horses. It was invented by Boston socialite Joshua Crane Jr, and first played in Jul 1902 at the Ardsley Polo Club in Tarrytown, New York, USA. The original version of the game soon died out amid jokes about hospitals "congested with concussed millionaires". It was revived following the introduction of the relatively cheap Model T Ford in 1908, with the violent and chaotic matches proving popular at state fairs and carnivals.

The teams are named for Florence's historic parishes. This game is between Santa Maria Novella (in red) and San Giovanni (in green).

JUL 28 — In 2024, Christian Roberto López Rodríguez (ESP) popped on his Crocs to claim the **fastest mile in foam clogs**. He covered the distance in 4 min 13.9 sec.

JUL 29 — A fossilized maiasaur became the **first dinosaur in space** in 1985. Astronaut Loren Acton took the remains of this hadrosaur with him on the Space Shuttle.

During the match, the ball is typically carried by a player at the centre of a huge scrum of teammates called a "hug".

ON THE RECORD

Hoose agen hoose,
toone agen toone,
if tho' meets a man,
knock 'im doone,
but tho' cannae
wound 'im!

– The rules of mob football, as traditionally declared by the master of ceremonies (known as the Fool) at the Haxey Hood game in North Lincolnshire

The Ashbourne game is started by a visiting dignitary, who throws the ball into the crowd. It earned its "royal" moniker in 1928, when the future King Edward VIII kicked off the game (and got a bloody nose in the ensuing mayhem!).

LONGEST-RUNNING "FOOTBALL" FIXTURE

The Royal Shrovetide Football game is contested each year between the "Up'ards" and "Down'ards" of Ashbourne in Derbyshire, UK. Local tradition dates the game's origins to the 12th century, though the oldest written reference is from 1683. It is held on Shrove Tuesday (a Christian feast day known elsewhere as Mardi Gras), which typically falls in February or March. The teams, which are of unlimited size, are named for the end of the town they start from. The aim of the game is to get the ball from the centre of Ashbourne to the site of the Clifton Mill (the Down'ards' goal) or the Sturston Mill (the Up'ards' goal). The rules prohibit the use of weapons and hiding the ball, but that's more or less where they end.

JUL 30 Stuntman Luke Aikins (USA) pulled off the **highest skydive without a parachute** in 2016, plummeting 25,000 ft (7,600 m) into a giant net in California, USA.

JUL 31 The **largest fruit crumble** was baked at La Ruée 2016, a festival in Tracadie, New Brunswick, Canada. The gigantic dessert weighed 498 kg (1,097 lb 14 oz).

Pyramids

TYPES OF PYRAMID

True pyramid
Perhaps the best-known kind of pyramid has smooth triangular sides that meet to form a pointed pinnacle.

Stepped pyramid
The earliest stone pyramids had a flat top and comprised several concentric levels that could be scaled on the outside.

Ziggurat
Inspiring stepped pyramids, these Mesopotamian oblong platforms were topped with a temple accessed by a ramp.

Tumulus
A more rudimentary form that requires fewer building materials, tumuli are hill-like burial mounds of soil or grit.

Oldest pyramid

Constructed *c.* 2630 BCE by Pharaoh Djoser's royal architect, Imhotep, the Djoser Step Pyramid at Saqqara, Egypt, has long been recognized as the undisputed earliest pyramid.

More recently, some archaeologists have suggested that similar structures may have been built in the same period at Caral – one of the Americas' earliest cities – in western Peru.

The **oldest true pyramid** today is the Red Pyramid, part of the Dahshur complex (see also the Bent Pyramid, opposite) south of Cairo, Egypt. It was constructed *c.* 2575–2563 BCE during the reign of Pharaoh Sneferu (aka Soris). Its design likely evolved from the earlier Meidum Pyramid, near Memphis in Egypt – a seven-level stepped pyramid that likely collapsed during attempts to retrofit it with smooth sides.

First diving expedition beneath a pyramid

In Jan 2019, American archaeologist Pearce Paul Creasman donned scuba gear to explore the flooded tomb of Kushite King Nastasen, situated beneath his pyramid in Nuri, Sudan. While it would have been dry when excavated *c.* 315 BCE, over the centuries the water table of the nearby River Nile has risen. During the dive, Creasman found ceramic figurines and even a toe bone that may have belonged to the king.

LARGEST...

Ziggurat ever

Built for the Elamite King Untas in the 13th century BCE, the five-storey Ziggurat of Chogha Zanbil in Iran originally stood 53 m (174 ft) high – twice the height of the UK's Buckingham Palace – and had a footprint of 11,000 m^2 (118,400 sq ft).

The **largest surviving** example is the Ziggurat of Ur (now Muqayyar) in Iraq with a 61 x 45.7-m (200 x 150-ft) base, though it has undergone fairly extensive restoration work.

Maya pyramid

La Danta ("The Tapir") is a stepped pyramid that reaches 72 m (236 ft) high, breaking out of the dense jungle canopy in northern Guatemala. It is the largest structure at the extensive El Mirador site – a Maya metropolis that at its peak (300 BCE to 150 CE) was home to more than 100,000 people.

Tumulus

The burial mound of the Mermnad King Alyattes, located at Bin Tepe in western Türkiye, stands 63 m (207 ft) tall and was built using 785,000 m^3 (27.7 million cu ft) of soil and stone. It may have taken more than 2,000 labourers two-and-a-half years to complete, starting *c.* 560 BCE.

Most pyramids (country)

Sudan had at least 230 still-standing pyramids as of 2025, all built during the Kingdom of Kush (*c.* 780 BCE to 330 CE). These are typified by steep-sided examples at royal burial sites near the ancient city of Meroë (above). By comparison, neighbouring Egypt (see opposite) has at most 140 extant pyramids.

Largest pyramid

The Great Pyramid of Cholula, aka Tlachihualtepetl ("man-made mountain"), in Puebla, Mexico, has a volume of *c.* 4.45 million m^3 (157.1 million cu ft) – 70% larger than Giza's Great Pyramid (see right). It was worked on by several cultures – including the Olmec – from the 3rd century BCE. It is now mostly obscured within a hill, with a 16th-century church sat on top.

Largest Buddhist temple

Built from some 1.5 million stone blocks in the 8th/9th centuries CE, Borobudur in Central Java, Indonesia, is one of the most sacred monuments in Buddhism. A stepped pyramid/ziggurat hybrid, the 60,000-m^3 (2.12-million-cu-ft) structure – made up of nine terraces and topped with a bell-shaped stupa – was created during the Śailendra Dynasty.

AUG 1 Creative numismatist Milenko Topalov (SRB) presented the **smallest replica coin** in Serbia in 2022: a 2.73-mm-wide (0.1-in) ¼ Swiss franc, featuring Albert Einstein.

AUG 2 Designed by Belgian artist Paul Van Hoeydonck, an aluminium figurine entitled *Fallen Astronaut* is the **first sculpture on the Moon**, left by Apollo 15's crew in 1971.

MOST VISITED PYRAMID COMPLEX

In a typical year, more than 2.5 million tourists – greater than the entire population of central Paris, France – flock to the Giza Plateau, just outside of Egypt's capital, Cairo. This figure is set to increase with the long-awaited opening of the Grand Egyptian Museum (see p.127) nearby in 2025.

Giza is home to nine pyramids, but the standout star is, without doubt, the Great Pyramid of Khufu, which is the sole survivor from the original Seven Wonders of the World. When built some 4,600 years ago, it would have towered 146.7 m (481 ft), but even at its current slightly diminished height of 137.5 m (451 ft), it remains the **tallest pyramid**.

Greatest incline disparity in a pyramid
Also not far from Cairo is the earlier Dahshur necropolis, developed under the reign of Fourth Dynasty ruler Sneferu – widely acknowledged as the most prolific pyramid-building pharaoh. One of his architectural legacies is the Bent Pyramid. Partway through its completion, *c.* 2600 BCE, at a height of 47 m (154 ft), the angle of its sloping walls switches from 54° at the base to a shallower 43° at the top, likely as a result of structural issues.

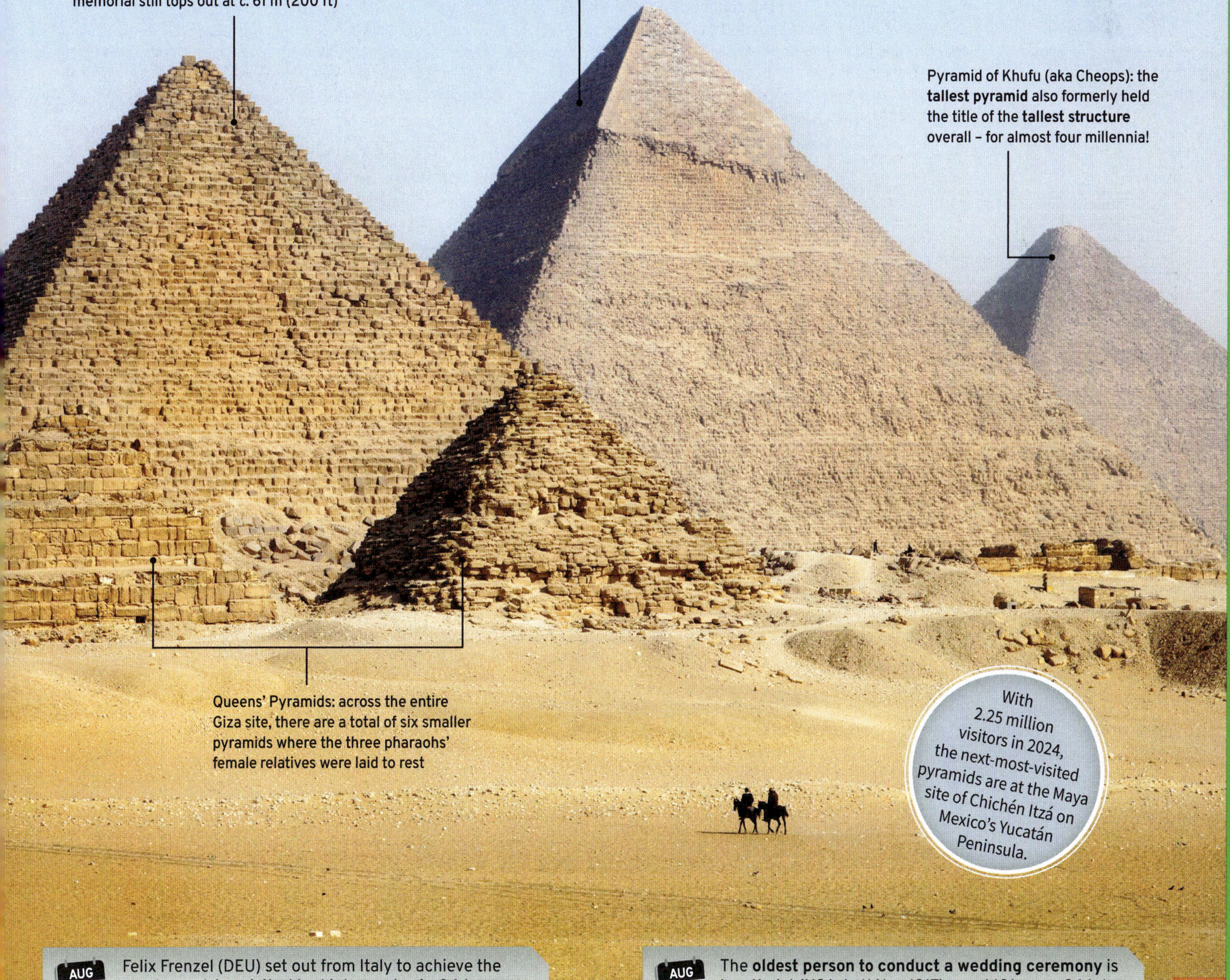

With 2.25 million visitors in 2024, the next-most-visited pyramids are at the Maya site of Chichén Itzá on Mexico's Yucatán Peninsula.

AUG 3 Felix Frenzel (DEU) set out from Italy to achieve the **most countries visited by kick scooter in 24 hours** (five), arriving home in Germany on this day in 2019.

AUG 4 The **oldest person to conduct a wedding ceremony** is Leo Kadet (USA, b. 11 Nov 1917), aged 101 years 266 days when he wed his granddaughter and her fiancé in 2019.

Tales of the Unexplained

Most common type of animal rain
Randall Cerveny, GWR's meteorology consultant, has collected hundreds of accounts of "anomalous rain", including showers of frogs, beans, spiders, coins and snakes. Small fish remain the most frequent flyers, however, with 78 historical examples of this peculiar precipitation and new ones emerging every few years.

It is believed that piscine rain occurs when tornado-like waterspouts suck shoals of fish into the air, but the similar phenomenon of the "meat shower" remains harder to explain. The **largest meat shower**, which dropped "half a wagon-load" of flying flesh on a farm in eastern Kentucky, USA, during the spring of 1876, has been blamed on everything from tornadoes to vomiting vultures. Witnesses reported that it tasted like mutton or venison.

I want to believe!
An Ipsos survey of the American public from Oct 2021 found the following proportions of people believe in the existence of...

Ghosts 36%

Witchcraft 21%

Psychic powers 36%

Aliens and UFOs 39%

Largest vampire epidemic
Between 1725 and around 1750, the people of the eastern and southern provinces of the Austrian Empire (present-day Hungary, Romania and the northern Balkans) waged war against what has come to be known as the "Great Vampire Epidemic". There are 30 documented cases of communities exhuming the recently dead in the belief that they were leaving their graves to prey on the living. Suspected undead were staked, beheaded and/or burned.

Oldest paranormal research organization
Two British institutions lay claim to this title. The Ghost Club is the oldest – founded in 1862 – but has been briefly disbanded and reformed a few times. The Society for Psychical Research, meanwhile, wasn't incorporated until 1882, but has operated continuously since its inception. Both investigate suspected hauntings, psychics and other supernatural phenomena.

First reported alien abduction
The earliest clear example of an alien abduction narrative was published in the *Evening Mail* of Stockton, California, USA, on 27 Nov 1896. Local politician Henry Shaw wrote of witnessing a "strange airship" and encountering "inhabitants of Mars, who have been sent to the Earth for the purpose of securing one of its inhabitants". The letter was printed during a wave of "mystery airship" sightings across the country, and an associated boom in early science-fiction stories (the source of the illustration below).

Most shots fired at UFOs
On the night of 24–25 Feb 1942, soldiers in California, USA, claimed to have sighted a fleet of mystery aircraft over Los Angeles. They responded by firing more than 1,400 three-inch (76-mm) anti-aircraft shells over several chaotic hours. No trace of any aircraft was found in the aftermath of what became known as the "Battle of Los Angeles".

Most common type of UFO sighted
Of the more than 1,600 cases reviewed by the All-domain Anomaly Resolution Office (AARO), 41.1% involve reports of spherical flying objects. The next most common sighting is simply of "lights" (30.3% of witness accounts). The AARO is the US government's official body for investigating what they call UAP (unidentified anomalous phenomena), established in 2022. The two most common types of UFO correlate with the two most frequent explanations, which is that the sightings turned out to be balloons (51.1%) or satellites (35.6%).

Oldest depiction of a ghost
The clay tablet known as BM 47817, unearthed in Iraq during the early 1880s, contains a 2,500-year-old guide to exorcising the restless spirits of the dead. The Babylonian cuneiform tablet bears an engraving of the ghost of an old man being led into the underworld by the spirit of a beautiful woman, summoned to stop him tormenting the living.

If he were sighted today, that Babylonian spook would be a strong contender for the **longest-lived ghost**, an old GWR category that has been awarded variously over the years to a spectral Roman soldier in York, UK, a Bronze Age horseman on Salisbury Plain, UK, and, most recently, by the "snake-demon" spirit of a suspected dinosaur in Rio Arriba, New Mexico, USA.

First "spirit photograph"
In Nov 1862, William Mumler (USA) published what he insisted was a photo of a ghost in the spiritualist newspaper *Banner of Light*. He went on to open his own specialized photographic studio, producing pictures of sitters reunited with the spirits of their departed loved ones. Even though Mumler was put on trial for fraud in 1869, no one was able to conclusively prove how these images were created.

AUG 5 The winner out of 8,238 players was crowned after the three-and-a-half-hour-long **largest game of musical chairs** at Singapore's Anglo-Chinese School in 1989.

AUG 6 On this day in 1991, British computer scientist Tim Berners-Lee published the **first website** as a guide to introduce people to the new-fangled World Wide Web.

LONGEST VIGIL SEEKING THE LOCH NESS MONSTER
In Jun 1991, Steve Feltham (UK) left his life as an alarm fitter in Weymouth, Dorset, and travelled to the opposite end of the UK to search for a mysterious creature that had fascinated him since childhood. He set up camp at Dores Beach, at the northern end of Loch Ness, and began a daily search for Nessie. As of Dec 2025, nearly 35 years later, his hunt continues. In that time he's seen some mysterious things, but no unambiguous plesiosaur head poking up above the waves.

The best-known picture of Nessie is the "Surgeon's Photograph", taken by Robert Wilson in 1934, though it is now widely believed to be a hoax based on a toy submarine and a model dinosaur. Despite his decades-long search, Feltham has not yet snapped a picture of this aquatic cryptid.

AUG 7 Fred Grzybowski (USA) bounced into the record books in 2011 on the **tallest pogo stick** – 2.91 m (9 ft 6.5 in) – at the International Busker Festival in Toronto, Canada.

AUG 8 On a visit to GWR's London HQ in 2018, nimble Nepali Thaneswar Guragai set the **fastest time to pass through a toilet seat three times:** 21.04 sec.

Round-Up

Largest log jam

In the late 19th century, lumberjacks in the United States transported freshly cut trees to sawmills by floating them down rivers. Sometimes logs would get caught, and pile up into rafts of timber called "log jams" (example pictured). The largest of these was recorded in May 1880, in Chippewa Falls, Wisconsin. Low water levels caused a log jam to form that extended 7 mi (11.2 km) upstream and comprised some 200 million board-feet (472,000 m^3) of timber. It finally broke up on 13 Jun, flooding nearby towns.

Largest surviving medieval world map

The Hereford *Mappa Mundi* was inked on to a stretched calfskin in around 1300 CE. It measures 1.58 x 1.33 m (5 ft 2 in x 4 ft 4 in) and is today on display at Hereford Cathedral in the UK. *Mappa Mundi* are diagram-like world maps, embellished with religious and mythical scenes, intended as teaching aids rather than navigational resources.

Largest Roman shoe

This 32.5-cm-long (1-ft 0.8-in) boot was uncovered in Jun 2025 by archaeologists from the Roman Army Museum at Vindolanda in Northumberland, UK. It was found during excavations at Magna, a fort near Hadrian's Wall, and would have belonged to a Roman soldier with size-13 (US-size-14, EU-size-49) feet.

Oldest known personal name

Around 5,120 years ago, a clerk called Kushim signed off on various contracts related to deliveries at a brewery in Uruk (present-day southern Iraq). These contracts, inscribed in cuneiform on clay tablets, are today held at the Schøyen Collection in Oslo, Norway. The **oldest named animal** was an Egyptian hunting dog, or Tesem, called Beha. He lived around 4,400 years ago.

Most intact sailing warship salvaged

Rendered top-heavy by design changes and ornate decoration, the Swedish warship *Vasa* capsized and sank on its maiden voyage in 1628. The wreck was raised from Stockholm Harbour in 1961 and found to have been preserved remarkably well in the cold mud, with 98% of its original structure intact. It is today on display at the Vasamuseet in Stockholm.

Largest sailing vessel

The *Thomas W Lawson* was a 145-m-long (475-ft) seven-masted schooner, commissioned in 1901 by its namesake, an eccentric American businessman and yachting enthusiast. Built to demonstrate that sail-powered cargo vessels were still viable in the 20th century, the cumbersome and slow ship ended up proving the opposite and sank in a storm off the south coast of the UK in Dec 1907.

The *France II* (launched in 1912) was slightly larger, but was built with diesel engines and only made a handful of journeys under sail after its engines were removed as a cost-cutting measure.

Longest-lived phantom island

Many old maps show a small island called Bermeja in the Gulf of Mexico, around 200 km (124 mi) north of the Yucatán Peninsula. The island was first charted by Spanish cartographer Alonso de Santa Cruz in 1539, and his colleague Alonso de Chaves provided a detailed description of Bermeja in a 1540 guide for navigators.

Despite generations of surveyors having tried and failed to find the island, it was not until 2009 that the Mexican government conceded that Bermeja did not exist. It was removed from official maps and the country's maritime borders were redrawn. Some suggest the island may have been a real place destroyed by an earthquake, but no evidence has been found to support this claim.

AUG 9 — Takayuki Koike (JPN) rode the **fastest 100 miles on a unicycle** in 1987. He covered the distance in 6 hr 44 min at an athletics track in Kanagawa, Japan.

AUG 10 — In 2014, Duncan Forster and Phillip Weicker (both CAN) drove *Carpool DeVille* at 52.28 mph (84.14 km/h) in Utah, USA – making it the **fastest motorized hot tub**.

Most trains wrecked
Between 1896 and 1932, showman "Head-on" Joe Connolly (USA) organized the violent destruction of 146 locomotives at state fairs and circuses across the USA. Deliberate train-wrecking was a surprisingly common spectator event during this period. Thousands of people would pay to see two empty, firecracker-filled trains smash into each other at speed.

Greatest distance travelled by a runaway train
At 5 p.m. on 27 Mar 1884, a strong gust of wind set eight heavily loaded boxcars trundling east from a railway yard in Akron, Colorado, USA. The uncrewed train accelerated as the line descended on to the Great Plains, forcing trains to duck into sidings as it screeched past at more than 60 km/h (37 mph). Two railroad engineers gave chase in a locomotive, eventually bringing the runaway boxcars to a stop near Benkelman, Nebraska, at 7.30 p.m. – some 156 km (97 mi) from Akron.

First electric Christmas tree lights
In Dec 1882, three months after the completion of the **first commercial power station**, inventor Edward Johnson added some festive cheer to his house of electrical marvels on East 36th Street in New York City, USA. Johnson, who was vice president of the Edison Illuminating Company, was not content with a simple string of lights – the whole tree was mounted on an electrically powered rotating base, which also incorporated a switching mechanism that caused the lights to cycle between different patterns.

The tree was just one of the wonders that Johnson would show off to visiting journalists. Others included a fire-alarm system, a sewing machine and – as one newspaperman breathlessly reported – wall-mounted controls that allowed Johnson to turn the lights on and off at the flick of a switch!

First documented use of mouth-to-mouth resuscitation
James Blair collapsed while trying to escape a mine fire in Alloa, Clackmannanshire, UK, on 3 Dec 1732. He was dragged from the mine 45 min later, cold to the touch and apparently dead. Local doctor William Trossach immediately began expired-air resuscitation on Blair and, after a few minutes, the injured miner could once again breathe unaided. Blair went on to make a full recovery, which Trossach later described in the Edinburgh Society's *Medical Essays and Observations*. It is believed that Trossach was applying a technique that had been known to midwives for centuries, but never written down or attempted on adults.

Another unexpected early pioneer was American founding father and scientist Benjamin Franklin, who in 1749 revived the victim of an apparently fatal electric shock (a chicken) using mouth-to-beak respiration.

Widest skirts
In the 1750s, the women of the French royal court began wearing ever-larger pannier skirts as part of a style of dress known as the *grand habit*. The flat-fronted skirt of the *grand habit* was up to 2.1 m (7 ft) wide and designed to show off luxurious fabrics and ornate embroidery. These conspicuous displays of wealth and patronage were supported by woven cane-and-fabric undergarments.

Most expensive suit of armour
American entrepreneur Barry Trupin paid £1.9 m ($3 m) for this suit of armour in 1983. It was made in the 1540s by Milanese master craftsman Giovanni Negroli, and its original owner was Henri II of France. It would have served as a fashion statement and art piece rather than functional armour for combat.

AUG 11 On this day in 2014, Italian escapologist Danilo Audiello (aka "Alexis Arts") freed himself in 2.84 sec to claim the record for the **fastest escape from a straitjacket.**

AUG 12 A Nissan Qashqai suspended from a crane in Paris, France, set the **highest bungee jump by a car**, rebounding from a 65-m (213-ft) drop in 2024.

SNAPSHOT

Largest Octopus

It might weigh the same as a St Bernard dog, but the giant Pacific octopus is no substitute for a family pet. And even if you adopted one, you'd certainly need something bigger than a paddling pool to accommodate this shape-shifting ocean heavyweight.

The giant Pacific octopus (*Enteroctopus dofleini*) may look like a real-life sea monster, but it's more curious than it is fearsome. Living in the chilly waters of the North Pacific, the "GPO" is the world's **largest octopus species**. The biggest specimen to have been reliably measured sported an arm span of 4 m (13 ft 1 in) and weighed an impressive 71 kg (156 lb 8 oz).

For the record, they may grow even larger than this. A decomposing specimen – hauled in by fishermen off British Columbia, Canada, in 1956 – was estimated to span more than 9 m (30 ft) and weigh 272 kg (600 lb). Today, this case is regarded as an unreliable "legendary maximum", however.

Like all octopuses, the GPO is a world-class escape artist: it has no bones, so can squeeze through gaps with the diameter of a doughnut. Its skin can change colour and texture in the blink of an eye, and it's smart – able to solve puzzles, open jars and even recognize human faces.

Indeed, the octopus is a masterpiece of ocean engineering. Those eight flexible limbs are lined with hundreds of suckers, each capable of gripping, tasting and exploring the world. Every arm can move independently, controlled by a mini "brain" of its own, while a central brain coordinates the whole package. Add in three hearts – two pumping blood to the gills and one to the rest of the body – and blue, copper-rich blood that helps it survive in cold, low-oxygen waters, and you've got a creature perfectly adapted for deep-sea life. But *not* backyard paddling pools!

AUG 13 — In 2023, Manikkuttan G S (IND) embarked on the **longest car journey in a single country** – 69,207 km (43,003 mi) – from Thiruvananthapuram, Kerala, India.

AUG 14 — The **first images of Earth** were taken in orbit by NASA's *Explorer 6* satellite on this day in 1959. The very first picture released was of the crescent Earth.

Octopuses (aka octopodes, but *not* octopi!) don't have tentacles, only arms. Tentacles are long sucker-tipped limbs found on cuttlefish and squids.

AUG 15 Ben Affleck (USA, b. 15 Aug 1972) was aged 43 years 223 days when *Batman v Superman: Dawn of Justice* premiered in 2016, making him the **oldest Batman actor**.

AUG 16 TV motorhead James May (UK) and 300 volunteers built the **longest slot-car track** – 4.752 km (2.953 mi) – at Brooklands Museum in Surrey, UK, today in 2009.

ICON Hari Budha Magar

Hari Budha Magar (NPL) is no stranger to hardship. His birthplace was what he describes as a "cowshed" without electricity or running water, located in an isolated village in the shadow of the Himalayas. But sometimes a challenging start in life can breed a formidable resilience.

Hari's innate grit would help him flourish as a Gurkha – a Nepali British Army division known for its tough troops. In 2010, while on duty, he stepped on a hidden explosive; as a result, both his legs had to be amputated above the knee. The recovery process would test his fortitude more than ever, and Hari – now a long-time UK resident with his family – has bravely spoken about the mental-health struggles of his "darkest years".

He found a renewed sense of purpose from an idea that many initially dismissed as a pipe dream: Hari wanted to take on the world's biggest mountains (aka the Seven Summits). It took six-and-a-half years, a court battle against the Nepali government to overturn a law banning certain disabled people from scaling Everest, and not least the gruelling slog of climbing the highest peak on each continent. But when he topped the 4,892-m (16,050-ft) Mount Vinson in Antarctica (main image and inset) on 6 Jan 2026, Hari had achieved what he'd set out to do, becoming the **first double amputee to climb the Seven Summits (Mont Blanc)**. For those who know him, there was never any doubt he would see his mission through.

Hari grew up in the remote Nepali village of Mirul in Rolpa District. Here, he is pictured with his father, Purai, and two younger brothers, Padam and Nanda. It was not an easy upbringing, with the family living in a basic hut with very few amenities, but it would instil in Hari a hardy spirit that would go on to prove an invaluable asset.

Hari's father dreamed of one of his sons joining the British Army's esteemed Gurkha regiment. Hari achieved this by the age of 19, going on to serve for 15 years as a team medic, sniper and section commander across five continents (he's pictured here in Brunei). His days as a soldier came to an abrupt end in Afghanistan in 2010, where an improvised explosive device claimed both his legs.

Any record-breaking mountaineer will tell you that paramount to success is being prepared for all eventualities – and that means packing like a pro! On top of standard gear such as ropes, poles, energy snacks and warm clothing, Hari always takes three sets of prostheses, each suited to different stages of making an ascent.

It's not all about scaling mountains. Since recovering from his injuries, Hari has tried many other adventurous pursuits including skydiving, rock climbing, skiing and kayaking. He's also taken part in adaptive team sports such as wheelchair rugby and basketball. In his view, "No matter how challenging your disability, with the right mindset anything is possible."

VITAL STATISTICS

Name	Hari Budha Magar
Birthplace	Mirul, Rolpa, Nepal
Birth date	30 Jul 1979
Current GWR titles	Multiple, including **first double amputee to climb the Seven Summits**
Accolades (all in 2024)	MBE; Pride of Britain Special Recognition Award; Soldiering On "Inspiration" Award

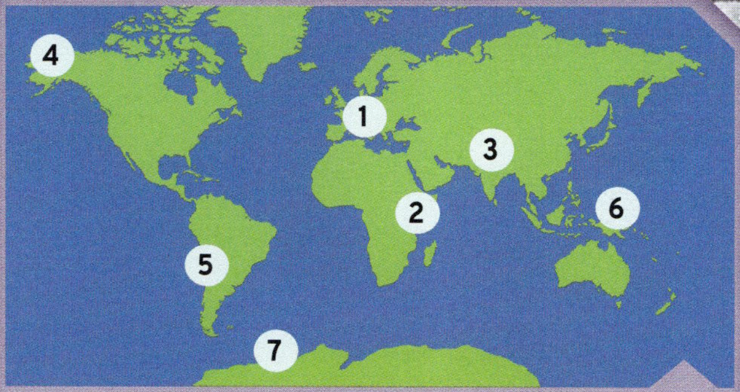

The Seven Summits challenge has several variants, depending on how continental borders are drawn. Hari opted, in order, for: Western Europe's highest peak, Mont Blanc (**1**); Kilimanjaro (Africa, **2**); Everest (Asia, **3**); Denali/McKinley (North America, **4**); Aconcagua (South America, **5**); Puncak Jaya (Oceania, **6**); and, finally, Vinson (Antarctica, **7**).

Discover all of GWR's incredible ICONS at **guinnessworldrecords.com/records/icons**

On 19 May 2023, aged 43, after more than a decade of planning, training and having to fight for the right just to make the attempt, Hari made history by becoming the **first double-above-knee amputee to climb Everest**. Not surprisingly, as a native of Nepal, where the world's **highest mountain** (known locally as Sagarmāthā, or "Goddess of the Sky") is highly venerated, the trailblazing alpinist received a hero's welcome on his triumphant return to the nation's capital, Kathmandu.

KIDS ZONE

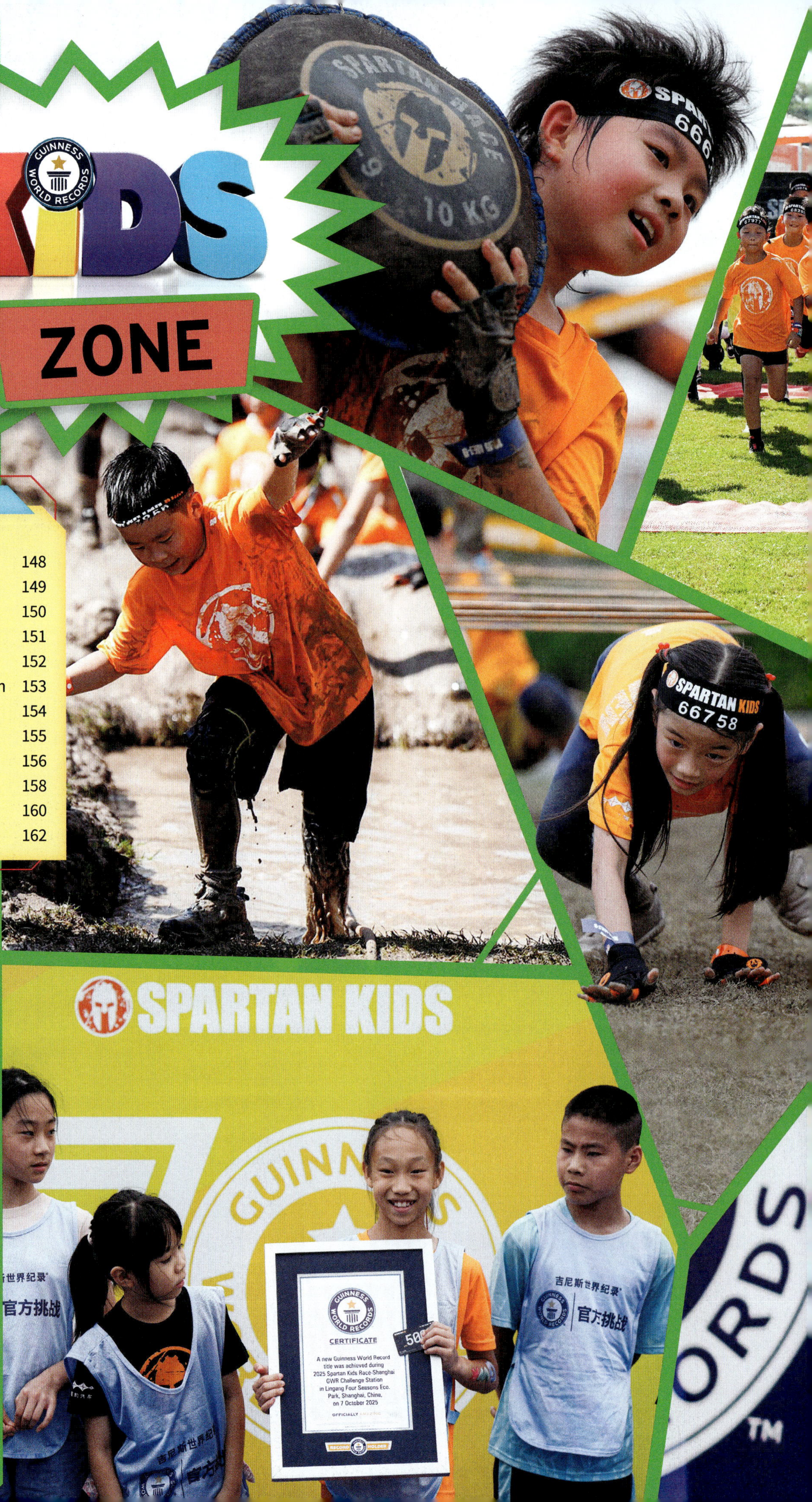

CONTENTS

Do you want to break a world record?
Now it's easier than ever to join the GWR family, thanks to our ever-expanding list of records exclusively for under-16s. Scan the QR code and discover your dream record on the GWR Kids site.

MOST FINISHERS IN A KIDS OBSTACLE RACE IN ONE WEEK

A total of 12,912 children crossed the finish line after wading through mud, swinging on monkey bars and negotiating a balance beam during the 2025 Spartan Kids Race. The annual challenge was held in both Beijing and Shanghai, China, between 1 and 7 Oct.

On the final day of the Shanghai event, three more records were set, all from our catalogue of under-16 titles. Eleven-year-old Hu Mai (CAN, above) achieved the **most burpees in 30 seconds** – 19 – while 10-year-old Wang Yiying (CHN; bottom left) took home two GWR certificates after recording the **fastest time to walk 50 m carrying a 5-kg weight** – 14.22 sec – and the **most star jumps in 30 seconds** – 62.

YOUNG ACHIEVERS Noah Williams

Many of us use computers without actually knowing how they work. Despite his tender age, Noah Williams (b. 5 Oct 2016) from Melbourne, Australia, is not among that number. The programming prodigy has always been interested in science, technology, engineering and mathematics (STEM), and by the age of six, he had learned the C++ language – a way of instructing devices what to do. Equipped with this complex skill, Noah began programming computers to help with mathematical calculations. At the age of 8 years 307 days, Noah became the **youngest computer programmer** after an independent firm published one of his programs for commercial use on 8 Aug 2025. The youngster is already at a professional level, and it's not just computers he's working on – he's also turned his hand to robots and drones!

When Noah isn't programming, he likes going for walks, playing piano and building LEGO® sets.

As of 2025, Noah had made between 10 and 15 computer programs, eight of which used C++ and Python codes.

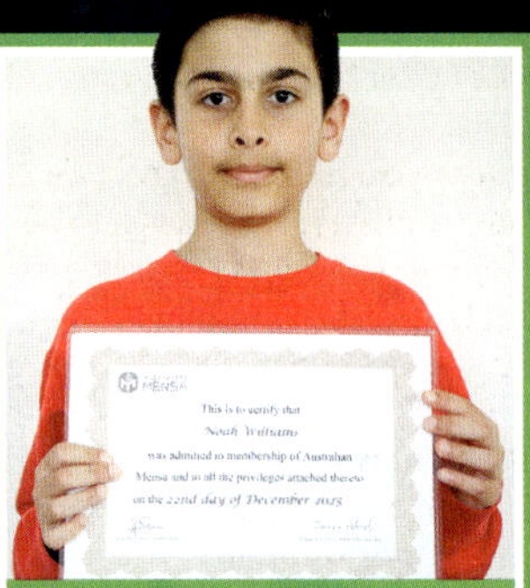

Aged seven, Noah joined the high IQ society, Mensa, after achieving an IQ score in the 99.9th percentile – placing him in the top 0.1% of the population.

What ignited your passion for STEM?
From a young age, I was interested in STEM and I bought lots of books to support my interest. I started with building shapes and circuits. Then I bought a micro:bit circuit kit so I could further enhance my programming skills. I just like how you get to explore and look forward to inventing something.

What do you enjoy most about programming computers?
You just need to learn the basics of coding and then the possibilities are endless! You can really let your imagination flow and get creative.

How did you celebrate after achieving your world record?
I had a really big party with my family.

What is your top tip for people wanting to learn how to program computers?
My number-one tip is to learn a programming language [e.g., C++, Python] and, when you get things wrong, keep trying and trying again until you fully debug [fix] the program.

What is your dream job?
I want to be a scientist and to go on the *International Space Station* [see pp.116–17].

Find out more about GWR's amazing younger record breakers and under-16 titles at **kids.guinnessworldrecords.com**

AUG 17 "Bathtubbing" is the sport of kayaking using a bath (with the plug in!). In 2013, Tony Bain (NZ) paddled the **fastest 100 m in a tub** in Cardiff, UK – 1 min 26.41 sec!

AUG 18 In 1982, "DC-2" became the **first robot to be arrested** after being used to distribute business cards illegally on North Beverly Drive in Los Angeles, California, USA.

YOUNG ACHIEVERS Kelia Mehani Gallina

Teahupo'o is regarded as one of the world's most dangerous surfing spots, but for Kelia Mehani Gallina (FRA, b. 10 Aug 2012), it is home and where she has learned the sport. Growing up in Tahiti, French Polynesia, summer is Kelia's favourite time of the year. Not only is that when her birthday falls, but it's also when pro surfers come to Teahupo'o to compete in the Tahiti Pro tournament. In Jul 2025, she took part in the Tahiti Pro Trials for the first time and, despite being the most junior entrant, she topped the podium. As a result, she was picked to be the women's wildcard for the main event, where she became the **youngest person to compete in the World Surf League Championship Tour** on 8 Aug 2025, aged 12 years 363 days. Nicknamed "Miss Teahupo'o", the surfing sensation placed ninth out of 12 female competitors.

Kelia spends five to six hours a day honing her surfing skills.

Ahead of the Paris 2024 Olympic Games, Kelia had the honour of carrying the prestigious Olympic torch through her home village of Teahupo'o, where the surfing events took place.

Do you remember surfing Teahupo'o for the first time?
My dad and his friend took me and my friend out to the reef and pushed me out into the small waves. I was four years old.

How do you feel when you're surfing?
I'm mostly happy because I'm usually with my friends. I get nervous sometimes when I'm in a heat/contest or when the waves are big at Teahupo'o, for example.

Have you had any significant injuries?
Yes, quite a few actually. I hit my face and my knee on the reef a few years ago. I just let them heal and then stretched to make them feel better.

Tell us about the moment you found out you had been named as the Tahiti Pro women's wildcard.
Well, I knew that was the prize after winning the Trials, but because I was under-age, I wasn't sure [if I'd get] in. But after a few days, we got an email saying that I [had]. I felt so happy and surprised.

How did it feel to compete in the Tahiti Pro event in the village you've grown up in?
It felt amazing, especially because it was in Teahupo'o, my home spot that I surf in every good-sized swell [a series of long, smooth waves].

What are your career goals?
I want to win the Tahiti Pro or win a world title – or both. I see myself on the World Championship Tour in 10 years' time.

Since the age of three, Kelia has been coached by her dad, Ryan, who is a keen surfer himself, hailing from Hawaii, USA.

AUG 19 Surveyed in 2009, the **largest garden gnome** stands 7.91 m (25 ft 11 in) tall. "Howard", built by Ron Hale (CAN), resides on a farm in British Columbia, Canada.

AUG 20 Josh Saunders pecked his partner Jenny Troy (both UK) on the cheek 146 times at GWR HQ in London, UK, in 2025 – the **most kisses by a pair in 30 seconds**.

Anvi Vishesh Agrawal

Everyone dreams of having a superpower, but Anvi Vishesh Agrawal (IND, b. 1 Oct 2019) thinks to unlock that power we need look no further than our own imaginations... The now six-year-old has proven that amazing things can happen as a result of being creative, such as achieving two GWR titles! On 11 Jun 2024, Anvi became the **youngest person to publish a bilingual book**, aged just 4 years 254 days. Her debut, *Little Girl's Big Emotions*, was written in both English and Spanish, and within the first week of publication over 1,160 copies were sold.

At the age of 5 years 96 days, the publishing prodigy demonstrated she had another power in her arsenal. By presenting at a public speaking event in Faridabad, Haryana, India, Anvi was recognized as the **youngest TEDx speaker (female)** on 5 Jan 2025.

Celebrating the release of her first book, *Little Girl's Big Emotions*, four-year-old Anvi hosted book-signing events at several popular bookstores in Delhi, India.

Anvi had never spoken on a large stage before her TEDx talk. Recalling how many people were in the audience, Anvi said: "A lot. Maybe 100? Enough to make me go 'Woah!' when I walked in."

Anvi enjoys painting, drawing and writing. These hobbies help her to process her emotions.

What inspired you to write *Little Girl's Big Emotions*?
Because my emotions were big – bigger than me! – sometimes I felt like a volcano. But then I learned emotions are okay and we just need to talk about them, instead of throwing toys out of the drawers. I made the book so other kids don't feel like aliens around their feelings. Instead, they can validate and express them in a calm way.

How did you decide on the topic for your TEDx talk?
I was sitting and thinking, "What do I have that nobody can take away?" And BOOM! My brain said "creativity".

When did you realize the importance of creativity?
During the COVID pandemic, my mum gave me finger paints and I made a huge mess on my feeding chair. But also a beautiful mess! Every time I felt happy, angry or bored, I'd just paint it out. My mum would say, "This is your superpower," and I'd reply, "Told ya."

How does it feel to be a two-time Guinness World Records title holder?
It feels like eating two ice creams at once – amazing and sweet! I'm super happy and now I want more world records.

What would you like to be when you're older?
A businesswoman! I want to make helpful things, sell them and then give some money to people who need it. I want to have my own office with slides and a spa.

If you were a superhero and you could have any superpower, what would it be?
To help everyone – even grumpy cats – because the world needs more helpers and I'd be the tiniest one with the biggest heart.

AUG 21 In 2024, soccer star Cristiano Ronaldo (PRT) uploaded his first YouTube video and set the record for the **most YouTube subscribers gained in 24 hours** – 19,729,827.

AUG 22 Built by Antony Edwards (UK), the **fastest lawnmower** reached a top speed of 230.446 km/h (143.193 mph) at Elvington Airfield in North Yorkshire, UK, in 2021.

YOUNG ACHIEVERS Bly Twomey

From the age of six, Bly Twomey (b. 27 Apr 2010) dreamed of representing Great Britain at the Paralympic Games. She may not have foreseen that it would happen quite so soon...

Bly was born with cerebral palsy, which restricts the movement in one side of her body, but she's never let it get in the way of her goals. Aged 11, she attended a holiday camp run by Brighton Table Tennis Club and instantly fell in love with the sport. Within six months, Bly was picked for the National Club League and, in 2022, she joined the British Para Table Tennis Development Squad. Fast-forwarding to 29 Aug 2024, the talented teen became the **youngest Paralympic table-tennis medallist** – aged 14 years 124 days – at the Paralympic Games in Paris, France. Playing in front of the biggest crowds of her career (including her family and 150 members of her club), she earned two bronze medals: one in singles and one in doubles (alongside Fliss Pickard). Considering Bly's skill and drive, these will surely be the first of many to come.

To commemorate Bly's success at the 2024 Paralympic Games, a sign at her local railway station in Brighton was temporarily modified to read "Welcome to Blyton".

Bly first met table-tennis world champion Will Bayley in 2021 after he returned from the Tokyo Paralympics with two silver medals. He is now her coach and mixed doubles partner.

Did you play many sports growing up?
I loved football, swimming, basketball, horse riding, dodgeball and tennis, but I gave most of them up once I discovered my love for table tennis. I realized this was the sport that was going to make my dreams come true.

Was there a key point when you realized that you could be a table-tennis pro?
When I had my first knock with Will Bayley (see right) after the Tokyo Paralympics in 2021, I smashed the ball past him and he was a bit shocked. He said I could be as good as him one day. That was a very memorable day for me.

How has this sport helped you develop as a person?
Table tennis has really helped me accept my disability and realize it's part of who I am and that it's okay to be different.

Tell us about the moment you found out you had been selected for Paris 2024.
I was sitting at the kitchen table and my mum told me and I started jumping up and down. I asked her how long till I'm playing and she said about six months. This felt like a lifetime, but I trained so hard and I was really proud to bring home two medals.

Of all the things you've done, which has been the most rewarding for you?
The best part about playing table tennis has been seeing all the different disabilities at the Paralympics as I never realized how many people there were like me.

What advice do you have for other kids?
Go out there and be the person you want to be. Everyone is born for a reason; now it's time for you to find yours.

Bly loves spending time with her identical twin sister, Ellis, when she's not competing or training.

Find out more about GWR's amazing younger record breakers and under-16 titles at **kids.guinnessworldrecords.com**

AUG 23 On this day in 2022, the world's **shortest dog** – Pearl – was measured in Orlando, Florida, USA, standing just 9.14 cm (3.59 in) tall from paw to shoulder.

AUG 24 The late US stuntman Ron Sarchian – nicknamed "World Record Ron" – achieved the **most tennis balls caught in one minute** (52) in California, USA, in 2018.

Max Alexander

Everyone wonders what they'll be when they grow up, but 10-year-old Max Alexander (USA, b. 25 Feb 2016) decided he couldn't wait until then to pursue his dream career. Aged four, Max announced to his parents that he was a "dressmaker" and sewed a frock for his sister. He began learning the basics of sewing from his mum, Sherri, and in 2021 he took up formal classes. In Nov 2023, Max showcased his first collection at Denver Fashion Week in Colorado, USA, making him the **youngest runway show designer**, aged just 7 years 266 days.

Since then, Max has grown his online store, selling everything from kaftans and charms to pyjamas and puffers. He's even created custom garments for celebrities, designed his own jewellery and gained over 13 million fans across his social-media platforms.

Reflecting on what it means to be the **youngest runway show designer**, Max told GWR: "It means a lot to me and [setting this title] really encouraged me to keep following my dreams."

What drives your approach to fashion?
Showing people how beautiful deadstock materials can become instead of going into landfill. It's better for our environment.

How involved are you in choosing the models and their looks?
The production companies provide the models, and I am as involved in hair and make-up as they will let me. It's important that [their looks] go with my dresses. I like the hair up so you can see the clothes.

Who are your biggest supporters?
My mum and Fern Mallis who is my "fashion godmother". She developed New York Fashion Week as we know it today.

Tell us about your Grounds for Change line, which earned you the bronze IDA Design Award in Women's Haute Couture.
My Uncle Eddy sent me some coffee-bean bags from his company Groundwork Coffee and I thought, "Ooh, I could make something out of this!" I want to encourage people to use recycled materials.

What does a day in your life look like?
I sometimes do sewing in the morning, then once I've finished school, I do sewing again.

What are your favourite colours and fabrics?
Burgundy, gold and butter yellow. Italian silk, chiffon, organza and anything floofy!

What are your career goals?
I want to be a designer, a restaurant owner, a chef, a car-wash owner and an engineer. I want to be the male Barbie with 250 different careers and an outfit for each one.

Max loves to give materials a new lease of life, as proven by his dress made entirely from ties (right).

Aged 10 years 6 days, Max ticked another career goal off the list as the **youngest runway show designer at Paris Fashion Week on 3 Mar 2026.**

The talented 10-year-old takes inspiration from "everything, everywhere", especially on holidays and beach trips!

Find out more about GWR's amazing younger record breakers and under-16 titles at **kids.guinnessworldrecords.com**

AUG 25 — Bryce Menzies (USA) made the **longest pickup-truck ramp jump** in New Mexico, USA, in 2016: 115.64 m (379 ft 4 in) – longer than an American football field!

AUG 26 — On this day in 2013, Silvio Sabba (ITA) claimed the **most dice stacked on the back of the hand in 30 seconds** – 23 – in Strumica, North Macedonia.

Carmela Chillery-Watson

When we think of female superheroes, fictional comic-book characters spring to mind. However, there's a real-life hero who's even more unstoppable: Carmela Chillery-Watson MBE (UK, b. 27 Mar 2014). When Carmela was four years old, she was diagnosed with a rare progressive muscle-wasting condition called LMNA-related congenital muscular dystrophy (L-CMD). But this only fuelled her inner fire to increase awareness of her disability. To date, she has raised a staggering £500,000 ($670,000) for Muscular Dystrophy UK, which funds research and supports around 110,000 people living with the condition. Her remarkable fundraising efforts saw her become the **youngest recipient of an MBE** (Member of the Most Excellent Order of the British Empire), aged 11 years 78 days on 13 Jun 2025.

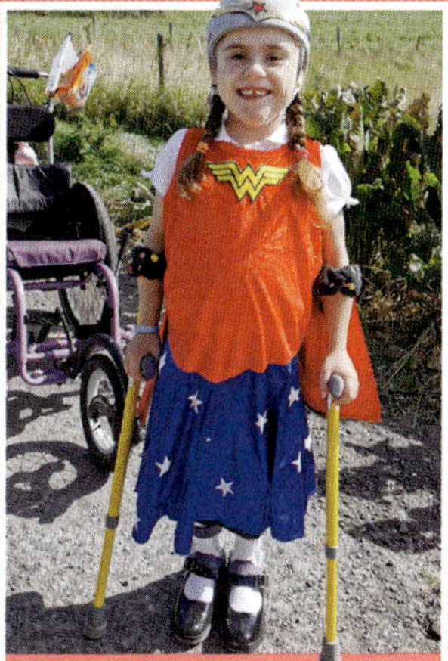

In 2020, six-year-old Carmela dressed up as Wonder Woman and trekked more than 300 km (186 mi) in 30 days. She covered c. 10 km (6 mi) per day, walking the first mile and completing the remainder in her wheelchair.

What was it like receiving the letter from King Charles that declared you had been awarded an MBE?
It was absolutely incredible. I was staring at it in shock, and knowing it [was] from royalty [took it to] another level.

How does it feel to set a GWR title?
Just wow! I was so excited to see Guinness World Records contact us. I was jumping up and down with joy!

Tell us about your day at Windsor Castle receiving your MBE medal.
I was nervous at first, but seeing the castle was so outstanding I forgot I was nervous. Then, I met Prince William and he was so nice to talk to. Inside the castle was so, so beautiful.

What do you remember about your Wonder Woman walk (see opposite)?
I found the challenge difficult, but I was so determined to help others I wanted to complete it.

Which has been your favourite fundraising project so far?
My Jurassic Coast walk because we got to see all the beautiful scenery [in Dorset, UK] since we just moved there.

What helps your condition the most?
Hydrotherapy, physiotherapy and gentle exercise.

What would be your dream job?
I have always loved art and I want to be a graphic designer.

What advice would you give to other kids living with illnesses and disabilities?
Don't focus on the bad things. Think of what you can do and live your life to the fullest.

Strutting down a catwalk had always been a dream of Carmela's, and in 2023 she made it happen at Bristol Fashion Week.

On 10 Dec 2025, William, Prince of Wales, presented Carmela with her MBE medal at Windsor Castle in Berkshire, UK.

AUG 27 A resounding 1,077 hooters were honked in unison to achieve the **largest car-horn ensemble** in 2023, by Ford Everest Club Philippines and Motul (both PHL).

AUG 28 In 2015, ReTuna Återbruksgalleria in Sweden opened its doors as the **first shopping mall for recycled goods**, selling everything from bikes to building materials.

Phoenix Giselle Hicks

Most of us learn about mindfulness later in life, but Phoenix Giselle Hicks (USA, b. 20 Jul 2019) mastered it early and is already sharing her wisdom with the world. When Phoenix was three months old, she went to her first yoga class with her mom, Sydney. By the age of four, she could keep up with the more advanced sessions at her mom's studio, and soon after they began teaching as a duo. Determined to become certified, the young *yogi* enrolled in training, and on 22 Jun 2025 she became the **youngest yoga instructor**, aged 5 years 337 days. She leads classes for all ages in Houston, Texas, USA.

When Phoenix isn't teaching, she's busy learning everything from business and ballet to science and piano. No matter what the task may be, Phoenix always rises to the challenge and flourishes with confidence, persistence and grace.

To become a yoga teacher, Phoenix had to complete 200 hr of training. This involved reading books, learning about anatomy, taking daily classes, doing teaching practice and attending a 10-day retreat.

How does it feel to teach classes alongside your mom?
I love teaching classes with my mom. She inspired me to be a yoga teacher, so it's fun when we get to teach together.

How do you prepare for your classes?
I start by practising my flow before class, then I do breathwork to make sure I'm calm and my energy is balanced.

What is it like leading a class?
When I'm teaching yoga, I feel honoured and proud that people allow me to lead them. It inspires me to see my community grow, be calm and find relaxation. I love helping people learn how to move their bodies mindfully.

What's your favourite yoga pose?
The tree pose, because it's fun to practise balancing and it can be a little tricky. I always remind my students that it's okay if you wobble or fall, just try your best.

Who is your biggest inspiration?
My mom, because she teaches me, supports me and encourages me to follow my dreams. She inspires me to be a leader and believe in myself.

What is one mindfulness tip you would give to other kids?
To take deep breaths when you feel upset, sad or angry. Just pause, breathe in slowly through your nose and breathe out through your mouth a few times. It helps your body relax and your mind feel calm. You can do it anywhere and anytime.

Where would you like to be in 10 years?
I'd like to be learning and preparing to become an astronaut. Beyond yoga, I have a big passion for STEM and love learning about planets and outer space.

Phoenix guided 11 children through a 30-min yoga lesson and gave an exclusive read-through of her book (right) at GWR HQ in London, UK, in Feb 2026.

In 2026, Phoenix published her first book, *Breathe*, which teaches kids how intentional breathing can help them to feel calm, safe and happy.

AUG 29 In 1965, Scott Carpenter made the **first phone call from the ocean floor to space** – checking in with the crew of the Gemini V spacecraft (all USA) from SEALAB II.

AUG 30 On this day in 2011, Japanese comedian Tomidokoro gave out his 50,361st embrace in Tokyo, Japan, to clutch the title for the **most hugs given in one month**.

YOUNG ACHIEVERS Jude Owens

When a child tries out one of their parents' hobbies, it's never guaranteed that they'll take to it. But for the UK's Jude Owens (b. 14 Dec 2022) and snooker, it turned out to be a match made in heaven.

At the age of two, Jude started playing miniature snooker, and within a year he'd progressed to full-sized tables – or "big snooks", as he calls it – and potted two GWR titles! Aged 2 years 261 days, he became the **youngest person to make a double pot** in Manchester, UK, on 1 Sep 2025. This is when two balls land in different pockets after a single strike of the cue (white) ball. By 12 Oct, he was the **youngest person to make a bank shot**, aged 2 years 302 days. For this, Jude hit a coloured ball off one of the table's cushions before it entered a pocket. With a sponsorship deal signed and recognition from snooker stars like Jimmy White, Jude is well on track to make his big break.

For now, Jude might need to climb on the snooker table to make some shots, but when we asked the talented toddler who would win a match between him and his dad, he still confidently replied: "Me!"

Q&A with Jude's dad, Luke Owens.

When did you notice that Jude had real talent?
I think I realized once he put the cue through his fingers and it was dead natural the way he did it. Also, when I uploaded a few videos to social media, I had some big outlets reaching out to us to use the content.

Do you have a background in snooker?
I'd like to think the talent is in the genes, but obviously Jude started a lot younger than me. I started playing when I was 10, and Jude started playing when he was two. I'd say Jude's got a lot more natural ability than myself.

Does he beat you at snooker?
He doesn't beat me at the moment, but I'd like to think that he would in the next few years easily.

How does Jude manage to play on regular-sized snooker tables?
At first, it was really difficult. We had to use stools from anywhere that we went, but we ended up sourcing a stool, which was mainly used for cooking, [and started] using it for [his] snooker shots.

Do you think he'll be a world champion?
As a father, you'd always hope that your kids do well in life, so that would be the biggest aspiration if he was to achieve that. It would be a great story.

Besides snooker, Jude enjoys watching *Octonauts*, supporting Manchester United and spending time with his family.

Jude was given star treatment with his very own walkout into the arena at the 2025 UK Championship, staged in York.

Find out more about GWR's amazing younger record breakers and under-16 titles at **kids.guinnessworldrecords.com**

AUG 31 In 2025, Nicola Smith (UK) topped six sponge cakes with buttercream, sprinkles and cherries in 52.01 sec – the **fastest time to decorate six cupcakes (under-16s)**.

SEP 1 In 2004, Striker the border collie clocked the **fastest time to open a car window by a dog** after training from his owner Francis V Gadassi (HUN) in Canada: 11.34 sec.

Kids Invent Stuff

Ruth Amos (UK), one of the engineering geniuses behind YouTube's "Kids Invent Stuff", is known for bringing her followers' ideas to life. After hosting a contest to find their next record-breaking contraption, they created the world's **largest hairdryer**, which measured 1.755 m long and 1.6 m tall (5 ft 9 in x 5 ft 3 in) on 22 Apr 2026.

The concept
Kiki (below right) suggested making the world's ***largest hairdryer*** *– one with enough force to topple over a chair!*

Thea (above) had the same idea and proposed that it could double up as a large leafblower.

BUILDING WITH THE BOSS
Ruth Amos gives us an insight into the competition, which sparked over 5,000 ideas and was supported by the engineering firm Accu and the Royal Commission for the Exhibition of 1851.

What were the biggest challenges you faced?
The hairdryer's size and weight. We moved it around on an engine hoist, but as it got bigger and heavier, it was really tricky to manoeuvre. [Ed: the hairdryer weighs roughly 80 kg (176 lb).]

How does this invention compare to the largest electric toothbrush?
The toothbrush is big and heavy, but the hairdryer is worse! It takes four people to lift and move it.

Why did the largest hairdryer win out over other entries?
It was such a fun invention idea. Thea and Kiki really thought about the invention brief and we loved the challenge of building something so big that was also functional.

What were some of the other most memorable entries?
There were so many amazing ideas! A giant lion that shoots out chicken nuggets, a banana car, a giant umbrella and the world's longest car.

SEP 2 — In 2024, multiple record holder Chinmay Sharma (IND) achieved the **fastest time to tie a martial-arts belt**, preparing himself for combat in just 4.33 sec.

SEP 3 — On this day in 2017, stunt driver Naji Bou Hassan (LBN) buckled up and performed five 360° spins in Lebanon – the **most simultaneous car donuts by the same driver**.

THE BUILD

To form the shape of the hairdryer, the team used metal ventilation ducts (with an industrial fan inside) and aluminium straps.

Once the core structure was in place, they filled the gaps with 14 cans of expanding foam and 12 litres (3.1 US gal) of car body-filler.

With the filler set, layers of resin and fibreglass matting were added. They then sanded the exterior, ready for painting.

BLOWN AWAY

Standing in the "Kids Invent Stuff" workshop in Sheffield, South Yorkshire, UK, Ruth proudly shows off her GWR certificate and her fully functional behemoth blowdryer, now painted and with all the finishing touches in place.

RUTH ALWAYS BREAKS RECORDS ON A GRAND SCALE. SHE HAS PREVIOUSLY MADE THE LARGEST ELECTRIC TOOTHBRUSH (2 M; 6 FT 7 IN) AND THE TALLEST 3D-PRINTED PLASTIC-BRICK CHRISTMAS TREE (1.81 M; 5 FT 11 IN).

SEP 4 — In 2022, Rohollah Doshmanziari (IRN) carefully piled up the **tallest stack of watermelons**, balancing four of the large fruits in a tower in Kazeroun, Iran.

SEP 5 — Self-taught acrobat Raymond Butler (USA) executed the **longest backwards somersault into a pair of trousers** – 2.59 m (8 ft 6 in), the length of a large sofa – in 2016.

KIDS School Together

FROM PAGES TO STAGES
"MC Grammar" (above) fell in love with books as a child and now he's sharing his passion with the next generation.

Which books did you enjoy most as a child?
I loved picture books. My favourite was *Where the Wild Things Are* by Maurice Sendak.

What do you love most about reading?
Think: just by opening a book you can learn anything and travel anywhere. Space, up a beanstalk, down into the deepest ocean, or into a world created purely by magic and imagination. You can also become anyone and anything. Whoever, whatever, wherever, whenever!

What did this record attempt mean to you?
Everything! My mission is to get young people reading and rapping. And that is exactly what we did. A jam-packed theatre full of good vibes and epic energy celebrating the magic and wonder of books and reading.

Any tips for someone thinking of "rap-reading"?
Choose a book you enjoy reading or exploring; then find a beat that gets you moving. There's no right way to rap a book. Just have fun and do it your way. You got this!

Largest air-drum ensemble
A total of 2,458 pupils and teachers banged imaginary drums in Bradford, West Yorkshire, UK, on 11 Nov 2025. That same day, 2,558 participants clapped, snapped, patted and stamped for the **largest body-percussion lesson**. The record attempts were part of the Bradford Schools Extravaganza, marking Bradford's designation as the UK City of Culture for 2025, and were organized by Bradford Music & Arts Service and the BBC Radio Leeds choir "Bantam of the Opera".

Largest creative-writing lesson
Once upon a time on 23 Jan 2026, Alif International School (SAU) brought together 378 students to study the art of creative composition in Riyadh, Saudi Arabia. The seven- to 14-year-olds were taught by qualified instructor Khaled Almaeena. The first half of the session focused on imagination, storytelling and creative expression, after which the pupils each penned a story of their own. The end.

Most floor-volleyball serves in three minutes (team)
Floor volleyball is a more inclusive seated version of the ball-and-net sport. On 4 Oct 2025, a six-person team from the Tottori School for the Visually Impaired (JPN) completed 46 successful serves in Japan. The attempt took part on the pupils' sports day and was partly organized in order to promote greater understanding about education for the visually impaired among the local community.

Largest rap lesson
On 2 Mar 2026, "MC Grammar" (aka Jacob Mitchell, UK) taught 859 people how to rap at the New Wimbledon Theatre in London, UK, for Wimbledon BookFest. Pupils and staff from 18 schools across the city learned how to choose a rapper name, write lyrics, rhyme to music and stay on beat during the 30-minute tutorial.

Most peppers on a single plant
Jason Loris (USA) grew a Carolina reaper chilli plant bearing 893 fruits on his farm in Amissville, Virginia, USA. On 17 Oct 2025, it was taken to the nearby Rappahannock County Elementary School in Washington, where the peppers were (carefully!) picked and counted by seventh-grade students for their farm-to-table class. They wore gloves, as this super-spicy variety was formerly the **hottest chilli pepper**.

Most people to sign up online for a beach clean-up in one hour
On 15 Sep 2025, Beach Heroes with Yaizuchuo High School (JPN) registered 1,680 eco-minded recruits, who committed to clear litter from local coastlines within two months. Respondents to the callout from the school – which is based in Shizuoka – came both from Japan and abroad.

Largest poetry lesson
The city of Nice in France assembled 525 students to study verse on 22 May 2025. Led by poet Sabine Venaruzzo, the outdoor lesson was held at the scenic Colline du Château, overlooking the Mediterranean Sea. Participants explored the idea of the ocean as a theme and a metaphor in poetry.

Most people solving rotating puzzle cubes simultaneously
On 9 Nov 2025, Guru Nanak Public School (IND) brought 5,434 people together to unscramble puzzle cubes in Bidar, Karnataka, India. The record attempt – which surpassed the previous mark of 3,997, also set by schoolchildren – was part of the institution's 50th anniversary celebrations.

Most people ice sledging simultaneously
On 11 Jan 2026, a group of 1,000 schoolkids propelled themselves across a frozen lake in Tieli, Heilongjiang, China, during their winter vacation. The mass ice-sledge was arranged by Heilongjiang Xiaoyao Baxian Lake Scenic Area Management (CHN) and took place in freezing conditions of -35°C (-31°F)!

SEP 6 — On this day in 2008, Slovakia beat Bulgaria by an emphatic 82–0 to register the **highest score in an international ice-hockey match** in Liepāja, Latvia.

SEP 7 — ERA TV's Channel 7 (KAZ) sponsored the **largest serving of doughnuts** – 856 kg (1,887 lb 2 oz) of traditional square *baursaks* – in Almaty, Kazakhstan, in 2014.

CLASS ACTS: SUPERLATIVE SCHOOL WORK

Record title	Total	Record holder(s)
1. **Largest human image of a submarine**	800 people	Elizabeth Public Schools and City of Elizabeth New Jersey (both USA)
2. **Largest game of "follow the leader"**	2,348 people	Logan-Rogersville School District (USA)
3. **Longest friendship bracelet**	852.19 m (2,795 ft 10 in)	Valley Creek Elementary School (USA)
4. **Most people performing a nursery rhyme in sign language**	242 people	Heathlands School for Deaf Children (UK)
5. **Most people doing scientific experiments simultaneously**	5,035 people	PACE Group (UAE)

Correct as of 10 Apr 2026

SEP 8 — The **first circumnavigation** was completed on this day in 1522 when the ship *Vittoria*, commanded by Juan Sebastián de Elcano (ESP), reached Seville, Spain.

SEP 9 — In 1963, a male bear named Ming-Ming (meaning "Bright") became the **first giant panda born in captivity**, at Beijing Zoo in China.

KIDS Quiz & Puzzles

Find all the answers on p.237

Emoji codebreakers
Since emojis were invented in 1999 by Japanese designer Shigetaka Kurita, they have gone on to be used around 10 billion times per day! Emojis often help us to express emotions, but in this game they depict five GWR titles. Can you guess them? Hint: all the record holders are green!

1
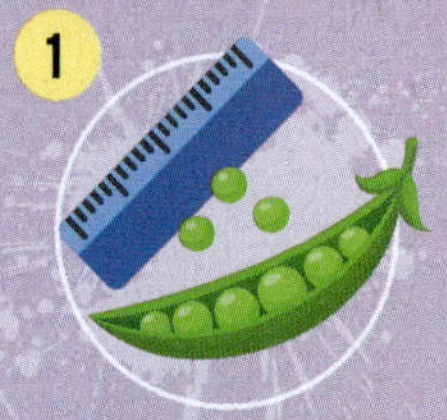

2

3

4

5

Scan here for more quizzes
See yourself as a GWR genius? Put your knowledge to the test on everything from dancing dogs to prehistoric poop on the GWR Kids website.

1. The **greatest distance to blow a pea** was recorded by David Rush (USA) on 8 Oct 2022. Was it longer or shorter than a bowling lane?
A) Longer B) Shorter

2. The **highest-grossing Christmas movie at the global box office** is *Dr. Seuss' The Grinch* (USA, 2018), which had earned $514,602,427 (£385 m) by 13 Oct 2025. In which fictional village is the animated film set?
A) Whoville
B) Thneedville
C) Grinchville

3. The **fastest time to identify all national flags** is 2 min 55 sec, set by Adam Saeed (BHR) on 5 Aug 2023. Which of these countries has green in its flag?
A) India B) Argentina C) Denmark

4. Cola (CHN) set the **most tricks performed by a parrot in one minute** (21) on 27 Jun 2025. Which of these tricks did Cola *not* perform?
A) Pushing a mini trolley
B) Front-flipping on to a deckchair
C) Skating on a fingerboard

5. TRUE OR FALSE?
Uranus – the **first planet discovered by telescope** – is also known as the "green planet" because its atmosphere consists largely of methane – the same gas that's found in farts!

6. The **best-selling videogame** is *Minecraft*. What are these green mobs called?
A) Enders B) Creepers C) Miners

7. Ashrita Furman (USA) has held the GWR title for the **fastest time to peel and eat a kiwi fruit** since 10 Dec 2008. Did he complete this fuzzy feat in under six seconds?
A) Yes B) No

8. The **most people dressed as Peter Pan** – 534 – was achieved by CRUK Relay for Life Kirriemuir (UK) on 12 Aug 2017. What is Peter Pan's fairy companion called?
A) Silvermist B) Flora C) Tinker Bell

9. Mario is the **best-selling videogame character**. *Wahoo!* What is his brother called?
A) Luigi B) Lucio C) Link

10. TRUE OR FALSE?
Bamboo – the **fastest-growing plant** – can shoot up the equivalent height of a toddler in a single day.

SEP 10 Operational since 2008, the Large Hadron Collider was designed to mirror conditions after the Big Bang. The 27-km (16.7-mi) ring is the **largest scientific instrument**.

SEP 11 In 2013, a space rock of around 400 kg (880 lb) struck the Moon, releasing the equivalent of some 15 tonnes (33,000 lb) of TNT – the **largest recorded lunar impact**.

Spot the difference
It's behind you! The **largest walking robot** – measuring 15.7 m (51 ft 6 in) long and 8.2 m (26 ft 10 in) tall – was unleashed by creators Zollner Elektronik (DEU) at a festival in Zandt, Germany, in 2012. Can you identify five differences between these photos of "Fanny" the fire-breathing dragon?

Merch search
This picture is brimming with artefacts from the **largest collection of *The Legend of Zelda* memorabilia** (see pp.78–79), alongside their owner, Constantine Adams. Can you find these six objects?

SEP 12 In 1998, Alfred A E Wolfram (USA) bestowed the **most kisses in eight hours**, pecking 11,030 people on the cheek at the Minnesota Renaissance Festival, USA.

SEP 13 On this day in 2009, a group of 1,503 high-kickers came together in Glasgow, UK, for the **largest can-can dance**, in an event organized by IRN-BRU.

Youngest videogame developer (male)
Max Baker (UK, b. 31 May 2014) was 10 years 357 days old when he made his five-level platformer, *Gravity Parkour 2.0*, in Penarth, UK, on 23 May 2025. He was inspired to set this record after reading about the **youngest female videogame developer**, Simar Khurana (CAN), in *GWR 2025*!

How did you find out your record had been approved?
My family brought my laptop into the kitchen and said I got an email. I opened up my emails, and immediately I saw one saying my attempt had been accepted! I started jumping up and down, and my little brother Clark did laps around the house.

How did you celebrate?
We had a nice dinner and I had fizzy grape juice in a fancy wine glass.

What do you enjoy most about making videogames?
I enjoy how you can dream up a game and bring your idea to life!

What is the biggest challenge you face when coding?
I find demotivation quite a challenge. Sometimes, there's a really hard problem and I can't find a way to solve it, so I get frustrated. Taking a break always helps though.

Join the GWR family!
We want to see your skills, so scan the QR code and explore our ever-growing range of records for kids.

Youngest music producer
Victoria Isaac (IND, b. 22 Apr 2017) was aged 8 years 160 days when her debut album, *Musically Fantastic*, was released in Chennai, India, on 29 Sep 2025. The multi-instrumentalist has already found her niche, which she calls "skate-dance music" – i.e., playing the violin while simultaneously dancing on roller-skates!

Youngest individually credited Grammy winner
Aura Valentina Simmons, aka Aura V (USA, b. 5 Jul 2017), was only 8 years 211 days old when she co-won Best Children's Music Album for *Harmony* (2025) at the 68th Grammy Awards in Los Angeles, California, USA, on 1 Feb 2026. The record was a joint project with her father, FYÜTCH (b. Harold Simmons II; formerly known as Future the Artist).

Aura surpassed the previous mark of 9 years 66 days, which was set by Blue Ivy Carter – the daughter of record-breaking musicians Beyoncé and Jay-Z – in 2021.

Longest time to balance a spoon on the nose
Matilda Brown (UK/AUS) kept a level head – and a spoon on her nose – for 59 min 56.60 sec in Eastbourne, East Sussex, UK, on 23 Aug 2025. Supported by her family and spectators at The Saffrons Sports Club, the nine-year-old told GWR: "It was so exciting to do it with so many people cheering me on. I felt really proud of myself for giving it my very best."

Most viewed YouTube Shorts video
A compilation of mind-boggling trick shots and challenges posted by "Colin Amazing" on 17 Dec 2024 had been watched 4.6 billion times as of 10 Mar 2026. The stars of the channel are brothers Colin and Owen End (both USA), who hail from a wider clan of sibling YouTubers known as the "That's Amazing" family, from Whitefish Bay, Wisconsin, USA.

Most wheels on a skateboard
Brothers Philip and Magnus Schmidt-Höck, helped by their father Jesper (all DNK), assembled a stretched-out skateboard with 60 wheels in Augustenborg, Denmark, on 26 Jul 2025. After sourcing the equipment from specialist companies, the trio spent a weekend building the board and testing it out on their street.

Youngest FIDE-rated chess player
On 2 Nov 2024, the International Chess Federation (FIDE) assigned Anish Sarkar (IND, b. 26 Jan 2021) a classical rating of 1555. The child prodigy was 3 years 281 days old when he placed 24th of 140 in an under-nines tournament. He is pictured above with Norwegian chess megastar Magnus Carlsen.

Fastest time to type the first 500 decimal places of Pi from memory on a tablet computer
Fan Yuchen (CHN) relayed 500 numbers in just 2 min 7.46 sec in Chengdu, Sichuan, China, on 23 Nov 2025. The sixth-grade student started memorizing the digits four months earlier.

UNDER-16 TITLES

Most star jumps in one minute
Seven-year-old Jordan Meyer (ZAF) jumped for joy after achieving 118 jumping jacks in Hermanus, South Africa, on 23 Mar 2026. That's almost two every second!

Most baseball caps placed on the head in 30 seconds
Daiki Motojima (JPN) sported a sky-high stack of 34 hats in Tokyo, Japan, on 29 Aug 2025. At the same event, which was organized by the Foundation for Promoting Sound Growth of Children, three other youngsters also gained GWR glory: Bunshiro Koyama (JPN) achieved the **most clothes pegs scooped into a pot using two turners in 30 seconds** (855), while Hieu Dang Minh and Tu Dao Ngoc (both VNM) racked up the **most seated balloon passes in 30 seconds**: 215.

SEP 14 — Brandi Carbee and Natalie Svenvold (both USA) ended the **longest seesaw marathon** after 75 hr 10 min – more than three days! – in Washington, USA, in 2004.

SEP 15 — In 2007, Luo Jun (CHN) from the Zunyi Acrobatic Troupe nimbly negotiated the **tallest stack of chairs balanced on** – 11 – on a GWR TV show in Beijing, China.

Youngest person to land a BMX backflip
On 10 Oct 2025, aged just 5 years 313 days, Tsumugi Tamura (JPN, b. 1 Dec 2019) coolly somersaulted on his bike in Ama, Aichi, Japan. Two months later on 11 Dec, he also became the **youngest person to land a BMX flair** (comprising a backflip and a 180° mid-air turn), at the age of 6 years 10 days. It's Tsumugi's hope that his superlative biking skills will inspire more kids to pursue their dreams, no matter what age they are.

Most kick-scooter flairs in one minute
On 29–30 Aug 2025, two German youngsters showcased their striking skills on the set of *Guinness World Records – Die große Show der Weltrekorde* in Munich. Tom Buxbaum (above) executed 20 flairs (a backflip and a 180° turn in the air), while Orell Herzog (inset) achieved the **most bottle caps unscrewed with a kick in one minute** – 56.

Fastest three GWR "FREESTYLE5" football tricks
Benjamin Taylor (UK) dreams of becoming a pro freestyle footballer, and at 11 he's already got the ball rolling. On 22 Jan 2026, he aced a trio of trick combos in just 6.3 sec in Penarth, Vale of Glamorgan, Wales, UK. Benjamin improved on his own record – 8.55 sec – set in 2025. The skilful sequence, dubbed the "FREESTYLE5" and launched in the debut *GWR Football Edition*, involves bouncing the ball on the ground, touching it with each foot, catching it between the knees, then the ankles, before jumping and catching the ball in the hands.

Most aquatic species identified in one minute
Wildlife-loving six-year-old Dhruva Shankar (USA) correctly named 41 creatures native to watery habitats – from squids to sardines – when he was shown randomized photos in Fremont, California, USA, on 8 Feb 2026.

Most sunflowers picked in the *Minecraft* Sunflower Field in one minute
Using an Xbox controller, nine-year-old *Minecraft* megafan Arya Umar (AUS) plucked 99 virtual sunflowers in-game in Melbourne, Victoria, Australia, on 14 May 2025.

Fastest time to build a 10-toilet-roll pyramid
On 25 Jan 2026, Holden Tinsley (CAN) piled up 10 loo rolls in 5.47 sec in Burlington, Ontario, Canada. The 12-year-old had always dreamed of breaking a world record when reading his *GWR* books and spent four weeks honing his stacking skills.

Fastest time to arrange a chess set
On 18 Jul 2025, M D Junaid Hossain Siam (BGD) positioned the pieces ready for gameplay in 34.58 sec in Cumilla, Bangladesh. His time is less than four seconds off the **blindfolded** adult version of this title (see p.66).

Pro hooper Amazi (right, with GWR Editor-in-Chief Craig Glenday) holds the title for **most hula-hoops spun while on stilts** – see p.90.

Most hula-hoop rotations while standing on one leg in 30 seconds (under-16s)
On 11 Nov 2025, GWR and Read Manchester teamed up to host a fun session with record-breaking hooper Amazi, aka Mariam Olayiwola (above), at Wythenshawe Forum Library in Manchester, UK. Skye Shakespeare (inset) became the first holder of this title with a total of 13 spins, although, later in the day, her mark was beaten by nine-year-old Phoebe McCarthy (above, all UK), who raised the bar to 29.

SEP 16 At the last official count in 2013, the **largest collection of stickers** totalled 102,317, all acquired by Nidhi Bansal from Bassi Pathana, Punjab, India.

SEP 17 In 2024, Tim Maw and Neil Laughton (both UK) had a chess match 6,216 m (20,393 ft) up a mountain in Nepal – the **highest altitude playing a boardgame**.

Largest Land Vehicle

Imagine the chaos you'd cause if you took the world's biggest digger for a joyride! The 14,000-tonne (15,400-ton) Bagger 293 bucket-wheel excavator – a driveable earth-moving machine longer than a city block – is one vehicle that you definitely don't want to get stuck behind on your daily commute!

The traffic report would sound very different if the Bagger 293 ever joined the morning rush hour. This monster isn't just the **largest mobile industrial machine** – it's the **largest** and **heaviest land vehicle** on Earth. And yes, it's fully driveable, by just one operator.

Constructed by TAKRAF (DEU), the Bagger is a mine excavator that stands 94.5 m (310 ft) at its tallest, and extends to a length of 220 m (722 ft). Crucially – especially when contemplating a shortcut across a concrete flyover – it weighs an incredible 14,196 tonnes (31.3 million lb). That's heavier than 130 blue whales or more than 170 fully loaded Boeing 737s.

The largest among the Bagger fleet, the 293 was built to shift 240,000 m³ (8.4 million cu ft) of earth per day from an open-cast coal mine in northern Germany. That's enough to fill 100 Olympic swimming pools, scooped up by 18 buckets attached to a 21.6-m-wide (71-ft) wheel and conveyed away on a belt that runs the length of its boom.

If you did try to take the Bagger out for a spin on a public road, the first problem would be its speed. Flat out, it crawls along at 0.6 km/h (0.37 mph) – easily overtaken by even the slowest of pedestrians. Another major hindrance would be the fact that the Bagger has to be plugged in to work! Its electrical cable – as thick as a man's arm – draws on enough power to feed some 10,000 homes.

Then there's the width. This titanic terraformer is about 46 m (151 ft) across, so it would take up every lane of the motorway. You certainly wouldn't want to make a wrong turn – road signs, bridges and power lines wouldn't stand a chance. One thing that might surprise you is how smoothly it rides, thanks to its 12 caterpillar tracks, which spread its weight across the ground like a massive snowshoe. Still, the highway would need serious repairs once it passed. It's probably for the best that it remains in the mine…

In addition to the driver, the Bagger needs just four other operators, excavating the daily equivalent of 10,000 dump trucks.

SEP 18 In 2014, Ahmed Gabr (EGY) took the plunge to complete the **deepest scuba dive in sea water** – 332.35 m (1,090 ft 4.5 in) – in the Red Sea off Dahab in Egypt.

SEP 19 Born on this day in 1991, Sebastian Harris (USA) became the **youngest person to dive to the *Titanic***, aged 13 years 319 days, in the *Mir-2* submersible on 4 Aug 2005.

A smaller sibling of the Bagger 293 – the 288 – makes a cameo appearance in the movie *The Hunger Games: Catching Fire* (USA, 2013).

SEP 20 On this day in 1980, Kate Bush's (UK) third album *Never for Ever* gave the celebrated singer the **first UK No.1 studio album by a solo female artist**.

SEP 21 In 2014, a total of 364 pet owners spruced up their pooches in the **largest dog-grooming lesson**, overseen by Golden Rescue (CAN) in Alliston, Ontario, Canada.

ICON Jonathan the Tortoise

The remote South Atlantic island of St Helena is home to a living legend: one who preceded London's Tower Bridge, Paris's Eiffel Tower and New York's Statue of Liberty.

Jonathan, a Seychelles giant tortoise (*Aldabrachelys gigantea hololissa*), is the **oldest-known terrestrial animal**. He's one of several tortoises who live in the grounds of Plantation House, the residence of the island's governor. Jonathan – or "Jono" as he's known to locals – is thought to have hatched in around 1832, making him 194 years old as of 2026. And that's a conservative estimate. He was said to be "fully mature" (i.e., at least 50 years old) in 1882, when he arrived there from the Seychelles, so he may already have surpassed 200!

Intriguingly, Jonathan's cells don't appear to mutate in the way that those of humans do. And as cell mutation can cause cancers, his genes might help scientists develop cures for this devastating disease. To that end, his DNA is currently being analysed for any secrets it may unlock.

This senior shellback has lived through a multitude of global milestones, from the Industrial Revolution to the **first powered flight**, the **first Moon landing** and the emergence of the World Wide Web. Old age brings its drawbacks, of course: Jonathan has lost his sense of smell, while cataracts have dimmed his sight. His hearing remains sharp, however, and his former vet (see right) has speculated that he may even reach his 250th birthday. Here's hoping!

Taken some time in the 1880s, this vintage snap shows Jonathan (left) with a fellow tortoise. He was c. 122 cm (4 ft) long here, meaning that he was fully mature at the time this picture was taken. A note on the photograph describes the men behind them only as "good types of Saint Helenians".

In 1947, the young Princess Elizabeth came to pay her respects to Jonathan, along with other members of the British royal family, including the then king, George VI. The celebrated supercentenarian was born before Elizabeth's great-great-grandmother – Queen Victoria – came to the throne! When Queen Elizabeth II passed away in 2022, after seven decades as monarch (making her the **longest-reigning queen ever**), Jonathan was still going strong.

In the 1960s, Jonathan went through an unusually disruptive spell, toppling benches near a tennis court and stopping croquet matches by sitting on the balls! Vets put the bad behaviour down to loneliness, and today he lives alongside three other giant tortoises. He's shown with David (right), a youngster at "only" about 58 years old.

In Mar 2016, Joe Hollins – Jonathan's primary vet and carer at the time – gave the long-lived reptile a rare treat: his first clean in 184 years! "It's purely for aesthetic reasons," explained Hollins, who checked with experts beforehand to make sure he was using the right technique. "We want visitors to witness the tortoises in their true form, without the obstruction of moss and lichen on their shells." Tortoise shells are surprisingly sensitive. "When I was cleaning his rear half," Joe recalls, "he kept rotating to see what was going on!" The procedure can make the shell rather dry, though, so it will only be repeated if Jonathan gets really dirty.

VITAL STATISTICS

Name	Jonathan
Species	*Aldabrachelys gigantea hololissa*
Birthplace	Seychelles
Birth date	*c.* 1832
Age	*c.* 194 years old
Home	Plantation House, St Helena
Current GWR titles	**Oldest living land animal**
	Oldest tortoise

In 2022, St Helena marked the 190th birthday of their most famous four-legged resident with a collection of commemorative stamps. They included the first-known image of Jonathan.

Considered a national treasure on the island, Jonathan has inspired mementoes and toys aplenty, and features on the St Helenian five-pence coin (left) and, as of 2025, also the new King Charles III banknotes.

100%

Even older animals dwell in the sea. Greenland sharks (*Somniosus microcephalus*) can survive *c.* 392 years – the **longest lifespan for a vertebrate**.

Discover all of GWR's incredible ICONS at **guinnessworldrecords.com/records/icons**

ARTS & ENTERTAINMENT

CONTENTS

Sun Wukong was created by Wu Cheng'en for his 16th-century novel, *Journey to the West*. In the book, the primate protagonist has special powers, which he attains through philosophical learning. He can carry two mountains on his shoulders while running at "the speed of a meteor", recall every monkey ever born and transform himself into any animal or object.

LARGEST GATHERING OF PEOPLE DRESSED AS SUN WUKONG

To celebrate the first National Great Sage Culture and Arts Week, 262 people cosplayed as the legendary literary and religious figure Sun Wukong (aka the Monkey King) in Jiyuan, Henan, China, on 20 Sep 2025. The parade – organized by Wulongkou Scenic Area Development Co., Ltd (CHN) – was led by Chinese actor Liu Xiao Ling Tong (b. Zhang Jinlai; standing front and centre in inset), who is best known for playing the mythical monkey in the 1986 TV hit *Journey to the West* (CCTV, CHN).

Crafting

Tallest crochet sculpture
Over 200 people from the municipality of Vilamarxant in Valencia, Spain, came together to build a crochet Christmas tree that towered 23.5 m (77 ft 1 in) tall on 5 Jan 2024. After nine months of preparation, the colossal conifer comprised more than 10,000 hook-work squares, and became the centrepiece of the town's main plaza. Following the festive season, it was cut up to make blankets.

Most origami flowers made in one hour
Ivorian artist Mylene Amon fashioned 203 folded flowers in Abidjan, Côte d'Ivoire, on 1 Jul 2025. She wanted to inspire young women to dream big and reach for their goals.

Largest embroidery by a team
More than 600 Singaporeans contributed towards an embroidered artwork measuring 180.66 m² (1,944 sq ft) – nearly the size of a singles tennis court – which was displayed at Qixi Fest on 29 Aug 2025. Celebrating Singapore's 60th year of independence, the project took around 10,000 hours.

Largest donation of handmade pet toys
A total of 46,506 knitted and crocheted mice were made by readers of *Woman's Weekly* magazine (UK) between 7 May and 15 Sep 2025. Pictured below with the publication's editor, Geoffrey Palmer, the soft toys were donated to more than 500 cat rescue centres and charities.

Largest display of origami dogs
Aria Omkrets and his classmates from Campus Viktor Rydberg school (all SWE) folded 3,134 paper pooches in Stockholm, Sweden, on 7 May 2025. Aria realized his passion for the Japanese artform in 2023, and taught himself how to make origami pups after finding out that dogs were his second cousins' favourite animals.

Smallest handmade sculpture
Artist David A Lindon (UK) of Bournemouth in Dorset, UK, has produced record-breaking microsculptures of everything from famous paintings and book characters to invertebrates and mammals. But on 19 Aug 2025, he revealed his smallest artwork yet – a yellow smiley face measuring 0.01104 x 0.01233 mm, which is about the same size as most bacteria or a single grain of talcum powder! David surpassed his previous record by over 50%.

Largest display of crochet squares
Since 2016, Mother India's Crochet Queens (IND) have showcased their handiwork to claim six world records. Most recently, on 9 Mar 2025, the group unveiled 100,581 colourful patches of yarn in Chennai, Tamil Nadu, India. The squares – all adorned with distinctive designs – were later repurposed into clothes such as ponchos.
They also amassed the **largest display of crochet Christmas decorations** – 66,158, on 15 Sep 2019.

A MARATHON YARN
Combining two of her most-loved hobbies, Louise Warwick (UK) crafted the ***longest crochet chain while running a marathon****, measuring 145.8 m (478 ft 4 in) long in Manchester, UK, on 16 Apr 2023. She ran the 26.2-mi (42.1-km) race in 5 hr 55 min.*

For most people, running a marathon would be enough of a challenge. What was it like to run and crochet at the same time?
It was actually quite fun, if a marathon can ever be fun? Crocheting took my mind off running, and running took my mind off crocheting too. It was so good to hear people cheering me on and being amazed that I was crocheting and running at the same time.

How did you carry the chain?
I made a pinny to go round my waist that was big enough for it to be carried in. I also had a bag on my back, which I could pull the yarn from that I was using. My partner and our little boy popped up at various places to give me more yarn.

Was the chain heavy?
Yes! By about mile 19, I had quite bad back ache.

Where is the chain now?
My chain sits pride of place on my crafting table.

Largest marbling painting
On 5 Jul 2025, Moldovan artist Ludmila Cuptor created a 39.97-m² (430.23-sq-ft) *ebru* painting in Chișinău, Moldova, akin in area to 10 king-size beds. She made the marbled masterpiece using a traditional Turkish technique, which involves placing pigments on oily water before transferring the design on to canvas.

SEP 22 The **fastest kite** was clocked in 1989 flying at 193 km/h (120 mph). The modified Super 10 Flexifoil was flown by Pete DiGiacomo (USA) in Ocean City, Maryland, USA.

SEP 23 Aged 105 years 1 day, Hidekichi Miyazaki (JPN, b. 22 Sep 1910) ran in a Masters Athletics race in Kyoto, Japan, in 2015 to become the **oldest competitive sprinter**.

Emilia initially unveiled her supersized sculpture at The Glasgow School of Art's Degree Show in May 2025.

LARGEST SOCK-MONKEY SCULPTURE
Emilia Evans-Munton (UK) exhibited her 15.1-m-long (49-ft 6-in) sock monkey at the Field Maneuvers music festival in Dereham, Norfolk, UK, between 15 and 17 Aug 2025. The fine-art student used corduroy and straw to build the body, and recycled scaffolding board and thread for the eyes. Emilia told GWR: "I love sock monkeys and wanted to make a massive tribute to the epitome of craft and homemade love." She also described the puppet as an homage to childhood toys that get left behind.

Emilia's sock monkey became the ultimate chill-out spot for festivalgoers at Field Maneuvers.

SEP 24 The **cat with the most toes** is Jake of Bonfield, Ontario, Canada, who had 28 in total – seven on each paw – as counted by a veterinarian on this day in 2002.

SEP 25 Marcello Ferri (ITA) achieved the **heaviest weight lifted with the toes**, holding 80 kg (176 lb 6 oz) aloft with his left phalanges for at least 5 sec in Pesaro, Italy, in 2024.

Stained Glass

Largest mouth-blown stained-glass ceiling
Completed in 1990, this colourful canopy over the Victoria Quarter in Leeds, UK, spans 746.9 m² (8,039.5 sq ft). British artist Sir Brian Clarke designed the enormous installation as part of the 1980s renovation of this 19th-century shopping arcade, having been initially approached only to adorn both entrances with stained glass.

Largest collection of Tiffany stained-glass pieces
In 1969, Dr Egon Neustadt and his wife Hildegard opened their so-called "apartment-museum" – a New York townhouse full of lamps and windows made by the renowned art-glass designer Louis Comfort Tiffany. Today, their hoard – comprising *c.* 500,000 original stained-glass sheets and fragments – can be seen at the Queens Museum and The Neustadt Collection of Tiffany Glass in New York, USA. The pieces above are typical of the nature-inspired Art Nouveau style that made Tiffany & Co's reputation in the early 1900s.

DID YOU KNOW?

Stained-glass windows are traditionally made from glass, lead, cement and chalk.
The artist starts by drawing a "cartoon" – a full-sized sketch of the design to map out where the glass and lead strips will be placed. The glass is then cut to size so it will fit precisely in the lead outline. The artist proceeds to paint the pieces with a mixture of metallic oxides and ground glass. Different brushes and techniques are used to create texture. A wide brush would be utilized for shading (matting), for example, while highlights are added by dabbing a brush (stippling). To set the paint, the glass is heated in a kiln. After firing the glass shards, the artist arranges them on the cartoon and secures them with cut-to-size lead strips. The joints are soldered and glazing cement is scrubbed into the gaps to make the window waterproof. Finally, the artist applies a chalk mixture known as "whiting" to harden the cement before cleaning the panel and leaving it to cure for several days.

Oldest stained-glass windows
The windows in the southern clerestory of Augsburg Cathedral in Bavaria, Germany, have remained intact in their original setting since the latter half of the 11th century. They portray five Old Testament prophets and are thought to be part of a larger series, the rest of which are now missing. This Roman Catholic church also boasts medieval windows that depict the Virgin Mary.

As for the **oldest stained glass** that is no longer in its original form, painted fragments from the Basilica of San Vitale – a late antique church in Ravenna, Italy – have been dated between the 6th and 9th centuries. Alternatively, pieces from pre-850 CE – and potentially the 7th century – were excavated by Professor Rosemary Cramp (UK) at monastery sites in Monkwearmouth and Jarrow in Northumbria, UK, in the 1960s and 1970s.

Largest *dalle-de-verre* stained glass
The Resurrection Cemetery in Justice, Illinois, USA, is home to a multicoloured "scheme" (a series of windows) measuring 2,079 m² (22,378 sq ft) – akin to nearly five basketball courts! *Dalle-de-verre* is a technique that involves smashing thick slabs of glass with a hammer, piecing the fragments back together and then setting them in place with concrete and epoxy resin.

Largest modern stained-glass scheme
The exterior of the Santuário Dom Bosco in Brasília, Brazil, is a façade of white concrete and seemingly opaque arched windows. But inside, it is a kaleidoscope of light and colour. The church has 80 floor-to-ceiling windows with a total surface area of 2,200 m² (23,680 sq ft) – comparable to nearly two Olympic swimming pools! While even larger schemes may exist in certain medieval buildings, this is the biggest example constructed post-1500.

Most expensive stained-glass window sold at auction
On 19 Nov 2024, the Danner Memorial Window fetched $12.48 m (£9.87 m) at Sotheby's in New York City, USA. It was designed by Agnes Northrop, the leading window artist at Tiffany Studios. The artwork was commissioned by the First Baptist Church in Canton, Ohio, USA, where it was installed between 1913 and 1990. The 16-ft-tall (4.8-m) panel depicts the sun setting behind apple trees on an idyllic river bank.

First stained-glass car (prototype)
British artist Dominic Wilcox revealed his spin on the future of transport at London Design Festival in the UK on 18 Sep 2014. He believes that by 2059, safe self-driving cars will make things like clear windscreens and steering wheels obsolete. Wilcox created a copper-foiled stained-glass dome for his futuristic four-wheeler, and even put a single bed inside so the passenger could take a nap while being chauffeured!

SEP 26 — On this day in 2024, Abdulrahaman Saidu of Yobe, Nigeria, speedily snapped 897 portraits – the **most head-shot photographs taken in one hour.**

SEP 27 — The **first 3D feature film** – Nat G Deverich's five-reel melodrama *The Power of Love* – premiered at the Ambassador Hotel Theater in Los Angeles, USA, in 1922.

GREATEST STAINED-GLASS-TO-WALL RATIO

The Sainte-Chapelle in Paris, France, comprises 670 m² (7,211.8 sq ft) of stained-glass windows, making up *c.* 75% of the building's walls. There are 15 stained-glass bays – most of which are 15 m (49 ft 2.5 in) in height – that depict stories from the Old and New Testament as well as major historical events up to the 13th century. This royal chapel has endured floods, fires and the chaos of the French Revolution, and remains the most complete example of medieval stained-glass art in the world. Today, two-thirds of its windows are more than 700 years old.

King Louis IX commissioned the chapel to serve as a repository for relics linked to Jesus Christ, such as the Crown of Thorns.

SEP 28 In 2008, multitasking musician Gregor Fabry (DEU) executed seven aerial cartwheels – the **most sideflips while playing guitar in one minute** – in Vienna, Austria.

SEP 29 Sam Wakeling (UK) completed the **longest continuous unicycle ride** in Aberystwyth, UK, in 2007, covering 169.9 km (105.57 mi) without dismounting once!

Street Art

GRAFFITI STYLES

Since modern graffiti emerged in the 1960s, a plethora of writing styles has evolved. Below are four of the most common types that you're likely to see on a wall near you.

Tag

Often the entry point into graffiti as it focuses on speed over complexity. This means that tags tend to have less artistic cachet, however.

Throw-up (aka throwie)

A natural progression from tags, throw-ups comprise joined-up, rounded "bubble writing". They can be just outlines or filled in.

Stencil

Popularized by global street-art megastar Banksy, this style makes use of cutout templates for clear and consistent lettering.

Piece (aka wildstyle)

Short for "masterpiece", these works go all out on detail. They are typified by intricate interlocking letters, multiple colours and 3D shading.

First modern graffiti

In its most basic sense, graffiti – i.e., the act of etching or daubing words, symbols and pictures on surfaces in public places – can trace its roots to ancient cave art (see p.193). The present-day concept (typically involving spray-painted text and images in urban settings), however, emerged in the eastern USA in the mid-1960s, particularly in big cities such as Philadelphia and New York. Given its subversive, often illicit nature, resulting in most graffiti being anonymous or signed cryptically, it's difficult to pinpoint the precise originators of the artform, but widely cited pioneers from that period were "Cornbread" (aka Darryl McCray), "Julio 204" and "Taki 183" (aka Demetrius, surname unknown).

First gallery graffiti exhibition

Graffiti got its first "high art" treatment in Sep 1973, with an exhibition curated by Hugo Martinez, of the collective United Graffiti Artists, at the Razor Gallery in SoHo, New York City, USA. It paved the way for more long-term establishments such as Fun Gallery, in Manhattan's East Village in the 1980s.

Meanwhile, the **first street-art documentary** was the 45-min *Stations of the Elevated*, which debuted at 1981's New York Film Festival. It was directed by Manfred Kirchheimer (USA, b. DEU) and spotlighted the rising trend of graffitiing New York's subway train carriages.

Most expensive street art sold at auction

Untitled (1982), by Jean-Michel Basquiat (USA, 1960–88), fetched $110.5 m (£85.4 m) – including buyer's fees – at Sotheby's in New York City, USA, on 18 May 2017. The piece depicts a skull-like head with elements of graffiti drawn from Basquiat's origins as a street artist in downtown New York in the 1970s and 1980s, where he went by the name "SAMO".

On the topic of valuable street art, US artist David Choe was commissioned in 2005 to add street-art-style murals to the headquarters of then-startup Facebook in California, USA. Offered either $60,000 in cash or shares in the company for the work, Choe opted for the latter. It proved to be a very lucrative decision, as when the social-media company went public in 2012, his stock was worth *c.* $200 m (£126 m)!

Most followed street artist on Instagram

Anonymous British street artist Banksy had 13,868,797 fans on his official Instagram account as of 23 Feb 2026. He also boasts the **best-selling street-art book**: his 2005 title *Wall and Piece* has shifted in excess of 572,000 copies to date.

Largest mural by one artist

Muralist Alessandro Ciambrone (ITA) gave the 5,441.93-m² (58,576-sq-ft) concrete exterior of a prison a vibrant makeover in Santa Maria Capua Vetere, Caserta, Italy, as verified on 4 Jun 2025. The so-called *Wall of Freedom* features UNESCO World Heritage Sites from across the globe and historical quotes about peace, culture and human rights.

Longest career as a street-art photographer

Photojournalist Martha Cooper (USA) took her earliest shots of street art for a college project in 1962. She formally decided to specialize in this subject in 1978. Her work has featured in many exhibitions, magazines and books, including the seminal 1984 tome *Subway Art*, compiled with Henry Chalfant.

Most street-art locations tagged in a city

By the end of 2025, the Australian city of Melbourne had 3,474 individual pieces virtually logged on the online community Street Art Cities, established in 2016. This put it ahead of Paris, France (with 2,278) and Los Angeles, California, USA (2,187). Pictured is one of Melbourne's best-loved graffiti hotspots: Hosier Lane in the downtown Central Business District.

SEP 30 In 2013, Hiroyuki Yoshida (JPN) and Sandra Smith (USA) tied the knot while 130 m (426 ft) below the surface of a lake in Thailand: the **deepest underwater wedding**.

OCT 1 On this day in 2023, Mansour Naderi (IRN) got his head in the game to set the **tallest stack of hats worn while unicycling** – 1.44 m (4 ft 8 in) – in Shahr-e Rey, Iran.

LARGEST STREET-ART GALLERY

Housed in a vast converted shipyard building (left) in Amsterdam-Noord, Netherlands, the STRAAT Museum opened in Oct 2020. Its permanent collection boasts some 180 artworks – displayed over *c.* 8,000 m^2 (86,100 sq ft) – by some of the biggest stars in the genre, both local and international. The pieces, some of which are as vast as 15 x 7 m (49 x 23 ft), are mainly created on site with spray paint on polyester canvases, but there are also a few sculptures and more unusual installations, including a graffiti-covered truck suspended on chains from the ceiling girders!

Established by Alan Ket and Allison Freidin in Dec 2019, the Museum of Graffiti in the Wynwood district of Miami, Florida, USA, is the **first graffiti museum**, dedicated solely to typographic street art. It houses a collection of 250 artworks over 9,000 sq ft (836 m^2) of exhibition space and receives some 35,000 visitors per year.

OCT 2 Father-son team Harry and Carson Willemse (both CAN) presented the **longest asparagus** (3.517 m; 11 ft 6 in) at a show in Port Elgin, Ontario, Canada, today in 2004.

OCT 3 Peter Wayne Botha (NZ) bared his sole(s) to run the **fastest 100 km barefoot** in 8 hr 42 min 11 sec in 2015, during the Sri Chinmoy 24-Hour Race in New Zealand.

Balloon Art

**As per GWR guidelines, all balloons used must be biodegradable*

Largest balloon mosaic (image)
Measuring 515.17 m^2 (5,545 sq ft) – enough to cover two tennis courts – this cartoon-style artwork was unveiled by Fábricas Selectas del Centro and Globos Payaso (both MEX) in Mexico City on 10 Nov 2023. Made from 95,900 balloons, the homage to the Day of the Dead festival includes *calaveras* (skeletons), *cempasúchil* marigolds (aka "flowers of the dead") and Xoloitzcuintli dogs – said to be guides in the afterlife.

On the same day, the Mexican companies achieved the **most people making balloon sculptures simultaneously**: 457. In keeping with the Day of the Dead theme, the participants learned how to make marigolds using balloons.

Largest balloon sculpture of a Chinese dragon

In the Chinese zodiac, dragons symbolize energy, power and good luck. To honour the year of the dragon in 2024, artists Sze Tai Pang and Kun Lung Ho (both CHN) assembled a mythical beast that was 41.77 m (137 ft) long. The duo revealed their 38,000-balloon golden dragon at the tmtplaza shopping mall in Hong Kong, China, on 24 Jan.

Fastest time to make 100 balloon hats

Ryan Tracey (IRL) manipulated 100 balloons into headwear in 6 min 59 sec at the BBC TV studios in Glasgow, UK, on 16 Dec 2017. He attempted the record during the 100th episode of *Officially Amazing Goes Bunkers* and, afterwards, gifted the hats to the kids in the audience.

Britain's Got Talent semi-finalist Tracey also holds the records for the **most balloon sculptures made in one minute** – 14, on 7 Sep 2017 – and the **fastest time to model five balloon sculptures blindfolded** – 43.64 sec, on 20 Jan 2020.

Most balloons inflated by the nose in three minutes

Prolific record breaker Ashrita Furman (USA) blew up 28 balloons using this unconventional method in New York, USA, on 7 Dec 2013. Over 10 years later, another one of GWR's serial record holders, David Rush (USA), equalled the mark in Boise, Idaho, USA, on 30 Jan 2024. To find out more about this dynamic duo and their *many* skills, see pp.62–63.

Largest balloon sculpture of a landmark

Using more than 103,000 gold balloons, *21st Century Business Herald* (CHN) recreated a section of the Great Wall of China measuring 27.36 m (89 ft 9 in) long in Guangzhou, Guangdong, China, as presented on 22 Feb 2024.

Largest balloon sentence

Decoraciones Globos, which is run by Genesis Nieves, her sister Iravid and her husband Francisco (all VEN), formed 53 letters with 7,236 balloons in Miami, Florida, USA, on 25 Oct 2020. The line read: "Success has nothing to do with luck, it is a matter of consistency."

How long did it take to construct the balloon zoo?
After two months of preparation, we built the zoo in just 10 days. This was with the help of 200 volunteers, including local and international balloon artists.

How did you decide which animals to include?
I tried to include a mix of well-known animals and species endemic to each part of the world. The iconic animals, such as the giraffe and lion, are important to meet the audience's expectations, but the endangered species such as the black sable antelope or the strange-looking okapi help to widen people's perspective of the animal world.

Which were the largest and smallest animals?
The whale shark in the Great Barrier Reef area was the largest and the red fire ants in South America the smallest. We tried to create all animals life-size, but we had to scale up the 40 bug species so the audience could find them!

Any tips for new balloon artists?
The only limitation is your own imagination. Dream big and work hard. The sky is not the limit any more – it's where you'll build your next project!

Fastest 100-m balloon chain (team)
On 24 Sep 2019, a total of 90 employees from Procter & Gamble International Operations (CHE) linked together 494 balloons in 4 min 34 sec in Évian-les-Bains, France. When measured, the chain greatly exceeded the required length, coming in at 170.95 m (560 ft 10 in).

Largest balloon zoo
Fashioned from 469,845 balloons, this inflatable animal park and its 100-plus inhabitants were unveiled at the World Balloon Art Festival in Xiamen, Fujian, China, on 13 Oct 2017. Xiamen Jimei City Development Co and American Event Management Institute (both CHN) recruited Dutch artist Guido Verhoef (see Q&A above) to lead the project.

OCT 4 The British Overseas Airways Corporation (BOAC) began operating the **first transatlantic jet service** between the UK and the USA on this day in 1958.

OCT 5 In 2005, the **first shootout goal in NHL history** was scored by Daniel Alfredsson (SWE), playing for the Ottawa Senators against the Toronto Maple Leafs.

LARGEST BALLOON COSTUME

After eight-and-a-half hours of inflating and twisting roughly 650 balloons, Gergő Csatai (HUN) completed his giant inflatable giraffe, standing 421 cm (13 ft 9 in) tall in Szarvas, Békés, Hungary, on 1 May 2025. Csatai knew he wanted to build a cute animal, so he accessorized his giraffe with a pink tutu!

Csatai previously held the title for the **fastest time to model five balloon sculptures blindfolded** – 44.25 sec – but this has since been beaten by Ireland's Ryan Tracey in 2020 (see opposite).

The **largest balloon costume** title was previously held by Tom Kent (UK), who paraded around a Comic Con event as The Incredible Hulk in Liverpool, UK, on 13 Nov 2021. The 353-cm-tall (11-ft 7-in) suit was built in two days and popped at the Comic Con after-party.

To secure the record, Csatai had to prove he could walk in the inflatable giraffe suit.

OCT 6 Hussam Saraf (AUS) grafted the **most types of fruit on a tree** – five (plum, apricot, almond, peach and cherry) – as verified in Kialla, Victoria, Australia, in 2021.

OCT 7 In perhaps the ultimate bonding exercise, Jean-Noël and Bertrand "Zébulon" Roche (both FRA) became the **first father-and-son team to summit Everest** in 1990.

Avatar: Behind the Scenes

As of 18 Feb 2026, James Cameron's *Avatar* franchise remained the **highest-grossing movie series (average/movie)** following the release of *Avatar: Fire and Ash* (USA/CAN, 2025). The three sci-fi epics had grossed an average of $2,236,301,331 (£1.6 bn) at the global box office, according to The Numbers. Pictured below is a behind-the-scenes shot – and its equivalent film still – of Miles "Spider" Socorro (played by Jack Champion) on board an airborne gondola with 10-ft-tall (3-m) Na'vi on the alien planet Pandora.

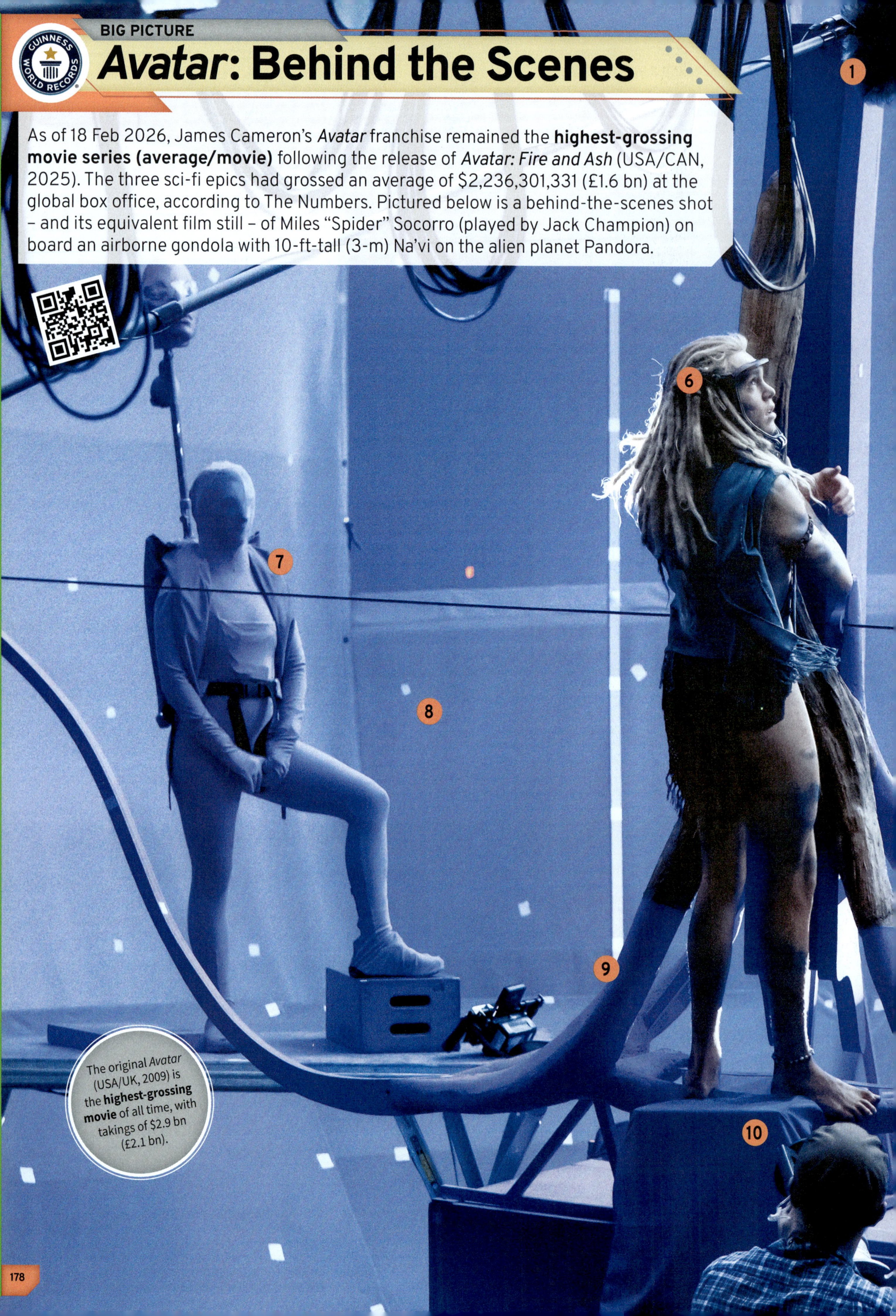

The original *Avatar* (USA/UK, 2009) is the **highest-grossing movie** of all time, with takings of $2.9 bn (£2.1 bn).

1: This boom microphone recorded the production sound (dialogue, ambience and natural SFX). Sometimes, actors also have hidden radio mics in their clothing or hair.

2: Live-action scenes were filmed in native stereo so the 3D effects could mimic human binocular vision. For this shot, the camera system was mounted on a crane.

3: This "flag" was used to block light and cast shadows on Champion, as if he had been surrounded by other objects and people in the live-action shot.

4: Each Wind Trader gondola comprises 2,000 computer-generated (CG) bamboo elements and 100 km (62 mi) of CG rope, faithfully realized from the production design.

5: In the completed film shot, Champion is the only live-action element. The gondola environment and the rest of the characters are fully computer-generated.

6: Champion's character wears a breathing mask as a human living on Pandora, but for much of the filming it was only the outer frame. The VFX team later added CG glass and its reflections.

7: In the live-action shot, this actor stood in for what would become a CG character. They wore a backpack rig with a suspended eyeline target for Champion to perform to.

8: By filming Champion's performance against a bluescreen set, it was easier to isolate him and place him in a completely CG environment for the final shot.

9: Partial set pieces like the gondola's crossbow were placed in the live-action shot so Champion had objects to interact with. They were later replaced with CG set pieces.

10: A member of the special-effects team disrupts Champion's hair and clothing with a "wind blower" as he's meant to be flying in this shot.

Star Wars

STAT WARS

GWR film consultant Stephen Follows has crunched the numbers on the Skywalker Saga to reveal which character is the ***most...***

Talkative

Anakin Skywalker has 857 dialogue lines over the course of the series.

Startled

Unsurprisingly, C-3PO has 241 lines of dialogue with at least one exclamation point.

Confused

Around 26% of Resistance pilot Poe Dameron's lines include at least one question.

Largest collection of *Star Wars* memorabilia

Retired journalist Steve Sansweet (USA) has been collecting all things *Star Wars* related since he was captivated by the first film in 1977. During his 15-year stint as Head of Fan Relations at Lucasfilm, Sansweet consolidated his hoard of *Star Wars* merchandise in a museum called Rancho Obi-Wan in California, USA. The number of unique items in Sansweet's collection has been estimated at around half a million, but the official GWR count (based on a subset that was photographed and catalogued in 2015) is a more modest 93,260 objects.

Longest-running videogame film licence

The **first official *Star Wars* videogame** was *Star Wars: The Empire Strikes Back* (Parker Brothers), which launched on the Atari 2600 in Jul 1982. Since then, more than 350 games (including ports) have been released on 36 platforms, including such classics as *TIE Fighter* (1994), *Knights of the Old Republic* (2003) and *LEGO Star Wars: The Skywalker Saga* (2022). On the slated release of *Star Wars: Galactic Racer* in late 2026, the franchise will have been a major force in gaming for more than 44 years.

Longest gap between *Star Wars* film appearances

Imperial commander Grand Moff Tarkin, played by British actor Peter Cushing, first appeared in *Episode IV: A New Hope* (1977). Cushing did not return to the role of the Death Star's commander until *Rogue One: A Star Wars Story* (2016), a full 39 years later. State-of-the-art visual effects allowed Cushing to appear despite having been dead for more than 20 years!

Most expensive *Star Wars* action figure

A pristine Rocket-Firing Boba Fett was sold by Goldin Auctions (USA) for $1.34 m (£1.03 m) on 18 Aug 2024. This prototype was made by toy company Kenner in 1979, ahead of the 1980 release of *Episode V: The Empire Strikes Back*. The design never went into production due to fears that the spring-loaded "rocket" projectiles could be a choking hazard.

Most actors to play one *Star Wars* character

The masked Sith Lord Darth Vader has been voiced by American actor James Earl Jones since the original movie in 1977. However, Lord Vader's on-screen presence has been handled by seven performers over the years. This includes actors David Prowse, Sebastian Shaw, C Andrew Nelson and Spencer Wilding, as well as stunt performers Bob Anderson, Gene Bryant and Daniel Naprous. The total rises to nine if Jake Lloyd and Hayden Christensen, who played Lord Vader before his turn to the Dark Side, are included.

Most appearances in the *Star Wars* series

The protocol droid C-3PO, played by British actor Anthony Daniels, has appeared in all nine of the Skywalker Saga movies and also made a cameo appearance in *Rogue One*. Over the course of these 10 films, C-3PO has spoken 648 lines of dialogue and interacted with 88 different characters.

Largest *Star Wars* costuming group

The 501st Legion was founded in 1997 as a club for *Star Wars* cosplayers. As of 18 Nov 2020, the Legion had a global membership of 14,141 people, united under the motto of "bad guys doing good". Its costumed members – who take inspiration from the "villainous or morally ambiguous" characters from a galaxy far, far away – make appearances at conventions, charity events and even occasionally as extras in *Star Wars* films and TV shows.

Most expensive *Star Wars* prop

On 4 Sep 2025, Darth Vader's lightsaber was auctioned off by Propstore in California, USA, for $3.6 m (£2.7 m). This prop was identified by its distinctive pattern of scratches, visible in the fight scenes of *The Empire Strikes Back* and *Return of the Jedi*. It broke a record that had been set two years earlier by the "Red Leader" X-Wing, a roughly 50-cm (1-ft 7-in) "hero" prop (a high-quality model used in close-ups). This miniature was used in the filming of *A New Hope*, and was sold by Heritage Auctions for $3.1 m (£2.55 m) on 15 Oct 2023.

OCT 8 Andrew Hellinga (AUS) completed the **greatest distance cycling backwards in 24 hours** – 337.6 km (209.77 mi) – in Norwell, Queensland, Australia, in 2013.

OCT 9 In 2021, Saul Hafting (CAN) solved the **most rotating puzzle cubes while on a pogo stick** – 211 – in Annapolis Royal, Nova Scotia, Canada.

HIGHEST-GROSSING SCIENCE-FICTION FILM SERIES
As of 2 Mar 2026, the 12 theatrically released films set in the *Star Wars* universe had earned a combined $10.37 bn (£7.7 bn) at the global box office. That figure will increase in May 2026 with the release of Jon Favreau's *The Mandalorian and Grogu*, and another movie – *Star Wars: Starfighter* – reportedly finished filming in Dec 2025. The **highest-grossing *Star Wars* movie** is 2015's *The Force Awakens*, which kicked off the blockbuster sequel trilogy. It alone took $2.05 bn (£1.52 bn) at the global box office during its theatrical run, according to The Numbers.

The phrase "I have a bad feeling" is said seven times over the course of the Skywalker Saga.

This artwork, painted by Tom Jung for *A New Hope*'s pre-release posters in 1977, became the **most expensive piece of *Star Wars* memorabilia** when it sold for $3.875 m (£2.9 m) on 11 Dec 2025. It was put on sale by Heritage Auctions (USA) on behalf of the family of Gary Kurtz (1940–2018), who was the producer of the first two *Star Wars* movies.

OCT 10 Born without arms, Jessica Cox (USA) became the **first woman to fly a plane with her feet** in 2008. She steers with one foot and manages controls with the other.

OCT 11 In 2015, serial record breaker Cherry Yoshitake (JPN) used just his teeth to claim the **most apples bobbed in one minute** – 37 – in Kakamigahara, Gifu, Japan.

Action Movies

Highest stunt bungee jump
British stuntman Wayne Michaels plummeted 220 m (721 ft) down the Verzasca dam in Switzerland for the opening sequence of the 1995 James Bond film *GoldenEye*.

Highest stunt freefall
For the 1982 movie *Highpoint*, Dar Robinson (USA) dropped 335 m (1,100 ft) from the CN Tower in Toronto, Canada, opening his parachute at just 90 m (295 ft).

Longest stunt stair fall
Joaquín Ortega (ESP) crashed down the 134 stone steps of the Escaleras de Bielva, which descends around 70 m (229 ft) down the side of a hill in northern Spain.

First action movie

Almost all films involve some sort of action and spectacle, meaning that "action" as a genre is notoriously difficult to pin down. The earliest clear ancestors of modern action movies, however, are the short films of British director James Williamson (active from around 1898 to 1910). His early films *Attack on a China Mission* (1900) and *Stop Thief!* (1901) are narrative shorts that include many action-movie staples such as chases, stunts, gun battles and fistfights.

Most commonly used movie weapon

As of 24 Feb 2026, users of the Internet Movie Firearms Database had logged 2,003 feature-film appearances by the Colt Single Action Army. This sturdy revolver, introduced in 1873 and still made today, is as ubiquitous in Westerns as it was in the actual Wild West. It made its movie debut in 1903 with *The Great Train Robbery* and has since been wielded by a cast of gunslingers that include Calamity Jane, Wyatt Earp and both Butch Cassidy and the Sundance Kid.

Fastest editing for a genre

Research carried out by GWR film consultant Stephen Follows in 2024 revealed that action is the fastest-cut genre, with an average shot length of just under 4 sec. Fast-paced fight scenes and chase sequences push the genre to the top of the rankings. The suspense-building shots of horror make it the **slowest**, with average shot lengths of 15.7 sec.

The **fastest editing for a film** is the Jean-Claude Van Damme action movie *Derailed* (2002), which crams 3,007 shots into its 79-min 59-sec runtime. That's an average shot length of 1.53 sec.

Highest-grossing action movie

As with the **first action movie**, there are a couple of possible candidates, because most blockbusters are arguably action films. The first is the all-time **highest-grossing movie**, *Avatar* (2009), which earned $2.92 bn (£2.22 bn) worldwide. If we restrict it to primarily live-action films, the record passes to 2019's *Avengers: Endgame,* which made $2.71 bn (£2.07 bn). Excluding films with a sci-fi or superhero theme, the record passes to 2015's *Furious 7* on $1.51 bn (£961.9 m; see below).

Largest film stunt explosion
On 29 Aug 2025, technicians on the set of thriller *7 Dogs* detonated the equivalent of 170.7 tonnes (188 tons) of TNT on set near Riyadh, Saudi Arabia. This big-budget blockbuster is the debut feature of Sela Studios, which hopes to put Saudi Arabia (where cinemas were only legalized in 2017) on the filmmaking map.

Highest-grossing action franchise
Over its more than 60-year history, the James Bond series has earned an estimated $7.87 bn (£5.87 bn) at the global box office. The top performing entry of the series' 25 films is 2021's *No Time to Die*, which was Daniel Craig's final appearance as the iconic super-spy. New series producers Amazon MGM are expected to announce a new film (and a new Bond!) in 2026.

Highest-grossing car-chase franchise
In the 25 years since the release of *The Fast and the Furious* (2001), the high-octane adventures of Dom Toretto's crew of street racers have earned $7.27 bn (£5.42 bn) at the global box office. The next instalment in the series, which will be called *Fast Forever,* is slated for release in 2028.

OCT 12 Don't look away! The **largest staring competition** saw 296 people lock eyes, in an event overseen by Hisense International (CHN) in Dartford, UK, in 2023.

OCT 13 Hats off to José Antonio Basteguieta (ESP), who unveiled the **largest beret** – a head-spinning 3.5 m (11 ft 4 in) in diameter – in Madrid, Spain, on this day in 2001.

DID YOU KNOW?

Tom Cruise prefers to do his own daredevil stunts.
In his 44-year Hollywood career, Cruise has free-climbed cliffs and skyscrapers, made dozens of parachute jumps, and clung on to the side of planes in flight. That's in addition to numerous examples of more day-to-day stunt work, including car crashes, knife fights and rooftop chases.

Tom Cruise made the jumps while also operating a chest-mounted camera rig called a SnorriCam.

MOST BURNING PARACHUTE JUMPS

During the tense final action sequence of 2025 spy thriller *Mission: Impossible – The Final Reckoning*, series protagonist Ethan Hunt (played by Tom Cruise) has to jump from a plane with a burning parachute. Rather than put this shot together on a green screen, or use a team of stunt performers, Cruise opted to make the jump for real. Furthermore, in order to get all the shots the director needed, Cruise (who is a licensed pilot and veteran skydiver) did it 16 times! The jumps were made on location in South Africa over nine shooting days between 14 Apr and 2 Dec 2022, under the supervision of stunt coordinator/2nd unit director Wade Eastwood and skydiving coordinator Allan Hewitt.

OCT 14 First lit in 2010, the Rheinquelle Lighthouse stands 2,046 m (6,713 ft) above sea level in Sedrun in the Swiss Alps. It is the **highest-altitude lighthouse**.

OCT 15 In 2003, China's Lieutenant Colonel Yang Liwei was sent into orbit in the *Shenzhou 5* spacecraft. His 21-hr 23-min mission was the **longest maiden spaceflight**.

Musicals

COMPANY
A MUSICAL COMEDY

For 10 years, GWR Editor-in-Chief (and Chair of The Stephen Sondheim Society) Craig Glenday has been tracking the tempo at which different singers perform the patter song "Getting Married Today", from the 1970 Sondheim musical *Company*.

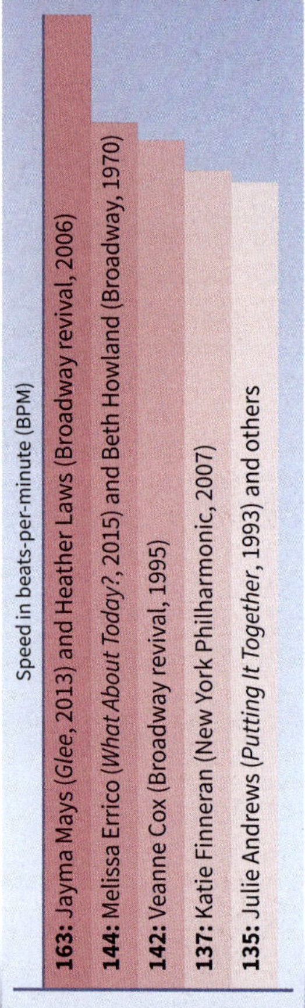

First "book" musical

The modern stage musical – which combines the elements of "book" (dialogue and structure), lyrics and music to tell a story – took shape in the first few decades of the 20th century. No one production can be singled out as the originator of the form, but the most complete and influential early example is *Show Boat* (1927) by Jerome Kern and Oscar Hammerstein II (both USA).

Most concurrent West End shows by a composer

Between 12 Jun 1991 and 20 Jun 1992, composer Andrew Lloyd Webber (UK) had five shows in London's West End. They were: *Cats*, *Starlight Express*, *The Phantom of the Opera*, *Aspects of Love* and *Joseph and the Amazing Technicolor Dreamcoat*. Between 24 and 28 Sep 1991, this total was brought up to six by a touring Japanese production of *Jesus Christ Superstar*.

Longest time in the same West End production

British actor Philip Griffiths joined the cast of *The Phantom of the Opera* on 21 Aug 1990, playing the combined parts of Monsieur Reyer and The Auctioneer. He remained in the role for 29 years 342 days, ending when the production was suspended during the COVID-19 pandemic.

Longest-running musical

The Fantasticks opened at the Sullivan Street Playhouse in Greenwich Village, New York City, USA, on 3 May 1960. This small-cast off-Broadway musical romance closed just shy of 42 years later on 13 Jan 2002. It was revived in 2006, and the new production went on to run for another decade.

Most Tony Awards for a musical

The Producers, by Mel Brooks and Thomas Meehan, won in 12 categories – including Best Musical – at the 55th Tony Awards on 3 Jun 2001. *Hamilton*, by Lin-Manuel Miranda, claimed the **most nominations** in 2016, with 16 (winning 11).

Hamilton also has the **most nominations at the Olivier Awards** (the West End equivalent of the Tony Awards), with its 2018 British production earning 13 nods – a feat matched by the 2024 London revival of *Fiddler on the Roof*. The record for **most wins** is jointly held by *Hamilton*, *Matilda the Musical* (in 2012), *Cabaret* (in 2022) and *Sunset Boulevard* (in 2024), each of which earned seven gongs.

Most visitors to a musical in a single theatre

On 19 Jan 2025, the German production of *Starlight Express* welcomed its 19-millionth ticket holder (inset). The show – written by Andrew Lloyd Webber and Richard Stilgoe – has run at the Starlight Express Theatre in Bochum, North Rhine-Westphalia, since 12 Jun 1988. The venue was custom built for the unique requirements of this musical, which involves the performers roller-skating through the audience.

Longest-running musical in the West End

Les Misérables (1980) was originally a concept album by French composer Claude-Michel Schönberg with lyricists Alain Boublil and Jean-Marc Natel. It was transformed into a theatrical blockbuster by impresario Cameron Mackintosh, whose production opened at the Barbican on 8 Oct 1985. Now at the Sondheim Theatre, it celebrated its 40th anniversary in 2025.

Highest international gross for a stage musical

Disney's *The Lion King* made its Broadway debut on 13 Nov 1997, in a production helmed by director Julie Taymor and Disney Theatrical Productions. The show made it to the West End in 1999, and its various resident and touring productions have since reached audiences in 24 countries and 100 cities. The combined earnings of these shows was $11.5 bn (£8.7 bn) as of 2 Nov 2025.

OCT 16 In 1976, Kathy Wafler carved the **longest apple peel** by painstakingly paring the skin from a cooking apple in one 52.5-m (172-ft) strip in Rochester, New York, USA.

OCT 17 Doug Hunt (CAN) balanced on top of the **tallest stilts** on this day in 2023, walking 10 steps on his 55-ft (16.7-m) legs in Brantford, Ontario, Canada.

Director Jon M Chu split the play into two movies because Act I's iconic finale, "Defying Gravity", didn't work in the middle of a film.

HIGHEST-GROSSING OPENING WEEKEND FOR A MOVIE BASED ON A STAGE MUSICAL

Between 21 and 23 Nov 2025, *Wicked: For Good* raked in $147 m (£112 m) at the global box office, breaking the record set by 2024's *Wicked*. The first part of the story remains the **highest-grossing film based on a play**, however, with worldwide earnings of $758 m (£566 m). The two films, starring Ariana Grande as Glinda (left) and Cynthia Erivo as Elphaba (right), adapt the first and second acts of *Wicked: The Untold Story of the Witches of Oz* (2003). The original Broadway production, which starred Kristin Chenoweth (below left) and Idina Menzel (below right), has become one of only a few shows to have ever earned more than $1 bn (£760 m) at the box office.

OCT 18 NASA astronauts Jessica Meir and Christina Koch (see pp.58–59) made the **first all-female spacewalk** in 2019, venturing outside the *International Space Station*.

OCT 19 The **first videogame tournament**, called the Intergalactic Spacewar Olympics, was held in 1972 at Stanford University in California, USA.

Music

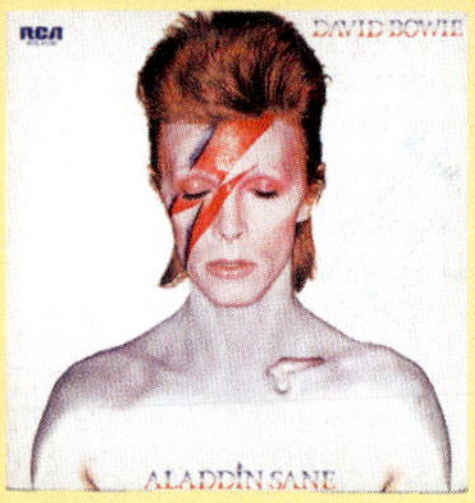

Most expensive album artwork sold at auction
The original image used for the cover of David Bowie's 1973 album *Aladdin Sane* sold for £381,400 ($498,551) at Bonhams auction house in London, UK, on 5 Nov 2025. The photo, which immortalized Bowie's iconic "lightning bolt" look, was taken by Brian Duffy (UK).

Most debuts at No.1 on the US albums chart
Since 2008, all 15 of Taylor Swift's (USA) No.1 albums on the *Billboard* 200 have debuted at the top of the chart. The run began with *Fearless*, while Tay's latest, *The Life of a Showgirl* (above), hit No.1 on 18 Oct 2025. The LP shifted an astonishing 4.002 million equivalent album units in its first week, also making it the **fastest-selling album in the USA**.

Most streamed track on Spotify (current year)
Chart-topping ballad "Die with a Smile", by Lady Gaga (b. Stefani Germanotta) and Bruno Mars (b. Peter Hernandez; both USA), amassed 1.7 billion streams on Spotify in 2025.

"Blinding Lights" by The Weeknd (CAN, b. Abel Tesfaye) remains the **most streamed track on Spotify** overall (5.3 billion, as of 4 Mar 2026). On 31 Aug 2025, it became the **first track to reach 5 billion streams** on the platform.

Most followed act on Spotify
Playback singer, composer and producer Arijit Singh (IND) had 175,204,852 Spotify fans, as of 4 Mar 2026. His closest rival, Taylor Swift, had 152.5 million.

For the fourth time since 2020, the **most streamed act on Spotify** is Bad Bunny (PRI, b. Benito Antonio Martínez Ocasio), with 19.8 billion streams in 2025.

Most UK No.1 albums
On 29 Jan 2026, Robbie Williams (UK) scored his 16th solo UK No.1 with *Britpop*. His album broke a record held for a quarter of a century by The Beatles (UK).

Most deliveries by UAV drones in one hour
On 19 Sep 2025, Cardi B, Atlantic Records, Wing and Walmart (all USA) dropped off 176 copies of the rapper's album *Am I the Drama?* in the Dallas-Fort Worth region.

Four days later, they followed up with the **most signed items sold in eight hours** – 2,463 LPs and CDs featuring Cardi's signature – in Cypress, Texas, USA.

Most consecutive Mercury Prize nominations from debut
The first four albums by British group Wolf Alice – *My Love Is Cool* (2015), *Visions of a Life* (2017), *Blue Weekend* (2021) and *The Clearing* (2025) – were all nominated for the UK's Mercury Prize. The four-piece band won the award in 2018 (inset) for *Visions of a Life*.

First producer to win the "Big Four" at the Grammys
At the 68th Grammy Awards ceremony on 1 Feb 2026, Jack Antonoff (USA) secured Record of the Year as the co-producer/engineer/mixer of "Luther" by Kendrick Lamar and SZA. In doing so, the Bleachers frontman completed his set of the "Big Four" trophies that aren't restricted by genre. He had previously won Album of the Year for Taylor Swift's *1989* (2016), *Folklore* (2021) and *Midnights* (2024); Song of the Year for "We Are Young" by fun. in 2013; and Best New Artist for his contributions to the latter pop-rock trio, also in 2013.

Most consecutive years with a Japanese No.1 single
The Japanese duo DOMOTO (formerly known as KinKi Kids) topped Japan's Oricon Singles Chart for 29 years – with 48 consecutive releases – between 1997 and 2025.

Longest marathon playing saxophone
From 22 to 23 Sep 2025, Elvis Nunes Sousa (PRT) blew his sax for 33 hr – more than six-and-a-half hours longer than the previous record – in Funchal, Madeira, Portugal.

Most *Billboard* Arabia charts topped by one song
"Fa9la", by Flipperachi (BHR, b. Hussam Aseem), had reached No.1 on four *Billboard* Arabia listings as of 1 Jan 2026. He topped the Arabic Hot 100, Arabic Artist 100, Khaleeji Top 50 and Arabic Hip Hop Top 50 charts.

Most weeks at No.1 on the UK Official Singles Chart by a songwriter
Sir Paul McCartney (UK) garnered a total of 104 weeks at No.1 between 1963 and 2023, with 29 hits: 18 as a member of The Beatles, one with Wings, two as a solo artist and eight as a credited songwriter for other acts.

First track to spend 100 weeks on the *Billboard* Hot 100
On 26 Jul 2025, "Lose Control" by singer-songwriter Teddy Swims (USA, b. Jaten Dimsdale) became the first track to reach a century of weeks on the US singles chart. It debuted at No.99 on 26 Aug 2023 and remained on the chart every week until 18 Oct 2025 – except for 4 Jan 2025 – with a week at No.1 on 30 Mar 2024. The 112-week run also gave "Lose Control" the **most cumulative weeks on the *Billboard* Hot 100**.

OCT 20 In 2015, the late Jim Bolin (USA) built the **largest mailbox** in Casey, Illinois, USA. It measured 36 x 14 ft (11 x 4.4 m). Visitors could climb inside via hidden stairs.

OCT 21 Hey Orgelbau (DEU) built the **loudest pipe organ** in Bavaria, Germany, in 2011. The Vox Maris played a 138.4 dBA note, making it louder than a chainsaw.

ON THE RECORD

"It is not possible to produce sound just with the prosthetic arm. I use my entire body to adjust the angle of the strings and change the strength of the sound. I attach a guide rod to prevent the bow from falling, and since I can't play it very hard, I attach a weight to [it] and use a cello bow"
– Manami Ito

Ito competed as a swimmer at the 2008 and 2012 Paralympics, and played her violin at the Tokyo 2020 opening ceremony (inset).

FIRST VIOLINIST WITH A FULL PROSTHETIC ARM
Manami Ito (JPN) lost her right arm in a traffic accident in 2004. Thanks to a customized artificial limb – and years of practice – she taught herself to play her beloved violin again, giving her first recital in 2012. Ito's drive to resume performing was partly motivated by her "desire to give back to the people who made [her] prosthetic arm", she told GWR. But there was another, very personal reason: "I remembered that I had not been able to fulfil a promise to my mom, who asked me, 'Play for me one day.' I decided to play the violin for my mom whatever way I could." GWR presented Ito with her certificate on 16 Nov 2025.

OCT 22 Housekeeper Chow Ka Fai (CHN) achieved the **fastest time to make a king-size bed** – a quick-fire 1 min 9 sec – at the Cordis hotel in Hong Kong, China, in 2018.

OCT 23 In 2018, Jafar Ashouri (IRN) performed the **fastest 100 m skipping with a jump rope** – 14.1 sec – in Shahroud, Iran. He spent eight months perfecting his speedy skip.

GAMING

Most Game Awards won by a videogame in a single year

Clair Obscur: Expedition 33 (Sandfall Interactive, 2025) picked up nine trophies at the 12th edition of The Game Awards in Los Angeles, California, USA, on 11 Dec 2025. The haul included gongs for the coveted categories of Best Role-Playing Game and Game of the Year. It also scored the **most Game Awards nominations** – a spectacular 13!

DDR DYNAMO!

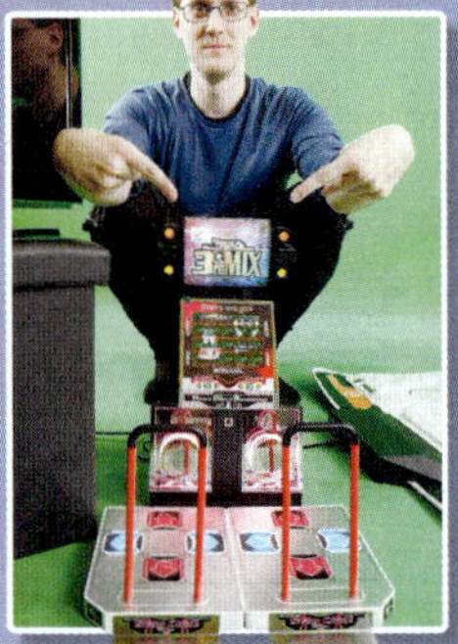

From 23 to 29 Oct 2024, "GrassHopper" (aka Szabolcs Csépe, HUN) played Dance Dance Revolution (DDR) *for 144 hr – the* ***longest videogame marathon****.*

What do you like most about *DDR*?
The choreography: each song has a unique flow, which gives the essence of "dancing" on the four foot panels.

What were your biggest challenges?
Overcoming the accumulating fatigue, plus getting the most out of rest and sleep breaks.

When you play friends at *DDR*, do you always win?
Yes, very often, against everyone except my big rival - my brother!

GWR TEAMS UP WITH ROBLOX FOR A RECORD-BREAKING FIRST

In *1% Win Obby* on Roblox, players had to navigate a glass bridge, knowing that half of its tiles would shatter under them! As they progressed, they unlocked new perks and rewards. Could they reach the end without tumbling?

Between 4 Nov and 14 Dec 2025, GWR invited Roblox users to attempt the platform's first official world records. Those who made it to the leaderboards were rewarded with a medal... and some even earned themselves a GWR title! On 4 Nov 2025, one gamer set the **fastest time to finish *1% Win Obby***, in 50.91 sec.

Later, two other players entered the record books for setting the **fastest times to complete *Cart Ride*** – 4 min 10.59 sec – and ***Ultimate Easy Obby*** – 5 min 48.96 sec. Virtual GWR Adjudicators (inset) made in-game appearances to present the digital certificates, which players could walk around with in a tote.

LARGEST ATTENDANCE FOR AN ESPORTS MATCH

A total of 62,196 people descended on the Tencent IEG TiMi Esports Center in Beijing, China, on 8 Nov 2025. Spectators watched the 2025 *Honor of Kings* King Pro League Grand Finals and joined in the celebrations for the game's 10th anniversary. GWR Adjudicators were present to hand over a certificate in front of the superlatively sized crowd.

OCT 24 In 2014, Google's senior vice president, Alan Eustace (USA), performed the **highest freefall parachute jump** – 41,422 m (135,898 ft) – above New Mexico, USA.

OCT 25 Cirque du Soleil performer Nicolas Montes de Oca (MEX) completed the **most handstands in one minute** – 41 – in Barcelona, Spain, in 2022.

Highest-grossing live-action movie based on a videogame

A Minecraft Movie (USA/SWE/NZ/CAN, 2025) had taken $961,187,780 (£712.2 m) worldwide as of 25 Feb 2026, according to The Numbers. The film also enjoyed the **highest-grossing opening weekend for a movie based on a videogame**, with global box-office earnings of $313.7 m (£243.1 m). Its stars include Danielle Brooks, Jack Black and Jason Momoa (far left to centre).

BEST-SELLING HEROINE

It's no surprise that games in the *Tomb Raider* series, fronted by adventuring archaeologist Lara Croft, have sold over 100 million units, as verified by Crystal Dynamics (the current developers) on 11 Oct 2024. Since 1996, Lara's starred in 12 main *Tomb Raider* titles, making her gaming's most successful heroine.

GAMER'S EDITION 2027

Check out our latest gaming bible, with: a section devoted to all-time essential records; must-know stats about the Nintendo Switch 2; the lowdown on the **youngest game developer**; and much, much more!

Most viewed trailer

Released on 6 May 2025, the second trailer for *Grand Theft Auto VI* (Rockstar Games, 2026) had more than 475 million views across all platforms. It confirms *GTA VI*'s status as the year's most highly anticipated game.

GTA VI's first reveal is still the **most viewed game trailer on YouTube in 24 hours** with 90,421,491 views, as confirmed on 5 Dec 2023.

OCT 26 — On this day in 2024, Price Schwanke (USA) built the **longest bridge in *Minecraft*** – comprising 44,444 blocks – in Lakeville, Minnesota, USA.

OCT 27 — The XIX Olympiad, which ended on this day in 1968, was held in Mexico City at 2,250 m (7,380 ft) above sea level – the **highest-altitude Summer Olympics**.

TV

MOST IN-DEMAND TV SHOWS OF 2025

Our selection of small-screen hits uses Parrot Analytics' "Demand Expressions per capita" metric, evaluating popularity in terms of viewing figures and engagement. The Voice USA's *37.6x rating means it was 37.6 times more popular than the average TV series, for example.*

Overall: *Stranger Things* (Netflix): 103.6x

Reality TV: *The Voice USA* (NBC): 37.6x

Romantic drama: *Heated Rivalry* (Crave): 45.7x

Documentary: *Formula 1: Drive to Survive* (Netflix): 20.5x

Children's TV show: *SpongeBob SquarePants* (Nickelodeon): 47.6x

Most in-demand debut for a TV show

HBO's *IT: Welcome to Derry* (USA) was 2025's most popular new TV series, according to data-science firm Parrot Analytics, with a global demand rating of 88.3x based on the 30 days after its premiere on 26 Oct 2025. A prequel to the chilling horror novel *It*, the series is set in 1962 and explores the origins of the malevolent clown Pennywise.

Most translated season for a streaming series

Season 1 of *The Chosen* – a crowdfunded dramatization of the life of Jesus Christ and his followers, supported by the NPO Come and See (both USA) – was produced in 125 languages, from Afrikaans to Waray. The feat was confirmed at the show's annual convention – ChosenCon – on 20 Feb 2026.

Oldest person to win a Daytime Emmy award

Veteran TV naturalist Sir David Attenborough (UK, b. 8 May 1926) received the gong for Outstanding Daytime Personality – Non-Daily at the age of 99 years 162 days on 17 Oct 2025. He won for his show *Secret Lives of Orangutans* (Netflix, USA).

Most phone numbers recalled in three minutes

Christian Schäfer (DEU) called the cellphones of 11 audience members (having memorized 200 phone numbers!) on *Guinness World Records – Die große Show der Weltrekorde* in Munich, Germany, on 30 Aug 2025. The memory master also holds the title for the **longest sequence of coins memorized** – 250.

Largest collection of *Stranger Things* memorabilia

As of 10 Jan 2026, Joey Avalos (USA) owned 2,301 items related to Netflix's hit sci-fi/horror series, which he keeps in Chandler, Arizona, USA. Avalos fell for the Duffer brothers' love letter to 1980s pop culture when it debuted in 2016. He began with an Eleven Funko POP! figure and then, "Like the Upside Down, my collection continued to spread throughout my house", he told GWR.

Youngest male actor to win a Primetime Emmy

Owen Cooper (UK, b. 5 Dec 2009) was just 15 years 283 days old when he bagged the Emmy for Outstanding Supporting Actor in a Limited or Anthology Series or Movie. The winning role was his screen debut as Jamie Miller in Netflix's miniseries *Adolescence*. The 77th Primetime Emmy Awards were held in Los Angeles, California, USA, on 14 Sep 2025.

Longest time between an original TV drama series and a reunion film with the same main cast

Landmark TV teen drama *Oretachi no Tabi* ("Our Journey"; NNN, JPN) debuted on 5 Oct 1975. After 50 years 96 days, its lead actors – Masatoshi Nakamura, Taisaku Akino, Ken Tanaka and Nana Okada – reprised their original roles for the film *50nenme no Oretachi no Tabi* ("Our 50-Year Journey", JPN), released on 9 Jan 2026.

Most capital cities named on a rollercoaster in one minute

For the 20th anniversary of game show *Postkodmiljonären* ("Postcode Millionaire"), Jonas von Essen named 48 capitals while riding a rollercoaster on 24 Nov 2025. Von Essen – a memory athlete and former top-prize winner on the *Who Wants to Be a Millionaire?* series – was joined by then-host Rickard Sjöberg (both SWE), who read out the country names.

Later that day, Sjöberg achieved his own GWR title (one of his bucket-list dreams) with the **fastest 10 m holding a balloon between the knees** – 3.91 sec. Both records were achieved in Gothenburg, Sweden.

Largest single set build on a reality TV show

"The City" in *Beast Games 2* (USA) occupied 162.95 ha (402.66 acres), as verified in Greenville, North Carolina, USA, in 2025. This mini-metropolis for contestants acted both as a living space and competition hub. Hosted by YouTube megastar and GWR ICON MrBeast (aka Jimmy Donaldson, USA; above), the show's second season also set competitive reality TV titles for the **most live cannons fired** (10) and **most supercars used** (also 10).

OCT 28 To be brief: the **shortest street** is Ebenezer Place in Wick, Caithness, UK, with a length of just 2.05 m (6 ft 9 in), as confirmed on this day in 2006.

OCT 29 In 2001, Francisco Javier Galán Marín (ESP) struck the **fastest kick of a soccer ball** – 129 km/h (80.1 mph) – at the studios of *El Show de los Récords* in Madrid, Spain.

MOST VIEWED FILM ON NETFLIX
Since its premiere on 20 Jun 2025, *KPop Demon Hunters* (USA) had logged more than 540 million views worldwide as of 22 Jan 2026. Remarkably, it had also stayed on Netflix's Top 10 movie listings for 31 weeks, as of that date.

The movie's totemic track "Golden" became a smash-hit single, topping the *Billboard* Hot 100 and charts worldwide. Its singers, shown above, are (left to right): Rei Ami (b. Sarah Yeeun Lee, KOR), EJAE (b. Kim Eun-jae, KOR/USA) and Audrey Nuna (b. Audrey Chu, USA), who perform as the fictional girl band HUNTR/X. "Golden" went on to become the **first K-pop track to win a Grammy**, picking up the trophy for Best Song Written for Visual Media at the 68th Annual Grammy Awards on 1 Feb 2026.

The movie secured yet more gongs on 15 Mar 2026, with Oscars for Best Animated Feature and Best Original Song ("Golden").

OCT 30 Le Salon du Chocolat (FRA) presented the **largest showcase of chocolate dresses** – 23 – on a catwalk in Paris, France, in 2008. Or should that be *chic*-olate?

OCT 31 To protest the refereeing in a previous game, Stade Olympique l'Emyrne netted the **most own goals in a football match** – 149 – vs AS Adema (both MDG) in 2002.

Round-Up

Celebrating a veteran singer
Tony Christie (UK, b. Anthony Fitzgerald, 25 Apr 1943) was aged 61 years 349 days on 9 Apr 2005, when his charity single "(Is This the Way to) Amarillo" and set *Definitive Collection* made him the **oldest male artist to top the UK singles and albums charts simultaneously**.

The 33 years 126 days between the chart debut of "Amarillo" on 20 Nov 1971 and its No.1 placing on 26 Mar 2005 also makes Christie the **male artist with the slowest climb to No.1 on the UK Official Singles Chart**. On 1 Dec 2025, GWR's Craig Glenday belatedly handed over the official certificates on the vintage crooner's farewell tour.

Most concurrent views for a podcast on YouTube
Hosted by brothers Travis and Jason Kelce, "New Heights" attracted 1.3 million simultaneous views on YouTube on 13 Aug 2025. The main draw was guest star Taylor Swift (soon to be Travis's fiancée), who chatted about her upcoming release *The Life of a Showgirl*. It would go on to become the **fastest-selling US album**, with first-week sales of 4.002 million equivalent album units on 3–9 Oct.

Most puppets at a film premiere
On 19 Nov 2025, a total of 127 puppets and their operators from the troupe 31 Minutos (CHL) took to the red carpet in Santiago de Chile. They were there to celebrate their Prime Video release *Calurosa Navidad*.

Longest *Super Mario* videogame marathon
Audrey Mina (JPN) spent 60 hr 17 min 58 sec engrossed in *Super Mario* games in Chiyoda, Tokyo, Japan, between 2 and 5 May 2025.

Most followers on Twitch
By 24 Feb 2026, Kai Cenat (USA) had accumulated 20.2 million fans on this live-streaming platform. He joined Twitch in Jan 2021, and his mix of comedy, gaming, celebrity cameos and "subathons" (live marathons driven by subscriptions and donations) secured him a loyal following.

Largest display of tree-root sculptures
Artist Chen Xing (CHN) has hewn 3,666 sculptures from the roots of trees, as verified in Tengchong, Yunnan, China, on 29 Dec 2025. Chen has operated a studio in Tengchong for two decades. Root carving is an ancient tradition in China, with origins dating back more than 2,000 years.

Largest knitted diorama
Creative Crafters Ireland unveiled a 15.92-m^2 (171.36-sq-ft) woollen recreation of the Emerald Isle at Carnew Community Care in County Wicklow, Ireland, on 30 Sep 2025. Aged from 65 to 90, the team of women spent more than four years on the diorama, which includes Irish provinces, landmarks and coastal features. The group had to down needles in 2020, owing to the COVID-19 pandemic. Sadly, when they resumed in 2022, two members – shown below in framed photos – had passed away.

NOV 1 Roll up, roll up! Shivganga Roller Skating Club (IND) assembled 308 sure-footed dancers for the **longest conga line on roller skates** in Belagavi, India, in 2019.

NOV 2 The **largest collection of coffee pots** – 27,390 in all – belongs to Robert Dahl (DEU), as verified in 2012. He stores the fine blend in Rövershagen, Germany.

Largest gathering dressed as screen characters
On 27 Sep 2025, a group of 874 cosplayers turned out as their favourite film and TV personas for an event organized by the Old Royal Naval College in Greenwich, London, and Elstree Studios (both UK). The celebration paid tribute to the college grounds being the UK's most-filmed heritage site; since 1925, it has appeared in 200-plus productions.

Most expensive 20th-century painting
Portrait of Elisabeth Lederer (1914–16), by the Austrian artist Gustav Klimt, fetched $236.4 m (£179.6 m) at Sotheby's New York, USA, on 18 Nov 2025. It is topped only by the **most expensive artwork** – Leonardo da Vinci's *Salvator Mundi* (*c.* 1499–1510), which realized $450.3 m (£343 m) in Nov 2017.

Fastest-selling PlayStation game
Helldivers II (Arrowhead Game Studios, 2024), which is published by Sony Interactive Entertainment, sold a combined 12 million units on PC and PlayStation in the 12 weeks from its launch on 8 Feb 2024. *Helldivers II* benefitted from a competitive price tag and by allowing cross-play between platforms.

Largest hand-tufted carpet
Patodia Contract (IND) unveiled a 12,464.29-m^2 (134,164.5-sq-ft) floor covering in the Kazakh capital of Astana on 19 Sep 2025. Crafted by more than 1,000 skilled artisans over some six months, it was later installed in the city's Grand Mosque.

Most expensive painting by a female artist
El sueño (La cama), or *The Dream (The Bed)* (1940), by Mexican artist Frida Kahlo, was snapped up by an undisclosed bidder for $54.7 m (£41.7 m), including fees, at Sotheby's New York, USA, on 20 Nov 2025. Kahlo's art rarely comes to market, as the Mexican government has declared her work an artistic monument, meaning that her pieces are now obliged to stay within her home country.

Oldest non-figurative painting
A stencilled hand with stylized, claw-like fingers, dated to at least 67,800 years ago, has been discovered with other Palaeolithic paintings in the Liang Metanduno cave on Muna Island in south-east Sulawesi, Indonesia. Details of the find were published in the journal *Nature* on 21 Jan 2026.

Highest-grossing PG film
Disney's *Zootopia 2* (aka *Zootropolis 2*; USA, 2025) had earned $1,710,396,118 (£1.27 bn) as of 20 Jan 2026, according to The Numbers. The film broke the $1-bn barrier just 17 days after its release.

Highest-grossing lead actress
As of 26 Jan 2026, the 18 movies in which Zoe Saldaña (USA) has played a lead role had earned $15,615,919,486 (£11.44 bn), according to The Numbers. Saldaña has starred in four of the 10 biggest box-office hits ever, including the three *Avatar* films (see pp.178–79).

As of the same date, the 57 movies starring Samuel L Jackson (USA) had taken $14,613,700,731 (£10.7 bn), making him the **highest-grossing lead actor**. Jackson's films include *Jurassic Park* (USA, 1993) and the Marvel blockbuster *Avengers: Endgame* (USA, 2019).

Bonnie Hunt (USA), who voices Bonnie Hopps in *Zootopia 2* (left), is the **highest-grossing actress in supporting roles**, with a cumulative gross of $9,095,165,716 (£6.66 bn) from 20 films.

Tallest LEGO®-brick fictional character
On 19 Nov 2025, a 10.07-m (33-ft) plastic-brick giant was presented by Bidaya FZ (UAE) in Abu Dhabi, UAE. The model depicted "Mansour", a 12-year-old Emirati character who's the star of a TV series of the same name and has become a popular icon among young Arabic audiences.

NOV 3 In 2010, the **largest burrito** – 5,799.44 kg (12,785 lb 9 oz) – was served up in Baja California Sur, Mexico, at an event arranged by CANIRAC La Paz (MEX).

NOV 4 François Gabart (FRA) set off in his trimaran *MACIF* for what would become the **fastest circumnavigation sailing solo** – 42 days 16 hr 40 min 35 sec – in 2017.

SNAPSHOT

Deepest Freedive

In 2007, on just a single breath, a daredevil freediver descended to a depth greater than the iconic Seattle Space Needle is tall – a record-breaking plunge that pushed the limits of equipment, safety planning and human physiology.

Freediver Herbert Nitsch (AUT) was no stranger to superlatives when he attempted his most audacious descent to date. It was 14 Jun 2007, and this celebrated diver and his team were in Greece's Saronic Gulf to improve upon the most challenging of Nitsch's many records – the **deepest no-limits freedive**.

This extreme sport, governed by AIDA – the International Association for the Development of Apnea – challenges divers to go as deep as possible while holding their breath. As per the rules, claimants may use any technology to help them travel vertically, and crucially must be conscious when they return to the surface!

Nitsch utilized a weighted sled to pull him feet-first into the Aegean Sea, past the limits of recreational scuba divers. After 105 sec, he came to a halt at an unprecedented 214 m (702 ft) – a depth that even the Greek summer sun could not reach. There, temperatures were near-freezing and the pressure was around 22 times that at the surface.

To visualize this depth, we've uprooted the 184.4-m-tall (605-ft) Space Needle from its home in central Seattle, Washington, USA, and lowered it on to the Greek seabed. While it only represents about 86% of the vertical distance that Nitsch travelled – it's about 10 storeys short – it clearly demonstrates just how deep he dived.

After the briefest of pauses, Nitsch triggered the ascent system that returned him to the surface. Not only was he fully conscious, he was now the holder of a new world record, and truly deserving of his nickname: "The Deepest Man on Earth".

The Space Needle was built as part of the 1962 World's Fair to symbolize Seattle's futuristic ambition.

Nitsch has dominated this record since 2005. Labelled here are the last four AIDA-certified deep-dive records, all set by Nitsch.

Nitsch equalized the pressure in his ears and sinuses by breathing into an empty Coca-Cola bottle, releasing small amounts of air as needed.

Following the ratification of Nitsch's record, no-limit dives were discontinued by AIDA, who cited the overwhelming risk factors and an increasing reliance on technology. This has not stopped divers going ever deeper, however, with Nitsch himself making the **deepest non-AIDA-certified no-limits freedive**, descending 253 m (830 ft) on 6 Jun 2012 off Santorini, Greece – a dive that left him with severe decompression sickness.

NOV 5 The Netherlands hit the **highest score in a World Korfball Championship final** – 32 – against Belgium in 2011.

NOV 6 In 2009, Cha Sa-soon (KOR) finally aced it after taking the **most driving theory tests** – on her 950th attempt!

NOV 7 The **fastest time to assemble Mr. Potato Head** is 4.75 sec, by Lim Kai Yi (MYS) on this day in 2024.

NOV 8 Paddy Doyle (UK) performed the **most squats in one hour** – 4,708 – in Birmingham, UK, in 2007.

ICON Shohei Ohtani

Los Angeles Dodgers star Shohei Ohtani (JPN) continues to build his legacy as one of the greatest players in the history of baseball. An ultra-rare "two-way" superstar who plays as both a pitcher and a designated hitter, "Shotime" has followed in the footsteps of one of the sport's most celebrated names, George "Babe" Ruth.

Shohei was born in 1994 in a farming town 300 mi (482 km) north of Tokyo. His father was an amateur baseballer and his mother played badminton. Shohei's performances in high-school baseball made waves both in Japan and beyond – but he had to work hard to prove that he could play as both a batter and a pitcher. Shohei made his pro debut at the age of 18, appearing as a right fielder for Nippon Professional Baseball side Hokkaido Nippon-Ham Fighters. He joined Major League Baseball (MLB) in 2018, winning two American League (AL) MVP awards with the Los Angeles Angels. In 2023, he signed a 10-year deal with the LA Dodgers worth $700 m (£557 m) – at that time, the **largest MLB contract**. Shohei propelled the Dodgers to back-to-back championships, his heroic postseason performances in 2025 only confirming his status as a once-in-a-generation talent.

VITAL STATISTICS

Name	Shohei Ohtani
Birthplace	Mizusawa, Iwate, Japan
Birth date	5 Jul 1994
Current GWR titles	Multiple, including the **first 50/50 MLB season**
MLB honours	• 5 x All-Star (2021–25) • 4 x MVP (2021, 2023–25) • 2 x World Series winner (2024–25)

On 21 Mar 2012, Shohei hit the 37th home run of his high-school career at the National High School Baseball Invitational Tournament in Japan. In August that same year, the 18-year-old made the headlines again when he unleashed a 99-mph (160-km/h) fastball in the Iwate regional tournament – at that time, the fastest-ever pitch by a Japanese high-school player.

In 2023, Shohei received his second unanimous American League MVP award with the LA Angels. He hit over .300 and led the AL in home runs (44) and total bases (325). On the mound, Shohei posted an ERA of 3.14 and struck out 167 batters in 132 innings. He became the first player in MLB to receive multiple unanimous MVP awards – and has since won two more with the LA Dodgers.

Shohei is a "two-way" player in more ways than one – he throws right-handed and bats left-handed!

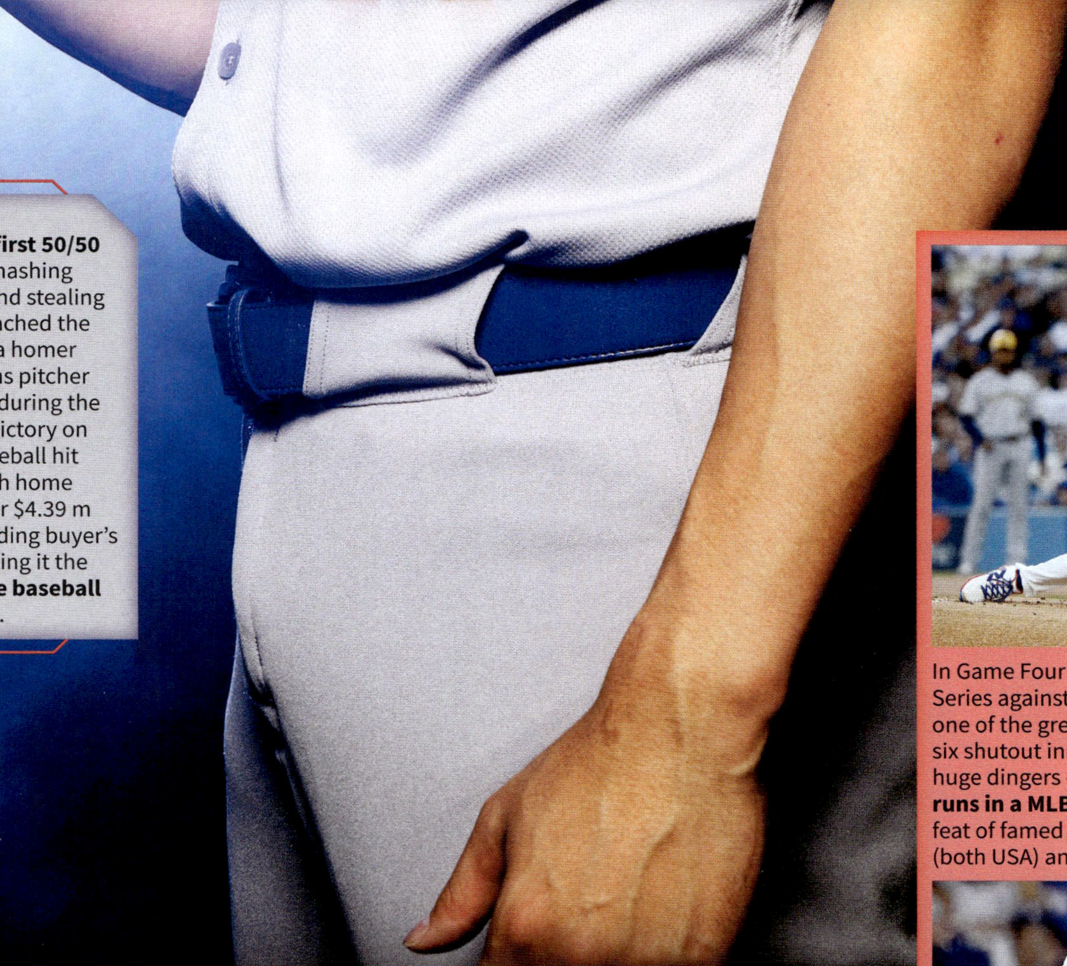

In 2024, Shohei completed the **first 50/50 MLB season**, smashing 54 home runs and stealing 59 bases. He reached the landmark with a homer off Miami Marlins pitcher Mike Baumann during the Dodgers' 20–4 victory on 19 Sep. The baseball hit for Shohei's 50th home run later sold for $4.39 m (£3.38 m), including buyer's premium – making it the **most expensive baseball sold at auction**.

On 27 Oct 2025, Shohei equalled the record for the **most extra-base hits in a World Series game** – four – tying Frank Isbell's (USA) feat for the Chicago White Sox in Game Five of the 1906 World Series. Shohei hit two home runs and two doubles against the Toronto Blue Jays. He also matched the record for the **most times safely reaching base in an MLB game** – nine.

Shohei's beloved dog Dekopin – aka Decoy – has found fame as the MLB's "Most Valuable Pet". In Jan 2024, the Kooikerhondje was presented with his own "visa" by the US embassy in Tokyo. Ahead of the LA Dodgers' game against the Baltimore Orioles on 28 Aug 2024, Decoy delivered the ceremonial first pitch to Shohei (right).

In Game Four of the 2025 National League Championship Series against the Milwaukee Brewers, Shohei produced one of the greatest games in baseball history. He pitched six shutout innings, striking out 10 batters, and hit three huge dingers – equalling the record for the **most home runs in a MLB postseason game**. Shohei matched the feat of famed sluggers such as Babe Ruth, Reggie Jackson (both USA) and Albert Pujols (DOM).

Discover all of GWR's incredible ICONS at **guinnessworldrecords.com/records/icons**

SPORTS

CONTENTS

Johannes Høsflot Klæbo's golden haul helped propel Norway to the top of the medal rankings at the 2026 Winter Olympics. The Scandinavian country was dominant throughout the Games, winning 18 events to surpass its own record for the **most gold medals won by a country at a single Winter Olympics.**

MILANO CORTINA 2026 MEDAL TABLE

Norway	18	12	11
USA	12	12	9
Netherlands	10	7	3
Italy	10	6	14
Germany	8	10	8

MOST GOLD MEDALS WON AT A SINGLE WINTER OLYMPICS
Johannes Høsflot Klæbo (NOR) made history at the 2026 Winter Olympics in Italy, winning all six of his cross-country skiing events. The previous best had been five, by speed skater Eric Heiden at the 1980 Games in Lake Placid, USA.

Klæbo's golden glut took his career total to 11 – earning him the outright record for the **most Winter Olympic gold medals**. Only one other athlete has won more Olympic titles: US swimmer Michael Phelps, who claimed 23 at four Summer Games between 2004 and 2016.

BIG PICTURE

Fastest F1 Pit Stop

Formula One pit stops are a blink-and-you'll-miss-it operation, demanding unbelievable speed and choreographed precision from more than 20 crew members. At the 2023 Qatar Grand Prix on 8 Oct, the McLaren Formula 1 Team (UK) completed the **fastest F1 pit stop** on driver Lando Norris's car in just 1.80 sec.

Winning formula

In 2025, McLaren claimed their first Formula One drivers' world championship for 17 years. Lando Norris (below) sealed the title in dramatic fashion, finishing third in the final race of the season in Abu Dhabi to ward off Red Bull's Max Verstappen and McLaren teammate Oscar Piastri.

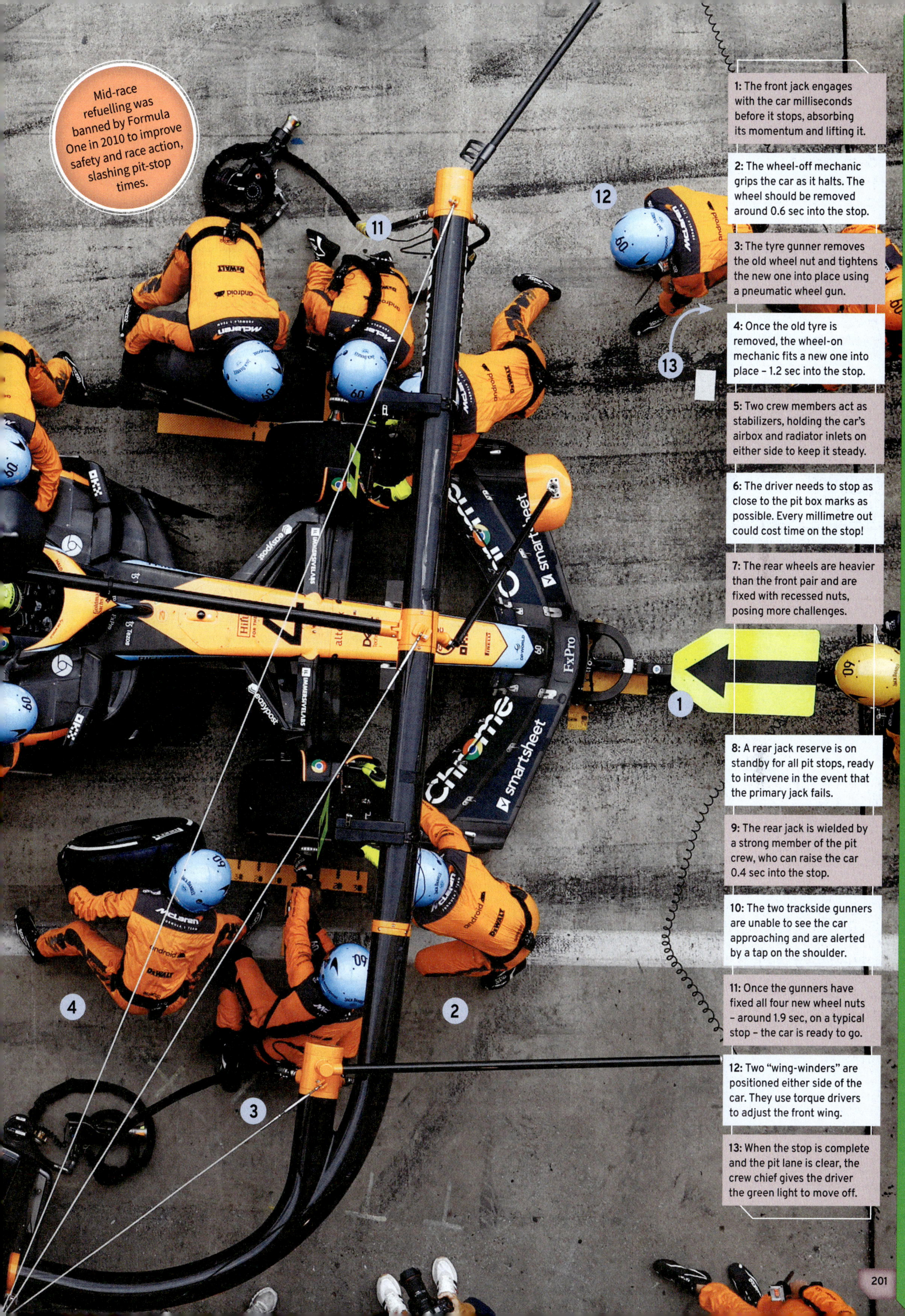

Mid-race refuelling was banned by Formula One in 2010 to improve safety and race action, slashing pit-stop times.

1: The front jack engages with the car milliseconds before it stops, absorbing its momentum and lifting it.

2: The wheel-off mechanic grips the car as it halts. The wheel should be removed around 0.6 sec into the stop.

3: The tyre gunner removes the old wheel nut and tightens the new one into place using a pneumatic wheel gun.

4: Once the old tyre is removed, the wheel-on mechanic fits a new one into place – 1.2 sec into the stop.

5: Two crew members act as stabilizers, holding the car's airbox and radiator inlets on either side to keep it steady.

6: The driver needs to stop as close to the pit box marks as possible. Every millimetre out could cost time on the stop!

7: The rear wheels are heavier than the front pair and are fixed with recessed nuts, posing more challenges.

8: A rear jack reserve is on standby for all pit stops, ready to intervene in the event that the primary jack fails.

9: The rear jack is wielded by a strong member of the pit crew, who can raise the car 0.4 sec into the stop.

10: The two trackside gunners are unable to see the car approaching and are alerted by a tap on the shoulder.

11: Once the gunners have fixed all four new wheel nuts – around 1.9 sec, on a typical stop – the car is ready to go.

12: Two "wing-winders" are positioned either side of the car. They use torque drivers to adjust the front wing.

13: When the stop is complete and the pit lane is clear, the crew chief gives the driver the green light to move off.

NFL

Most Super Bowl appearances

Super Bowl LX saw the New England Patriots reach "Super Sunday" for the 12th time – four more than any other NFL side. The Patriots have won six and lost six of their 12 appearances, tying the Pittsburgh Steelers for the **most Super Bowl wins.** Their latest visit ended in disappointment, with a 29–13 loss to the Seattle Seahawks.

Longest field goal

On 2 Nov 2025, Cam Little kicked a 68-yard field goal for the Jacksonville Jaguars against the Las Vegas Raiders. The record-breaking kick took place under the dome at Las Vegas's Allegiant Stadium. Little went on to record the second-longest NFL field goal, 67 yards, outdoors against the Tennessee Titans on 4 Jan 2026.

Most 200-yard rushing games

On 27 Dec 2025, Derrick Henry completed 200 yards rushing in a single NFL game for the seventh time. The Baltimore Ravens running back went for 216 yards and four touchdowns against the Green Bay Packers to break a three-way tie for the record. As of the end of the 2025 season, "King Henry" had compiled 13,018 career rushing yards – more than any other active player.

*all players USA

Fewest games to throw 250 touchdown passes

Patrick Mahomes chalked up his 250th TD pass in his 116th NFL game: a 37–20 win for the Kansas City Chiefs over the Baltimore Ravens on 28 Sep 2025. He beat Aaron Rodgers's previous record by five games. Mahomes became only the 28th player in league history to reach the mark.

Most passes completed in a game

On 16 Nov 2025, Arizona Cardinals quarterback Jacoby Brissett completed 47 passes during a 41–22 loss to the San Francisco 49ers. Brissett equalled the record set by Ben Roethlisberger for the Pittsburgh Steelers against the Cleveland Browns on 10 Jan 2021.

Brissett's teammate Trey McBride was also a record breaker in 2025, making the **most receptions by a tight end in a season** – 126. McBride generated 1,239 yards receiving and scored 11 touchdowns.

Most teams played for

Quarterback Josh Johnson joined his 14th NFL franchise in 2025, signing with the Washington Commanders. His nomadic career began in 2008 with the Tampa Bay Buccaneers. In 2015, Johnson was on the roster of four teams in a single season.

Youngest player to make 500 receptions

Justin Jefferson (b. 16 Jun 1999) was 26 years 90 days old when he reached 500 career catches on 14 Sep 2025, during the Minnesota Vikings' 22–6 defeat to the Atlanta Falcons. Remarkably, he tied the record of the Arizona Cardinals' Larry Fitzgerald, who reached the milestone at exactly the same age in 2009. Jefferson achieved the feat in 79 games, seven games fewer than Fitzgerald.

Most field goals in a Super Bowl game

Jason Myers kicked five field goals for the Seattle Seahawks at Super Bowl LX, held at Levi's Stadium in Santa Clara, California, on 8 Feb 2026. Myers was the only player to score in the first three quarters, adding two extra points to his five field goals to finish the game with 17 points. The Seahawks saw off the New England Patriots (see above left) 29–13 to claim their second championship title.

Most quarterback sacks in a season

On 4 Jan 2026, Myles Garrett of the Cleveland Browns tackled Joe Burrow to register his 23rd sack of the NFL season. He overtook the previous record of 22.5, by Michael Strahan and T J Watt. A two-time Defensive Player of the Year, Garrett logged his 100th career sack in 2024 – also on Cincinnati Bengals QB Burrow. Sacks became an official NFL statistic in 1982.

NOV 9 In 2009, a Norwegian branch of furniture retail giant IKEA baked the **largest gingerbread man.** It weighed in at a polar-bear-sized 651 kg (1,435 lb)!

NOV 10 The Emirates Minting Factory (UAE) unveiled the **largest gold bar** in 2024. The 300-kg (661-lb) ingot was worth approximately £20 m ($25.8 m).

MOST RUSHING TOUCHDOWNS BY A QUARTERBACK

Josh Allen crossed into the end zone 79 times between 2018 and 2025. He surpassed Cam Newton's record of 75 with an 8-yard score during the Buffalo Bills' 26–7 win over the Pittsburgh Steelers on 30 Nov 2025. Only running back Derrick Henry (see opposite) has more rushing TDs – 122 – among active players.

Standing 6 ft 5 in (1.95 m) tall, Allen is a dual-threat QB who has led the Bills to seven playoff appearances and five divisional titles. On 28 Dec 2025, he achieved the **fewest games to reach 300 touchdowns** – 127 – with a 2-yard run against Philadelphia.

Most rushing touchdowns by a quarterback in a season

In 2023, a pair of QBs set a new record by running in 15 touchdowns in a single NFL season: Josh Allen of the Buffalo Bills and Jalen Hurts of the Philadelphia Eagles (above). The previous mark of 14 – set by the Carolina Panthers' Cam Newton – had stood for 12 years.

NOV 11 In 2014, carpenter Devendra Suthar (IND) was confirmed as having the **most fingers and toes on a living person**: 28. He had 14 fingers and 14 toes.

NOV 12 French gymnast and circus pioneer Jules Léotard demonstrated the **first flying trapeze act** on this day in 1859, at Cirque Napoléon in Paris, France.

North American Sports

Fastest softball pitch
On 25 May 2025, a pitch from Karlyn Pickens of the Tennessee Lady Volunteers was clocked at 79.4 mph (127.7 km/h). The 6-ft 1-in (1.85-m) fireballer has been wowing coaches with her speed for years, hitting 60 mph (96 km/h) when she was just 12. Her record-breaking pitch was fired at the Nebraska Cornhuskers' Jordy Bahl in an NCAA Division I game.

Most home runs by a designated hitter in a Major League Baseball season
Kyle Schwarber of the Philadelphia Phillies went deep 56 times in 2025. He finished one clear of Shohei Ohtani (see pp.196–97). On 28 Aug, Schwarber became the 21st player to hit the **most home runs in an MLB match**, smashing four against the Atlanta Braves.

Most MVP awards won by a WNBA player
A'ja Wilson of the Las Vegas Aces was voted the best player in the league for a record fourth time in 2025. It was an extraordinary year for Wilson, who won her third WNBA championship as the Aces swept the Phoenix Mercury 4–0. She was voted Finals MVP and Defensive Player of the Year, and also led the league in scoring. On 25 Jun 2025, Wilson set a new record for the **fewest WNBA games to reach 5,000 points** – 238.

**all players USA, unless stated otherwise*

Fastest pitch thrown in an MLB postseason game
In Game 2 of the 2025 National League Wild Card Series between the San Diego Padres and the Chicago Cubs, Mason Miller produced a 104.5-mph (168.1-km/h) fastball to strike out Chicago's Carson Kelly. The previous record of 104.2 mph (167.6 km/h), by Aroldis Chapman, had stood for 15 years.

On 5 Aug 2025, Miller produced the **fastest MLB pitch to be hit for a home run** – 103.9 mph (167.2 km/h) – to Lourdes Gurriel Jr (CUB) of the Arizona Diamondbacks.

Fewest MLB games to reach 350 home runs
On 12 Jul 2025, Aaron Judge hit his 350th dinger in just his 1,088th game. The New York Yankees slugger beat Mark McGwire's previous record by 192 games.

Most total bases in an MLB game
Nick Kurtz of the Athletics racked up 19 total bases against the Houston Astros on 25 Jul 2025. He became the first rookie to hit four home runs – equalling the outright record for the **most home runs in an MLB match** (see right) – and also recorded a double and a single. Kurtz matched the figures of Shawn Green for the Los Angeles Dodgers against the Milwaukee Brewers on 23 May 2002.

Most points by a rookie in a WNBA game
Paige Bueckers scored 44 points for the Dallas Wings against the Los Angeles Sparks on 20 Aug 2025. She shot 17 of 21 from the field, scoring more than half of her team's points in an 81–80 loss. Cynthia Cooper of the Houston Comets also scored 44 points in the WNBA's inaugural season in 1997.

Youngest player to score 40 points in an NBA game
Cooper Flagg (b. 21 Dec 2006) was 18 years 359 days old when he put up 42 points for the Dallas Mavericks during their 140–133 overtime loss to the Utah Jazz on 15 Dec 2025. Flagg skipped a year of high school in order to begin his NBA career as soon as possible.

Most overtime goals in an NHL season
Leon Draisaitl (DEU) scored six OT goals for the Edmonton Oilers in 2024/25. He also set a new **postseason** record of four. Despite hitting game-winners in Games 1 and 4 of the Stanley Cup Finals, however, Draisaitl couldn't prevent the Oilers going down to a 4–2 series loss to the Florida Panthers (see below).

Sam Reinhart also scored the decisive goal in Game 7 of the 2024 Stanley Cup Finals – also against the Edmonton Oilers.

Most goals in an NHL Stanley Cup Finals game
Sam Reinhart (CAN) scored four times in Game 6 of the 2025 Stanley Cup Finals as the Florida Panthers powered to a 5–1 win over the Edmonton Oilers. Reinhart became only the sixth player – and the first since 1957 – to net four in a Finals match. The victory sealed a 4–2 series win for the Panthers, earning them back-to-back championships.

NOV 13 Dominic Cuzzacrea (USA) achieved the **highest pancake toss** in 2010. He caught a crepe flipped 9.47 m (31 ft 1 in) into the air in Cheektowaga, New York, USA.

NOV 14 In 2017, François Gabart (FRA) completed the **greatest distance sailed single-handedly in 24 hr** – 850.68 nautical mi (1,575.45 km) in the South Atlantic.

MOST NBA SEASONS PLAYED

On 18 Nov 2025, Los Angeles Lakers forward LeBron James took to the court to kick off his 23rd season in the NBA. The four-time champion had entered the league as the first overall pick of the 2003 NBA draft.

On 12 Feb 2026, James (b. 30 Dec 1984) became the **oldest NBA player to achieve a triple-double**, logging 28 points, 12 assists and 10 rebounds against the Dallas Mavericks at the age of 41 years 44 days.

Most points in an NBA overtime period

On 25 Dec 2025, Nikola Jokić (SRB) racked up 18 points in a five-minute OT period during the Denver Nuggets' 142–138 win over the Minnesota Timberwolves. This beat Stephen Curry's record of 17, which had stood since 2016. Jokić finished the game with a 56-point triple-double, also claiming 16 rebounds and 15 assists.

NOV 15 In 2012, Steve Jacobs (AUS) pulled on the **most pairs of underpants** – an elastic-stretching 266 – in Sydney, New South Wales, Australia.

NOV 16 The **first aeroplane flight over Antarctica** was made in 1928 by Hubert Wilkins (AUS) and Carl Ben Eielson (USA). They were flying a Lockheed Vega aircraft.

Soccer

Most goal involvements in a Major League Soccer postseason
Lionel Messi (ARG) scored six goals and set up nine more for Inter Miami during their 2025 playoff run. In the MLS Cup final against the Vancouver Whitecaps on 6 Dec, Messi laid on two assists as Miami won 3–1 to claim their first MLS championship. Tadeo Allende's (ARG) injury-time strike gave him the **most goals in an MLS postseason** – nine.

DID YOU KNOW?

Matches at the first UEFA Women's Euros only lasted for 70 min.
The inaugural tournament in 1984 was unrecognizable to today's competition. Instead of 16 teams, just four qualified for the finals. Sweden beat England 4–3 on penalties to become champions, after the two-legged final ended 1–1.

Most soccer matches played

On 20 Aug 2025, Brazilian goalkeeper Fábio (b. Fábio Deivson Lopes Maciel) stepped out to make his 1,391st professional appearance, overtaking the record of former England keeper Peter Shilton. Fábio played every minute of the 2025 Brazilian league season for Fluminense, extending his record to 1,419 games by the end of the year.

First £1-m women's soccer transfer

On 17 Jul 2025, Olivia Smith (CAN) broke one of the great historical barriers in football, signing for Arsenal from Liverpool for £1 m ($1.3 m). The 20-year-old had enjoyed a standout WSL campaign with Liverpool, scoring seven league goals in 20 appearances. Her record for the **most expensive women's transfer fee** did not last for long, however, as the following month Mexico's Lizbeth Ovalle moved from Tigres UANL to Orlando Pride for £1.1 m ($1.4 m).

Smallest country by population to qualify for the FIFA World Cup

On 18 Nov 2025, the Caribbean island of Curaçao held Jamaica to a 0–0 draw to book their place at the 2026 FIFA World Cup – despite being a nation of just 156,115 people. Curaçao, aka the "Blue Wave", surpassed the feat of Iceland (population: 337,669) in qualifying for the 2018 tournament.

Youngest winner of a FIFA men's international tournament

Gilberto Mora (MEX, b. 14 Oct 2008) won the 2025 CONCACAF Gold Cup at the age of 16 years 265 days. His Mexico team defeated the USA 2–1 in the final on 6 Jul in only Mora's third international game. He beat the record of Spain's Lamine Yamal, who won the 2024 UEFA Euros aged 17 years 1 day.

Youngest player in the UEFA Champions League

Max Dowman (UK, b. 31 Dec 2009) was 15 years 308 days old when he came on for Arsenal during their 3–0 victory over Slavia Prague on 4 Nov 2025. The skilful midfielder became the first 15-year-old to play in the Champions League.

Fewest matches to score 100 goals in the English Premier League
Erling Haaland (NOR, b. UK) reached a century of English league goals in his 111th game, Manchester City's 5–4 win over Fulham on 2 Dec 2025. Haaland's tally included eight hat-tricks and the **most goals in an EPL season** – 36 – from his debut 2022/23 campaign.

Most wins of the Ballon d'Or Féminin

Aitana Bonmatí (ESP) was voted the best women's footballer on the planet for the third successive year in 2025, finishing ahead of her Spain teammate Mariona Caldentey and England's Alessia Russo. Bonmatí was named Player of the Tournament at the 2025 UEFA Women's Euros and UEFA Women's Champions League Player of the Season, despite losing both finals with Spain and Barcelona, respectively.

Most wins of the Women's Africa Cup of Nations

On 26 Jul 2025, Nigeria staged a dramatic 3–2 comeback win over hosts Morocco to claim their 10th WAFCON title. The Super Falcons also won the first two African Women's Championships in 1991 and 1995, but these tournaments are not usually included in official WAFCON statistics.

Most goalscorers for a team at a UEFA Women's European Championship
A total of 11 players found the net for England at the 2025 Women's Euros. The Lionesses successfully defended their title from 2022, beating Spain in the final after a penalty shootout. Six different players scored in a single game: the 6–1 romp over Wales in the group stages.

NOV 17 In 2014, the **longest fingernail** was measured at 197.8 cm (6 ft 6 in). It belonged to Shridhar Chillal (IND), who stopped trimming the nails of his left hand in 1952.

NOV 18 The **most expensive jeans** were sold at auction for $412,750 (£332,166) in 2023. The pair of blue Levi's had been worn by Nirvana frontman Kurt Cobain.

HIGHEST MARGIN OF VICTORY IN A UEFA CHAMPIONS LEAGUE FINAL

On 31 May 2025, Paris Saint-Germain (FRA) earned their first Champions League title in style, demolishing Inter Milan 5–0 at Munich's Allianz Arena. The previous biggest final win had been during the European Cup era (1955–92), when Real Madrid defeated Eintracht Frankfurt 7–3 in 1960. PSG were spearheaded by Man of the Match Désiré Doué, who produced the **most goal involvements in a UEFA Champions League final**, scoring twice and setting up Achraf Hakimi for PSG's first goal.

For even more facts and stats on the beautiful game, check out the ***Guinness World Records Football Edition 2027***.

Most wins of the European Cup/UEFA Champions League with different clubs by a manager

Paris Saint-Germain's victory in 2025 was a second title for coach Luis Enrique (ESP, centre), who had also masterminded Barcelona's path to glory in 2015. He is one of seven managers to lift the hallowed trophy with two different clubs, including Pep Guardiola (ESP) and Carlo Ancelotti (ITA).

NOV 19 The Indian Army's Tornadoes motorcycle team achieved the **most people on a motorbike** in 2017. A total of 58 riders balanced on a single 500-cc Royal Enfield.

NOV 20 In 2005, the Japanese spacecraft *Hayabusa* touched down on the 500-m-long (1,640-ft) asteroid Itokawa. This is the **smallest space rock landed on.**

Athletics

Fastest women's 1,500 m

On 5 Jul 2025, Faith Kipyegon (KEN) clocked 3 min 48.68 sec at the Prefontaine Classic in Eugene, Oregon, USA. It was the third successive year that she had broken the world record over the distance.

On 16 Sep 2025, Kipyegon extended her record for the **most wins of the women's 1,500 m at the World Athletics Championships** with her fourth title. She finished almost three seconds clear of the field.

Youngest men's long jump world champion

Mattia Furlani (ITA, b. 7 Feb 2005) was 20 years 222 days old when he won gold at the 20th World Athletics Championships in Tokyo, Japan, on 17 Sep 2025. His fifth-round jump of 8.39 m (27 ft 6 in) was enough to see off the field. Furlani surpassed the great Carl Lewis, who was 22 when he leapt to glory at the first World Athletics Championships in 1983. It was the Italian's second global title of the year, having also taken indoor gold on 23 Mar in Nanjing, China.

Farthest women's T62 long jump

Two-time Paralympic champion Fleur Jong (NLD) leapt 6.86 m (22 ft 6 in) on 7 Jun 2025 while competing at the International Golden Roof Challenge. This urban athletics event was staged in the heart of Innsbruck, Austria, on "The FlySwat" – a mobile athletics facility that complies with World Athletics' record-eligibility regulations.

Farthest men's discus throw

On 13 Apr 2025, Mykolas Alekna (LTU) hurled the discus 75.56 m (247 ft 10 in) at the Oklahoma Throws Series World Invitational in Ramona, USA. He broke his own world record twice, opening with a 74.89-m (245-ft 8-in) effort in the first round before going even farther in the fourth.

Highest men's pole vault

Armand Duplantis (SWE, b. USA) cleared 6.30 m (20 ft 8 in) at the World Athletics Championships on 15 Sep 2025. He had already won the gold – his eighth global title in a row – before taking on the record height. It was the fourth time that year that the high-flying Swede had set a new mark in the event, and his 14th overall.

In Feb 2025, Duplantis released his debut music single, "Bop". It racked up more than 2 million streams on Spotify.

Most World Athletics Championships appearances

Race walker João Vieira (PRT) took to the start line at his 14th world championships on 13 Sep 2025. The 49-year-old finished 20th in the 35 km race walk in Tokyo. Vieira (b. 20 Feb 1976) first entered the championships in 1999. Twenty years later, aged 43 years 221 days, he became the **oldest medallist** in its history, winning silver in Doha, Qatar.

Fastest men's T12 100 m

On 28 Sep 2025, Salum Ageze Kashafali (NOR, b. COD) won gold at the World Para Athletics Championships in New Delhi, India, in a time of 10.42 sec. The Congolese-born sprinter competes in the T12 classification for athletes with visual impairment. He first broke the 100 m record in 2019 – in his first-ever race as a Paralympian.

Fastest men's 35 km road walk

At the 2025 European Race Walking Team Championships in Poděbrady, Czechia, Massimo Stano (ITA) walked 35 km in 2 hr 20 min 43 sec, surpassing the previous best by almost a minute. Stano is an Olympic gold medallist over 20 km from the COVID-delayed 2020 Games.

Fastest women's New York City Marathon

On 2 Nov 2025, Hellen Obiri (KEN) ran 26.2 mi (42.1 km) through the streets of the Big Apple in 2 hr 19 min 51 sec. She took almost three minutes off the previous women's record, by Margaret Okayo, which had stood since 2003. It was Obiri's second triumph in New York in three years.

Sharon Lokedi (KEN) finished second behind Obiri, also running inside record time. On 21 Apr 2025, Lokedi completed the **fastest women's Boston Marathon**, coming home in 2 hr 17 min 22 sec and smashing the course record by more than two-and-a-half minutes.

Fastest women's London Wheelchair Marathon

Catherine Debrunner (CHE) claimed her third London Marathon title in 1 hr 34 min 18 sec on 27 Apr 2025. She broke her own course record by more than four minutes. Debrunner also holds numerous track world records in the T53 category, including the **fastest 100 m** – 15.20 sec – and the **fastest 400 m** – 49.02 sec.

NOV 21 The **most expensive movie prop** is Robby the Robot, from the 1956 sci-fi film *Forbidden Planet*. It fetched $5.375 m (£4.06 m) at Bonhams New York, USA, in 2017.

NOV 22 On this day in 2006, Li Jingguan (CHN) executed the **most somersaults in one minute** – 65 – at the Shaolin Tagou Martial Arts School in Dengfeng, Henan, China.

MOST WINS OF THE MEN'S 200 M AT THE WORLD ATHLETICS CHAMPIONSHIPS
On 19 Sep 2025, Noah Lyles (USA) claimed his fourth consecutive world championship 200 m title, crossing the line in 19.52 sec in Tokyo, Japan. The flamboyant sprinter matched the feat of Usain Bolt (JAM), who also won four in a row between 2009 and 2015 (see below right). Lyles has dominated his 200 m rivals at the world championships, clocking the fourth-best time in history – 19.31 sec – in 2022. But Olympic glory in the event has eluded him, earning two bronze medals in 2021 and 2024.

Most Diamond League men's track titles
Lyles is a six-time champion on the elite athletics circuit, winning five 200 m titles (in 2017–19, 2022 and 2025) and one in the 100 m (2019). He stands just one behind the overall **men's** record of seven Diamond League titles, shared by pole vaulter Renaud Lavillenie (FRA) and triple jumper Christian Taylor (USA).

Bolt out of the blue
Usain Bolt (JAM) won the first of his four 200 m world championships in style on 20 Aug 2009, running the **fastest 200 m** in 19.19 sec in Berlin, Germany. The 22-year-old broke his own world record of 19.30 sec, which he had set at the Beijing Olympics exactly one year earlier. Bolt won three of his eight Olympic gold medals over 200 m and still holds four of the seven fastest-ever times for the event.

NOV 23 Strongman Kevin Fast (CAN) got into the pre-Christmas spirit with the **heaviest sleigh pulled** – 16,500 kg (36,376 lb 4 oz), in Cobourg, Ontario, Canada, in 2020.

NOV 24 Keith Jorgenson and Nestor's Bakery (both CAN) served up the **longest doughnut** – 5.842 m (19 ft 2 in) – in Saskatoon, Saskatchewan, Canada, in 2015.

SPORTS

Cricket

Youngest batter to score a century in all three men's international formats
On 30 Sep 2025, Zimbabwe opener Brian Bennett (b. 10 Nov 2003) scored 111 in a T20 match against Tanzania to complete his set of international hundreds aged 21 years 324 days. He had already made 169 in an ODI against Ireland and Test tons against Afghanistan and England.

Youngest player to score a men's T20 century
Teenage sensation Vaibhav Sooryavanshi (IND, b. 27 Mar 2011) was just 14 years 32 days old when he blasted a 35-ball century for Rajasthan Royals against Gujarat Titans in the IPL on 28 Apr 2025. He broke the previous IPL record, held by compatriot Manish Pandey since 2009, by more than five-and-a-half years.

Most Test wickets by a left-arm fast bowler
Mitchell Starc (AUS) had dismissed 433 Test batsmen as of 7 Mar 2026. He surpassed Wasim Akram's total of 414 during the Second Test of the 2025/26 Ashes series, reaching 418 wickets in his 195th Test innings as a bowler. Starc was dominant throughout the Ashes, named Player of the Series and finishing as the leading wicket-taker with 31. His career total of 433 means that he is currently tied for the **most Test wickets by a left-arm bowler** outright, with Sri Lanka's Rangana Herath.

Most runs in a Men's T20 World Cup
Sahibzada Farhan plundered 383 runs from six visits to the crease at the 2026 tournament. The Pakistan opener produced scores of 47, 73, 0, 100 not out, 63 and 100 to surpass Virat Kohli's record of 319 runs – also in six innings – from 2014. Farhan became the first player to hit two centuries at a Men's T20 World Cup tournament.

Most wickets at the Women's Cricket World Cup
Marizanne Kapp (ZAF) dismissed 44 batters across five tournaments between 2009 and 2025. The South African medium-pacer took 12 wickets at the 2025 edition, moving past Jhulan Goswami's previous record of 43 during the semi-final against England – when she returned career-best figures of 5 for 20.

Also in 2025, Kapp's teammate Laura Wolvaardt scored the **most runs in a Women's Cricket World Cup tournament** – 571, at an average of 71.37 per innings.

Most sixes in men's international cricket
Rohit Sharma (IND) had cleared the boundary rope 650 times as of 7 Mar 2026. The total included the **most men's ODI sixes** – 357 – and the **most men's T20I sixes** – 205. Sharma had also hit 88 sixes in Test matches. He surpassed Pakistan batter Shahid Afridi's ODI record of 351 during a 50-over match against South Africa on 30 Nov 2025.

The **most sixes in men's Test cricket** is 136, by England captain Ben Stokes in 120 matches.

Fastest women's T20 century
On 17 Oct 2025, Kiran Navgire (IND) blitzed a century from 34 balls for Maharashtra against Punjab in a Senior Women's T20 Trophy match in Nagpur, India. Navgire finished 106 not out from 35 balls, bludgeoning seven sixes and 14 fours. Remarkably, her teammates contributed just seven runs as Maharashtra chased down Punjab's score of 110 for 6.

Best bowling figures in a women's T20 International
On 9 Apr 2026, Brazil's Laura Cardoso became the first player – male or female – to take nine wickets in a T20I. The right-arm medium-fast bowler finished with figures of 9 for 4 from her three overs against Lesotho in Botswana.

Most wickets in a men's over
During Indonesia's T20 match against Cambodia in Bali on 23 Dec 2025, Gede Priandana became only the fourth male player to dismiss five batsmen in a single over of professional cricket. He matched the feat of Neil Wagner (NZ) for Otago in 2011, Al-Amin Hossain (BNG) for UCB-BCB XI in 2013 and Karnataka's Abhimanyu Mithun (IND) in 2019.

Most men's Test catches by a fielder
England's Joe Root had taken 216 catches in 163 matches as of 7 Mar 2026 – more than any other non-wicketkeeper in Test history. He moved past Rahul Dravid's previous record of 210 with a spectacular one-handed grab to dismiss India's Karun Nair at Lord's on 11 Jul 2025 (pictured).

As of 7 Mar 2026, Joe Root stood just one catch ahead of Australia's Steve Smith, who had reached 215.

NOV 25 — Scouts Australia organized the **largest piggyback race** in 2012 in Pascoe Vale South, Victoria, Australia. The jovial jamboree had 1,274 participants.

NOV 26 — In 2019, David Smith Jr (USA) reached the **greatest height by a human cannonball**, soaring 27.12 m (89 ft) in Riyadh, Saudi Arabia, before landing on an airbed.

HIGHEST SUCCESSFUL RUN CHASE IN A WOMEN'S ONE-DAY INTERNATIONAL (ODI)

In a pulsating Women's Cricket World Cup semi-final on 30 Oct 2025, India successfully chased down Australia's total of 338, scoring 341 for 5 with nine balls to spare. This was the highest target reached in the 1,519 women's ODIs played to that date. India's innings was anchored by Jemimah Rodrigues (127 not out, below right) and captain Harmanpreet Kaur (89). The remarkable game, held at DY Patil Sports Academy in Navi Mumbai, India, also produced the **most aggregate runs in a Women's Cricket World Cup match** – 679.

Most wickets in a Women's Cricket World Cup match
Alana King (AUS) took seven wickets for just 18 runs against South Africa on 25 Oct 2025. The leg-spinner tore through the South African batting line-up, who crumbled from 32 for 0 to 97 all out. Australia won the game at Holkar Cricket Stadium in Indore, India, by seven wickets.

Most centuries at the Women's Cricket World Cup
England skipper Nat Sciver-Brunt has hit five World Cup hundreds. She claimed the outright record with a knock of 117 against Sri Lanka in Colombo on 11 Oct 2025. Sciver-Brunt's previous tons came against Pakistan, New Zealand (both 2017) and Australia (twice in 2022 – including 148 not out in the final).

NOV 27 — In 2012, Nick "The Lick" Stoeberl (USA) was verified as the owner of the **longest tongue.** His 10.1-cm-long (3.9-in) licker can hold five ring doughnuts!

NOV 28 — Retro-running Achim Aretz (DEU) completed the **fastest half marathon run backwards** in 2009, finishing in 1 hr 40 min 29 sec in Essen, Germany.

Racket Sports

DID YOU KNOW?

Badminton shuttlecocks are among the fastest objects in sport. Made from 16 overlapping feathers attached to a cork base, these aerodynamic projectiles can reach speeds of 550 km/h (342 mph) – that's 150 km/h (93 mph) faster than a Formula One car.

Most women's singles titles at the BWF World Championships
Akane Yamaguchi (JPN) won her third title at the 2025 Badminton World Federation World Championships in Paris, defeating Chen Yufei 21–9, 21–13 in the final on 31 Aug. Yamaguchi matched the feat of Carolina Marín (ESP), who won in 2014–15 and 2018.

Youngest tennis player to complete a career men's singles Grand Slam

On 1 Feb 2026, Carlos Alcaraz (ESP, b. 5 May 2003) won the Australian Open to complete his set of the four Grand Slam singles titles at the age of just 22 years 272 days. Alcaraz defeated Novak Djokovic at the Rod Laver Arena to claim his seventh Slam in total – two each at Wimbledon, the French Open and the US Open, and one at the Australian Open.

Most prize money won by a tennis player at a single tournament

On 18 Oct 2025, Jannik Sinner (ITA) beat Carlos Alcaraz to retain his title at the second edition of the Six Kings Slam in Riyadh, Saudi Arabia, and once again land the biggest-ever payday in tennis history: a staggering $6 m (£4.4 m). The exhibition event – not sanctioned by the Association of Tennis Professionals (ATP) – saw six players compete for a total prize pot of $13.5 m (£10.05 m).

At the 2025 Women's Tennis Association (WTA) Finals, also staged in Riyadh, Elena Rybakina (KAZ, b. RUS) set a new **women's** record of $5.23 m (£3.98 m). She went through the tournament undefeated, beating Aryna Sabalenka 6–3, 7–6 in the final on 8 Nov.

Youngest wheelchair tennis player to complete a Career Golden Slam

Tokito Oda (JPN, b. 8 May 2006) won all four Grand Slam singles titles and a Paralympic gold medal by the age of 19 years 121 days. He completed the set at the US Open on 6 Sep 2025, defeating his doubles partner Gustavo Fernández in the final.

Most women's singles titles at the Real Tennis World Championship

A precursor to lawn tennis that originated in the Middle Ages, this racket sport is played on an indoor asymmetric court. The walls form part of the playing area and are punctuated by sloping roofs and openings. Claire Fahey (UK) claimed her eighth consecutive world title on 31 May 2025, defeating Lea Van Der Zwalmen in Newport, Rhode Island, USA.

Alongside her sister, Sarah Vigrass, Fahey has won the **most women's doubles titles as a pairing** – five – as well as three titles with Tara Lumley.

Highest earnings in a women's tennis season
World No.1 Aryna Sabalenka (BLR) banked $15,008,519 (£11.4 m) in prize money in 2025. She won the US Open and WTA 1000 events in Miami and Madrid, and also reached Slam finals in Melbourne and Paris. Sabalenka surpassed Serena Williams's previous record of $12.3 m (£7.6 m) at the season-ending WTA Finals.

Most wins of the Sudirman Cup

Badminton's world mixed team championship was first contested in 1989. Each tie consists of up to five matches: men and women's singles, men and women's doubles and mixed doubles. China earned its 14th title with a 3–1 final win over South Korea on 4 May 2025 in Xiamen, Fujian, China. South Korea (four titles) and Indonesia (one) are the only other countries to have lifted the trophy.

Most wins of the women's PSA Squash Tour Finals

On 28 Jun 2025, Nouran Gohar (EGY) secured her fourth end-of-season squash title in five years. She defeated Olivia Weaver 11–10, 9–11, 11–8, 11–3 in Toronto, Ontario, Canada.

Most wins of the PSA Women's World Championships

On 17 May 2025, Nour El Sherbini (EGY) claimed her eighth Professional Squash Association (PSA) world championship, defeating her compatriot Hania El Hammamy 11–5, 11–9, 4–11, 11–7 in Chicago, Illinois, USA. El Sherbini equalled the total of Malaysia's Nicol David, who won eight titles between 2005 and 2014.

Nicknamed "The Warrior Princess", El Sherbini is a squash prodigy who won the world junior championship aged just 13.

NOV 29 *Ker-ching!* Vytautas Jakštas and Domas Jokubauskis (both LTU) completed the **largest coin pyramid** – using 1,000,935 coins – in Vilnius, Lithuania, in 2014.

NOV 30 On this day in 2021, the island nation of Barbados officially removed the UK's Queen Elizabeth II as head of state, becoming the **newest republic**.

Jannik Sinner and Carlos Alcaraz combined to win all eight men's singles Grand Slams in 2024 and 2025.

LONGEST FRENCH OPEN MEN'S SINGLES TENNIS FINAL

On 8 Jun 2025, Carlos Alcaraz (ESP) and Jannik Sinner (ITA) engaged in a gruelling clay-court battle at Stade Roland Garros that lasted for 5 hr 29 min. Alcaraz, the defending French Open champion, saved three match points in the fourth set to win 4–6, 6–7, 6–4, 7–6, 7–6, following the tournament's first-ever championship tie-break. The final set alone lasted 1 hr 17 min. It was Alcaraz's fifth Grand Slam singles triumph in five finals. Sinner would have his revenge at Wimbledon a month later, defeating Alcaraz 4–6, 6–4, 6–4, 6–4 in the final in another epic encounter.

DEC 1 In 2012, a head-spinning 528 performers took part in the **largest breakdance**. The event was organized by the Mecenatpolis shopping mall in Seoul, South Korea.

DEC 2 A total of 70,080 players had their eyes down for the **largest bingo game**, staged by supermarket chain Almacenes Éxito in Bogotá, Colombia, in 2006.

Target Sports

Most Archery World Cup wins in men's recurve
On 19 Oct 2025, Brady Ellison (USA) claimed his sixth men's recurve title, defeating Marcus D'Almeida in the final in Nanjing, Jiangsu, China. It was the 36-year-old's first World Cup win for six years. Recurve bows are the traditional bowstyle used at the Olympic Games and can fire arrows at speeds of up to 200 km/h (124 mph).

DID YOU KNOW?

Curling is one of the world's oldest team sports. It is believed to have originated on the icy lochs of Scotland in the early 16th century. The 1565 painting *The Bird Trap*, by Flemish master Pieter Bruegel the Elder, depicts people curling on a frozen river.

Most Mosconi Cup appearances
First held in 1994, the Mosconi Cup is an annual nine-ball pool contest between the USA and Europe. Shane Van Boening (USA) – aka "The South Dakota Kid" – played in his 19th tournament in 2025, held at Alexandra Palace in London, UK, on 3–6 Dec. He moved two clear of Team Europe's Ralf Souquet and the USA's Johnny Archer.

Highest score in ISSF Women's 10 m Air Rifle
On 14 Sep 2025, Peng Xinlu (CHN) scored 255.3 points in the final of an International Shooting Sport Federation World Cup event in Ningbo, Zhejiang, China. Aged just 16, she was making her debut in the competition.

The **men's** record also fell in Ningbo, to Danilo Sollazzo (ITA), who shot a score of 255 on 11 Sep. Sollazzo claimed his third World Cup gold medal in style, surpassing runner-up Sheng Lihao's previous best of 254.5 points.

Most wins of the World Women's Curling Championship
Canada's women are 19-time world curling champions. They secured their latest title on 23 Mar 2025 in Uijeongbu, South Korea. The team of (above, left to right) Rachel Homan, Tracy Fleury, Emma Miskew, Sarah Wilkes and alternate Rachelle Brown beat Switzerland in the final for the second year in a row.

Most 147 breaks in snooker
A 147 break is the highest possible in a standard frame of snooker, and requires players to pot 15 blacks with 15 reds before clearing up the colours. At the 2025 Saudi Arabia Snooker Masters on 15 Aug, Ronnie O'Sullivan (UK, b. 5 Dec 1975) compiled two maximums in two hours against Chris Wakelin to take his career total to 17. At the age of 49 years 253 days, "The Rocket" became the **oldest player to make a 147 break**.

Most century breaks in a snooker season
Judd Trump (UK) made 107 centuries in 2024/25. "The Ace in the Pack" rounded off the season with 14 at the 2025 World Snooker Championship to pass Neil Robertson's 2013/14 record of 103. At the British Open in Sep 2024, Trump became only the third player in history, after Ronnie O'Sullivan (above) and John Higgins, to reach 1,000 centuries.

Highest break in women's snooker
Bai Yulu (CHN) compiled a break of 145 against Wang Xinzhong on 2 Nov 2025 in a pre-qualifier at the International Championship in Nanjing, Jiangsu, China. The 22-year-old potted 13 blacks and two pinks with the reds before clearing up the colours, leaving her just two points shy of a maximum.

Most World Croquet Championships
On 26 Oct 2025, Reg Bamford (ZAF) won his sixth croquet world crown. He went through the tournament in Florida, USA, without dropping a game. Bamford matched the feat of Robert Fulford (UK), who won six titles from 1990 to 2023.

Most Horseshoe Pitching World Championships
Alan Francis (USA) secured his 29th men's world title – and his 13th consecutively – on 2 Aug 2025. He won all 15 of his matches in Sandy, Utah, USA.

Emma Miskew was part of Canada's 2017 world championship team who made history by going undefeated in the tournament.

DEC 3 Unmanned NASA spacecraft *Pioneer 10* carried out the **first flyby of Jupiter** in 1973. It passed by the gas giant at a distance of 130,000 km (80,778 mi).

DEC 4 In 2022, fitness fanatic Hayley Payton (UK) completed the **most burpees in one minute (female)** – 44, or one every 1.3 sec – in Milton Keynes, UK.

Lowest 72-hole score on the PGA Tour
Scottie Scheffler (USA) took 253 shots to complete four rounds at the CJ Cup Byron Nelson on 1–4 May 2025. He finished on 31 under par at TPC Craig Ranch in McKinney, Texas, USA. Scheffler matched the PGA Tour record of Justin Thomas (USA) at the 2017 Sony Open and Ludvig Åberg (SWE) at the RSM Classic in 2023.

Lowest round on the PGA Tour
Jim Furyk (USA) completed 18 holes in just 58 shots on 7 Aug 2016 at the Travelers Championship in Cromwell, Connecticut, USA. He carded 10 birdies and an eagle to complete his round in an astonishing 12 under par. It was the lowest of an estimated 1.5 million rounds shot on the PGA Tour at that point.

LOWEST 72-HOLE SCORE TO PAR ON THE PGA TOUR
On 5 Jan 2025, Hideki Matsuyama (JPN) carded a 35-under-par total score of 257 (65–65–62–65) at The Sentry tournament on Maui, Hawaii, USA. His four rounds contained 33 birdies and two eagles. Matsuyama sank a birdie with his final putt to eclipse Cameron Smith's previous Tour record of -34, also shot at The Sentry. The stunning Kapalua Plantation Course is the only par-73 on the PGA Tour and is famous for its low scores.

DEC 5 Rob Peterson (USA) hit the **most consecutive tennis serves** – 8,017 – at Port Aransas, Texas, USA, in 1998. He served for 10 hr 7 min without a single double fault.

DEC 6 In 2017, travel blogger Lindsay Nemeth (CAN) reached Tokyo DisneySea, completing the **fastest time to visit all Disney theme parks**, in a 75-hr 6-min fairytale tour.

SPORTS

Round-Up

Oldest Winter Olympic individual gold medallist
Elana Meyers Taylor (USA, b. 10 Oct 1984) was 41 years 129 days old when she won the women's individual bobsleigh (monobob) at the 2026 Milano Cortina Games on 16 Feb. Having previously won three Olympic silvers and two bronze, Meyers Taylor claimed her first gold medal at her fifth Winter Games.

The **men's** record also fell at the 2026 Games – to snowboarder Benjamin Karl (AUT, b. 16 Oct 1985), who won the parallel giant slalom on 8 Feb at the age of 40 years 115 days. He successfully defended his title from four years earlier.

Most Winter Olympic medals in freestyle skiing
Freestyle skiing debuted at the Winter Olympics in 1992 and comprises seven events: aerials, moguls, dual moguls, ski cross, halfpipe, slopestyle and big air. At the 2026 Games, Eileen Gu (CHN, b. USA) won a gold in halfpipe and silvers in big air and slopestyle to take her career medal tally to six (three golds and three silvers).

Fastest average speed at a World Rally Championship event
Kalle Rovanperä (FIN) won the 2025 Rally Finland in Jyväskylä with an average speed of 129.95 km/h (80.74 mph). The two-time world champion finished 39.2 sec clear of the field in his Toyota GR Yaris Rally1 after four days of racing. Rally Finland is known as the "Grand Prix on Gravel", owing to its fast roads.

Most Winter Olympic medals in short-track speed skating
Arianna Fontana (ITA) won 14 medals between 2006 and 2026. At the 2026 Winter Games, the 35-year-old home favourite claimed a gold in the 2,000 m mixed relay and silvers in the 500 m and 3,000 m relay to become Italy's most decorated Olympian.

Most Winter Olympic gold medals in the men's luge
Tobias Arlt and Tobias Wendl (both DEU) claimed their seventh career Olympic title at Milano Cortina, as part of Germany's triumphant team relay. Arlt and Wendl, nicknamed the "Bayern Express", had won the doubles and the team relay events at the three previous Olympics.

Fastest men's 15 m speed climb
On 3 May 2025, Sam Watson (USA) conquered the wall in 4.64 sec at an IFSC World Cup event in Bali, Indonesia. It was his second world record of the day, having clocked 4.67 sec in the semi-finals.

Aleksandra Mirosław (POL) set a new **women's** record of 6.03 sec on 24 Sep 2025. She was competing at the IFSC Climbing World Championships in Seoul, South Korea.

Most laps completed in a backyard ultramarathon
Backyard ultras challenge competitors to complete a run of 6.706 km (4.16 mi, or 100 mi divided by 24) every hour until only one runner remains. Winners can only complete one more lap than the second-placed runner. On 21–26 Jun 2025, Australian firefighter Phil Gore ran 119 laps at the Dead Cow Gully Backyard Masters, staged on a cattle farm outside Nanango in Queensland. Gore outlasted Sam Harvey (118 laps), covering 495 mi (797 km) across six days.

The **women's** record also fell in 2025, to Sarah Perry (UK). She completed 95 laps at the Backyard Ultra Individual World Championship in Bell Buckle, Tennessee, USA – a total of 395 mi (635 km) over five days.

Youngest winner of the UIM–ABP Class Pro World Endurance Championships
Boanerges Ratag (IDN, b. 2 Feb 2009) became an aquabike world champion at the age of 16 years 194 days on 15 Aug 2025. He was crowned following the Grand Prix of Indonesia, staged on Sumatra's Lake Toba.

Youngest X Games men's medallist
Ema Kawakami (JPN, b. 8 Sep 2014) was just 10 years 293 days old when he claimed a bronze in the men's Skateboard Vert at X Games Salt Lake City 2025. He is also the **youngest X Games competitor** outright – aged 9 years 294 days in 2024.

DEC 7 Kevin Strahle, aka competitive eater "LA Beast", battled brain freeze to wolf down the **most ice lollies eaten in one minute** – six – in 2017.

DEC 8 In 2024, the curtain fell on Taylor Swift's *The Eras Tour*. It raked in $2,077,618,725 (£1.62 bn) from 149 shows, making it the **highest-grossing music tour**.

Fastest average speed at a Formula One Grand Prix
On 7 Sep 2025, Max Verstappen (NLD, b. BEL) won the Italian Grand Prix with an average speed of 250.706 km/h (155.781 mph) over 53 laps. The previous day, the Red Bull racer and four-time world champion had completed the **fastest average speed for a Formula One lap** – 264.682 km/h (164.466 mph) – during qualifying.

Fastest indoor women's 800 m
On 19 Feb 2026, Keely Hodgkinson (UK) clocked 1 min 54.87 sec at a World Athletics Indoor Tour Gold meeting in Liévin, France. The previous indoor record of 1 min 55.82 sec had stood since 3 Mar 2002 – the day Hodgkinson was born. The reigning 800 m Olympic champion, her best time outdoors is 1 min 54.61 sec – currently the seventh fastest time in history.

Youngest Formula One driver to qualify in pole position
Kimi Antonelli (ITA, b. 25 Aug 2006) was 19 years 201 days old when he qualified fastest for the Chinese Grand Prix in Shanghai on 14 Mar 2026. He finished 0.222 sec ahead of his Mercedes teammate George Russell. Antonelli went on to claim his maiden race win the following day – in just his 26th F1 start – to become the second-youngest winner in championship history.

Most UFC women's title-bout wins
Valentina Shevchenko (KGZ) racked up her 11th title-fight victory at UFC 322 on 16 Nov 2025, defeating Zhang Weili by unanimous decision. She equalled the record of Amanda Nunes (BRA), who won eight title bouts at bantamweight and three at featherweight between 2016 and 2023. A two-time flyweight champion, Shevchenko has defended her belt on nine occasions.

Most tries in a rugby union Six Nations Championship tournament
France winger Louis Bielle-Biarrey touched down nine times during the 2026 Six Nations. The 22-year-old beat his own shared record of eight with a four-try haul against England in the final match of the tournament; France won a thrilling encounter 48–46 to seal the championship with the last kick of the match. Bielle-Biarrey has scored 18 tries in just 14 Six Nations games, with scores in his last 10 consecutive matches.

Most tries in the National Rugby League
On 13 Mar 2026, Alex Johnston (AUS) wrote his name into the NRL record books with his 213th try for the South Sydney Rabbitohs. He surpassed Ken Irvine's record of 212 tries, which had stood for 53 years following his retirement in 1973. Johnston's history-making try sparked a pitch invasion that halted play for 15 min.

Most women's downhill race wins at the FIS Alpine Ski World Cup
Lindsey Vonn (USA) claimed her 45th downhill victory in Zauchensee, Austria, on 10 Jan 2026. Her second win of the 2025/26 World Cup season, it capped a remarkable comeback for the 41-year-old eight-time champion, who returned to the sport after a six-year absence following knee surgery.

Highest attendance at a women's rugby union match
The final of the 2025 Women's Rugby World Cup at Twickenham Stadium in London, UK, drew a crowd of 81,885. They saw England defeat Canada 33–13, with an opening try from tournament star Ellie Kildunne (left). The Red Roses extended their record for the **most consecutive wins in women's international rugby union** to 33.

DEC 9 In 2021, music teacher Pandit Sudarshan Das (UK) performed the **longest drum roll**, lasting… (wait for it) a staggering 16 hr 41 min 50 sec in London, UK.

DEC 10 High-school senior Raul Rosas Jr (USA, b. 8 Oct 2004) became the **youngest UFC fight winner** in 2022. He defeated Jay Perrin at the age of 18 years 63 days.

Athletics

Fastest men's 400 m
South Africa's Wayde van Niekerk made history at the 2016 Olympic Games in Rio de Janeiro, becoming the first man to win 400 m gold running in the outside lane 8 – and in a world-record time of 43.03 sec. Van Niekerk broke the mark of 43.18 sec set by the USA's Michael Johnson, which had stood for almost 17 years.

TRACK EVENTS – MEN

Event	Time/Distance	Name & Nationality	Location	Date
50 m	5.56 sec	Donovan Bailey (CAN)	Reno, USA	9 Feb 1996
60 m	6.34 sec	Christian Coleman (USA)	Albuquerque, USA	18 Feb 2018
100 m	9.58 sec	Usain Bolt (JAM)	Berlin, Germany	16 Aug 2009
200 m	19.19 sec	Usain Bolt	Berlin, Germany	20 Aug 2009
400 m	43.03 sec	Wayde van Niekerk (ZAF)	Rio de Janeiro, Brazil	14 Aug 2016
800 m	1 min 40.91 sec	David Rudisha (KEN)	London, UK	9 Aug 2012
1,000 m	2 min 11.96 sec	Noah Ngeny (KEN)	Rieti, Italy	5 Sep 1999
1,500 m	3 min 26.00 sec	Hicham El Guerrouj (MAR)	Rome, Italy	14 Jul 1998
Mile	3 min 43.13 sec	Hicham El Guerrouj	Rome, Italy	7 Jul 1999
2,000 m	4 min 43.13 sec	Jakob Ingebrigtsen (NOR)	Brussels, Belgium	8 Sep 2023
3,000 m	7 min 17.55 sec	Jakob Ingebrigtsen	Chorzów, Poland	25 Aug 2024
5,000 m	12 min 35.36 sec	Joshua Cheptegei (UGA)	Fontvieille, Monaco	14 Aug 2020
10,000 m	26 min 11.00 sec	Joshua Cheptegei	Valencia, Spain	7 Oct 2020
One hour	21,330 m	Mo Farah (UK, b. SOM)	Brussels, Belgium	4 Sep 2020
50 m hurdles	6.25 sec	Mark McKoy (CAN)	Kobe, Japan	5 Mar 1986
60 m hurdles	7.27 sec	Grant Holloway (USA)	Albuquerque, USA	16 Feb 2024
110 m hurdles	12.80 sec	Aries Merritt (USA)	Brussels, Belgium	7 Sep 2012
400 m hurdles	45.94 sec	Karsten Warholm (NOR)	Tokyo, Japan	3 Aug 2021
3,000 m steeplechase	7 min 52.11 sec	Lamecha Girma (ETH)	Paris, France	9 Jun 2023
4 x 100 m relay	36.84 sec	Jamaica	London, UK	11 Aug 2012
4 x 200 m relay	1 min 18.63 sec	Jamaica	Nassau, The Bahamas	24 May 2014
4 x 400 m relay	2 min 54.29 sec	USA	Stuttgart, Germany	22 Aug 1993
4 x 800 m relay	7 min 2.43 sec	Kenya	Brussels, Belgium	25 Aug 2006
4 x 1,500 m relay	14 min 22.22 sec	Kenya	Nassau, The Bahamas	25 May 2014
Distance medley	9 min 14.58 sec*	Brooks Beasts (USA)	Eugene, USA	19 Apr 2024

pending ratification by World Athletics

TRACK EVENTS – WOMEN

Event	Time/Distance	Name & Nationality	Location	Date
50 m	5.96 sec	Irina Privalova (RUS)	Madrid, Spain	9 Feb 1995
60 m	6.92 sec	Irina Privalova	Madrid, Spain	11 Feb 1993
			Madrid, Spain	9 Feb 1995
100 m	10.49 sec	Florence Griffith Joyner (USA)	Indianapolis, USA	16 Jul 1988
200 m	21.34 sec	Florence Griffith Joyner	Seoul, South Korea	29 Sep 1988
400 m	47.60 sec	Marita Koch (GDR)	Canberra, Australia	6 Oct 1985
800 m	1 min 53.28 sec	Jarmila Kratochvílová (TCH)	Munich, West Germany	26 Jul 1983
1,000 m	2 min 28.98 sec	Svetlana Masterkova (RUS)	Brussels, Belgium	23 Aug 1996
1,500 m	3 min 48.68 sec	Faith Kipyegon (KEN)	Eugene, USA	5 Jul 2025
Mile	4 min 7.64 sec	Faith Kipyegon	Fontvieille, Monaco	21 Jul 2023
2,000 m	5 min 19.70 sec	Jessica Hull (AUS)	Fontvieille, Monaco	12 Jul 2024
3,000 m	8 min 6.11 sec	Wang Junxia (CHN)	Beijing, China	13 Sep 1993
5,000 m	13 min 58.06 sec	Beatrice Chebet (KEN)	Eugene, USA	5 Jul 2025
10,000 m	28 min 54.14 sec	Beatrice Chebet	Eugene, USA	25 May 2024
One hour	18,930 m	Sifan Hassan (NLD, b. ETH)	Brussels, Belgium	4 Sep 2020
50 m hurdles	6.58 sec	Cornelia Oschkenat (GDR)	East Berlin, East Germany	20 Feb 1988
60 m hurdles	7.65 sec	Devynne Charlton (BHS)	Glasgow, UK	3 Mar 2024
100 m hurdles	12.12 sec	Tobi Amusan (NGA)	Eugene, USA	24 Jul 2022
400 m hurdles	50.37 sec	Sydney McLaughlin-Levrone (USA)	Paris, France	8 Aug 2024
3,000 m steeplechase	8 min 44.32 sec	Beatrice Chepkoech (KEN)	Fontvieille, Monaco	20 Jul 2018
4 x 100 m relay	40.82 sec	USA	London, UK	10 Aug 2012
4 x 200 m relay	1 min 27.46 sec	USA	Philadelphia, USA	29 Apr 2000
4 x 400 m relay	3 min 15.17 sec	USSR	Seoul, South Korea	1 Oct 1988
4 x 800 m relay	7 min 50.17 sec	USSR	Moscow, USSR	5 Aug 1984
4 x 1,500 m relay	16 min 27.02 sec	Nike/Bowerman Track Club (USA)	Portland, USA	31 Jul 2020
Distance medley	10 min 36.50 sec	USA	Nassau, The Bahamas	2 May 2015

Fastest women's 5,000 m
At the 2025 Prefontaine Classic in Eugene, Oregon, Beatrice Chebet (KEN) clocked 13 min 58.06 sec to become the first woman to break the 14-min barrier in a track 5,000 m. It was another world record for Chebet at Hayward Field, where she had run the **fastest 10,000 m** – 28 min 54.14 sec – the previous year.

Fastest mixed 4 x 400 m relay
At the 2024 Olympic Games in Paris, the US team of Vernon Norwood, Shamier Little, Bryce Deadmon and Kaylyn Brown won their 4 x 400 m semi-final in 3 min 7.41 sec. They became the new holders of the only mixed world record recognized by World Athletics.

DEC 11 Lawrence Stump (USA) created the **largest ukulele** – 3.99 m (13 ft 1 in) long – as confirmed in Lansing, Michigan, USA, on this day in 2015.

DEC 12 Saugat Bista (NPL, b. 6 Jan 2007) – the **youngest professional movie director** – was 7 years 340 days old when his film *Love You Baba* was released in 2014.

FIELD EVENTS – MEN

Event	Distance/Score	Name & Nationality	Location	Date
High jump	2.45 m	Javier Sotomayor (CUB)	Salamanca, Spain	27 Jul 1993
Pole vault	6.30 m	Armand Duplantis (SWE, b. USA)	Tokyo, Japan	15 Sep 2025
Long jump	8.95 m	Mike Powell (USA)	Tokyo, Japan	30 Aug 1991
Triple jump	18.29 m	Jonathan Edwards (UK)	Gothenburg, Sweden	7 Aug 1995
Shot	23.56 m	Ryan Crouser (USA)	Los Angeles, USA	27 May 2023
Discus	75.56 m	Mykolas Alekna (LTU)	Ramona, USA	13 Apr 2025
Hammer	86.74 m	Yuriy Sedykh (USSR)	Stuttgart, Germany	30 Aug 1986
Javelin	98.48 m	Jan Železný (CZE)	Jena, Germany	25 May 1996
Decathlon*	9,126 points	Kevin Mayer (FRA)	Talence, France	15–16 Sep 2018

**100 m: 10.55 sec; LJ: 7.80 m; S: 16.00 m; HJ: 2.05 m; 400 m: 48.42 sec; 110 m H: 13.75 sec; D: 50.54 m; PV: 5.45 m; J: 71.90 m; 1,500 m: 4 min 36.11 sec*

Longest men's triple jump
Jonathan Edwards (UK) hopped, skipped and jumped 18.29 m (60 ft) at the 1995 World Athletics Championships in Gothenburg. The record distance – longer than two double-decker buses – celebrated its 30th anniversary in 2025 with no sign of it being beaten.

Highest women's high jump
Yaroslava Mahuchikh (UKR) cleared 2.10 m (6 ft 10 in) at a Diamond League event in Paris on 7 Jul 2024. She broke a record that had stood since 1987, 14 years before she was born. Mahuchikh went on to claim her first Olympic high jump gold medal in Paris the following month.

FIELD EVENTS – WOMEN

Event	Distance/Score	Name & Nationality	Location	Date
High jump	2.10 m	Yaroslava Mahuchikh (UKR)	Paris, France	7 Jul 2024
Pole vault	5.06 m	Yelena Isinbayeva (RUS)	Zurich, Switzerland	28 Aug 2009
Long jump	7.52 m	Galina Chistyakova (USSR)	Leningrad, USSR	11 Jun 1988
Triple jump	15.74 m	Yulimar Rojas (VEN)	Belgrade, Serbia	20 Mar 2022
Shot	22.63 m	Natalya Lisovskaya (USSR)	Moscow, USSR	7 Jun 1987
Discus	76.80 m	Gabriele Reinsch (GDR)	Neubrandenburg, Germany	9 Jul 1988
Hammer	82.98 m	Anita Włodarczyk (POL)	Warsaw, Poland	28 Aug 2016
Javelin	72.28 m	Barbora Špotáková (CZE)	Stuttgart, Germany	13 Sep 2008
Heptathlon*	7,291 points	Jackie Joyner-Kersee (USA)	Seoul, South Korea	23–24 Sep 1988
Decathlon†	8,358 points	Austra Skujytė (LTU)	Columbia, USA	14–15 Apr 2005

**100 m H: 12.69 sec; HJ: 1.86 m; S: 15.80 m; 200 m: 22.56 sec; LJ: 7.27 m; J: 45.66 m; 800 m: 2 min 8.51 sec*

†100 m: 12.49 sec; LJ: 6.12 m; S: 16.42 m; HJ: 1.78 m; 400 m: 57.19 sec; 100 m H: 14.22 sec; D: 46.19 m; PV: 3.10 m; J: 48.78 m; 1,500 m: 5 min 15.86 sec

SHORT TRACK EVENTS – MEN

Event	Time/Score	Name & Nationality	Location	Date
200 m	19.92 sec	Frankie Fredericks (NAM)	Liévin, France	18 Feb 1996
400 m	44.57 sec	Kerron Clement (USA)	Fayetteville, USA	12 Mar 2005
800 m	1 min 42.67 sec	Wilson Kipketer (DNK, b. KEN)	Paris, France	9 Mar 1997
1,000 m	2 min 14.20 sec	Ayanleh Souleiman (DJI)	Stockholm, Sweden	17 Feb 2016
1,500 m	3 min 29.63 sec	Jakob Ingebrigtsen (NOR)	Liévin, France	13 Feb 2025
Mile	3 min 45.14 sec	Jakob Ingebrigtsen	Liévin, France	13 Feb 2025
3,000 m	7 min 22.91 sec	Grant Fisher (USA)	New York City, USA	8 Feb 2025
5,000 m	12 min 44.09 sec	Grant Fisher	Boston, USA	14 Feb 2025
5,000 m race walk	18 min 7.08 sec	Mikhail Shchennikov (RUS)	Moscow, Russia	14 Feb 1995
Heptathlon*	6,645 points	Ashton Eaton (USA)	Istanbul, Türkiye	9–10 Mar 2012
4 x 200 m relay	1 min 22.11 sec	Great Britain & Northern Ireland	Glasgow, UK	3 Mar 1991
4 x 400 m relay	3 min 1.51 sec	Houston (USA)	Clemson, USA	9 Feb 2019
4 x 800 m relay	7 min 11.30 sec	HOKA NJ/NY Track Club (USA)	Boston, USA	25 Feb 2018

**60 m: 6.79 sec; LJ: 8.16 m; S: 14.56 m; HJ: 2.03 m; 60 m H: 7.68 sec; PV: 5.20 m; 1,000 m: 2 min 32.77 sec*

Fastest men's short track mile
On 13 Feb 2025, Jakob Ingebrigtsen (NOR) broke two world records in the same indoor race in Liévin, France. The two-time Olympic champion ran a mile in 3 min 45.14 sec and also completed the **fastest men's short track 1,500 m** in 3 min 29.63 sec.

Fastest women's short track 200 m
Merlene Ottey (JAM) ran a single lap of an indoor track in 21.87 sec on 13 Feb 1993. She remained the only woman to have broken 22 sec in the event as of 2025. Ottey, pictured in 1995, transferred her allegiance to Slovenia in 2002 and enjoyed a career of astonishing longevity, competing internationally until the age of 52.

SHORT TRACK EVENTS – WOMEN

Event	Time/Score	Name & Nationality	Location	Date
200 m	21.87 sec	Merlene Ottey (JAM)	Liévin, France	13 Feb 1993
400 m	49.17 sec	Femke Bol (NLD)	Glasgow, UK	2 Mar 2024
800 m	1 min 54.87 sec	Keely Hodgkinson (UK)	Liévin, France	19 Feb 2026
1,000 m	2 min 30.94 sec	Maria Mutola (MOZ)	Stockholm, Sweden	25 Feb 1999
1,500 m	3 min 53.09 sec	Gudaf Tsegay (ETH)	Liévin, France	9 Feb 2021
Mile	4 min 13.31 sec	Genzebe Dibaba (ETH)	Stockholm, Sweden	17 Feb 2016
3,000 m	8 min 16.60 sec	Genzebe Dibaba	Stockholm, Sweden	6 Feb 2014
5,000 m	14 min 18.86 sec	Genzebe Dibaba	Stockholm, Sweden	19 Feb 2015
3,000 m race walk	11 min 40.33 sec	Claudia Iovan (ROM)	Bucharest, Romania	30 Jan 1999
Pentathlon*	5,055 points	Nafissatou Thiam (BEL)	Istanbul, Türkiye	3 Mar 2023
4 x 200 m relay	1 min 32.41 sec	Russia	Glasgow, UK	29 Jan 2005
4 x 400 m relay	3 min 23.37 sec	Russia	Glasgow, UK	28 Jan 2006
4 x 800 m relay	8 min 5.89 sec	USA	New York City, USA	3 Feb 2018

**60 m H: 8.23 sec; HJ: 1.92 m; S: 15.54 m; LJ: 6.59 m; 800 m: 2 min 13.60 sec*

DEC 13 In 1983, the Detroit Pistons racked up the **highest score in an NBA match,** beating the Denver Nuggets 186–184 in a triple-overtime thriller.

DEC 14 The **largest falcon-racing tournament** featured 2,654 birds and was achieved on this day by the Saudi Falcons Club in Riyadh, Saudi Arabia, in 2023.

Athletics & Cycling

ATHLETICS – ROAD RACING

MEN		Time	Name & Nationality	Location	Date
Mile		3 min 51.3 sec	Elliot Giles (UK)	Düsseldorf, Germany	1 Sep 2024
5 km		12 min 49 sec	Berihu Aregawi (ETH)	Barcelona, Spain	31 Dec 2021
10 km		26 min 24 sec	Rhonex Kipruto (KEN)	Valencia, Spain	12 Jan 2020
Half marathon		57 min 30 sec	Yomif Kejelcha (ETH)	Valencia, Spain	27 Oct 2024
Marathon		2 hr 35 sec	Kelvin Kiptum (KEN)	Chicago, USA	8 Oct 2023
50 km		2 hr 38 min 43 sec	C J Albertson (USA)	San Francisco, USA	8 Oct 2022
100 km		6 hr 5 min 35 sec	Aleksandr Sorokin (LTU)	Vilnius, Lithuania	14 May 2023
WOMEN		**Time**	**Name & Nationality**	**Location**	**Date**
Mile	women-only	4 min 20.98 sec	Diribe Welteji (ETH)	Riga, Latvia	1 Oct 2023
5 km	women-only	14 min 13 sec	Beatrice Chebet (KEN)	Barcelona, Spain	31 Dec 2023
	mixed	13 min 54 sec	Beatrice Chebet	Barcelona, Spain	31 Dec 2024
10 km	women-only	29 min 27 sec	Agnes Ngetich (KEN)	Herzogenaurach, Germany	26 Apr 2025
	mixed	28 min 46 sec	Agnes Ngetich	Valencia, Spain	14 Jan 2024
Half marathon	women-only	1 hr 5 min 16 sec	Peres Jepchirchir (KEN)	Gdynia, Poland	17 Oct 2020
	mixed	1 hr 2 min 52 sec	Letesenbet Gidey (ETH)	Valencia, Spain	24 Oct 2021
Marathon	women-only	2 hr 15 min 50 sec	Tigst Assefa (ETH)	London, UK	27 Apr 2025
	mixed	2 hr 9 min 56 sec	Ruth Chepngetich (KEN)	Chicago, USA	13 Oct 2024
50 km	women-only	3 hr 30 sec	Emane Seifu (ETH)	Gqeberha, South Africa	26 Feb 2023
	mixed	2 hr 59 min 54 sec	Desiree Linden (USA)	Dorena, USA	13 Apr 2021
100 km	mixed	6 hr 33 min 11 sec	Tomoe Abe (JPN)	Lake Saroma, Japan	25 Jun 2000

Fastest women-only marathon
At the 2025 London Marathon, Tigst Assefa (ETH) set a new best time of 2 hr 15 min 50 sec for an exclusively female field. She is a previous holder of the outright women's marathon record, running 2 hr 11 min 53 sec with male pacemakers at the 2023 Berlin Marathon.

Greatest distance run in 48 hours
Ultrarunner Matthieu Bonne (BEL) covered 485.099 km (301.426 mi) at the 2025 UltraPark Weekend 48 Hour race, staged on a 1.5-km-long (0.9-mi) circuit through Park Wolności in the Polish city of Pabianice. Bonne averaged 5 min 56 sec per km (including breaks), smashing a record that had stood for 29 years.

ATHLETICS – ULTRA LONG-DISTANCE

MEN	Time/Distance	Name & Nationality	Location	Date
50 km	2 hr 38 min 43 sec	C J Albertson (USA)	San Francisco, USA	8 Oct 2022
50 mi	4 hr 48 min 21 sec	Charles Lawrence (USA)	Vienna, USA	11 Nov 2023
100 km	6 hr 5 min 35 sec	Aleksandr Sorokin (LTU)	Vilnius, Lithuania	14 May 2023
100 mi	10 hr 51 min 39 sec	Aleksandr Sorokin	Tel Aviv, Israel	7 Jan 2022
6 hours	98.496 km	Aleksandr Sorokin	Bedford, UK	23 Apr 2022
12 hours	177.410 km	Aleksandr Sorokin	Tel Aviv, Israel	7 Jan 2022
24 hours	319.614 km	Aleksandr Sorokin	Verona, Italy	16–17 Sep 2022
48 hours	485.099 km	Matthieu Bonne (BEL)	Pabianice, Poland	30 May–1 Jun 2025
6 days	1,045.519 km	Matthieu Bonne	Balatonfüred, Hungary	5–11 Sep 2024
WOMEN	**Time/Distance**	**Name & Nationality**	**Location**	**Date**
50 km	2 hr 59 min 54 sec	Desiree Linden (USA)	Dorena, USA	13 Apr 2021
50 mi	5 hr 31 min 57 sec	Courtney Olsen (USA)	Vienna, USA	10 Nov 2024
100 km	6 hr 33 min 11 sec	Tomoe Abe (JPN)	Lake Saroma, Japan	25 Jun 2000
100 mi	12 hr 42 min 40 sec	Camille Herron (USA)	Vienna, USA	11 Nov 2017
6 hours	85.49 km	Nele Alder-Baerens (DEU)	Münster, Germany	11 Mar 2017
12 hours	153.60 km	Satu Lipiäinen (FIN)	Kokkola, Finland	20 May 2023
24 hours	278.621 km	Sarah Webster (UK)	Albi, France	18–19 Oct 2025
48 hours	436.371 km	Patrycja Bereznowska (POL)	Pabianice, Poland	30 May–1 Jun 2025
6 days	928.577 km	Stine Rex (DNK)	Aabybro, Denmark	31 Aug–6 Sep 2025

ATHLETICS – RACE WALKING

MEN	Time	Name & Nationality	Location	Date
20,000 m	1 hr 17 min 25 sec	Bernardo Segura (MEX)	Bergen, Norway	7 May 1994
30,000 m	2 hr 1 min 44 sec	Maurizio Damilano (ITA)	Cuneo, Italy	3 Oct 1992
50,000 m	3 hr 35 min 27 sec	Yohann Diniz (FRA)	Reims, France	12 Mar 2011
20 km road	1 hr 16 min 10 sec	Toshikazu Yamanishi (JPN)	Kobe, Japan	16 Feb 2025
35 km road	2 hr 20 min 43 sec	Massimo Stano (ITA)	Poděbrady, Czechia	18 May 2025
50 km road	3 hr 32 min 33 sec	Yohann Diniz	Zurich, Switzerland	15 Aug 2014
WOMEN	**Time/Distance**	**Name & Nationality**	**Location**	**Date**
10,000 m	41 min 56 sec	Nadezhda Ryashkina (USSR)	Seattle, USA	24 Jul 1990
20,000 m	1 hr 26 min 52 sec	Olimpiada Ivanova (RUS)	Brisbane, Australia	6 Sep 2001
20 km road	1 hr 23 min 49 sec	Jiayu Yang (CHN)	Huangshan, China	20 Mar 2021
35 km road	2 hr 37 min 15 sec	Maria Pérez (ESP)	Poděbrady, Czechia	21 May 2023
50 km road	3 hr 59 min 15 sec	Hong Liu (CHN)	Huangshan, China	9 Mar 2019

Fastest men's 20 km road walk
On 16 Feb 2025, Toshikazu Yamanishi (JPN) won the Japanese 20 km Race Walking Championships in Kobe in 1 hr 16 min 10 sec. He wrestled the world record from his compatriot, Yusuke Suzuki, who had held it for almost a decade. Yamanishi is a two-time world champion and Olympic bronze medallist.

DEC 15 In 2018, the Friends of Portsmouth (USA) spread Christmas cheer by assembling the **most people carolling** – 1,880 – in Portsmouth, Ohio, USA.

DEC 16 Jyoti Amge (IND) celebrated her 18th birthday in 2011 with a new record – **shortest woman.** She was measured at 62.8 cm (2 ft 0.7 in) in Nagpur, India.

Fastest women's 1 km time trial
In 2025, the UCI extended the women's time trial distance from 500 m to 1 km to match the men's event. At the UCI Track Cycling World Championships in Santiago on 25 Oct 2025, Hetty van de Wouw (NLD) broke her own world record twice, setting a time of 1 min 3.121 sec in the final.

TRACK CYCLING

MEN	Time/Distance	Name & Nationality	Location	Date
200 m flying time trial	8.857 sec	Matthew Richardson (UK)	Konya, Türkiye	15 Aug 2025
500 m flying time trial	24.564 sec	Jeffrey Hoogland (NLD)	Aguascalientes, Mexico	31 Oct 2023
1 km time trial	55.433 sec	Jeffrey Hoogland	Aguascalientes, Mexico	31 Oct 2023
4 km individual pursuit	3 min 59.153 sec	Jonathan Milan (ITA)	Copenhagen, Denmark	18 Oct 2024
750 m team sprint	40.949 sec	Netherlands	Saint-Quentin-en-Yvelines, France	6 Aug 2024
4 km team pursuit	3 min 39.977 sec	Denmark	Konya, Türkiye	2 Feb 2026
One hour	56.792 km	Filippo Ganna (ITA)	Grenchen, Switzerland	8 Oct 2022
WOMEN	**Time/Distance**	**Name & Nationality**	**Location**	**Date**
200 m flying time trial	9.759 sec	Emma Finucane (UK)	Konya, Türkiye	2 Feb 2026
500 m flying time trial	27.063 sec	Emma Hinze (DEU)	Berlin, Germany	17 Aug 2024
1 km time trial	1 min 3.121 sec	Hetty van de Wouw (NLD)	Santiago, Chile	25 Oct 2025
4 km individual pursuit	4 min 19.461 sec	Josie Knight (UK)	Konya, Türkiye	4 Feb 2026
500 m team sprint	31.804 sec	China	Tokyo, Japan	2 Aug 2021
750 m team sprint	45.186 sec	Great Britain	Saint-Quentin-en-Yvelines, France	5 Aug 2024
4 km team pursuit	4 min 2.808 sec	Great Britain	Konya, Türkiye	2 Feb 2026
One hour	50.455 km	Vittoria Bussi (ITA)	Aguascalientes, Mexico	10 May 2025

TRACK PARA-CYCLING

MEN		Time/Distance	Name & Nationality	Location	Date
200 m flying time trial	C5	10.381 sec	Blaine Hunt (UK)	Saint-Quentin-en-Yvelines, France	20 Oct 2022
	C4	10.298 sec	Korey Boddington (AUS)	Brisbane, Australia	14 Feb 2025
	C3	10.356 sec	Korey Boddington	Cambridge, New Zealand	13 Feb 2026
	C2	11.212 sec	Alexandre Léauté (FRA)	Saint-Quentin-en-Yvelines, France	20 Oct 2022
	C1	11.641 sec	Li Zhangyu (CHN)	Rio de Janeiro, Brazil	21 Mar 2024
	B	9.568 sec	Neil Fachie & Matt Rotherham (both UK)	Brisbane, Australia	7 Apr 2018
1 km time trial	C5	1 min 1.557 sec	Alfonso Cabello (ESP)	Izu, Japan	26 Aug 2021
	C4	1 min 1.466 sec	Jody Cundy (UK)	Aguascalientes, Mexico	12 Apr 2014
	C3	1 min 2.397 sec	Korey Boddington	Cambridge, New Zealand	12 Feb 2026
	C2	1 min 7.944 sec	Alexandre Léauté	Saint-Quentin-en-Yvelines, France	31 Aug 2024
	C1	1 min 8.347 sec	Li Zhangyu	Izu, Japan	27 Aug 2021
	B	58.038 sec	Neil Fachie & Matt Rotherham	Izu, Japan	28 Aug 2021
3 km pursuit	C3	3 min 15.488 sec	Jaco van Gass	Saint-Quentin-en-Yvelines, France	30 Aug 2024
	C2	3 min 24.298 sec	Alexandre Léauté	Saint-Quentin-en-Yvelines, France	30 Aug 2024
	C1	3 min 31.338 sec	Li Zhangyu	Saint-Quentin-en-Yvelines, France	29 Aug 2024
4 km pursuit	C5	4 min 13.934 sec	Dorian Foulon (FRA)	Saint-Quentin-en-Yvelines, France	31 Aug 2024
	C4	4 min 17.700 sec	Archie Atkinson (UK)	Saint-Quentin-en-Yvelines, France	1 Sep 2024
	B	3 min 55.396 sec	Tristan Bangma & Patrick Bos (both NLD)	Saint-Quentin-en-Yvelines, France	29 Aug 2024
One hour	C5	51.471 km	William Bjergfelt (UK)	Konya, Türkiye	14 Aug 2025
WOMEN		**Time/Distance**	**Name & Nationality**	**Location**	**Date**
200 m flying time trial	C5	11.605 sec	Marie Patouillet (FRA)	Saint-Quentin-en-Yvelines, France	20 Oct 2022
	C4	11.519 sec	Kate O'Brien (CAN)	Milton, Canada	31 Jan 2020
	C3	12.506 sec	Wang Xiaomei (CHN)	Rio de Janeiro, Brazil	23 Mar 2024
	C2	13.123 sec	Flurina Rigling (CHE)	Glasgow, UK	8 Apr 2023
	C1	13.367 sec	Qian Wangwei (CHN)	Glasgow, UK	8 Jun 2023
	B	10.609 sec	Sophie Thornhill & Helen Scott (both UK)	Brisbane, Australia	5 Apr 2018
1 km time trial	C5	1 min 12.028 sec	Claudia Cretti (ITA)	Rio de Janeiro, Brazil	16 Oct 2025
	C4	1 min 10.806 sec	Tara Neyland (AUS)	Rio de Janeiro, Brazil	17 Oct 2025
	C3	1 min 14.630 sec	Emily Petricola (AUS)	Rio de Janeiro, Brazil	17 Oct 2025
	C2	1 min 20.020 sec	Sabrina Custódia (BRA)	Rio de Janeiro, Brazil	16 Oct 2025
	C1	1 min 25.366 sec	Tahlia Clayton-Goodie (AUS)	Rio de Janeiro, Brazil	18 Oct 2025
	B	1 min 4.623 sec	Sophie Thornhill & Helen Scott	Brisbane, Australia	7 Apr 2018
3 km pursuit	C3	3 min 41.692 sec	Wang Xiaomei	Saint-Quentin-en-Yvelines, France	29 Aug 2024
	C2	3 min 45.133 sec	Daphne Schrager (UK)	Saint-Quentin-en-Yvelines, France	29 Aug 2024
	C1	4 min 10.941 sec	Frances Brown (UK)	Glasgow, UK	6 Aug 2023
4 km pursuit	B	4 min 32.697 sec	Sophie Unwin & Jenny Holl (both UK)	Rio de Janeiro, Brazil	17 Oct 2025
One hour	C5	45.502 km	Sarah Storey (UK)	London, UK	28 Feb 2015

Fastest men's para-cycling 200 m flying time trial (C3)
Korey Boddington (AUS) won sprint gold at the 2026 Oceania Track Championships in 10.356 sec. He improved his own record from the 2025 UCI Para-cycling Track World Championships (above).

Fastest women's para-cycling 1 km time trial (C2)
Sabrina Custódia clocked 1 min 20.020 sec on 16 Oct 2025 to become the first Brazilian to break a para-cycling world record. She also claimed her first world championship gold medal, at the age of 44.

DEC 17 Piotr Lichwala (USA) embarked on a berry-bolting banquet in 2023, gobbling the **most raspberries eaten in one minute** – 95 – in Springfield, Illinois, USA.

DEC 18 In 2024, strongman Harald Riise (NOR) executed the **most pull-ups in a wheelchair in one minute**, completing 25 in Bærum, Norway.

Freediving, Rowing & Skating

*see pp.194–95

FREEDIVING				
MEN'S DEPTH DISCIPLINES	**Depth**	**Name & Nationality**	**Location**	**Date**
Constant weight with fins	136 m	Alexey Molchanov (RUS)	Limassol, Cyprus	29 Sep 2023
Constant weight with bifins	127 m	Alexey Molchanov	Soufrière, Dominica	1 Dec 2025
Constant weight without fins	103 m	Petar Klovar (HRV)	Sharm El-Sheikh, Egypt	26 May 2025
Variable weight	156 m	Alexey Molchanov	Bonaire, Caribbean Netherlands	28 Mar 2023
Free immersion	135 m	Petar Klovar	Limassol, Cyprus	27 Sep 2023
No limit	214 m	Herbert Nitsch (AUT)*	Spetses, Greece	9 Jun 2007
DYNAMIC APNEA	**Distance**	**Name & Nationality**	**Location**	**Date**
With fins	319 m	Ming Jin (CHN)	Goyang, South Korea	9 Nov 2025
With bifins	298 m	Guillaume Bourdila (FRA)	Wakayama, Japan	28 Jun 2025
Without fins	250 m	Mateusz Malina (POL)	Dębica, Poland	1 May 2022
STATIC APNEA	**Time**	**Name & Nationality**	**Location**	**Date**
Duration	11 min 35 sec	Stéphane Mifsud (FRA)	Hyères, France	8 Jun 2009

WOMEN'S DEPTH DISCIPLINES	Depth	Name & Nationality	Location	Date
Constant weight with fins	123 m	Alessia Zecchini (ITA)	Camotes Islands, Philippines	24 May 2023
Constant weight with bifins	111 m	Alenka Artnik (SVN)	Long Island, The Bahamas	30 Jul 2023
Constant weight without fins	86 m	Kateryna Sadurska (UKR)	Soufrière, Dominica	23 Nov 2025
Variable weight	130 m	Nanja van den Broek (NLD)	Sharm El-Sheikh, Egypt	18 Oct 2015
Free immersion	103 m	Sanda Delija (HRV)	Mabini, Philippines	4 May 2025
No limit	160 m	Tanya Streeter (USA)	Turks and Caicos Islands	17 Aug 2002
DYNAMIC APNEA	**Distance**	**Name & Nationality**	**Location**	**Date**
With fins	280 m	Zsófia Törőcsik (HUN)	Wakayama, Japan	2 Jul 2025
With bifins	259 m	Zsófia Törőcsik	Wakayama, Japan	28 Jun 2025
Without fins	213 m	Julia Kozerska (POL)	Jeju, South Korea	13 Jun 2023
STATIC APNEA	**Time**	**Name & Nationality**	**Location**	**Date**
Duration	9 min 22 sec	Heike Schwerdtner (DEU)	Stockholm, Sweden	4 May 2025

Deepest women's freedive constant weight without fins
Kateryna Sadurska (UKR) achieved a depth of 86 m (282 ft) at the 2025 Blue Element freediving event in Dominica. A former world championship medallist in artistic swimming, Sadurska returned to the surface on a single breath without the aid of fins or propulsion devices.

Fastest women's lightweight single sculls
Imogen Grant (UK) rowed 2,000 m in 7 min 23.36 sec at the final regatta of the 2022 Rowing World Cup, held in Lucerne, Switzerland. She also holds the record for the **lightweight double sculls** – 6 min 40.47 sec – alongside Emily Craig (UK).

Fastest mixed double sculls
The 2025 World Rowing Championships saw the debut of mixed-gender boats in the double sculls and eights. Margaret Cremen and Fintan McCarthy (both IRL) won the mixed double sculls final on 28 Sep, rowing 2,000 m in 6 min 24.22 sec.

ROWING (2,000 M)				
MEN	**Time**	**Nationality**	**Location**	**Date**
Single sculls	6 min 30.74 sec	New Zealand	Poznań, Poland	18 Jun 2017
Double sculls	5 min 59.72 sec	Croatia	Amsterdam, Netherlands	29 Aug 2014
Quadruple sculls	5 min 32.03 sec	Netherlands	Tokyo, Japan	28 Jul 2021
Coxless pairs	6 min 8.50 sec	New Zealand	London, UK	28 Jul 2012
Coxless fours	5 min 37.86 sec	Great Britain	Lucerne, Switzerland	25 May 2012
Coxed pairs	6 min 33.26 sec	New Zealand	Amsterdam, Netherlands	29 Aug 2014
Coxed fours	5 min 58.96 sec	Germany	Vienna, Austria	24 Aug 1991
Eights	5 min 18.68 sec	Germany	Poznań, Poland	18 Jun 2017
MEN'S LIGHTWEIGHT	**Time**	**Nationality**	**Location**	**Date**
Single sculls	6 min 39.56 sec	Italy	St Catharines, Canada	18 Aug 2024
Double sculls	6 min 5.33 sec	Ireland	Tokyo, Japan	28 Jul 2021
Quadruple sculls	5 min 42.75 sec	Greece	Amsterdam, Netherlands	29 Aug 2014
Coxless pairs	6 min 22.91 sec	Switzerland	Amsterdam, Netherlands	29 Aug 2014
Coxless fours	5 min 43.16 sec	Denmark	Amsterdam, Netherlands	29 Aug 2014
Eights	5 min 30.24 sec	Germany	Montreal, Canada	13 Aug 1992

WOMEN	Time	Nationality	Location	Date
Single sculls	7 min 7.71 sec	Bulgaria	Seville, Spain	21 Sep 2002
Double sculls	6 min 37.31 sec	Australia	Amsterdam, Netherlands	29 Aug 2014
Quadruple sculls	6 min 5.13 sec	China	Tokyo, Japan	28 Jul 2021
Coxless pairs	6 min 47.41 sec	New Zealand	Tokyo, Japan	28 Jul 2021
Coxless fours	6 min 14.36 sec	New Zealand	Amsterdam, Netherlands	29 Aug 2014
Eights	5 min 52.99 sec	Romania	Tokyo, Japan	28 Jul 2021
WOMEN'S LIGHTWEIGHT	**Time**	**Nationality**	**Location**	**Date**
Single sculls	7 min 23.36 sec	Great Britain	Lucerne, Switzerland	9 Jul 2022
Double sculls	6 min 40.47 sec	Great Britain	Varese, Italy	17 Jun 2023
Quadruple sculls	6 min 15.95 sec	Netherlands	Amsterdam, Netherlands	29 Aug 2014
Coxless pairs	7 min 17.02 sec	Poland	St Catharines, Canada	24 Aug 2024

MIXED	Time	Nationality	Location	Date
Double sculls	6 min 24.22 sec	Ireland	Shanghai, China	28 Sep 2025
Eights	5 min 34.46 sec	Romania	Shanghai, China	28 Sep 2025

DEC 19 — In 2018, the Dubai Mall (Emaar Malls) in the UAE unveiled the **largest Christmas bauble**. The outsized ornament had a diameter of 4.68 m (15 ft 4 in).

DEC 20 — Guy Schott (USA) completed the **most chin-ups in one minute** – 57 – in 2008. He performed the feat at the Sonoma YMCA in Santa Rosa, California, USA.

SPEED SKATING

MEN	Time/Points	Name & Nationality	Location	Date
500 m	33.61 sec	Pavel Kulizhnikov (RUS)	Salt Lake City, USA	9 Mar 2019
500 m x 2	1 min 8.23 sec	Jenning de Boo (NLD)	Heerenveen, Netherlands	14 Feb 2025
1,000 m	1 min 5.37 sec	Jordan Stolz (USA)	Salt Lake City, USA	26 Jan 2024
1,500 m	1 min 40.17 sec	Kjeld Nuis (NLD)	Salt Lake City, USA	10 Mar 2019
3,000 m	3 min 32.42 sec	Metoděj Jílek (CZE)	Salt Lake City, USA	26 Oct 2025
5,000 m	5 min 58.52 sec	Sander Eitrem (NOR)	Inzell, Germany	24 Jan 2026
10,000 m	12 min 25.69 sec	Davide Ghiotto (ITA)	Calgary, Canada	25 Jan 2025
Sprint combination	136.065 points	Kai Verbij (NLD)	Calgary, Canada	25–26 Feb 2017
Small combination	146.365 points	Erben Wennemars (NLD)	Calgary, Canada	12–13 Aug 2005
Big combination	144.740 points	Jordan Stolz	Inzell, Germany	9–10 Mar 2024
Team sprint	1 min 16.98 sec	USA	Calgary, Canada	26 Jan 2025
Team pursuit	3 min 32.49 sec	USA	Salt Lake City, USA	16 Nov 2025

WOMEN	Time/Points	Name & Nationality	Location	Date
500 m	36.09 sec	Femke Kok (NLD)	Salt Lake City, USA	16 Nov 2025
500 m x 2	1 min 13.98 sec	Femke Kok	Heerenveen, Netherlands	15 Feb 2025
1,000 m	1 min 11.61 sec	Brittany Bowe (USA)	Salt Lake City, USA	9 Mar 2019
1,500 m	1 min 49.83 sec	Miho Takagi (JPN)	Salt Lake City, USA	10 Mar 2019
3,000 m	3 min 52.02 sec	Martina Sáblíková (CZE)	Salt Lake City, USA	9 Mar 2019
5,000 m	6 min 39.02 sec	Natalia Voronina (RUS)	Salt Lake City, USA	15 Feb 2020
Sprint combination	146.390 points	Nao Kodaira (JPN)	Calgary, Canada	25–26 Feb 2017
Mini combination	153.776 points	Joy Beune (NLD)	Salt Lake City, USA	9–10 Mar 2018
Small combination	154.580 points	Cindy Klassen (CAN)	Calgary, Canada	18–19 Mar 2006
Team sprint	1 min 24.02 sec	Netherlands	Salt Lake City, USA	13 Feb 2020
Team pursuit	2 min 50.76 sec	Japan	Salt Lake City, USA	14 Feb 2020

MIXED	Time	Nationality	Location	Date
Mixed relay	2 min 54.05 sec	Netherlands	Calgary, Canada	23 Nov 2025

Fastest speed skating men's 5,000 m
On 24 Jan 2026, Sander Eitrem (NOR) won gold at the ISU Speed Skating World Cup in Inzell, Germany, in 5 min 58.52 sec. He became the first skater to break the six-minute barrier in the men's 5,000 m, beating Timothy Loubineaud's record of 6 min 0.23 sec, set just two months earlier.

Fastest short-track speed skating women's 500 m
Xandra Velzeboer (NLD) set the only short-track world record at the 2026 Winter Olympics, winning her 500 m semi-final in 41.399 sec. Velzeboer went on to win the final in 41.609 sec. Four days later, she added the 1,000 m title – her third career Olympic gold.

SPEED SKATING – SHORT TRACK

MEN	Time	Name & Nationality	Location	Date
500 m	39.505 sec	Wu Dajing (CHN)	Salt Lake City, USA	11 Nov 2018
1,000 m	1 min 20.875 sec	Hwang Dae-heon (KOR)	Salt Lake City, USA	12 Nov 2016
1,500 m	2 min 7.943 sec	Sjinkie Knegt (NLD)	Salt Lake City, USA	13 Nov 2016
5,000 m relay	6 min 28.625 sec	Hungary	Calgary, Canada	4 Nov 2018

WOMEN	Time	Name & Nationality	Location	Date
500 m	41.399 sec	Xandra Velzeboer (NLD)	Milan, Italy	12 Feb 2026
1,000 m	1 min 25.958 sec	Suzanne Schulting (NLD)	Salt Lake City, USA	4 Nov 2022
1,500 m	2 min 14.354 sec	Choi Min-jeong (KOR)	Salt Lake City, USA	12 Nov 2016
3,000 m relay	4 min 2.809 sec	Netherlands	Beijing, China	23 Oct 2021

MIXED	Time	Nationality	Location	Date
2,000 m relay	2 min 35.339 sec	Netherlands	Beijing, China	14 Mar 2025

FIGURE SKATING

MEN	Points	Name & Nationality	Location	Date
Short programme	113.97	Nathan Chen (USA)	Beijing, China	8 Feb 2022
Free skating	238.24	Ilia Malinin (USA)	Nagoya, Japan	6 Dec 2025
Combined total	335.30	Nathan Chen	Torino, Italy	6–7 Dec 2019

WOMEN	Points	Name & Nationality	Location	Date
Short programme	87.42	Kamila Valieva (RUS)	Sochi, Russia	26 Nov 2021
Free skating	185.29	Kamila Valieva	Sochi, Russia	27 Nov 2021
Combined total	272.71	Kamila Valieva	Sochi, Russia	26–27 Nov 2021

PAIRS	Points	Name & Nationality	Location	Date
Short programme	84.41	Sui Wenjing & Han Cong (CHN)	Beijing, China	18 Feb 2022
Free skating	158.13	Riku Miura & Ryuichi Kihara (JPN)	Milan, Italy	16 Feb 2026
Combined total	239.88	Sui Wenjing & Han Cong	Beijing, China	18–19 Feb 2022

ICE DANCE	Points	Name & Nationality	Location	Date
Rhythm dance	93.91	Madison Chock & Evan Bates (USA)	Tokyo, Japan	13 Apr 2023
Free dance	138.41	Madison Chock & Evan Bates	Tokyo, Japan	14 Apr 2023
Combined total	232.32	Madison Chock & Evan Bates	Tokyo, Japan	13–14 Apr 2023

Highest figure skating score in men's free skating
Ilia Malinin (USA) was awarded a score of 238.24 points for his free skate routine at the ISU Grand Prix Final 2025 in Nagoya, Japan. His programme included seven quad jumps and a backflip. The "Quad God" duly won his third successive Grand Prix Final gold medal.

DEC 21 The **first crossword puzzle** appeared in 1913. Compiled by Arthur Wynne (UK), it was included in the Sunday "Fun" section of US newspaper *The New York World.*

DEC 22 In 1991, the Klinck Automatic Weather Station in central Greenland recorded the **lowest temperature in Earth's northern hemisphere**: -69.6°C (-93.3°F).

Swimming

LONG COURSE (50-M POOL)				
MEN	**Time**	**Name & Nationality**	**Location**	**Date**
50 m freestyle	20.88 sec	Cameron McEvoy (AUS)	Shenzen, China	20 Mar 2026
100 m freestyle	46.40 sec	Pan Zhanle (CHN)	Paris, France	31 Jul 2024
200 m freestyle	1 min 42.00 sec	Paul Biedermann (DEU)	Rome, Italy	28 Jul 2009
400 m freestyle	3 min 39.96 sec	Lukas Märtens (DEU)	Stockholm, Sweden	12 Apr 2025
800 m freestyle	7 min 32.12 sec	Zhang Lin (CHN)	Rome, Italy	29 Jul 2009
1,500 m freestyle	14 min 30.67 sec	Bobby Finke (USA)	Paris, France	4 Aug 2024
50 m backstroke	23.55 sec	Kliment Kolesnikov (RUS)	Kazan, Russia	27 Jul 2023
100 m backstroke	51.60 sec	Thomas Ceccon (ITA)	Budapest, Hungary	20 Jun 2022
200 m backstroke	1 min 51.92 sec	Aaron Peirsol (USA)	Rome, Italy	31 Jul 2009
50 m breaststroke	25.95 sec	Adam Peaty (UK)	Budapest, Hungary	25 Jul 2017
100 m breaststroke	56.88 sec	Adam Peaty	Gwangju, South Korea	21 Jul 2019
200 m breaststroke	2 min 5.48 sec	Qin Haiyang (CHN)	Fukuoka, Japan	28 Jul 2023
50 m butterfly	22.27 sec	Andrii Govorov (UKR)	Rome, Italy	1 Jul 2018
100 m butterfly	49.45 sec	Caeleb Dressel (USA)	Tokyo, Japan	31 Jul 2021
200 m butterfly	1 min 50.34 sec	Kristóf Milák (HUN)	Budapest, Hungary	21 Jun 2022
200 m medley	1 min 52.69 sec	Léon Marchand (FRA)	Singapore	30 Jul 2025
400 m medley	4 min 2.50 sec	Léon Marchand	Fukuoka, Japan	23 Jul 2023
4 x 100 m freestyle relay	3 min 8.24 sec	USA	Beijing, China	11 Aug 2008
4 x 200 m freestyle relay	6 min 58.55 sec	USA	Rome, Italy	31 Jul 2009
4 x 100 m medley relay	3 min 26.78 sec	USA	Tokyo, Japan	1 Aug 2021
WOMEN	**Time**	**Name & Nationality**	**Location**	**Date**
50 m freestyle	23.61 sec	Sarah Sjöström (SWE)	Fukuoka, Japan	29 Jul 2023
100 m freestyle	51.71 sec	Sarah Sjöström	Budapest, Hungary	23 Jul 2017
200 m freestyle	1 min 52.23 sec	Ariarne Titmus (AUS)	Brisbane, Australia	12 Jun 2024
400 m freestyle	3 min 54.18 sec	Summer McIntosh (CAN)	Victoria, Canada	7 Jun 2025
800 m freestyle	8 min 4.12 sec	Katie Ledecky (USA)	Fort Lauderdale, USA	3 May 2025
1,500 m freestyle	15 min 20.48 sec	Katie Ledecky	Indianapolis, USA	16 May 2018
50 m backstroke	26.86 sec	Kaylee McKeown (AUS)	Budapest, Hungary	20 Oct 2023
100 m backstroke	57.13 sec	Regan Smith (USA)	Indianapolis, USA	18 Jun 2024
200 m backstroke	2 min 3.14 sec	Kaylee McKeown	Sydney, Australia	10 Mar 2023
50 m breaststroke	29.16 sec	Rūta Meilutytė (LTU)	Fukuoka, Japan	30 Jul 2023
100 m breaststroke	1 min 4.13 sec	Lilly King (USA)	Budapest, Hungary	25 Jul 2017
200 m breaststroke	2 min 17.55 sec	Evgeniia Chikunova (RUS)	Kazan, Russia	21 Apr 2023
50 m butterfly	24.43 sec	Sarah Sjöström	Borås, Sweden	5 Jul 2014
100 m butterfly	54.60 sec	Gretchen Walsh (USA)	Fort Lauderdale, USA	3 May 2025
200 m butterfly	2 min 1.81 sec	Liu Zige (CHN)	Jinan, China	21 Oct 2009
200 m medley	2 min 5.70 sec	Summer McIntosh	Victoria, Canada	9 Jun 2025
400 m medley	4 min 23.65 sec	Summer McIntosh	Victoria, Canada	11 Jun 2025
4 x 100 m freestyle relay	3 min 27.96 sec	Australia	Fukuoka, Japan	23 Jul 2023
4 x 200 m freestyle relay	7 min 37.50 sec	Australia	Fukuoka, Japan	27 Jul 2023
4 x 100 m medley relay	3 min 49.34 sec	USA	Singapore	3 Aug 2025
MIXED	**Time**	**Name & Nationality**	**Location**	**Date**
4 x 100 m freestyle relay	3 min 18.48 sec	USA	Singapore	2 Aug 2025
4 x 100 m medley relay	3 min 37.43 sec	USA	Paris, France	3 Aug 2024

Fastest men's 200 m individual medley
At the 2025 World Aquatics Championships in Singapore, Léon Marchand (FRA) clocked 1 min 52.69 sec to smash a record that had stood since 2011. Swimmers in this event have to complete one 50-m leg each in butterfly, backstroke, breaststroke and freestyle.

Fastest women's 400 m freestyle
On 7 Jun 2025, Summer McIntosh (CAN) touched home in 3 min 54.18 sec to reclaim the women's 400 m freestyle world record from Australia's Ariarne Titmus. It was one of three world records that the 18-year-old McIntosh set during the Canadian Trials in Victoria.

Fastest women's 800 m freestyle
GWR ICON Katie Ledecky (USA) swam 16 lengths of the pool in 8 min 4.12 sec at the TYR Pro Swim Series in Florida on 3 May 2025. She broke her own mark from the 2016 Rio Olympics, which she had set at the age of 19. It was Ledecky's first long-course world record over any distance in almost seven years.

DEC 23 — The **first electric-powered aircraft** took to the skies in 2007. The Electra F-WMDJ flew for 48 min around the French Alps, powered by a 25-hp (18-kW) motor.

DEC 24 — In 1997, British strongman John Evans stood for 10 sec with the **greatest weight balanced on the head** – 188.7 kg (416 lb) – in the form of 101 bricks!

SHORT COURSE (25-M POOL)

MEN	Time	Name & Nationality	Location	Date
50 m freestyle	19.90 sec	Jordan Crooks (CYM)	Budapest, Hungary	14 Dec 2024
100 m freestyle	44.84 sec	Kyle Chalmers (AUS)	Kazan, Russia	29 Oct 2021
200 m freestyle	1 min 38.61 sec	Luke Hobson (USA)	Budapest, Hungary	15 Dec 2024
400 m freestyle	3 min 32.25 sec	Yannick Agnel (FRA)	Angers, France	15 Nov 2012
800 m freestyle	7 min 20.46 sec	Daniel Wiffen (IRL)	Bucharest, Romania	10 Dec 2023
1,500 m freestyle	14 min 6.88 sec	Florian Wellbrock (DEU)	Abu Dhabi, UAE	21 Dec 2021
50 m backstroke	22.11 sec	Kliment Kolesnikov (RUS)	Kazan, Russia	23 Nov 2022
100 m backstroke	48.16 sec	Hubert Kós (HUN)	Toronto, Canada	25 Oct 2025
200 m backstroke	1 min 45.12 sec	Hubert Kós	Toronto, Canada	23 Oct 2025
50 m breaststroke	24.95 sec	Emre Sakçı (TUR)	Gaziantep, Türkiye	27 Dec 2021
100 m breaststroke	55.28 sec	Ilya Shymanovich (BLR)	Eindhoven, Netherlands	26 Nov 2021
200 m breaststroke	1 min 59.52 sec	Caspar Corbeau (NLD)	Toronto, Canada	25 Oct 2025
50 m butterfly	21.32 sec	Noè Ponti (CHE)	Budapest, Hungary	11 Dec 2024
100 m butterfly	47.68 sec	Josh Liendo (CAN)	Toronto, Canada	23 Oct 2025
200 m butterfly	1 min 46.85 sec	Tomoru Honda (JPN)	Tokyo, Japan	22 Oct 2022
100 m medley	49.28 sec	Caeleb Dressel (USA)	Budapest, Hungary	22 Nov 2020
200 m medley	1 min 48.88 sec	Léon Marchand (FRA)	Singapore	1 Nov 2024
400 m medley	3 min 54.81 sec	Daiya Seto (JPN)	Las Vegas, USA	20 Dec 2019
4 x 50 m freestyle relay	1 min 21.80 sec	USA	Hangzhou, China	14 Dec 2018
4 x 100 m freestyle relay	3 min 1.66 sec	USA	Budapest, Hungary	10 Dec 2024
4 x 200 m freestyle relay	6 min 40.51 sec	USA	Budapest, Hungary	13 Dec 2024
4 x 50 m medley relay	1 min 29.72 sec	Italy	Melbourne, Australia	17 Dec 2022
4 x 100 m medley relay	3 min 18.68 sec	Neutral Athletes B	Budapest, Hungary	15 Dec 2024
WOMEN	**Time**	**Name & Nationality**	**Location**	**Date**
50 m freestyle	22.83 sec	Gretchen Walsh (USA)	Budapest, Hungary	15 Dec 2024
100 m freestyle	49.93 sec	Kate Douglass (USA)	Toronto, Canada	25 Oct 2025
200 m freestyle	1 min 49.36 sec	Mollie O'Callaghan (AUS)	Toronto, Canada	24 Oct 2025
400 m freestyle	3 min 50.25 sec	Summer McIntosh (CAN)	Budapest, Hungary	10 Dec 2024
800 m freestyle	7 min 54.00 sec	Lani Pallister (AUS)	Toronto, Canada	25 Oct 2025
1,500 m freestyle	15 min 8.24 sec	Katie Ledecky (USA)	Toronto, Canada	29 Oct 2022
50 m backstroke	25.23 sec	Regan Smith (USA)	Budapest, Hungary	13 Dec 2024
100 m backstroke	54.02 sec	Regan Smith	Budapest, Hungary	15 Dec 2024
		Regan Smith	Westmont, USA	18 Oct 2025
200 m backstroke	1 min 57.33 sec	Kaylee McKeown (AUS)	Toronto, Canada	25 Oct 2025
50 m breaststroke	28.37 sec	Rūta Meilutytė (LTU)	Melbourne, Australia	17 Dec 2022
100 m breaststroke	1 min 2.36 sec	Rūta Meilutytė	Moscow, Russia	12 Oct 2013
		Alia Atkinson (JAM)	Doha, Qatar	6 Dec 2014
		Alia Atkinson	Chartres, France	26 Aug 2016
200 m breaststroke	2 min 12.50 sec	Kate Douglass	Budapest, Hungary	13 Dec 2024
50 m butterfly	23.72 sec	Gretchen Walsh	Carmel, USA	11 Oct 2025
100 m butterfly	52.71 sec	Gretchen Walsh	Budapest, Hungary	14 Dec 2024
200 m butterfly	1 min 59.32 sec	Summer McIntosh	Budapest, Hungary	12 Dec 2024
100 m medley	55.11 sec	Gretchen Walsh	Budapest, Hungary	13 Dec 2024
200 m medley	2 min 1.63 sec	Kate Douglass	Budapest, Hungary	10 Dec 2024
400 m medley	4 min 15.48 sec	Summer McIntosh	Budapest, Hungary	14 Dec 2024
4 x 50 m freestyle relay	1 min 32.50 sec	Netherlands	Eindhoven, Netherlands	12 Dec 2020
4 x 100 m freestyle relay	3 min 25.01 sec	USA	Budapest, Hungary	10 Dec 2024
4 x 200 m freestyle relay	7 min 30.13 sec	USA	Budapest, Hungary	12 Dec 2024
4 x 50 m medley relay	1 min 42.35 sec	Australia	Melbourne, Australia	17 Dec 2022
4 x 100 m medley relay	3 min 40.41 sec	USA	Budapest, Hungary	15 Dec 2024
MIXED	**Time**	**Name & Nationality**	**Location**	**Date**
4 x 50 m freestyle relay	1 min 27.26 sec	Italy	Lublin, Poland	4 Dec 2025
4 x 50 m medley relay	1 min 35.15 sec	USA	Melbourne, Australia	14 Dec 2022

Fastest short course men's 100 m butterfly
On 23 Oct 2025, Canada's Josh Liendo set his first swimming world record in 47.68 sec at the World Aquatics Swimming World Cup in Toronto. Liendo, who won a silver medal in the 100 m butterfly at the 2024 Olympics in Paris, beat the previous best by 0.03 sec.

Fastest short course men's 200 m backstroke
Hubert Kós (HUN) touched home in 1 min 45.12 sec in Toronto on 23 Oct 2025, breaking a record that had stood for almost a decade. Kós completed the "Triple Triple" at the 2025 Swimming World Cup, winning all three backstroke events at each of the three stages.

Fastest short course women's 50 m butterfly
On 11 Oct 2025, Gretchen Walsh (USA) beat her own world record with a time of 23.72 sec in Carmel, Indiana, USA. Walsh won seven golds at the 2024 short course world championships and holds the **most current swimming world records** – nine, in five individual and four relay events.

DEC 25 In 2017, Beijing Hyundai and Mohe Tourism Bureau (both CHN) finished the **longest wish list to Santa** in Mohe, Heilongjiang, China. It consisted of 124,969 wishes.

DEC 26 Tottenham striker Harry Kane (UK) helped himself to a Boxing Day hat-trick in 2017 to complete the **most English Premier League goals in a calendar year** – 39.

Weightlifting & Waterskiing

WEIGHTLIFTING – MEN

	Category	Weight	Name & Nationality	Location	Date
60 kg	Snatch	-	-	-	-
	Clean & Jerk	173 kg	Theerapong Silachai (THA)	Chonburi, Thailand	13 Dec 2025
	Total	-	-	-	-
65 kg	Snatch	-	-	-	-
	Clean & Jerk	181 kg	Hampton Morris (USA)	Cali, Colombia	14 Jul 2025
	Total	324 kg	Muhammed Furkan Özbek (TUR)	Førde, Norway	4 Oct 2025
71 kg	Snatch	160 kg	Yueji He (CHN)	Førde, Norway	5 Oct 2025
	Clean & Jerk	195 kg	Weeraphon Wichuma (THA)	Chonburi, Thailand	14 Dec 2025
	Total	347 kg	Weeraphon Wichuma	Chonburi, Thailand	14 Dec 2025
79 kg	Snatch	166 kg	Abdelrahman El-Sayed (EGY)	Riyadh, Saudi Arabia	10 Nov 2025
	Clean & Jerk	205 kg	Rizki Juniansyah (IDN)	Chonburi, Thailand	15 Dec 2025
	Total	365 kg	Rizki Juniansyah	Chonburi, Thailand	15 Dec 2025
88 kg	Snatch	177 kg	Yeison López (COL)	Førde, Norway	7 Oct 2025
	Clean & Jerk	215 kg	Ro Kwang-ryol (PRK)	Førde, Norway	7 Oct 2025
	Total	387 kg	Yeison López	Førde, Norway	7 Oct 2025
94 kg	Snatch	182 kg	Alireza Moeini (IRN)	Førde, Norway	9 Oct 2025
	Clean & Jerk	222 kg	Karlos Nasar (BGR, b. FRA)	Førde, Norway	9 Oct 2025
	Total	-	-	-	-
110 kg	Snatch	196 kg	Akbar Djuraev (UZB)	Førde, Norway	10 Oct 2025
	Clean & Jerk	-	-	-	-
	Total	428 kg	Akbar Djuraev	Førde, Norway	10 Oct 2025
+110 kg	Snatch	-	-	-	-
	Clean & Jerk	-	-	-	-
	Total	-	-	-	-

Heaviest men's 79 kg total
At the 2025 SEA Games, Rizki Juniansyah (IDN) lifted a combined 365 kg: 160 kg in the snatch and the **heaviest men's 79 kg clean & jerk** – 205 kg. The 79 kg class is part of a new programme of bodyweight categories introduced by the International Weightlifting Federation (IWF) from 1 Jun 2025.

Heaviest women's 77 kg total
At the 2025 IWF World Championships in Førde, Norway, Olivia Reeves (USA) lifted a combined 278 kg to set new world records in every event at 77 kg. The 22-year-old had won Olympic gold the previous year, competing in the 71 kg weight class. She took up weightlifting at the age of 13.

WEIGHTLIFTING – WOMEN

	Category	Weight	Name & Nationality	Location	Date
48 kg	Snatch	-	-	-	-
	Clean & Jerk	122 kg	Ri Song-gum (PRK)	Førde, Norway	2 Oct 2025
	Total	213 kg	Ri Song-gum	Førde, Norway	2 Oct 2025
53 kg	Snatch	-	-	-	-
	Clean & Jerk	-	-	-	-
	Total	-	-	-	-
58 kg	Snatch	-	-	-	-
	Clean & Jerk	-	-	-	-
	Total	236 kg	Kim Il-gyong (PRK)	Førde, Norway	4 Oct 2025
63 kg	Snatch	111 kg	Ri Suk (PRK)	Førde, Norway	5 Oct 2025
	Clean & Jerk	142 kg	Ri Suk	Førde, Norway	5 Oct 2025
	Total	253 kg	Ri Suk	Førde, Norway	5 Oct 2025
69 kg	Snatch	120 kg	Song Kuk-hyang (PRK)	Førde, Norway	7 Oct 2025
	Clean & Jerk	150 kg	Song Kuk-hyang	Førde, Norway	7 Oct 2025
	Total	270 kg	Song Kuk-hyang	Førde, Norway	7 Oct 2025
77 kg	Snatch	123 kg	Olivia Reeves (USA)	Førde, Norway	8 Oct 2025
	Clean & Jerk	155 kg	Olivia Reeves	Førde, Norway	8 Oct 2025
	Total	278 kg	Olivia Reeves	Førde, Norway	8 Oct 2025
86 kg	Snatch	-	-	-	-
	Clean & Jerk	-	-	-	-
	Total	-	-	-	-
+86 kg	Snatch	-	-	-	-
	Clean & Jerk	-	-	-	-
	Total	-	-	-	-

Heaviest women's 63 kg total
Ri Suk (PRK) won gold at the 2025 IWF World Championships with a combined total of 253 kg from her snatch and clean & jerk. North Korea were a dominant force throughout the tournament, setting multiple world records and winning an incredible 17 gold medals – 14 clear of their nearest rivals.

DEC 27 Joshua Regrello (TTO) embarked on the **longest steelpan-playing marathon** in 2024. He beat out rhythms for 31 hr in San Fernando, Trinidad and Tobago.

DEC 28 In 2021, the **most southerly game of musical chairs** took place at 89.9°S, near the South Pole. The 15 hardy competitors were led by Cindy Y Chang (USA/JPN).

PARA POWERLIFTING – MEN

	Weight	Name & Nationality	Location	Date
49 kg	183.5 kg	Lê Văn Công (VNM)	Mexico City, Mexico	4 Dec 2017
54 kg	205 kg	Sherif Osman (EGY)	Dubai, UAE	6 Apr 2014
59 kg	211 kg	Sherif Osman	Rio de Janeiro, Brazil	9 Sep 2016
65 kg	222 kg	Yi Zou (CHN)	Hangzhou, China	24 Oct 2023
72 kg	232 kg	Bonnie Bunyau Gustin (MYS)	Paris, France	6 Sep 2024
80 kg	242 kg	Roohallah Rostami (IRN)	Paris, France	6 Sep 2024
88 kg	251 kg	Abdelkareem Khattab (JOR)	Dubai, UAE	29 Aug 2023
97 kg	270 kg	Abdelkareem Khattab	Paris, France	7 Sep 2024
107 kg	255 kg	Aliakbar Gharibshahi (IRN)	Cairo, Egypt	16 Oct 2025
+107 kg	310 kg	Siamand Rahman (IRN)	Rio de Janeiro, Brazil	14 Sep 2016

Heaviest men's para powerlift 107 kg
Aliakbar Gharibshahi (IRN) lifted 255 kg at the World Para Powerlifting Championships in Cairo on 16 Oct 2025. He went on to attempt a further lift at 260 kg but was unable to complete it. Gharibshahi is a three-time world champion and won a gold medal at the 2024 Paralympics.

Heaviest women's para powerlift 45 kg
Guo Lingling (CHN) secured her fifth world championship title in style in 2025, lifting 125 kg in Cairo to break her own world record by 1 kg. She is the only female para powerlifter to hold current world records in two weight categories: 41 kg and 45 kg. Guo has also won Paralympic gold medals at both weights.

PARA POWERLIFTING – WOMEN

	Weight	Name & Nationality	Location	Date
41 kg	123 kg	Guo Lingling (CHN)	Hangzhou, China	23 Oct 2023
45 kg	125 kg	Guo Lingling	Cairo, Egypt	14 Oct 2025
50 kg	131 kg	Esther Oyema (NGA)	Gold Coast, Australia	10 Apr 2018
55 kg	135 kg	Rehab Ahmed (EGY)	Tbilisi, Georgia	22 Jun 2024
61 kg	150 kg	Onyinyechi Mark (NGA)	Paris, France	6 Sep 2024
67 kg	147 kg	Cui Jianjin (CHN)	Cairo, Egypt	15 Oct 2025
73 kg	151 kg	Kafila Almaruf (NGA)	Dubai, UAE	26 Aug 2023
79 kg	154 kg	Miaoyu Han (CHN)	Paris, France	7 Sep 2024
86 kg	159 kg	Feifei Zheng (CHN)	Tbilisi, Georgia	25 Jun 2024
+86 kg	168 kg	Folashade Oluwafemiayo (NGA)	Cairo, Egypt	16 Oct 2025

WATERSKIING – MEN

Event	Record	Name & Nationality	Location	Date
Slalom	2.5 buoy 9.75-m line	Nate Smith (USA)	Covington, Louisiana, USA	7 Sep 2013
Tricks	13,020 points	Jake Abelson (USA)	Polk City, Florida, USA	14 Jun 2025
Jump	77.4 m (253 ft 11 in)	Ryan Dodd (CAN)	Palm Bay, Florida, USA	1 Jul 2017
Ski fly	95.09 m (311 ft 11 in)	Freddy Krueger (USA)	Grand Rapids, Michigan, USA	7 Aug 2015
Overall	2,716.07 points	Joel Poland (UK)	Polk City, Florida, USA	12 Oct 2025
Barefoot slalom	20.6 crossings in 30 sec	Keith St Onge (USA)	Bronkhorstspruit, South Africa	6 Jan 2006
Barefoot tricks	13,350 points	David Small (UK)	Napanee, Ontario, Canada	14 Aug 2018
Barefoot jump	29.9 m (98 ft 1 in)	David Small	Brandenburg, Germany	11 Aug 2010

Most points in men's waterskiing tricks
On 14 Jun 2025, Jake Abelson (USA) became the first waterskier to break the 13,000-point barrier for tricks – at the age of just 17. He scored 13,020 at the Bill Wenner Memorial Record tournament on Lake Grew in Florida.

WATERSKIING – WOMEN

Event	Record	Name & Nationality	Location	Date
Slalom	5 buoy 10.25-m line	Regina Jaquess (USA)	Tuscaloosa, Alabama, USA	15 Sep 2023
Tricks	11,450 points	Erika Lang (CAN)	Rio Linda, California, USA	7 Jun 2025
Jump	61.3 m (201 ft 1 in)	Jacinta Carroll (AUS)	Polk City, Florida, USA	31 Oct 2021
Ski fly	69.4 m (227 ft 8 in)	Elena Milakova (RUS)	Pine Mountain, Georgia, USA	26 May 2002
Overall	2,581.39 points	Hanna Straltsova (USA)	Polk City, Florida, USA	15 Jun 2025
Barefoot slalom	17.2 crossings in 30 sec	Ashleigh Stebbeings (AUS)	Perth, Australia	8 Oct 2014
Barefoot tricks	10,100 points	Ashleigh Stebbeings	Mulwala, Australia	13 Mar 2014
Barefoot jump	23.4 m (76 ft 9 in)	Ashleigh Stebbeings	Canungra, Australia	19 Feb 2017

Most overall points in women's waterskiing
On 15 Jun 2025, Hanna Straltsova (USA) beat Natallia Berdnikava's overall record of 2,581.12 – which had stood since 2012 – by 0.27 points at the Bill Wenner Memorial Record tournament. Straltsova skied five buoys on an 11.25-m-long rope, scored 8,890 in tricks and jumped 59.8 m (196 ft 2 in).

Most points in women's waterskiing tricks
Erika Lang (CAN) scored 11,450 points at the Bell Acqua Lake 3 Record Trick event in California on 7 Jun 2025. It was the seventh world record that Lang had set in the event. Competitors have two runs to perform tricks such as turns, flips and rotations, and are judged on technique and flair.

DEC 29 Lizanne Wilmot (CAN) cycled the **fastest 1 km on a penny farthing (female)** in 2024. She clocked 1 min 52.75 sec in Devonport, Tasmania, Australia.

DEC 30 In 2021, Alexander Schulz (DEU) set out on the **longest blindfolded slackline walk**, covering 1,712 m (5,616 ft) over the Cañón del Sumidero in southern Mexico.

Stop Press

The following entries were approved and added to our database after the official closing date for this year's submissions.

Most expensive cake stand
On 23 Oct 2025, a luxurious cake pedestal sold for £15,000 ($20,020) in Poole, Dorset, UK. Made by Prop Options in association with Renshaw (both UK), it featured mirror-polished stainless steel and 30,000 hand-embellished Swarovski crystals.

Largest Day of the Dead altar
On 1 Nov 2025, a 3,695-m² (39,772-sq-ft) *ofrenda* for the departed was displayed by Municipio de Ixtlahuacán de los Membrillos (MEX) in Jalisco, Mexico. More than 3,800 people worked on the altar, which was set in a cemetery, serving as a perfect bridge between life and death.

Most nationalities in a soccer exhibition match
In advance of the 2026 World Cup, FIFA brought together players from 68 nations – ranging from Argentina to Zimbabwe – for a one-off game in Rabat, Morocco, on 5 Nov 2025. Altogether, 83 athletes took part, each of whom saw at least 10 min of play on the pitch.

Youngest TEDx speaker (female)
Aged just 5 years 52 days, Laranyaa Agarwal (IND, b. 5 Oct 2020) gave a speech titled "Tiny but Mighty" at the event *Decoding Tomorrow: From Vision to Reality* in Palwal, Haryana, India, on 26 Nov 2025. She spoke of her journey from being born a growth-restricted baby to becoming a symbol of strength and determination. Laranyaa surpassed her compatriot Anvi Vishesh Agrawal (see p.150).

Most subscribed YouTube cooking channel
Nick DiGiovanni's (USA) "Nick's Kitchen" channel had 35.7 million followers, as of 30 Mar 2026. The youngest-ever *MasterChef* finalist, Nick has a smorgasbord of GWR titles, including **largest chicken nugget** – 20.9 kg (46 lb 3 oz) – cooked up with fellow culinary influencer, the late Lynn Davis (JPN).

Largest collection of *The Legend of Zelda* memorabilia
As of 21 Feb 2026, Anne Martha Harnes (NOR) had 4,000 mementoes of Nintendo's acclaimed franchise, as verified in Ålesund, Norway. Anne was inspired by the game's 40th anniversary in 2026 to regain a record that she first claimed in 2016. Her updated haul narrowly surpassed that of the previous holder (see pp.78–79).

Smallest QR code
Balint Hajas (HUN), Erwin Peck, Christian Pflaum, Alexander Kirnbauer, Paul Heinz Mayrhofer, Martin Kunze and Thomas Schachinger (all AUT) created a QR code measuring just 1.977 square micrometres, as verified in Vienna, Austria, on 3 Dec 2025. It links to the research group's official web page.

Oldest unicycle rider
Extending her own record, Linda Jarrett (USA, b. 31 May 1956) was aged 69 years 189 days when she pedalled her one-wheeler on stage during a performance of *The Children's Nutcracker* in Lindsay, California, USA, on 6 Dec 2025.

Most libraries visited in 24 hours
Sujoy Kumar Mitra and Prateek Choraria (both IND) checked in at 42 book repositories in New Delhi, India, between 9 and 10 Dec 2025.

Fastest time to peel and slice a pineapple
On 10 Dec 2025, Slovakia's Dominika Gasparova prepared a pineapple in only 11.43 sec in Wisbech, Cambridgeshire, UK. The attempt took place at the Del Monte factory, where Dominika works.

Longest churro
Ariel Acosta-Rubio and María Alejandra Bravo (both USA, b. VEN) – founders of the Churromania franchise – presented a 153.21-m (502-ft 7-in) deep-fried pastry in Hialeah, Florida, USA, on 12 Dec 2025. It took 1.5 hr to prepare the supersized churro, but only 4 min to cook it.

Longest Christmas stollen
On 18 Dec 2025, Sky Radio (NLD) entered into the festive spirit with a 79.95-m (262-ft 3-in) spiced bread in Haarlem, Netherlands.

Most messages to Santa collected in 24 hours
Capitale de Noël, Kado Ghamloush and Whish Money (all LBN) gathered up 2,924 Christmas wish lists in Batroun, Lebanon, on 20–21 Dec 2025.

Farthest flight by a paper aircraft
Liu Liwen – helped by Tang Shuai, Yang Shian, Huang Yizhou, Qiao Yuchen and Wang Chenghao (all CHN) – launched a paper plane a distance of 98.43 m (322 ft 11 in) on 28 Dec 2025. The attempt took place in Shanghai, China, and surpassed the previous record by more than 10 m (32 ft 9 in).

Most expensive comic
A copy of *Action Comics* #1 (DC Comics, 1938) – featuring Superman's debut – realized $15 m (£11.15 m) in a private sale brokered by Metropolis Collectibles/ComicConnect on 9 Jan 2026.

Fastest time to solve a 3x3x3 rotating puzzle cube while blindfolded
On 10 Jan 2026, Charlie Eggins (AUS) completed a classic puzzle cube in 11.67 sec with his eyes covered in Sydney, New South Wales, Australia.

Most Oscar nominations for a film
On 22 Jan 2026, horror flick *Sinners* (USA, 2025) earned 16 Academy Award nods, including the coveted Best Picture and Best Director categories.

Largest flower word
On 24 Jan 2026, Navsari Municipal Corporation (IND) spelled out the town's name using a total of 95,280 blooms in Gujarat, India.

Largest display of cheese varieties
On 28 Jan 2026, Elie Makhlouf (LBN) presented an array of 1,189 cheeses in Dubai, UAE. They ranged from Swiss Vacherin Fribourgeois and Dutch Veldhuyzen Extra to 81 unique types of cheddar.

Longest professional hairdressing marathon
Trained coiffeur Joshua Babatunde Aiyenuro (NGA) devoted 72 hr to creating stylish hairdos in Nasarawa State, Nigeria, on 29 Jan 2026.

Largest smartphone photography competition
As verified on 29 Jan 2026, a group of 15,988 sharp-shooters entered the "India #withGalaxy" contest, arranged by Samsung in Gurugram, Haryana, India.

Most escape rooms attended in 24 hours
Raychel Garcia, Steven Hepsworth, Ona Delussey, Victor Hui and Richard Corbett (all USA) – aka "The Florida Keys" – sleuthed their way out of 41 different escape rooms between 5 and 6 Feb 2026. All of the sites were in Orlando, Florida, USA.

DEC 31 On New Year's Eve 2015, Yuriy Yaniv (UKR) set off the **largest sparkler candle:** 10,000 fireworks in a 50-kg (110-lb) bundle that produced a huge tower of sparks.

Largest tropical greenhouse
Edenya is a 40,447-m² (435,367-sq-ft) hothouse within Pairi Daiza zoo, as verified in Brugelette, Belgium, on 6 Feb 2026. The indoor paradise features a 17-m-tall (55-ft 9-in) waterfall and one of Europe's largest butterfly sanctuaries.

Fastest half marathon in a non-racing wheelchair (female)
On 8 Feb 2026, Jack Clemit (UK) completed the Goodwood Running GP Half Marathon in 1 hr 39 min 27 sec in Chichester, West Sussex, UK, improving on the previous record by 16 min.

First non-English-language Super Bowl half-time show
Puerto Rico's Bad Bunny (b. Benito Antonio Martínez Ocasio) performed a mostly Spanish-language medley at the Apple Music Super Bowl LX Halftime Show in Santa Clara, California, USA, on 8 Feb 2026. The 14-min set drew a TV audience of 128.2 million.

Most mouse clicks in one minute
"Yigox" (aka Yiğit Arslan), supported by Logitech G (both TUR), tapped a Pro X2 Superstrike mouse 760 times in Istanbul, Türkiye, on 10 Feb 2026.

Loudest billboard
A replica stock-car engine embedded into an advertising hoarding emitted a 133.7-dBC roar for an event organized by NASCAR (USA) in New York City, USA, as confirmed on 10 Feb 2026.

Tallest church
The Sagrada Família in Barcelona, Spain, topped out at 172.5 m (565 ft 11 in) on 20 Feb 2026. Masons completed the external work to the basilica 144 years after it was started, though it will take up to two more years to finish the interior.

Fastest Welsh stepdance medley
Tudur Phillips (UK) executed five steps based on traditional Welsh folk dances in 28.47 sec in Cardiff, UK, on 22 Feb 2026. The record was set in anticipation of St David's Day (1 Mar 2026).

Most clothes collected in 24 hours
On 25 Feb 2026, Gulf Bank (KWT) amassed 59.1 tonnes (65.1 tons) of donated clothing in Kuwait City, which was distributed to people in need by the Kiswa charity association.

Highest-altitude skydive landing
After leaping from a plane with a parachute, Tanaboworn Sirikunakornkun (THA) touched down at an elevation of 5,442 m (17,854 ft) on Chile's Ojos del Salado volcano on 14 Mar 2026.

Most kick-scooter flairs in one minute
Improving on his own record that he set live on German TV in 2025 (see p.163) by one, young teen Tom Buxbaum (DEU) executed 21 backflips on his scooter in Siegen, Germany, on 20 Mar 2026.

Highest-earning *EA Sports FC/FIFA* player
"Nicolas99FC", aka Nicolas Villalba (ARG), had banked $851,431 (£635,438) in prize money from 54 soccer eSports contests, as of 25 Mar 2026.

Longest table-tennis serve
Surpassing his own record, Osman Gürcü (TUR) delivered a serve while standing 17.5 m (57 ft 4 in) away from the ping-pong table in Denizli, Türkiye, on 27 Mar 2026.

Largest serving of guacamole
Municipio de Tancítaro (MEX) whipped up a 6,800.5-kg (14,992-lb 8-oz) batch of avocado dip in Michoacán, Mexico, on 10 Apr 2026.

Oldest manatee ever
Romeo (b. *c.* 1955), a West Indian manatee (*Trichechus manatus*), was at least 71 years old as of 2026. A more typical lifespan for these aquatic mammals is 30–40 years, especially in the wild. Since Jun 2025, he has resided at the Gulfarium on Fort Walton Beach, Okaloosa Island, Florida, USA.

Most Bundesliga titles won by a player
On 19 Apr 2026, Manuel Neuer won Germany's top soccer league for the 13th time with Bayern Munich (2013–23, 2025–26), matching Thomas Müller (both DEU) in 2010, 2013–23 and 2025, also with Bayern.

Oldest zoological society
The Zoological Society of London (ZSL) marked its 200th anniversary on 29 Apr 2026. Today, the ZSL cares for *c.* 20,000 animals across two sites: London Zoo in Regent's Park and Whipsnade Zoo in Bedfordshire. The former pioneered the **first public aquarium** (1853–2019). It is also the location of the **first insect house** (1881) and **children's zoo** (1938), though neither now exist in their original form.

Special *Winter Games Express* chocolate bars were later sold to raise funds for the charity Associazione Cure Palliative.

Longest chocolate sculpture
On 26 Jan 2026, a 55.27-m (181-ft 3-in) chocolate model of a vintage steam locomotive and 22 carriages was unveiled in Milan, Italy. Dubbed the *Winter Games Express* – in anticipation of the Milano Cortina 2026 Olympics – the choco choo-choo was created by chocolatier Andrew Farrugia from the Institute of Tourism Studies (both MLT) and the Italian pastry-chef association Consorzi Pasticceri di Bergamo-Brescia.

Index

Bold entries in the index indicate a main entry on a subject; **BOLD CAPITALS** indicate an entire chapter.

BEHIND THE SCENES

Consultants

Each year, we collaborate with dozens of experts who know their subjects inside out. The learned specialists who contributed to *GWR 2027* excel in everything from stained glass, Egyptology and North American sport, to musicals, gemstones, poisonous plants and street art.

For a full list, visit **guinnessworldrecords.com/records/partners**

Jasmine Allen is the curator and director of The Stained Glass Museum in Ely, Cambridgeshire, UK. She specializes in stained glass from 1800 to the present, and has published widely in this field. Her book *Windows for the World: Stained Glass and the International Exhibitions 1851–1900* (2018) focused on the exhibition of post-medieval stained glass in an international context. Jasmine is also an Honorary Freeman of the Worshipful Company of Glaziers and Painters on Glass, and committee member of the Glaziers Trust as well as the Stained Glass Repository.

Mark Aston has long served as a Science & Technology consultant for *GWR*. A retired scientist and engineer, with a background specializing in optical physics and astrophysics, he brings nearly 40 years of experience of high-technology science and engineering to ensure *GWR*'s sci-tech records are accurate and informative. Mark's varied career across both academia and commercial enterprises led to a lively career in new technology development.

Ian Failes is the founder of *befores & afters*, a visual-effects and animation eMagazine, print publication and podcast destination. He has also contributed to a plethora of magazines and websites such as *fxguide*, Cartoon Brew, *VFX Voice*, *3D Artist*, *3D World*, *Syfy*, *Digital Arts*, *MovieMaker* and Polygon, and co-hosts the *VFX Notes* visual podcast. Ian is a regular on the conference circuit, at events such as FMX, SIGGRAPH, Trojan Horse Was a Unicorn and SPARKFX. His debut book – *Masters of FX* – was published in 2015.

David Fischer has been *GWR*'s senior North American sports consultant since 2006. He has written for *The New York Times* and *Sports Illustrated for Kids*, and has worked at *Sports Illustrated*, *The National Sports Daily* and NBC Sports. David has authored several books, including *Tom Brady: A Celebration of Greatness on the Gridiron* (2021), *The New York Yankees of the 1950s: Mantle, Stengel, Berra, and a Decade of Dominance* (2019) and *The Super Bowl: The First Fifty Years of America's Greatest Game* (2015).

Stephen Follows is a world-leading film-industry analyst and researcher. He seeks to discover how the film industry operates and to use that knowledge to help filmmakers get their films made and seen. His work has covered gender equality, applied creativity, AI innovation and film education.

Melanie-Jayne Howes, Senior Research Leader at the UK's Royal Botanic Gardens, Kew, is an expert in natural product chemistry, pharmacognosy and bioactive molecules. At Kew, she researches the chemistry of plants and fungi to understand the scientific basis for their uses, particularly those in medicine, food and human health, and leads a team investigating plant and fungal chemistry. She is also a Chartered Chemist and a Visiting Senior Lecturer at the Institute of Pharmaceutical Science at King's College London. She has penned over 80 publications on plant chemistry and bioactivity, including the Kew Pocketbook on *Poisonous Plants* (2024), co-written with Eliot Jan-Smith.

8000ers.com
Eberhard Jurgalski has developed the system of "Elevation Equality", a method of classifying mountain ranges and peaks. His website has become the main source of altitude statistics for the Himalayas and Karakoram ranges.

CANNA UK National Giant Vegetables Championship
A pinnacle in the calendar of competitive gardeners is the Malvern Autumn Show, held each year in Worcestershire, UK. Head judge Sebastian Suski conducts the assessments.

Council on Tall Buildings and Urban Habitat
Based in Chicago, Illinois, USA, the CTBUH is the world's leading resource for professionals focused on the design, construction and operation of tall buildings and future cities.

Great Pumpkin Commonwealth
The GPC cultivates the growing of giant pumpkins – among other prodigious produce – by establishing universal standards and regulations that ensure quality of fruit and fairness of competition.

International Ice Swimming Association
Founded by Ram Barkai, the IISA was established in 2009 with a vision to formalize swimming in icy water – i.e., below 5°C (41°F). It has put in place rules to allow for maximum safety, and to regulate swim integrity in terms of distance, time and conditions.

International Slackline Association
The mission of the ISA is to support and develop slackline communities of all sizes, in addition to providing governance for slacklining as a competitive sport.

The IRONMAN® Group
The IRONMAN Group is the largest operator of mass-participation sports in the world. It provides more than a million people annually the benefits of sport via its offerings across triathlon, cycling, running and trail/dirt events.

LongeviQuest
LongeviQuest (LQ) is a global research organization that verifies the ages of the world's oldest people. Founded in 2022 by leading experts, LQ focuses on supercentenarians – people who have reached 110 years of age. With researchers across five continents, LQ confirms longevity records worldwide while preserving the life stories and insights of these extraordinary individuals.

Major League Eating
MLE is a body that oversees professional eating contests globally. The organization developed the sport of competitive eating and coordinates the governing body, the International Federation of Competitive Eating.

MonumentalTrees.com
Tim Bekaert is the administrator of this community website listing tens of thousands of photos, girth and height measurements for noteworthy trees. It also records the location details of often otherwise undocumented remarkable specimens around the world.

The Numbers
TheNumbers.com is the web's biggest database of cinema box-office information, with figures on 50,000 movies and around 200,000 people in the film industry. It was founded in 1997 by Bruce Nash and is visited by more than 8 million people every year.

Ocean Rowing Society International
The ORSI was established in 1983 by Kenneth F Crutchlow and Peter Bird, later joined by Tom Lynch and Tatiana Rezvaya-Crutchlow. The organization documents all attempts to row the oceans and major bodies of water, and classifies, verifies and adjudicates ocean-rowing achievements.

Parrot Analytics
Parrot Analytics is the leading global content demand analytics company for the modern multi-platform TV business. It tracks more than 1.5 billion daily expressions of demand in more than 100 languages and 200 countries.

Polar Expeditions Classification Scheme
PECS is a grading and labelling system for extended, unmotorized polar journeys that is overseen by a committee of polar-expedition specialists, managed by Eric Philips. Polar regions, modes of travel, routes and forms of aid are defined under the scheme, giving expeditioners guidance on how to classify, promote and immortalize their journeys.

Royal Botanic Gardens, Kew
RBG Kew (aka Kew Gardens) in Richmond, London, UK, is a world-famous scientific organization, globally respected for its outstanding collections as well as its scientific expertise in plant diversity, conservation and sustainable development in the UK and around the world. Its remit includes all aspects of botany and fungal research.

The UK & International Timing Association
The UK & ITA was established in 2013 when Straightliners and SPEE3D united to enhance and promote land-speed record breaking in the UK and Europe. It ensures that land-speed contenders can compete on equal terms.

World Cube Association
The WCA governs competitions for mechanical puzzles that are operated by twisting groups of pieces, such as the Rubik's Cube. Its mission is to have more events in more countries, all participating under fair and equal conditions.

World Freestyle Football Association
Founded in 2017 and now with 119 member countries, the WFFA is the world governing body for the sport of freestyle football. Its main mission is to grow awareness of, and participation in, freestyle football worldwide. The WFFA is the official organizer of a wide range of freestyle-football championships including first-class tournaments such as the World Freestyle Football Championship, the Pulse Series, the Super Ball World Open and the NextGen World Championship. The WFFA has been established upon a backbone of community development and education: this means it recognizes the power this exciting sport has to inspire healthy, active lifestyles for young people all over the world. Aside from growing the sport as a full-time profession for the athletes, the WFFA is committed to teaching key life skills through freestyle football.

World Meteorological Organization
Based in Geneva, Switzerland, this UN body is the global authority on weather, climatology and hydrology, for both the purposes of science and advising policy. Dr Randall Cerveny is a President's Professor in Geographical Sciences who specializes in weather and climate. He has held the position of Rapporteur of Weather and Climate Extremes for the WMO since 2007.

Alexandra Jones is the founder and president of Jones Archaeology Consulting. She earned her PhD in Historical Archaeology from the University of California, Berkeley, in 2010. Her research centres on African diaspora archaeology, community archaeology and public outreach. With more than 16 years of experience as an archaeology educator, Jones is dedicated to making archaeological knowledge accessible to all. She previously served as Archaeology Field School Director for the PBS series *Time Team America*, leading field schools for junior-high and high-school students. Dr Jones is president of the Society of Black Archaeologists, president of the St Croix Archaeological Society and chair of the USA's Cultural Property Advisory Committee.

Cedar Lewisohn is an artist, writer and currently works as a curator at the Southbank Centre in London, UK, having held previous curatorial roles at the Museum of London, Hangar Bicocca (Milan), Birmingham Museums, Northwestern (Qatar), Tate Britain and Tate Modern. Cedar curated the landmark *Street Art* exhibition at Tate Modern in 2008. He has written for and edited many periodicals and is the author of the books *Street Art* (2008) and *Abstract Graffiti* (2011).

Lisa Martland is a writer and editor who began her career with a decade on staff at *The Stage* as critic, chief sub-editor and deputy editor. She is the founder/publisher of one of the UK's top theatre websites, Musical Theatre Review, which celebrated its 10th anniversary in 2023. Other roles include sub-editor and reviewer at *Musicals Magazine* and editor for the My Theatre Mates and StageFaves websites.

Helen Molesworth is a jewellery historian and gemmologist whose 25-year career has spanned the global jewellery industry from auctions to academic posts. She spent 10 years as a specialist at Christie's and Sotheby's, where she managed such important sales as that of HRH Princess Margaret's heirlooms in 2006. Helen has travelled to mine sites and salerooms all over the world in search of gems. She is now the Senior Jewellery Curator at the UK's V&A Museum, where she curated *Cartier* in 2025, and her book – *Precious, The History and Mystery of Gems Across Time* – launched in 2024.

Barry Rice is an astrobiologist who spans two main scientific disciplines: astronomy and botany. He worked for 10 years at The Nature Conservancy and has engaged in fieldwork, focusing on carnivorous plants, for more than 25 years. He has served for over two decades as an editor for the journal of the International Carnivorous Plant Society, and has authored two books on carnivorous plants, as well as many supporting chapters and research papers – mostly focusing on the genera *Utricularia*, *Drosera*, *Darlingtonia* and *Sarracenia*.

Ramy Romany is a world-renowned Egyptologist and best-selling author whose lifelong passion for ancient history began in his documentary-filmmaking family in Cairo. Before turning 20, he had already filmed, produced and been featured in more than 100 documentaries about ancient Egypt. After relocating to Los Angeles, he continued his mission to shine a light on his ancient civilization, becoming a trusted expert and host of major archaeological series on Discovery, National Geographic and BBC among others, captivating global audiences with his insight and storytelling.

Karl P N Shuker has a PhD in Zoology and Comparative Physiology from the University of Birmingham, UK, and is a Scientific Fellow of the Zoological Society of London, a Fellow of the Royal Entomological Society and a Member of The Society of Authors. He has penned 25 books as well as hundreds of articles covering many aspects of natural history. Karl's work has an emphasis on anomalous animals, including new, rediscovered and unrecognized species.

Chris Stokes is a former president of the British Branch of the International Glaciological Society and is now a professor at Durham University, UK. His expertise lies in glaciers and their response to climate change, and his research spans from monitoring small mountain glaciers over the last few decades to large-scale reconstructions of continental ice sheets over millennia. In the last 20 years, Chris has published more than 140 scientific papers and served on the editorial boards of *Geology* (2018–21) and *The Cryosphere* (2012–24).

Matthew White is *GWR*'s lead music, cricket and tennis consultant, formulating 1,200-plus new and updated records. Additionally, between 2007 and 2026, he pored over an estimated 85,000 published records as proofreader and fact-checker for the world's **best-selling annual.** In 2002, Matthew landed his dream job as a member of the team that produced the final four editions of the *Guinness Book of British Hit Singles & Albums* – the much-missed "bible of pop" that soundtracked his adolescence.

World Open Water Swimming Association
Founded in 2005, WOWSA is an international governing body for the sport of open-water swimming. It provides membership and certification programmes as well as publications and online resources to cater to all levels of outdoor swimmer.

World Sailing Speed Record Council
The WSSRC was recognized by the International Yacht Racing Union (now World Sailing) in 1972. The council of experts draws members from Australia, France, Great Britain and the USA.

World Sport Stacking Association
As the official worldwide governing body for sport stacking, the WSSA – founded in 2001 – promotes the standardization and advancement of sport-stacking rules, records and events.

World UltraCycling Association
WUCA is a non-profit organization dedicated to supporting ultracycling across the world. It holds the largest repository of cycling records for all bike types, and certifies successful rides for its members.

Xpogo
Xpogo works with the best extreme pogo-sticking athletes in the world, with the goal of growing the sport of extreme pogo through touring, competitions and athlete development. The Xpogo jumpers bounce on air-powered pogo sticks, which enable them to achieve incredible height, bounding several feet in the air, performing stunts and flips and chasing records to push the limits of the sport.

Thanks also to...
Alex Liu, Alnwick Garden (Angela Blythe, Ian McAllister), Amanda Malpass, Ambrose Greenway, Andy Garrett, Antarctic Logistics & Expeditions (Steve Jones), Boston Dynamics (Kerri Neelon), Boston University (David Carballo), Bridgestone World Solar Challenge (Judi Lalor), Carenza Lewis, Cassidy Zachary, Chris Martin, Dennis Crowley, Eljas Oksanen, Ellen Swift, Ghost Club of Great Britain (Alan Murdie), Griffin Museum of Science and Industry, Gulfarium (Patrick Berry), Holly Nicholls, Internet Movie Firearms Database, Jaclyn Swope, Jim Singh, Joe Hollins, Jonathan McDowell, Kitty Abel Smith, Kris Lockyear, Kristen Metzger, London Museum (Michel Stocco, Bree Wilkinson), Mark O'Shea, Meijin Kroon, MOLA, NASA (Rachel Kraft, Kelly Perry), National Research Council of Italy (Stefano Mammola), Rebecca Byers, Roland Sigrist, Roman Army Museum (Sonya Galloway), Sky Elements (Hayes Walsh, Preston Ward), Society for Psychical Research (Tom Ruffles), St Helena Government (Danni Thomas), Terri Calleson, Thaneswar Guragai, The Alfred Russel Wallace Correspondence Project (George Beccaloni), The American Center of Research (Pearce Paul Creasman), The Numbers (Brian Ellerman), The Shipley School, University of Arizona (Takeshi Inomata), University of Lincoln (Fernando Montealegre-Zapata), University of the Peloponnese (Anna Lazarou), V&A (Louis Copplestone), Warner Brown, World Cube Association (Kyle Hayles), Wouter de Herder, WUCA (Larry Oslund)

Acknowledgements

SVP Brand Strategy & Global Publishing
Nadine Causey

Editor-in-Chief
Craig Glenday

Publishing Director
Jane Boatfield

Senior Managing Editor
Adam Millward

Senior Editors
Tom Beckerlegge, Alice Bell (*Gamer's Edition*), Ben Hollingum

Editor
Caitlin Hyem

Layout Editor
Rob Dimery

Senior Picture Editor
Abby Taylor

Picture Editors
Saffron Fradley, Alice Jessop

Proofreading & Fact-Checking
Matthew White

Editorial Intern
Allison Dolan

VP Global Production & Supply Chain
Patricia Magill

Production & Distribution Manager
Thomas McCurdy

Senior Talent Researcher
Charlie Anderson

Design
Paul Wylie-Deacon and Richard Page at 55design.co.uk

Cover Design
Paul Wylie-Deacon and Richard Page at 55design.co.uk

Indexer
Rob Gibson

Head of Commissioned Content
Michael Whitty

Original Photography
Thomas Abrahams, Ian Bowkett, Paul Michael Hughes, Erik Isakson, Peter Jülich, Trudy Lee, Max & Sophia, Ahmed Sarandaz Rathore

3D Artwork
Joseph O'Neil

Production Consultants
Yannick Laag, Astrid Renders, Kevin Sarney, Julia Seebach, Dennis Thon

Printing & Binding
Mohn Media Mohndruck GmbH, Gütersloh, Germany

Global Marketing Director
Nicholas Brookes

Senior Content Manager
Eleonora Pilastro

Senior Marketing Executive
Nicole Dyer-Rainford

CRM Marketing Manager
Jody Ho

Head of Global Brand Communications
Amber-Georgina Maskell

Senior PR Manager (UK & International)
Anna Hammersley

PR Manager (UK & International)
Madalyn Bielfeld

Global Sales Director
Joel Smith

Senior Key Account Manager
Mavis Sarfo

International Sales Manager
Alexandra Bielikova

Director of Brand Strategy
Lucy Hunter

Head of Brand Management
Juliet Dawson

Brand Manager
Jack Brockbank

Head of Design
Rebecca Fisher

Senior Designer
Kelsey Bell

Designer
Aaron Quinn

Reprographics
Resmiye Kahraman and Louise Pinnock at BORN Group

British Library Cataloguing-in-publication data:
a catalogue record for this book is available from the British Library

UK: 978-1-80650-022-2
US: 978-1-80650-025-3
US (Costco): 978-1-80650-041-3
CAN: 978-1-80650-031-4
AUS: 978-1-80650-035-2

Records are made to be broken – indeed, it is one of the key criteria for a record category – so if you find a record that you think you can beat, tell us about it by making a record claim. Always contact us before making a record attempt.

Sustainability

At Guinness World Records, we continue to run our business in the most sustainable, environmentally conscious way we can. As part of that commitment, the pages of this book are printed on a paper produced as close as possible to our printing partner, Mohn Media, which comes from Sappi Ehingen Mill in Germany. Sappi is a leading global producer of graphic papers, embracing sustainability and high environmental performance. Sappi is committed to the UN Sustainable Development Goals and continues to invest in CO_2-neutral production. GWR is committed to ethical and responsible sourcing of paper, as well as ink. We also work to ensure that all our supply-chain partners meet the highest international standards for sustainable production and energy management. For more information, please contact us.

PEFC/04-31-1033

GWR has a very thorough accreditation system for records verification. However, while every effort is made to ensure accuracy, GWR cannot be held responsible for any errors contained in this work. Feedback from our readers on any point of accuracy is always welcomed.

GWR uses metric and imperial measurements. Exceptions are made for some scientific data where metric measurements are universally accepted, and some sports data. Where a specific date is given, the exchange rate is calculated according to the currency values at the time. Where only a year date is given, the exchange rate is calculated from 31 Dec of that year.

Appropriate advice should always be taken when attempting to break or set records. Participants undertake records entirely at their own risk. GWR has complete discretion over whether or not to include a record attempt in any of its publications. Being a GWR record holder does not guarantee you a place in any Guinness World Records publication.

Printed in Germany by Mohn Media

Guinness World Records Limited's authorized representative in the European Union is Mohn Media Mohndruck GmbH, Carl-Bertelsmann-Straße 161M, 33311 Gütersloh, Germany

www.mohnmedia.de

Registered address: Ground Floor, The Rookery, 2 Dyott Street, London, WC1A 1DE

THE JIM PATTISON GROUP

OFFICIALLY AMAZING

Global President
Alistair Richards

Entertainment: Alexia Argeros, Sean Coogan, Fiona Gruchy-Craven, Paul O'Neill, Alan Pixsley

Governance
Alison Ozanne

Global Finance: Tanjila Begum, Elizabeth Bishop, Jess Blake, Arianna Cracco, Lisa Gibbs, Gianluca Halil, Kimberley Jones, Natsumi Ogawa, Kirtan Patel

Finance Business Partnering: Tom Jones, Maryana Lovell, Lorenzo Di Sciullo

Global Legal: Mathew Alderson, Sarah Elgeti, Greyson Huang, Matthew Knight, Jiayi Teng

IT & Global Operations
Rob Howe

Project Management: Caroline Brouwer

Digital Technology & IT: Mohamed Hanad Abukar, Zainab Alabi, Emman Chaudhry, Oliver Hickie, Veronica Irons, Apon Majumder, Sohail Malik, Ajoke Oritu, Priya Ponnusamy, Vishrutha Soora, Carolyn Sudding, Alex Waldu

Central Records Services
Mark McKinley

Customer Support: Joanne Brent, Megan Bruce, Clea Lime, Ryan Masserano, Mufidah Mustafa, Mariana Sinotti, Melissa Wooton

Data Quality Management: Erin Branney, Thomas Marshall, Will Sinden

Global People & Culture
Stephanie Lunn

London: Olivia Herrera, Gurpreet Kaur, Monika Tilani

Americas: Jennifer Olson

Beijing: Crystal Xu, Nina Zhou

Dubai: Shilpa Kurian

Tokyo: Emiko Yamamoto

TV & Digital
Katie Forde

TV & Digital: Karen Gilchrist

Video Production & Design: Fran Morales, Dan Peters, Dominic Punt

Commissioned Content: Michael Whitty

Talent & Creative: Nana Asante, Will Munford, Dave Wilson

Social Media: Emma Salt, Dan Thorne

Website Content: Vassi Bakogianni, Vicki Newman

GWR for Business
Marco Frigatti, Charles Wharton

Global Commercial Sales Lead: Fay Edwards

Global Records Creative & Adjudication Leads: Karen Hamzeh, Ted Li

Brand Communications
Doug Male, Amber-Georgina Maskell

London: Madalyn Bielfeld, Anna Hammersley

Americas: Kylie Galloway, Amanda Marcus

Beijing: Echo Zhan, Yvonne Zhang

Dubai: Maram Al Isawi, Mohamed Foudil Bouadda, Hassan Ibrahim

Tokyo: Kazami Kamioka, Theo-Haryo Putro, Masakazu Senda

Ecommerce & Product
Scott Shore

London: Jackie Angus, Cat Blyth, Harry Bristow, Sara Kali, Athina Kontopoulou, Aled Mann, Rebecca Ward

Beijing: Richard Guo

Tokyo: Hiroyuki Tanaka

Global Marketing & Demand Generation
Angelique Begarin

London: Amina Addow, William Baxter-Hughes, Melissa Brown, Mohamad Kaddoura, Alexandra Moldoveanu

Americas: Winchelle Jean-Pierre

Beijing: Theresa Gao, Nicole Kang

Dubai: Enas Abduljabbar, Shaddy Gaad

Tokyo: Takumi Otsubo, Eri Yuhira

International offices

Beijing
Carlos Martinez

Commercial Account Services: Catherine Gao, Linda Li, Luna Liu, Jing Ran, Amelia Wang, Elaine Wang

Editorial: Angela Wu

Records Creative Team: Fay Jiang, Chloe Liu, Jingjing Liu, Vertin Pang, Vanessa Tao, Kaia Wang, Peng Wang, Alicia Zhao

Dubai
Talal Omar

Commercial Account Services: Sara Abu-Saad, Hazal Altunoglu, Khalaf Bin Badi AlDosari, Naser Batat, Daniel Hickson, Jana Tannir, Kamel Yassin

Records Creative Team: Maha Alem, Sarah Alkholb, Reem Al Ghussain, Tarek El-Saoudi, Salma Sobeh

London
Sam Prosser

Commercial Account Services: Nick Adams, Monika Drobina, Sirali Gandhi, Charlize Jelley, Spoorthy Prakash, Nikhil Shukla, Lucia Sinigagliesi, Nataliia Solovei, Precious Taiwo

Records Creative Team: Muhammad Ahmed, Shreya Bahuguna, Lewis Blakeman, Andrew Fanning, Veronika Hanl, Apekshita Kadam, Francesca Raggi, Sohini Sinha

Americas
Nicole Pando

Commercial Account Services: Isabella Barbosa, Mackenzie Berry, Brittany Carpenter, Carolina Guanabara, Ralph Hannah, Kim Partrick, Callie Smith, Joana Weiss

Records Creative Team: Raquel Assis, Amelis Escalante, Lianett Fernandez, Maddison Kulish, Alba (Niky) Pauli, Carlos Tapia Rojas

Tokyo
Kaoru Ishikawa

Commercial Account Services: Jonathan Caleb, Minami Ito, Takuro Maruyama, Yumiko Nakagawa, Nana Nguyen, Yuki Sakamoto, Wei Watanabe, Masamichi Yazaki

Records Creative Team: Saif Almannaei, Caycee Dolan, Shiori Hatsuda, Aki Makijima, Mai McMillan, Momoko Omori, Naomi-Emily Sakai, Aoi Shimizu

Quiz & Puzzles answers (pp.160–61)

Quiz: 1. A: Longer. A standard bowling lane is 18.3 m (60 ft) long, whereas the greatest distance to blow a pea is 25.89 m (84 ft 11 in), achieved by David Rush (USA) in Boise, Idaho, USA, on 8 Oct 2022 **2.** A: Whoville **3.** A: India **4.** C: skating on a fingerboard **5.** True: Uranus is also known as the "green planet" **6.** B: Creepers **7.** A: Yes. Ashrita Furman (USA) peeled and ate a kiwi in 5.35 sec in New York, USA, on 10 Dec 2008 **8.** C: Tinker Bell **9.** A: Luigi **10.** True: certain species of bamboo can grow up to 91 cm (3 ft) in a 24-hour period.

Emoji codebreakers:

1. Longest pea pod: 180 mm (7 in), grown by Graham Barratt (UK) and measured on 2 Jul 2025.

2. Fastest time to slice a cucumber: 13.4 sec, by Norman Johnson (UK) on 3 Apr 1983.

3. Smelliest plant: *Amorphophallus titanum* can be smelled up to half a mile (0.8 km) away.

4. Most lights on a Christmas tree: 194,672, set by Kiwanis Malmedy/Haute Fagnes Belgium on 10 Dec 2010.

5. Most expensive emerald sold at auction: 7.765 m Swiss francs (see p.30) for the Aga Khan Emerald on 12 Nov 2024.

Acknowledgements
55Design (Hayley Wylie-Deacon, Tobias Wylie-Deacon, Rueben Wylie-Deacon, Vidette Burniston, Lewis Burniston, Jay Page, Ellice Page, Bruno, Zeus, Buster, Macy), 360 Food Partners (Ian Brocklehurst, James Mawer), Alliance National (Shad Williams, Sam Owen), Atlas Creative (MaKayla Hartter, Cody Flaherty), Atmosphere TV (Lin Nguyen, Sebastian Quinn), Banijay (Helen Greatorex), Blooming Color Inc, Brave Bison (Greg Hollands, Ed Hunt, Adam Raw, Martin Ruffell, Bo Yee Leung), Ian Briscoe, Martin Brock, Lance Burnett, Cepac Ltd, Codex Solutions Ltd, Constantin Film (Alexander Pelzer), Copenhagen GWR Museum (Henri Sokou, Phyllis Calloway), Cuarzo (Sonia Perez), DataWorks Plus, Sophia Dittmann, DVAD (David de Bie), Egg Soldiers (Stefan Cosser, Jemma Jackson), Ezoic (Claire Johnson), Sean Fitzgerald, FJT Logistics Ltd (Ray Harper), Fraser Direct Distribution Services Ltd, Grafit Display Hire Ltd (Antonia Johnston, Paul Harrison), Greenspan (Tim Donell, Ryan Palmer, Jamie Davenport), Violetta Gringersch, Roger Hawkins, Matt Hillman, Kathryn Hubbard, IAAPA (Lane Vento), Ithaca interns (Sarah Mooney, Sonya Mukhina, Anna Phelps), Kay Elliott (John Barclay, Liam Ellis, Adam Wicks, Valentina Parente, Owen Nichols), Orla Langton, Lavingtons (Paul Mansell), Left Brain Games, Macmillan Distribution, Ray & Jen Mansell, Silvia Martini, Mather & Co (Paul Lee, Matt Melling, Yasmin Wan, Iona Gibson), ME engineers (Goyo Marta, Matthew Jackson, Venitza de Klerk, Phil White, Cashel Brown), Meta (Dan Biddle), Mohn Media (Yannick Laag, Astrid Renders, Kevin Sarney, Julia Seebach, Jeannette Sio, Dennis Thon), Momentum Engineering (Pamela Ewang, Ed Lofts, Abigail Matthews), MSC Cruises (Steve Leatham, Matteo Mancini, Christine Kerber, Antony James, Andrea Correale, Mihaela Carlan, Carlos Ponzetto, Biagio De Girolamo, Gianluca Russo), Museum of Discovery & Science (Andrea Hart, Andi Fuentes, Kayla Sanders, Joe Cox), Matthew Musson, NeoXperiences (Boris Courte), Newmark (Mike McChesney), Alastair North, Joseph O'Neil, Alice Pagan, Nigel Perry, Duncan Phillips, Ping Leisure Communication Ltd (Claire Owen), Precision Proco, Prestige Design (Jackie Ginger), The Production Suite (Beverley Williams, Zoe Vaux-Thompson, Barry Mason), Propworks (Emma Banwell, Dan Lee, Rosie Young, Annie Lumby, Charlie Stoddart, Flo Minchella, Pauline McGrath, Jess Way), Ripley Office (Jim Pattison Jr, John Corcoran, Clay Stewart, William Anthony, Tacita Barrera, Brian Relic, Todd Hougland), Iain Robertson, Sappi, Science North (Ashley Larose, Marc Gareau, Pamela Therrien, Kris Gurnsey), Jasmine Selbie, Snap Finger Click (Flo Burchill, Hope Dangerfield, Ed Gladwin, Joanne Haslam, Martijn van der Meulen), Stark RFID, Taboola (Liane Lederer), Francis Tessendorf, Uncoded (Matt Spence), Uplause (Veli-Pekka Marin, Jussi Marin), Gabriela Ventura, Colin & Susie Walker

Official adjudicators
Camila Borenstain, Thomas Bradford, Joanne Brent, Sarah Casson, Marc Cote, Swapnil Dangarikar, Kanzy El Defrawy, Brittany Dunn, Michael Empric, Fumika Fujibuchi, John Garland, Şeyda Subaşı Gemici, Andrew Glass, Iris Hou, Monica Hu, Austin Johnson, Kazuyoshi Kirimura, Lena Kuhlmann, Maggie Luo, Chloe McCarthy, Rishi Nath, Mbali Nikos, Hannah Ortman, Pravin Patel, Justin Patterson, Glenn Pollard, Susana Reyes, Alfredo Arista Rueda, Emi Saito, Paulina Sapinska, Carl Saville, Tomomi Sekioka, Tina Shi, Brian Sobel, Minyoung Sohn, Hanane Spiers, Richard Stenning, Kayo Takeyama, Natalia Ramirez Talero, Raafat Tawfik, Lala Teranishi, Anouk De Timary, Aynee Toorabally, Sonia Ushirogochi, Lorenzo Veltri, Xiong Wen, Angela Wu, Peter Yang, Jacob Yip

Abbreviations

AFG Afghanistan
ALB Albania
AND Andorra
ARG Argentina
ARM Armenia
ASM American Samoa
AUS Australia
AUT Austria
AZE Azerbaijan
BEL Belgium
BGD Bangladesh
BGR Bulgaria
BHR Bahrain
BHS The Bahamas
BIH Bosnia and Herzegovina
BLR Belarus
BOL Bolivia
BRA Brazil
BRB Barbados
CAN Canada
CHE Switzerland
CHL Chile
CHN China
CIV Côte d'Ivoire
CMR Cameroon
COL Colombia
CPV Cape Verde
CRI Costa Rica
CUB Cuba
CZE Czechia
DEU Germany
DJI Djibouti
DNK Denmark
DOM Dominican Republic
DZA Algeria
ECU Ecuador
EGY Egypt
ERI Eritrea
ESP Spain
EST Estonia
ETH Ethiopia
FIN Finland
FJI Fiji
FRA France
GEO Georgia
GHA Ghana
GIN Guinea
GRC Greece
GTM Guatemala
GUY Guyana
HND Honduras
HRV Croatia (Hrvatska)
HTI Haiti
HUN Hungary
IDN Indonesia
IND India
IRL Ireland
IRN Iran
IRQ Iraq
ISL Iceland
ISR Israel
ITA Italy
JAM Jamaica
JOR Jordan
JPN Japan
KAZ Kazakhstan
KEN Kenya
KHM Cambodia
KOR Korea, Republic of
KWT Kuwait
LBN Lebanon
LBR Liberia
LKA Sri Lanka
LTU Lithuania
LVA Latvia
MAR Morocco
MCO Monaco
MDA Moldova
MDG Madagascar
MEX Mexico
MLI Mali
MMR Myanmar
MNE Montenegro
MNG Mongolia
MOZ Mozambique
MRT Mauritania
MUS Mauritius
MWI Malawi
MYS Malaysia
NAM Namibia
NGA Nigeria
NIC Nicaragua
NLD Netherlands
NOR Norway
NPL Nepal
NZ New Zealand
PAK Pakistan
PER Peru
PHL Philippines
PNG Papua New Guinea
POL Poland
PRI Puerto Rico
PRT Portugal
PRY Paraguay
QAT Qatar
ROM Romania
RUS Russian Federation
SAU Saudi Arabia
SDN Sudan
SEN Senegal
SGP Singapore
SHN Saint Helena
SMR San Marino
SOM Somalia
SRB Serbia
SSD South Sudan
SVK Slovakia
SVN Slovenia
SWE Sweden
SWZ Eswatini
SYC Seychelles
SYR Syrian Arab Republic
THA Thailand
TKM Turkmenistan
TON Tonga
TTO Trinidad and Tobago
TUN Tunisia
TUR Türkiye
TZA Tanzania
UAE United Arab Emirates
UGA Uganda
UK United Kingdom
UKR Ukraine
URY Uruguay
USA United States of America
UZB Uzbekistan
VEN Venezuela
VNM Vietnam
VUT Vanuatu
WSM Samoa
YEM Yemen
ZAF South Africa
ZWE Zimbabwe

Picture Credits

Cover Hao_Stocker/Shutterstock, bells7/Shutterstock, Martin Pelanek/Shutterstock, Petr Smagin/Shutterstock, homydesign/Shutterstock, AY Amazefoto/Shutterstock, New Africa/Shutterstock, Vac1/Shutterstock, Guaxinim/Shutterstock, FotoRequest/Shutterstock, SamSamFM/Shutterstock, NosorogUA/Shutterstock, BartTa/Shutterstock, Smileus/Shutterstock, Thx4Stock team/Shutterstock, Davizro Photography/Shutterstock, Kaiskynet Studio/Shutterstock, Breck P Kent/Shutterstock, JIANG HONGYAN/Shutterstock, panda3800/Shutterstock, Dmitrij Skorobogatov/Shutterstock, Martina_L/Shutterstock, Richard Bradbury/GWR, Anton Starikov/Shutterstock, Tetiana Rostopira/Shutterstock, ang intaravichian/Shutterstock, beast01/Shutterstock, mrpstock/Shutterstock, Alexander_P/Shutterstock, masa44/Shutterstock, Stephen Coyne/Alamy, Narupon Nimpaiboon/Shutterstock, Valentina Razumova/Shutterstock, stockphoto-graf/Shutterstock, MilenaWi/Shutterstock, Byjeng/Shutterstock, urfin/Shutterstock, Kurit afshen/Shutterstock, S K Chavan/Shutterstock

Endpapers Alexander_P/Shutterstock, New Africa/Shutterstock, Narupon Nimpaiboon/Shutterstock, stockphoto-graf/Shutterstock, Kaiskynet Studio/Shutterstock, Breck P Kent/Shutterstock, SamSamFM/Shutterstock, Marvel/Disney/TCD/Prod.DB/Alamy, Pixel-Shot/Shutterstock, Smileus/Shutterstock, ifiStudio/Shutterstock, Petr Smagin/Shutterstock, Universal/Courtesy Everett Collection/Alamy, Igor Link/Shutterstock, AY Amazefoto/Shutterstock, Hao_Stocker/Shutterstock, BartTa/Shutterstock, Davizro Photography/Shutterstock, Walt Disney Productions/Allstar Picture Library/Alamy, NosorogUA/Shutterstock, Guaxinim/Shutterstock, beast01/Shutterstock, mrpstock/Shutterstock, Stephen Coyne/Alamy, Thx4Stock team/Shutterstock, panda3800/Shutterstock, Byjeng/Shutterstock, urfin/Shutterstock, Kurit afshen/Shutterstock, JIANG HONGYAN/Shutterstock, S K Chavan/Shutterstock, Martina_L/Shutterstock, FotoRequest/Shutterstock, MilenaWi/Shutterstock, Anton Starikov/Shutterstock, Hseena/Shutterstock, Richard Bradbury/GWR, bells7/Shutterstock, homydesign/Shutterstock, Vac1/Shutterstock, masa44/Shutterstock, seeshooteatrepeat/Shutterstock, Jim Henson Productions/Everett Collection Inc/Alamy, Dmitrij Skorobogatov/Shutterstock, Tetiana Rostopira/Shutterstock, Lucasfilm/Disney/Alamy, Valentina Razumova/Shutterstock, ang intaravichian/Shutterstock

1 Fiona M Donnelly/Shutterstock

2 Traveller MG/Shutterstock

4 masa44/Shutterstock, BartTa/Shutterstock, beast01/Shutterstock, Dmitrij Skorobogatov/Shutterstock, Kaiskynet Studio/Shutterstock, Glenn Murphy, Damen

5 Kevin Schafer/Alamy, Mr Methane, Marek R Swadzba/Shutterstock, Traveller MG/Shutterstock, Jim Henson Productions/Everett Collection Inc/Alamy, homydesign/Shutterstock, beast01/Shutterstock, Davizro Photography/Shutterstock, mrpstock/Shutterstock, Alexander_P/Shutterstock

6 (UK) BBC, Jed Leicester for London Marathon Events/Vitality Westminster Mile, Craig Glenday/Guinness World Records

7 (UK) Madalyn Bielfeld/GWR

8 (UK) BBC, Michael Bowles/GWR

9 (UK) AFCB/Amy Maidment, Lexy Ilsley/Manchester City FC, BHAFC/Paul Hazlewood

6 (CAN) Jay Patel/Sports Press Photo/SPP/Shutterstock

9 (CAN) Andrea Masini/Insidefoto via ZUMA

6 (USA) Gilbert Flores/Penske Media via Getty Images

7 (USA) Max Touhey/Courtesy Queens Museum New York, etorres/Shutterstock, Jaromír Jirman/CimiPhoto

8 (USA) Erik Isakson/GWR, Polina Raulina/GWR, Vladimir Molnar/GWR

9 (USA) iD_studio/Shutterstock

10 Sergey Nivens/Shutterstock, Courtesy of the Dubai Marathon

11 Madalyn Bielfeld/GWR, Alex Broadway/Getty Images, Alex Davidson/Getty Images, Anna Phelps/GWR, Abby Taylor/GWR

10 (USA) Kampee Patisena/Getty Images, Frank Micelotta/PictureGroup for Disney, Arfin Studio/Shutterstock, 279photo Studio/Shutterstock, Oksana Mizina/Shutterstock, Andrey Chuprinov/Shutterstock, Karramba Production/Shutterstock, pics five/Shutterstock, Anucha Tiemsom/Shutterstock, Chris Willson/Alamy

11 (USA) Katya Slavashevich/Shutterstock, Paul.vsky/Shutterstock, Ink N Propeller/Shutterstock, Iana Alter/Shutterstock

12 Matt Hillman/GWR

13 Matt Hillman/GWR, Paul Michael Hughes/GWR, Ali Spagnola

14 Brien Adams/GWR, Paul Michael Hughes/GWR, Pandora Pictures/Shutterstock

16 Alan Dyer/VWPics/Universal Images Group via Getty Images, Macrovector/Shutterstock, Photoongraphy/Shutterstock

17 CHINE NOUVELLE/SIPA/Shutterstock, Elena11/Shutterstock

18 George Rose/Getty Images, Deb Snelson/Getty Images, Michal Hykel/Shutterstock, JoeyPhoto/Shutterstock

19 MB Photography/Getty Images, David Zentz/Getty Images

20 David Anchondo, Orangée/Wikimedia Commons, Adi Prima/Anadolu via Getty Images, Ami.M/Shutterstock

21 ASalanova/Shutterstock

22 Piemags/Nature/Alamy, Blue Planet Archive LLC/Alamy, blickwinkel/Hartl/Alamy, Liu Lixin/China News Service/VCG via Getty Images

23 Adam Millward/GWR, Paul Grover/Shutterstock

24 Jeremiah Harris, Domonick Gravine/RedLeaf Exotics, Margaret Whittaker

25 Phil Wilkinson/Alamy, Margaret Whittaker

26 Steve Gschmeissner/Science Photo Library/Alamy

27 Tagide deCarvalho, University of Maryland, Baltimore County, Tobetv/Shutterstock

28 Dr. Alexey Yakovlev, Marko Von Der Osten/imageBROKER/Shutterstock, Alberto Carrera/Alamy, Holger Kirk/Shutterstock

29 Worraket/Shutterstock, TommyK/Alamy

30 Luis Acosta/AFP via Getty Images, Corbis via Getty Images, AFP via Getty Images, *South China Morning Post* via Getty Images, Björn Wylezich/Alamy Stock Photo

33 Adam Millward/GWR, Egton Bridge Old Gooseberry Society

34 Royal Botanic Gardens Kew, Corbis/VCG via Getty Images, EQRoy/Shutterstock

35 Sipa US/Alamy Stock Photo, Future Publishing/Getty Images

36 Caroline Chaptini, Dr. Fernando Vargas-Salinas

37 Adam Millward/GWR, Radu Frenţiu

38 Jerome LABOUYRIE/Shutterstock

39 Joseph O'Neil/GWR

40 PUBG Mobile/YG Entertainment, YG/Netflix © 2020, Frazer Harrison/Getty Images for Coachella

41 Martin Lelievre/AFP via Getty Images, Victoria Jones/Alamy, Xavier Collin/Image Press Agency/Alamy, John V Esparza

42 Brien Adams/GWR

43 Brien Adams/GWR

44 LongeviQuest, The Marinho family, PA Images/Alamy

45 Luis Miguel Soriano, Ian Dawson - Nord

46 rangizzz/Shutterstock, Irina Gutyryak/Shutterstock, EKKAPHAN CHIMPALEE/Shutterstock, schankz/Shutterstock, happymay/Shutterstock, Karramba Production/Shutterstock, Dr. Jack Ashby/Nottingham Trent University, Craig Glenday/GWR, Paul Michael Hughes/GWR, Dan Thorne/GWR

47 pics five/Shutterstock, Di Studio/Shutterstock, Craig Glenday/GWR, Paul Michael Hughes/GWR

48 Paul Michael Hughes/GWR

50 Olivier Ramonteu/GWR, Afsana Roji/Shutterstock, Shaikh Aman12/Shutterstock, LabluWay/Shutterstock, PixelAura Creative/Shutterstock

51 Erik Isakson/GWR

52 Paul Michael Hughes/GWR

55 Trudie Lee/GWR, Jon Enoch/GWR

56 Ron Edge Collection, Mark Schwettmann/Shutterstock, Joseph O'Neil/GWR

57 National Trust

58 Robert Markowitz/NASA-Johnson Space Center, Keegan Barber/NASA, NASA

59 NASA

60 Emanuele Tedesi/GWR

61 Emanuele Tedesi/GWR

62 Ranald Mackechnie/GWR

63 James Ellerker/GWR, David Fisher/Shutterstock, Paul Michael Hughes/GWR, Sam Christmas/GWR

65 Paul Michael Hughes/GWR

66 Antony Jones/Getty Images for World Chess, How Hwee Young/EPA-EFE/Shutterstock

67 Caterpillar Inc

68 Marcelo Maragni/Red Bull Content Pool, Joyn/Claudius Pflug

69 Peter Jülich/GWR

70 Ahmed Sarandaz Rathore/GWR

71 Ian Bowkett/GWR

74 Habuild Healthtech Pvt Ltd

77 Richard Clatworthy/Jamie Oliver Enterprises Ltd

78 Jeremy Norwood/Norwood Photography

80 Adam Millward/GWR, GetThis/Shutterstock, Stock_Ninja/Shutterstock, Shopno dana/Shutterstock

81 Sofia Brandes & Max Slobodda/GWR, Paul Michael Hughes/GWR

82 Julian Krakowiak/Alamy, koya979/Shutterstock, Galaxy Entertainment Group

83 Jeppe Gustafsson/Shutterstock, Ragnar Th Sigurdsson/Arctic Images/Alamy, udaya fire/Shutterstock

84 Anadolu/Getty Images, Valda Kalnina/EPA/Shutterstock, Associated Press/Alamy Stock Photo

85 hjochen/Shutterstock, Graham Hunt/Alamy Stock Photo, Geoff Moore/Shutterstock, Graham Hunt/Alamy Stock Photo

86 Madalyn Bielfeld/GWR, Christopher Polk/Shutterstock, YummyBuum/Shutterstock, TAW4/Shutterstock

87 YummyBuum/Shutterstock, A Zhuravleva/Shutterstock, xpixel/Shutterstock, Don Arnold/Getty Images for Nickelodeon Australia, Brett Hemmings/Getty Images for Nickelodeon Australia, Nick N A/Shutterstock, mitsuap/Shutterstock, New Africa/Shutterstock, YummyBuum/Shutterstock

90 Z-project, Craig Glenday/GWR, Joyn/Claudius Pflug, Joyn/Claudius Pflug

91 Ian Bowkett/GWR

93 Joep Buijs Photography

94 Aurelien Droux

95 Valentin Rapp

96 Ali Spagnola, Jack Leach/Goldin Auctions, FabViews

97 Erik Isakson/GWR, Thomas Abrahams/GWR

98 Joseph O'Neil/GWR, Josh Landis/U.S. National Science Foundation

99 Mattschwarz/Shutterstock

100 WWE/WWE via Getty Images, Rich Freeda/WWE via Getty Images, Rich Freeda/WWE via Getty Images

101 Rob Kim/Getty Images, Amazon MGM Studios/Shutterstock, Ethan Miller/Getty Images, Rich Freeda/WWE via Getty Images

102 Vera C. Rubin Observatory/NSF/DOE/NOIRLab/SLAC/AU, Vera C. Rubin Observatory/NOIRLab/SLAC/NSF/DOE/AURA/P Horálek

103 NSF–DOE Vera C. Rubin Observatory, FotoYakov/Shutterstock

104 NASA, Ben Hollingum/GWR, Breaking The Walls/Shutterstock, ONYXprj/Shutterstock, Photo_Pix/Shutterstock, happymay/Shutterstock, Inspiration GP/Shutterstock, Mitand73/Shutterstock

105 ZUMA Press, Inc./Alamy, NASA, Yuen Man Cheung/Alamy, NASA

106 MICRO.S/Shutterstock, Anterovium/Shutterstock, Karramba Production/Shutterstock, happymay/Shutterstock, Tatahnka/Shutterstock, showcake/Shutterstock, Juhku/Shutterstock, Ben Hollingum/GWR, NASA, Thomas Trompeter/Alamy, NASA

107 Thomas Bethge/Shutterstock, ArthurStock/Shutterstock, mdbildes/Shutterstock, Sasin Paraksa/Shutterstock, SpaceX/UPI/Shutterstock